A
Man of
Sentiment

Philippe-Joseph Aubert de Gaspé as a young man, from a drawing by an unidentified artist. Public Archives Canada. C-19199

A
Man of
Sentiment

The Memoirs of
Philippe-Joseph Aubert de Gaspé
1786-1871

Translated and annotated
by Jane Brierley

Véhicule Press

MONTRÉAL

DOSSIER QUÉBEC

This book has been published with the help of a grant from the Canadian Federation for the Humanities, using funds provided by the Social Sciences and Humanities Research Council of Canada and a translation grant from the Canada Council.

Dossier Québec Series Editor: Simon Dardick
Cover design: JW Stewart
Typeset and printed by Les Éditions Marquis Ltée

First published in French, 1866 (Ottawa: G.E. Desbarats)
© 1988 by Jane Brierley for the introduction, annotations and translation.
All rights reserved.
Dépôt légal, Bibliothèque nationale du Québec &
the National Library of Canada, 1st trimester, 1988

Canadian Cataloguing in Publication Data

Aubert de Gaspé, Philippe, 1786-1871
[Mémoires. English]
   A man of sentiment

(Dossier Québec series)
Translation of: Mémoires.

   1. Aubert de Gaspé, Philippe, 1786-1871—Biography.
2. Quebec (Province)—History—19th century.
3. Novelists, Canadian (French)—19th century—Biography.
I. Brierley, Jane, 1935-   . II. Title. III. Title: Mémoires. English.

PS8401.U24Z53 1988   971.4'02   C88-090341-1
PQ3919.G3Z47 1988

Canadian distribution:

Publications Department
University of Toronto Press
5201 Dufferin Street
Downsview, Ontario
M3H 5T8

U.S. distribution:

University of Toronto Press
340 Nagel Drive
Buffalo, New York
14225-4731

Véhicule Press, P.O.B. 125, Place du Parc Station
Montreal, Quebec, Canada H2W 2M9

Printed in Canada

For John, Sarah, and Tim

A gentle gaiety, seasoned with the old
French wit, animated this fine group, of
which Monsieur de Gaspé was the soul.
His unfailing verve, his original mind, his
wide knowledge, and his talent for
narration made one forget the passing
hours in his company.

H.-R. Casgrain, *De Gaspé et Garneau*

"Do not think, young sir, that I
compliment or congratulate you on having
a kind heart. On the contrary, happy is
he—a thousand times happy—who
possesses a heart of brass, since he is
constrained to live among men."

de Gaspé, *Mémoires*

TABLE OF CONTENTS

TRANSLATOR'S NOTE

In translating and editing this work my aim has been to transmit the freshness and conversational charm of de Gaspé's style in a manner that strikes a responsive chord in the English reader. The complete text of the 1866 edition has been translated. Of equal consideration has been the fact that this is a document of historical as well as literary interest, and many of the details and incidents bring a vivid reality to everyday scenes that we can usually only glimpse through the charts and quantitative analyses of the New History. Every effort has been made to express correctly the reality that de Gaspé knew.

The author's footnotes to the original edition now appear as endnotes, indicated by superior numbers where they occurred in the original text. The translator's annotations are shown by superior capital letters and will, it is hoped, provide readers with background information enlarging their knowledge and appreciation of the setting and the work.

Essentially, the text follows the format of the 1866 edition, although on a few occasions de Gaspé's one-sentence paragraphs (he had a great many) have been incorporated in the previous or following paragraphs. The arrangement of dialogue has generally been treated in accordance with English usage, although in several places I have followed de Gaspé's style (usually a colon followed by a new paragraph) to preserve the emphasis that the passage seemed to deserve.

In the matter of place names, I have preserved the French style of "Saint-Thomas" with a hyphen rather than "St. Thomas," thereby avoiding confusion with similar names outside Quebec. De Gaspé's use of hyphens in names of persons is not always consistent. I have followed his usage or eliminated inconsistencies within the body of the translation, but used the style given in reference works in the annotations. Of the many other editorial decisions that had to be made, I will only say that all were taken bearing in mind the spirit of the author and the quality of communication that his work merits.

ACKNOWLEDGEMENTS

I would like to acknowledge my special thanks to Dr. Alec Lucas, Professor Emeritus of McGill University, for giving unstintingly of his time, advice, and encouragement in connection with this work. I also wish to thank Dr. Yvan Lamonde, former Director of the French Canada Studies Program at McGill University, and a Quebec historian whose special interests include the autobiographical literature of French Canada, for his interest and kindness in discussing the historical field and suggesting research resources.

Mrs. Jacqueline Beaudoin-Ross, Curator of Costume for the McCord Museum of McGill University, was extremely helpful in providing me with information regarding dress, particularly the uniform worn by students at the Quebec Little Seminary in early times. Mrs. Norma Morgan made available to me material from a historical bibliography of references to Canadian costume that she was in the process of preparing while a graduate student at Concordia University of Montreal.

A number of people have offered helpful comments and advice over the years of preparation, and to all of these I am grateful. Among others, Maître Jacques Riverin of Chicoutimi, former president of the Quebec Chamber of Notaries, gave me a first-hand description of the Little Seminary uniform, essentially unchanged from de Gaspé's day until the 1940s. Judge Hélène Baillargeon-Côté suggested possible sources for popular Canadian chansons, and Robert Meadowcroft unearthed passages in Sterne. My special thanks go to Principal Jacques Castonguay of Collège militaire royal de Saint-Jean, whose vigilance has preserved an important collection of de Gaspé's papers, and who has very kindly offered permission to reproduce manuscript pages from an early draft of the *Mémoires* to illustrate this book, as well as other material. I would also like to thank, among others the McLennan Library, the Department of Rare Books and Special Collections, and the McCord Museum of Canadian History, all of McGill University; the Musée du Québec, the National Gallery of Canada, the Public Archives of Canada, the Musée du Séminaire de Québec, the Château Ramezay Museum of Montreal, the Art Gallery of Ontario, and the Archives nationales du Québec for their generous cooperation.

I also gratefully acknowledge the assistance of the Canada Council, through a grant-in-aid for the translation, and the Canadian Federation for the Humanities, in granting assistance for publication.

INTRODUCTION

A little to the west of the town of Saint-Jean Port-Joli on the South Shore of the Saint Lawrence, a narrow road forks inland beside a steep bluff. The road rises gently to a flat expanse covered with wild grasses and a tangle of trees and bushes that rustle in the hot wind of a summer's day. Beyond this flat place, narrow meadows stretch toward the Saint-Louis hills some miles off, where the popular summer cottage resort of Lac Trois-Saumons lies hidden. There is no obvious sign of habitation—no decayed shed, no rusted plowshare—nothing. The place has an air of being swept clean. Time and nature have done their work well. But for those who hold the key and who listen carefully, the distant chink of horses' hobbles and the far-off cries of rambunctious children seem to float in the wind, and in the glare of the brilliant sunshine—perhaps it is a trick of the light—the faint stripes of a picket fence shimmer against the outline of a long, many-windowed house. A shadow flickers at one of the windows, as of someone sitting at a table, writing.

Here stood the manor house of Saint-Jean Port-Joli, once the home of Philippe-Joseph Aubert de Gaspé (1786-1871), sixth and last seigneur and the fifth of that name,[1] author of the novel *Les Anciens Canadiens* and of these *Memoirs*, one of our great autobiographical legacies.[2] The house was destroyed by fire in April 1909, one hundred and fifty years after its predecessor was razed on the orders of General Wolfe. Fortunately at least two photographs and an engraving of the later building exist, mute witnesses of time past that make it possible to reconstruct both sides of the house.[3] They show a long building with a steeply-pitched pavilion roof and two gabled wings extending forward

19

at each end. A picket fence surrounds a garden in front. Behind the house is a small paddock enclosed by a split-rail fence.

Time past need not be time lost—not if we have a key. The *Memoirs* are just such a key, a symbolic, imaginative recollection, a testimony of a personality, and of times, places, and outlooks that are otherwise beyond our intuitive grasp, however much we may claim to understand or appreciate them intellectually or, like the New History, to analyze them from a documentary standpoint. The reader—post-industrial, post-atomic, post-Vatican II, post-Vietnam—cannot easily divest himself of a present-minded mentality when encountering evidence of bygone periods. Even the most skilled historians have difficulty doing so.

These memoirs are not, however, the story behind great events, despite the title. De Gaspé's autobiographical work constitutes a precious literary heritage that evokes and transmits a consciousness of an individual and of a time. If we remember that de Gaspé was born before the French Revolution, and spent long evenings listening to his family talk of earlier days, this consciousness extends very far back indeed.

The original *Mémoires* were published in 1866. Their seventeen chapters totaled over 550 pages, a monumental undertaking for a man in his seventies. Publication itself was an exacting task, given the attendant revision and correction of proofs. De Gaspé wrote to his grandson Raoul de Beaujeu, on February 18, 1866: "I began correcting the final chapter of my work last week and hope to be finished and rid of it in a few days, as I am thoroughly fed up with these interminable proofs."[4] The letter continued with self-deprecating but tart humour, "If my chapter on the Recollets has been approved by such a competent judge as Mr. Stephens, I am confident that our good Canadians will swallow the others without balking. In the meantime please give him my best regards and don't show him this scribble, otherwise he may lose his enormous respect for the author of *Les Anciens Canadiens*."[5]

A number of people had read de Gaspé's work in progress, among them his relative and younger friend who also acted as literary adviser, the historian Abbé Henri-Raymond Casgrain. Various clues in the *Memoirs* indicate that he had been working for a number of years on material that was eventually included. The publication of *Les Anciens Canadiens* in 1863 acted as a great stimulus to the author, however.

Abbé Casgrain wrote that as he and de Gaspé were reading the proofs for the first edition of the novel, "Each passage . . . gave rise in Monsieur de Gaspé's mind to an inexhaustible fund of commentary on men and things of yesteryear. Monsieur de Gaspé had not even begun to read before memories were flying forth, like birds taking wing. He drew up to the firescreen . . . a small mahogany table on which he was accustomed to write. It was a great favourite of his. 'This small table . . . is an old family piece that I grew up with and that my mother always used and treasured, for Lady Dorchester gave it to her as a present. No English governor is better remembered in Canada than Lord Dorchester. . . .'"[6]

Although de Gaspé began his career as a man of letters at an advanced age, he had an abiding love of story and literature. "During the long evenings, if the conversation began to flag, he would open his handsome bookcase, take out a volume, and with some passage chosen from Racine, Molière, Shakespeare, or others, would entertain his listeners by reading aloud, for which he had an incomparable talent. This form of amusement was so attractive to himself and his family that he had translated into French, and copied in his own hand, almost all the works of Walter Scott, which he used to read aloud in the evenings. . . . The talent of Monsieur de Gaspé had been perfected over a long period by the thorough study of the great masters."[7]

Great and humble alike stimulated de Gaspé's sense of story and narrative. "Sometimes, to vary the entertainment, he would have Augustin, the miller, come with his son Tintin, and get them to tell stories to the children" down by the shore.[8] The shore and the river are in fact a constant theme in de Gaspé's work. Below the bluff near the manor house, the salt-water tides of the twenty-five-mile-wide Saint Lawrence wash the rocks along the shoreline. Various small groups of islands can be seen in the vista across the river to the huge capes of the North Shore, where, as de Gaspé writes in chapter 6, the Laurentian chain rise—"an immense green serpent whose gigantic head, Cap Tourmente" is visible in the distance. Walks after supper with members of the family along the river's edge where a cool breeze lessened the summer's heat, conversations with the Indians who were in the habit of beaching their canoes and building cabins there, flower-picking forays with the children: to all of these activities, the river formed a backdrop. The Abbé Casgrain described how de Gaspé would often go out, "a book under his arm, to sit on the seashore at the foot of his small cape, near the clear spring that bubbled up from the rock. There he used to spend long hours in reading, reflexion and reverie."[9]

De Gaspé's world was not confined to the rural South Shore, however. He spent much of his youth and later life in the city of Quebec, which, although it was a colonial outpost, reproduced in miniature the social structure typical of communities influenced by Western European culture in the late eighteenth and early nineteenth centuries, and which has been portrayed imaginatively in such novels as Thackeray's *Vanity Fair*, Austen's *Pride and Prejudice*, or even Tolstoy's *War and Peace*. Indeed, there is a strong resemblance in the *Memoirs* to the world of Tolstoy: the semi-feudal setting, the snowy winters and hot summers, the dinners at officers' messes, the balls in the capital, the closeness to nature on the country estate, and the unsophisticated worth of the peasant/habitant who acts as mentor to his superior in the social scale of the time. Those familiar with Tolstoy's three autobiographical fragments will notice not only similarities of social context—childhood years in the country estate, separation from family in order to be educated in the capital, entry into society—but also a similar observant sensitivity. De Gaspé's evocation in chapter 3 of an October evening at the manor house, with children playing, mother busy supervising supper, father seeing to the horses in the stable, and the visit of two Recollets, succeeds in creating an ambiance reminiscent of Tolstoy's poignant description of similar scenes from childhood, to cite but one example.[10]

De Gaspé's parents were members of an elite Quebec society that gravitated toward the military and administrative establishments after the Conquest, much as they had under French rule. In general, the de Gaspé family and their connections were highly conservative in their politics and loyal to the legitimate power, Great Britain—a loyalty that was reinforced by the horrors of regicide and the French Revolution. It must be remembered that to the eighteenth-century mind, legitimate authority represented an important political and moral principle, and according to the rules of the game, legitimate authority now resided in the British monarch. Moreover, his new subjects had sworn a solemn oath of loyalty to the king and his representatives—no light matter in those days.

The gentry of New France, unlike their counterparts in Europe, were permitted to engage in trade or join a profession, as well as hold public office. After the Conquest, when the French-Canadian elite were generally far from wealthy and in many cases suffered extreme financial hardship as a result of the Seven Years' War in Canada, the emoluments attached to public posts were often an important addition to their income. Their loyalty was all the more bound up with their interests in that the Quebec Act specifically exempted them from the religious requirements for public office-holders set forth in the Test Act, an exemption not accorded at that time to Roman Catholics in other British domains. However, although the gentry's loyalty had an undeniably pragmatic side, their highly developed concept of honour, in keeping with the social and religious traditions of the time, also acted as a strong psychological force, and it is important to keep this in mind when reading the *Memoirs*.

Despite the French-Canadian gentry's lack of wealth, they nevertheless combined a ceremonious way of life with a vivacity of manner that contrasted sharply with the more staid English customs and temperament, and this quality made their company particularly attractive to the British military and administrative elite in the city of Quebec. Conspicuous among the king's representatives was Sir Guy Carleton, later Lord Dorchester, and his wife, the Lady Maria Howard, daughter of the Earl of Effingham. Lady Dorchester was "small and fair, upright and extremely dignified, and was ceremonious to a degree that in her old age almost amounted to eccentricity. She had been brought up and educated at Versailles, which may be held to account for her partiality for the French at Quebec, and may possibly have influenced her husband in the same direction."[11]

De Gaspé's parents and the Dorchesters were on intimate terms. De Gaspé's uncle on his mother's side, the "celebrated chevalier" Charles de Lanaudière, was aide-de-camp to Lord Dorchester and had been present at the courts of Versailles and St. James. As a family the de Lanaudières seem to have been stimulating company: witty, well read, and of a highly individual turn of mind, as the *Memoirs* show. The English felt their attraction, and Governor Simcoe's wife, for example, recorded that she spent the winter of 1791-1792 enjoyably in Quebec, often in the company of de Gaspé's maternal aunt, Madame François Baby, whom she mentions repeatedly in her diary.[12]

De Gaspé was keenly aware of a family heritage of resourcefulness and distinguished service to the colony of New France. His earliest Canadian forebear on his father's side was the enterprising Charles Aubert de la Chesnaye, who arrived at Quebec in 1655 at the age of twenty-two and soon prospered as a trader, eventually acquiring seigneuries up and down the Saint Lawrence River, including that of Saint-Jean Port-Joli in 1686. The "Lettres de noblesse de Charles Aubert de la Chesnaye" issued by Louis XIV in 1693[13] praised him for his commercial, civil, and military contribution, including his courage and valor in fighting the Iroquois, among others. Charles had eighteen children by his marriages to Catherine-Gertrude Couillard, Marie-Louise Juchereau de la Ferté, and Marie-Angélique de la Ronde. It was the third son of Marie-Louise, Pierre Aubert (1672-1731)— Aubert being the family name—who purchased the seigneurie of Saint-Jean Port-Joli from his father's debt-burdened estate in 1709 and took the surname "de Gaspé," possibly with reference to the seigneurie of Percé in which the family had an interest.[14]

Pierre's second wife was Madeleine-Angélique Legardeur de Tilly (he traveled to Rome for the necessary dispensation, as she was a cousin of his first wife), by whom he had three surviving children: two girls, who became nuns, and Ignace-Philippe (1714-1787). The latter was born at Saint-Antoine de Tilly, where his parents had settled, and it was he who built the first manor house at Saint-Jean Port-Joli, burnt in the summer of 1759 by the English. Long before 1759, however, Ignace-Philippe had experienced the hardships of war. Known as "the soldier-seigneur," he had taken part in the Indian wars, in the conflict reflected in North America in 1744 by the War of the Austrian Succession, and finally in the "War of the Conquest" or the Seven Years' War in North America. Even after the Conquest, serving his new British king, Ignace-Philippe took part in the repulse of the American invasion of Quebec in 1775-76. Captain de Gaspé was named chevalier or knight of the Royal and Military Order of Saint Louis on March 24, 1761, after thirty-three years of loyal service to the French crown, a circumstance that de Gaspé proudly recorded in the "note" at the end of chapter 5. Interestingly enough, he was one of the few Canadian officers commended by Montcalm, who was an exponent of the formal combat tactics used in Europe and generally unappreciative of the guerilla-like manoeuvres of Canadian troops.[15]

24

In 1745, Philippe-Ignace married Marie-Anne Coulon de Villiers, sister of that Villiers de Jumonville who was, according to family tradition, coldly murdered by George Washington in a frontier skirmish.[16] The sixth-born, Pierre-Ignace (1758-1823), continued the line. His early childhood was spent in the Trois-Saumons mill near Saint-Jean Port-Joli, where the family had taken refuge for about five years after the burning of the first manor house. By 1766 they were installed in the new manor house, and it was this building that de Gaspé knew.

Pierre-Ignace undertook the real development of the seigneurie, purchasing the fief of L'Islet-à-Peau for additional river frontage, clearing land, and building roads to the inland concessions. His interest and involvement in the development of the seigneurie earned him the respect and affection of the habitants, and at his death the *Quebec Gazette* reported: "Just and liberal towards his censitaires, he never, during the period of forty years that he managed his seigneuries, undertook a single suit against them."[17] In a society that abounded in lawsuits, this was high praise and evidence of conspicuous harmony between seigneur and censitaire, especially since Pierre-Ignace was a stern man in many respects, as his son recorded.

De Gaspé's grandfather and father had, with difficulty, managed to reestablish the family on a sound financial footing after the Conquest and were consequently in a position to live as nobles. "In Canada, this meant feeding oneself from the land, owning a 'manor house,' occasionally organizing fine receptions, occupying the seigneurial pew, and taking precedence over laymen in religious ceremonies."[18] On January 26, 1786, Pierre-Ignace married Catherine Tarieu de Lanaudière. Her mother was Catherine Le Moyne de Longueuil, daughter of the Baron de Longueuil of Montreal; her father was Charles-François Tarieu de Lanaudière, seigneur of La Pérade and son of the now famous heroine Madeleine Jarret de Verchères. The new bride's father was essentially a successful entrepreneur. His home had been considered a centre of polite society in Quebec before the Conquest, and, not surprisingly, he soon established excellent relations with the British administration.

Philippe-Joseph Aubert de Gaspé was born in the city of Quebec on October 30, 1786, two hundred years ago. A brother, Antoine-Thomas (1790-1824), and a sister, Catherine (1796-1803) were the only others to survive infancy. Of the latter, de Gaspé wrote a touching note to chapter 11 of *Les Anciens Canadiens* that was typical of the nostalgic sensitivity of mother and son. He described how, when he was about seventeen, he found his mother in tears over a shoe belonging to his little sister, who had died some ten years before. "After the child's death my family felt it necessary to get rid of all the objects that might feed my mother's grief if she saw them; but with ingenious tenderness she had smuggled away this little shoe, unknown to everyone."[19]

In character De Gaspé was affectionate, imaginative, candid, and trusting to the point of guilelessness, qualities that he retained in adulthood. He writes humorously of his lack of vigilance in financial dealings in his childhood, but at various points expresses the shame and heartbreak that this caused him in later life. "You belong to the de Lanaudières on your mother's side," a ruined man says to the young de Gaspé in chapter 17. "Do not think, young sir, that I compliment or congratulate you on having a kind heart. On the contrary, happy is he—a thousand times happy—who possesses a heart of brass, since he is constrained to live among men." Even so, de Gaspé's kind heart and scapegrace antics earned him many friends while boarding at Quebec's Little Seminary and later as a young bachelor and articled law clerk.

The education offered by the Little Seminary was remarkably well rounded, in comparison with the generally poor state of education in the colony. It included Latin, modern languages, some sciences, and mathematics. The boys rose early, had a strict timetable, a simple diet, and were expected to perform various duties and chores. The strictness of the regime was relaxed on Thursdays, when the boys had a half-holiday. In warm weather this was usually spent walking to La Canardière, a beach near the city, for swimming and games. The long summer vacation was spent at the seminary's farms at Saint-Joachim, near Cap Tourmente downriver from Quebec. These Thursdays and summer holidays were a source of great happiness to de Gaspé. His enthusiastic participation in hikes and hunting expeditions also gave his keen eye a chance to record the landscape and the activities of his companions, and over sixty years later he found these scenes rising to the surface of his memory with a vividness that he was able to recreate in literary terms.

After completing the five-year course at the Little Seminary in 1804, de Gaspé boarded for two years with the Reverend John Jackson, an Anglican clergyman who ran a school in Quebec. During this period, he also attended philosophy courses at the Grand Seminary, the senior branch of the Quebec Seminary intended primarily for the education of future priests. The purpose of boarding with the Reverend Jackson was to learn English, and it was here that he first encountered such authors as Shakespeare and Sterne. As he explained in chapter 16, the highly original style and mood of Sterne particularly attracted him. Earthy, farcical, homely, and touching—Sterne's mastery of anecdote is echoed throughout the *Memoirs*, whether de Gaspé is writing about a gossiping shrew being pelted with horse manure, or a South Shore swain struggling with a bundle that his North Shore super-lass has handled with ease. Moreover, de Gaspé appears to have drawn inspiration for his first chapter from the rambling and whimsical—not to say whacky—opening of *Tristram Shandy* as a model for autobiographical narration. Indeed, the arrangement of his first chapter may be thoroughly puzzling to the reader who is unaware of this possibility, and it is perhaps worth digressing briefly to provide some insight into the imaginative and creative level on which de Gaspé operated.

"As my life and opinions are likely to make some noise in the world," wrote Sterne facetiously, ". . . right glad I am, that I have begun the history of myself in the way I have done." Sterne's "way" was a nonsensical, roundabout anecdote on how he came to be conceived. He then introduced himself with bitter humour:

> On the fifth day of *November*, 1718 . . . was I *Tristram Shandy*, Gentleman, brought forth into this scurvy and disastrous world of ours. . . . for I can truly say, that from the first hour I drew my breath in it . . . I have been the continual sport of what the world calls Fortune. [20]

De Gaspé took a similar approach, first with a whimsical anecdote ("Fanchette's Corner") to justify his avoidance of chronological narrative, [21] then with a story about his grandmother's nose, and finally with the assertion that, "As I am my own oldest contemporary, I am obliged to consider my humble self first in this account." With the same bitter humour as Sterne, he continued,

> The cry of pain that I gave upon opening my eyes to the light must have been grievous indeed. . . . I cannot write the history of my contemporaries without speaking of my own

27

life. . . . The reader will therefore pardon my introducing myself on the very day of my birth. On the 30th of October in the year 1786 . . . a very puny little being first opened his eyes to the light."

De Gaspé was not sent to learn English for his literary edification, however, but in order to acquire a useful asset. When his two years were up, he became an articled clerk in the office of Attorney-General Jonathan Sewell, and finished his legal training in the office of Olivier Perrault. By his own account he led a delightful bachelor life with his many French and English friends, his office hours being mitigated by mess dinners, racing, parties at the homes of hospitable families such as the de Salaberrys and the Sewells, and attendance at official balls. He became a full-fledged lawyer in 1811, and after some years' practice was appointed sheriff of Quebec in 1816. In the meantime he had performed militia duties in Quebec City during the War of 1812, acted as official government French translator, and married Suzanne Allison, the daughter of a British officer. Her mother was a member of the distinguished French-Canadian Baby family of Upper Canada. It is perhaps worth remarking that de Gaspé did not portray his wife in his *Memoirs*, apart from a brief mention of her beauty and virtue. Mother, aunts, and female cousins are drawn with vivid touches, so this omission cannot be from any reluctance to "allude to a lady in these memoirs," a "Rubicon" that he readily crossed at the end of chapter 1.

Everything seemed to smile on this pleasant young man, yet on November 14, 1822, six years after his appointment as sheriff, he was relieved of his office as a result of a debt to the crown that he was unable to reimburse. He was a ruined man, forced to retreat to the manor house of Saint-Jean Port-Joli, where his mother received him after the death, in February 1823, of his father. With him went his wife and family of seven children, later to expand to thirteen. The role of de Gaspé's mother in sheltering her son and his family has yet to be evaluated. In addition to her more tender qualities, she was a woman of intellect and sound judgment. On the death of her husband she became co-seigneuresse with her son of Saint-Jean Port-Joli and L'Islet-à-Peau, retaining the usufruct or life use of the other half, which was thus saved from confiscation.

De Gaspé did not refer explicitly to his financial débâcle in his memoirs, although he gave a sensitively-drawn account of the ruined

Mr. Ritchie in chapter 17. The Abbé Casgrain, however, was of the opinion that "Monsieur de Gaspé painted himself in *Les Anciens Canadiens* under the pseudonym of Monsieur d'Egmont," also a ruined man. "I will not try . . . mitigate the extent of my follies . . . but one thing is certain: I could have met my own expenses, but not those of my friends. . . . my signature was at the disposal of all the world. That . . . was my greatest mistake."[22]

So bitter was this experience that de Gaspé could only refer to it obliquely and symbolically, portraying the anguish of betrayal in his account of old Mr. Ritchie (who, unlike de Gaspé, never succeeded in outliving his humiliation), and in his evocation of moods of dark reverie, despondency, and painful brooding, particularly during his retirement to the country. The poignant regrets of characters in two legends recounted in the *Memoirs* reflect an emotional truth. These legends, in chapters 7 and 13, were ostensibly told by the old habitants Laurent Caron and Romain Chouinard, whose simple but honest and serviceable wisdom de Gaspé emphasized.

Debtor's prison loomed, and the final blow came in 1838 with the execution of a judgment delivered against him in October 1834 on behalf of the crown for the sum of £1,974 14s. This occurred in the wake of a sentence involving a sum of £1,169 14s., plus the outstanding interest since 1823, handed down against Joseph François Perreault,[23] for whom he had acted as guarantor and who in turn sued de Gaspé for the amount, which the latter could not pay. The possibility of such an execution had been hanging over him for years, and he had tried to avert it by legal means, without success. There is some suggestion that the law was interpreted with undue harshness in his case because of the prevailing mood of repression during and immediately after the 1837-38 Rebellion.[24]

In May 1838 de Gaspé entered the Quebec prison, there to remain until October 1841. His wife and children were given a home in his mother's house nearby.[25] The period of his imprisonment was further embittered by the sudden death of his oldest son in Halifax on March 7, 1841. This was Philippe-Ignace-François, author of "the first French-Canadian novel."[26] The younger de Gaspé, a parliamentary reporter and a journalist for the *Quebec Mercury* and *Le Canadien*, had himself spent a month in prison following threatened violence to a member of the legislative assembly, Dr. Edmund Bailey O'Callaghan, whom he felt had questioned his integrity.[27]

The darkest moments were now past, however. "On July 20, 1841, de Gaspé requested parliament to set him free. The request was referred to a committee composed of Attorney-General Ogden, and members Christie, Hamilton, Neilson, de Salaberry, Viger, Berthelot, and Quesnel. The committee submitted a favourable report. . . . On September 4, 1841, the governor sanctioned an *Act for the relief of Philip Aubert de Gaspé*."[28]

De Gaspé looked back on this event, again in the persona of Monsieur Egmont, commenting with sardonic humour on the committee's hairsplitting deliberations. "In the end, they very politely showed me the door."[29]

With the death of his mother and an aunt in 1842, de Gaspé received a double inheritance that put his financial affairs on a sound footing. Although his wife died in 1847, he began to take a renewed interest in life, becoming involved in a cultural renaissance that was taking place in the city. "He met the historians and archeologists of the old capital, among others François-Xavier Garneau, Georges-Barthélemi Faribault, and the commissary general James Thompson Jr. The conversation of all these veterans usually turned on the antiquities of Quebec. Gaspé more than any others, because of his lengthy absence, was able to gauge the manifold changes that had taken place. . . . It was before this circle, as well as in family reunions, that he related his memories before writing them down."[30]

De Gaspé's seclusion in the country may have reflected comparative material poverty, but it provided unsuspected riches for the future writer. The comfortable circle that gathered around the candlelight after supper in the old manor house included, apart from his thirteen children, the author and his wife, Mrs. Allison (his mother-in-law, née Thérèse Baby), his mother, and his aunt, Marie Louise Olivette de Lanaudière. The conversation must have often turned to the days of de Gaspé's childhood and earlier. His own contributions to the conversation and his talent for narration were described by the Abbé Casgrain.[31]

Casgrain was admittedly one of de Gaspé's greatest admirers and tended to mythologize his subject. The young daughter of de Gaspé's notary and business manager perhaps provided a more objective view in a rare glimpse of the author from a different angle. "Almost every day in the summer we used to see Monsieur de Gaspé arriving or else would pay him a visit. I was just a little girl, you understand,

and he used to tease me about my clothes or my dolls. I still seem to hear his sardonic laugh, and yet at the same time his distinguished manner commanded respect. I remember the attack of whooping cough in his seventies. He was writing his first book, *Les Anciens Canadiens*, at the time, and almost didn't finish it. Each of his coughing fits had me shaking all over, and I used to hide behind my parents."[32]

The publication of the novel in 1863 was a resounding success, and the first edition was quickly followed by a second, revised and corrected by the author, in 1864. Laudatory comments came from as far afield as the *Dublin Review*, quoted in Henry J. Morgan's 1867 *Bibliotheca Canadensis*. The writer who could produce such gratifying results had by no means exhausted his material, however, and de Gaspé was now preparing a new work for publication. In 1866 the *Mémoires* appeared and were considered a "solid" success.[33] Morgan quoted an extract from a review in the *Revue canadienne* signed "S. Lesage" that concluded, "A skilful and sensitive observer, he has been able to make a judicious choice from the infinite amount of material that must have presented itself to his memory." In a paper read in 1867 before the Quebec Literary and Historical Society, Dr. W. J. Anderson made liberal use, with acknowledgement, of de Gaspé's account of the de Salaberry family.[34] Almost immediately the content of this paper was included in a biographical sketch of Charles-Michel de Salaberry, "the hero of Chateauguay," in William Notman's *Portraits of British Americans*, again with acknowledgement of de Gaspé as the source.[35]

The abundance of praise accorded the nostalgic and historical element in de Gaspé's work should not be allowed to obscure its value as literature. Although he called his work *Mémoires* in keeping with the French tradition, the book is in fact one of Canada's great autobiographies,[36] in which the author evokes in imaginative terms both the outer and inner landscapes through which he has passed, imparting to his readers not only a picture of the society of a certain period of Canadian history, but also an implicit account of the human journey.

Writing in the middle of the nineteenth century, during what a modern critic has referred to as "the classical age of autobiography" ushered in by Rousseau's *Confessions*, Goëthe's *Poetry and Truth*, and Wordsworth's *Prelude*,[37] de Gaspé combined the literary heritages of France and Great Britain, both of which had contributed to the development of the genre. Even his style, a discursive prose exhibiting the "natural speaking style" that Northrop Frye saw as an ingredient of autobiography,[38] reflected his debt to literary precursers of the genre. Apart from the great memoir writers of France whom he mentioned or quoted, such as the Sieur de Joinville, d'Argenson, and Madame de Staal de Launay, is it possible to discern an affinity with the major proponent of the genre: Rousseau. Indeed, the latter's autobiographical works, *Confessions* (1781) and *Rêveries du promeneur solitaire* (1782) offer some striking similarities in subject and treatment. Rousseau, for example, recounts a fire seen as a child, beginning, "One Sunday when I was at Mamma's, a building belonging to the Franciscans, which adjoined her house, caught fire. This building contained their oven, and was crammed to the roof with dry faggots."[39] In a passage in chapter 3 of the *Memoirs*, de Gaspé echoes not only the details and the prose rhythm of Rousseau, but also the narrative flow and point of view, as the opening sentences indicate: "I was in school at the old bishop's palace near the Lower Town gate when the tocsin sounded from the cathedral belfry. . . . The roofs were as dry as tinder, and that of the Recollets' church had the added attraction of being covered with tufts of green moss."

Similarities in imagery and mood are especially evident in passages from Rousseau's *Rêveries* and de Gaspé's *Memoirs* where, in a woodland retreat, each seeks solace from the injustices of their fellow men. Rousseau writes of having been "transported brusquely" to the shores of Lac de Bienne. "Beneath the forest shade I felt forgotten, free, and untroubled, as though I no longer had enemies, or as though the greenery of the woods were protecting me from their attacks. . . . Not many travellers frequent the country, but it is attractive to the solitary thinker who likes . . . to commune with himself in a silence broken only by the eagle's cry, the intermittent twittering of a few birds, and the roar of mountain torrents."[40]

De Gaspé describes the "shrill, piercing call" of loons on Lac Trois-Saumons, and in chapter 7 goes on to say: "The profound and religious silence that reigns in this solitude is what first strikes the visitor. He experiences a feeling of well-being and security, much as a man who . . . finds himself suddenly transported to some restful haven far from the malicious attacks of men." Rousseau's imagery appears again in chapter 14: "Often I sought the forest calm. . . .

There I met only friends; their church-like silence quieted my thoughts, and the roar of the storm added nothing to my agony."

The literary affinities to be found in de Gaspé's work are numerous, and not surprising given the evidence of wide reading in the *Memoirs*. The details of his literary debt to Scott, in particular, have still to be explored. While acknowledging these influences, we must nevertheless recognize that the Memoirs constitute a genuine literary creation, carefully thought out to provide an impression of immediacy. It may be, as he avers in the first and last pages of the work, that he originally set out to use up the notes left over from his novel, although recent critical theory would consider this apologia typical of the true autobiographer. In any event, taken as a whole the work achieves a "rhythm of continuity"[41] that denotes a sustained professional approach by the author to his craft. There are four major divisions, each fairly consistent in mood, that together reflect the pattern of his life: the nostalgic account of childhood and family reminiscences (chapters 1 to 5); exuberant youth and young manhood accompanied by success and popularity (chapters 6 to 11); retreat from the city and a lively social environment to a relatively poor and isolated rural existence, bringing a growing appreciation of the humbler, more elemental aspects of life (chapters 12 to 14); and finally the return to active society (chapters 13 to 17), represented by a sort of literary coda that is tempered by nostalgia and an awareness of approaching death, in which he seems to take stock of the distance he has traveled and the changes that have occurred. "Bonsoir la compagnie," he says, in a final farewell to his readers.

De Gaspé died at the Quebec home of his son-in-law, Judge Andrew Stuart, husband of Elmire-Charlotte.[42] The Abbé Casgrain was present, and wrote that "the supreme moment of the good old man formed a truly biblical scene." The author was "surrounded by his children and grandchildren, who filled the room in which he lay dying, and whom he saw kneeling around his death-bed. . . . His mind was as lucid, his speech as clear, as in his finest days. . . . 'I won't forget you in my prayers,' said I, coming close to him. 'Nor I, in eternity,' he replied, pressing my hand affectionately." After further prayer, his children and grandchildren came "one after the other, to give a last kiss to the icy forehead of the old man, who spoke a loving word to each. Finally, he joined his hands, raised his eyes, then closed them, and like his Saviour gave a deep sigh. That was the end. The pallor of death spread over his face, which became placid and as white as marble."[43]

Thus passed Philippe-Joseph Aubert de Gaspé, one of the "fathers of the prose fiction tradition" in Canada,[44] and a Canadian of old.

J.B.,
Montreal, September 1987

CHAPTER ONE

And I have hearkened back to these things
for you, so that those who possess this
book may firmly believe its record of what
I have truly seen and heard.

Memoirs of the Sire de Joinville [A]

I detest prefaces, although this does not prevent me from reading them, contrary to a great many who deprive themselves of this privilege. Like our great satirist Boileau when invited to an unappetizing dinner, I feel that a preface resembles a host asking his guests derisively if they would mind excusing him. [B]

This being said, I don't quite know how to begin, not wishing to be so contradictory as to criticize in others what I find myself constrained to do in commencing this chapter.

A great many of my friends, who have read *Les Anciens Canadiens* [C] with feelings of patriotism rather than strict judgment, have been kind enough to reproach me for not having begun to write forty years ago. Was this meant as a compliment, or a piece of barbed wit?

Experience notwithstanding, I have never been able to convince myself that people mean to hurt anyone deliberately, particularly an old man. I therefore took this remark at face value and set myself to write.

If I may risk an "Irish bull"—or an Irish pun—let me say that, since I am my own oldest contemporary, I am obliged to consider my

35

humble self first in this account. I really ought to recall every detail of my life from the very day of my birth, for the cry of pain that I gave upon opening my eyes to the light must have been grievous indeed.

Whether or not I may be criticized for beginning with myself matters little to me. I cannot write the history of my contemporaries without speaking of my own life, bound up as it is with those whom I have known since childhood. My own story will therefore be the frame within which I crowd my memories.

The reader will forgive me for beginning with a tale. At my age, I take nothing seriously save death; the rest is but a comedy that often turns to tragedy. "Thus he who thought to catch is caught," runs the refrain of an old Canadian song.

FANCHETTE'S CORNER

> Put it in the corner....I forgot to put it in the corner.
>
> *A Tale Told by my Grandmother*

Once upon a time there was a woman named Fanchette. She was a slattern if ever there was one, and left everything lying about the house. Whenever anyone reproached her, she always replied, "I forgot to put it in the corner. Put it in the corner." The poor corner was overflowing with the accumulated rubbish of twenty years.

If one of her little ones banged his nose and cried piteously while clasping it with both hands, Fanchette would take the child in her arms and say, by way of consolation, "Don't cry, my love. I forgot to put that nasty log in the corner, and it tripped you."

One day, as Fanchette's oldest daughter came out of her room dressed for a ball with her hair powdered white, she stumbled over a bucket. Headfirst into a pail of dirty water she went, spilling it all over her. She emerged in a flood of tears, coated from head to foot in starch-paste. The mother, leaving a pan filled with boiling fat on the fire, hurried toward her. "Never mind, my sweet. I forgot to put that horrid bucket and that wretched pail in the corner."

The short-sighted grandfather came running to see what all the fuss was about, tripped, and sat down in the middle of the frying fat, screeching like a tenderfoot being roasted by his enemies. The daughter tried to unstick his trousers, part of which had become glued to the unwilling martyr, and in the process skinned the old fellow like an

36

eel. By way of consolation, Fanchette wailed the whole time: "It's all my fault, dear Papa; I forgot to put my pan in the corner . . . of the fireplace. I won't forget next time."

In the evening her husband returned from work and fell over a toolbox left on the doorstep, giving himself a lump on the forehead as big as a hen's egg. Swearing like a man possessed, he shouted to his wife to bring the vinegar bottle to bathe the bruise. Fanchette ran to the larder; the sound of breaking crockery was heard, and the husband bawled out, "Where the devil are you with that vinegar!"

"It's nothing, my dear," answered Fanchette. "I left the bottle on the counter and unfortunately I broke it; but it doesn't matter—brine is just as good for bumps on the head. I'm off to the cellar to get some."

In her hurry to get there, the hapless Fanchette caught her legs on something and fell headlong into the cellar, breaking her neck.

I told my mother this tale one day. She laughed heartily, being a particularly tidy and well-organized woman herself, and asked me where I'd heard it.

"My grandmother told me," said I.

"Don't be silly," she replied. "You were barely three years old when my mother-in-law died, and my own mother passed away shortly after you were born."[1]

"All the same, I knew my grandmother—I mean the one who died last," I retorted. "She had a big pair of silver spectacles. They pinched so tightly that it was almost impossible to loosen them. I used to grab them with my small hands, and had I been strong enough I might have pulled her nose off." And forthwith I gave a graphic description of my grandmother's nose, a nose à la Villiers de L'Isle-Adam, such as must have adorned her ancestor, the Grand Master of the Order of Saint John of Jerusalem: in a word, a nose worthy of the knights of old. "For you often told me," I added, "that in family conversation a respectable nose was always referred to as a nose à la Villiers de L'Isle-Adam in memory of our revered forebear."[2]

My mother's laughter rang out. "Don't you know, my dear boy, that in days gone by all old ladies used to wear spectacles without sides, jokingly called *pince-nez*? You must be confusing ones seen recently with your grandmother's, which you couldn't possibly remember."

"What do you mean, couldn't remember!" I expostulated. "I remember how she used to take me on her lap in the evening and let me play with her rosary and all its medals."

I proceeded to give an exact description of it.

"Pooh!" scoffed my mother. "All rosaries were like that then; you're just imagining things."

"Just imagining things!" I cried indignantly. "As if every child didn't remember at least one grandmother out of two! Well then, madame," said I, bowing low, "will you do me the honour of accompanying me into the drawing room?"

My mother laughingly acquiesced to this gallant invitation, and we passed into the drawing room.

"In this room, one evening, I saw a dead person covered with a white sheet. On a little table over there," and I showed her the place, "stood two lighted tapers, and between them a crucifix, a goblet of water, and a little pine branch. My father was kneeling here weeping. You were on your knees too, holding me in your arms, and you motioned to me not to make any noise, pointing to my father."

"Impossible," said my mother to herself. "He was only three years old. But then no one has died in this house since his grandmother, almost fifteen years ago."

In the end we both gave ground. My dear mother granted me my memories of my grandmother's nose, spectacles, rosary, and medals, and for my part I was obliged to confess that I had invented the anecdote attributed to my grandmother.

The reader may suppose, with reason, that I am rambling somewhat. I feel bound to defend myself against an imputation so injurious to my self-respect as an author. There were several anecdotes, no doubt insignificant, that I neglected to mention in *Les Anciens Canadiens*. Being a stubborn old man, I was determined to set them down somewhere. In the midst of this quandary an ingenious solution came to mind. I will imitate that dear Fanchette, thought I, and make of this present work a corner, like hers, for everything that passes through my head, whether about Canadians old or new.[1] After all, the only cost is the labour, and the worst that could happen would be to break my neck like Madame Fanchette. I shan't be any tidier, what's more, and will pile in my anecdotes as they occur, with no fixed plan apart from a vague chronological order—and even this I don't undertake to observe faithfully.

38

The reader will therefore pardon my introducing myself on the very day of my birth. On the 30th of October in the year 1786, in a house within the walls of Quebec where the archbishop's palace now stands, a puny little thing first opened his eyes to the light. He was tenacious of life, however, for he is holding a pen today at the age of seventy-nine. After howling night and day without interruption for three months beneath the rooftree of his maternal grandmother, widow of the Chevalier Charles Tarieu de Lanaudière,[E] the little Philippe Aubert de Gaspé was transported to Saint-Jean Port-Joli. Here he was taken to a house of somewhat modest appearance, which nevertheless presumed to replace the opulent manor house of an earlier age, razed by our English friends in 1759.

I cannot explain why I should remember my paternal grandmother before my father and mother. Could it be that the old lady's sudden disappearance left a gap in my life? The fact is, I have no memory of my father and mother until the day I saw them kneeling beside my grandmother's body. I surely knew nothing of death, and yet there remains the impression that the lifeless body covered with a white shroud was that of my paternal grandmother, and that I would never see her again.

Childhood was full of charm for me. I cared nothing for the past and still less for the future. I was happy: what more could I want? Each evening I reluctantly left my playthings; but the certainty of seeing them on the morrow consoled me, and I would be up at dawn to resume the games of the previous day.

At dusk I used to roam around the manor courtyard, finding infinite amusement in building miniature castles in Spain, and giving fantastic names to the trees dominating the magnificent promontory to the south of the seigneurial domain. My imagination would seize upon some resemblance to a living being, and in this way I created a whole menagerie of men, women, and children, as well as domestic animals, wild beasts, and birds. Should the night be calm and clear, I felt no anxiety for my beloved menagerie. But if the wind howled or the rain poured down in torrents, or if thunder shook the cape to its very foundations, I was filled with anxiety for my friends. It seemed to me that they were fighting a great battle among themselves, and that the strong were devouring the weak. I was relieved to find them safe and sound in the morning.

One fine day I found myself carried, as if by magic, to the city of Quebec. I must have been very young, for I have no idea how I made the journey. I was in the Place d'Armes and a regiment was being drilled—the regiment of his Royal Highness, the Duke of Kent, father of our gracious sovereign, Queen Victoria. I suppose the prince must have been pointed out to me; but in those days I judged men by the amount of noise they made, as many are wont to do nowadays. Thus it was that the only two actors in this novel spectacle who attracted my attention, and whom I recall today, were the bass drummer and the huge black who waved two steel plates above his head, banging them rhythmically, one against the other.

According to my parents, I was blessed with a prodigious memory during my childhood. As to my powers of intellect, I will let the reader decide. By the age of six, I knew all the fables of the good La Fontaine by heart; I had memorized the cities of the world, even those of China, I believe; and I had enough knowledge of history to try the patience of even the most inveterate pedants. Lady Simcoe,[F] who had the reputation of being a bluestocking,[3] once said to my mother, "Be so good as to bring your son when you come for tea this evening. I am told he is quite a scholar."

I was paraded through the drawing rooms of Quebec like some rare little animal. What a pity Barnum wasn't yet born: he would have purchased the little creature for a fabulous sum. In a word, Pic de la Mirandole[G] was a perfect dunce compared to my mother's son Philippe.

In all seriousness, however, it appears that my memory was astonishingly good. It seems to me that I have always been able to read. A quite natural circumstance led my mother to begin teaching me. Happening to have me on her lap one day while reading, she took my hand in hers and pointed to several strange-looking letters, naming three or four. A fortnight later, when I was again on her lap and she was holding a book, I gave a shout of joy and unhesitatingly named my new friends with the funny faces. O luckless Philippe! Laziest of children! You had just sealed your fate, your enslavement. How many canings, lessons, and punishments were your treacherous friends to bring down upon your unsuspecting head? Their number is legion!

The most sanguine predictions as to my future were already being made when, alas! an inopportune attack of typhoid fever at the age of seven brought me to death's door. The doctor who saved my life predicted that I would lose my prodigious memory as a result of this cruel malady. His prophesy was partly accurate, since for the remainder of my studies I displayed a very ordinary memory, rather unpromising than otherwise. Nevertheless, when it comes to events witnessed, conversations that seem perfectly trivial, or places and objects, I can vouch for its phenomenal nature. Even the most insignificant things observed from the age of three onward are as vivid to me now as they were then.

What makes me believe this capacity for recall to be so exceptional is that very few of my contemporaries, after a space of forty or fifty years, can remember the anecdotes about our childhood that I recount to them. How is one to account for this type of memory? With me, both the senses of sight and sound must be struck at the same time. When going over my lessons aloud, I learned them twice as fast as when studying silently. I leave it to the physiologists to answer the question. Even so, I wouldn't wish such a memory on my worst enemy. For every ten kind or flattering words, one remembers a hundred harsh comments that still have the power to make one's cheeks burn after a lapse of three-quarters of a century.

I was talking recently to my old and witty friend, Dr. Painchaud.[11] "Do you remember," said I, "how we were the two best swimmers at the Quebec Seminary, and how the masters refused to let us have a deciding race when swimming at La Canardière?[i] We agreed to put it off until the first suitable opportunity. Don't you remember how, a few days before the August vacation, having some time off as was usual at that season, we rushed down to the old Palace beach, where the river waters had risen to within a few feet of the king's woodyard?"[j]

"I'm afraid I don't," said my friend.

"Can't you remember how the tide was beginning to ebb, and how a schooner was putting out to sea with a canoe lashed behind, aided by the current and two huge oars?[k] And do you remember how, in spite of the distance, we agreed to swim out to the schooner, sure of being able to rest in the canoe if we became tired, and that after a tremendous effort we arrived at the same time?"

"I don't recall it," said the doctor again.

"What! Only sixty-three years since this escapade, and you've forgotten what a risk we both took? Let me refresh your memory.

"Do you remember that we had barely grasped the canoe when a brute of a man threatened us with a long pole? That we let go in our

41

This rare photograph of the front of the de Gaspé manor house at Saint-Jean Port-Joli was taken about 1885. The building was destroyed by fire in 1909. Photographer unknown. Public Archives Canada. PA-14845

The seigneurial mill on the Trois-Saumons river, where de Gaspé's grandfather took refuge with his family after Wolfe's soldiers burned the original manor house in 1759. Photo. Public Archives Canada. PA-36853

terror? And that it was only after a life-and-death struggle that we reached the shore and lay motionless on the sand for what seemed an age?"

My old friend had forgotten the whole episode, even though his memory was certainly more acute than mine as a student at the seminary, which we began and finished together. As for me, I remember the very colour of the pole the bully held: it was cherry wood.

Near the Quebec law courts one day, I happened to meet a stranger asking for directions. After a somewhat drawn-out conversation, he told me his name was Riverin.

"Have you ever lived in Saint-Jean Port-Joli?" I asked.

"Yes, for three or four years, according to what my father told me; but I was too young to remember."

"And yet you're the same age as I am," I replied. "My mother always told me so. I remember you as though it were yesterday, after more than sixty-six years. You used to come and play with me often. Your father was a widower and lived in a house belonging to mine, near our Trois-Saumons mill. The last time I saw you was just before you left. We were in the courtyard, opposite the window to the northeast of the front door of the manor. I can still remember that we were very absorbed in making two little wooden horses eat from a manger, improvised from the bottom of a broken bottle filled with grass and water. Whether because of the excitement of such an ingenious discovery, or through mere clumsiness, I pressed my hand down hard on the makeshift manger. The cut on my finger left a scar that I still bear. I was just four years old at the time."

Monsieur Riverin had forgotten everything.

Let us return, however, to the attack of typhoid, then known in Canada as putrid fever. If nothing else, this story serves to illustrate the ways in which God moves to save the life of a human creature.

For three days I had given hardly any sign of life, and was expected to die at any moment. The country doctor who was treating me had probably never been near a medical school, for he had not the slightest idea what my illness was, and the treatment he made me undergo was more likely to kill than cure. He was one of those surgeons who, in days gone by, were given the title *frater*,[4] which is perhaps the equivalent of a "hospital-mate" or English orderly. The frater may well have performed the same function in French army hospitals.

43

Any frater whom I knew in childhood always administered such huge pills that they had to be split in four to be swallowed. This didn't prevent them from frequently curing the sick. The habitants were loud in their praises of the frater, and thought him a clever surgeon, a pleasure to deal with, and one who really knew his business when it came to purging. The doctors in our present progressive century consider bile a myth, and consequently administer almost invisible globules for pills. This doesn't prevent them from also effecting the occasional cure, and so everyone is happy.

A short anecdote concerning a frater seems appropriate here. One evening, a French-Canadian maidservant of Lady Dorchester's[L] had taken a remedy prescribed by her French doctor (all fraters were French). The maid had promptly gone into terrifying convulsions, and the Château Saint-Louis was in an uproar. The governor's family doctor was sent for in all haste. He declared that he could prescribe nothing until he knew what the unfortunate woman had swallowed. Lord Dorchester rushed to meet the frater who had been urgently summoned. "What on earth have you given this poor girl? She's dying!" said the governor.

"Your Excellency," replied the Aesculapius, "they were good little English remedies; I know nothing about them."

This Aesculapius was named Soupirant.[M]

The governor's physician was able to save the girl's life, despite the good little English remedies that the frater had administered in all ignorance of what they contained. Soupirant's exceptionally naïve reply to Lord Dorchester went the rounds of Quebec for six months, affording the citizens much amusement.

This naturally brings me back to my own case. I was believed to be dying, and one evening my sobbing mother said, "The very evening before he fell ill, the poor darling was playing on the carpet near me in my room, and I heard him say to himself, 'If I were Dr. Oliva's little boy, I wouldn't die, even if I were very sick.'"

My father hesitated not an instant. Fifteen minutes later two messengers had their feet in the stirrups and were heading for Quebec at full gallop—one to warn the doctor and the other to arrange for relays of carriages. A generous reward awaited those who spared neither men nor horses.

I don't know whether they spared the horses, but as far as men were concerned, I know that my father's miller, who was very attached to our family, rode all the way to Quebec. For a fortnight after this he could not sit down—it kept him all the more on his toes for his customers, you might say.

Here is what inspired the comment that saved my life at the age of seven.

My father often used to visit his friend Dr. Oliva[N] in the little town of Saint-Thomas, before the latter moved to Quebec. On one of these visits he found the entire family in a state of great affliction. Frederick, the doctor's eldest son, was on the point of death.

"Tomorrow my child will be no more," said the celebrated physician to his friend.

"Have you no resource in your healing art to save the life of a child with such a sound constitution?" asked my father.

"Yes," answered the doctor, "there is one very slight chance, but my wife would never consent to her child undergoing such harsh treatment. If he died as a result, people would say I killed him, and everyone would point to me as my own son's executioner."

"Have you told her how desperate your son's case is?" countered my father.

"She knows the child will be dead by tomorrow morning," said Dr. Oliva.

"Madame Oliva is a woman of character and superior judgment," said my father. "She knows your skill and will agree to anything. If the mother consents, you oughtn't to worry about village gossips."

Upon this they entered the sick child's room, where they found the mother and several of her friends, as well as neighbours from the town of Saint-Thomas. The doctor examined the child, shaking his head sadly.

"So it has come at last," said the poor mother. "Can't you do something more—you whom I've seen perform such wonderful cures?"

"There's one possibility, my dear wife," said the doctor, "but you'd never consent."

"What is it? Tell me quickly!"

"Bring in a tub of ice-cold water and plunge the child in it."

The visitors let out horrified cries. Madame Oliva rose calmly and said to them, "Come with me into another room. This precious child's life is as dear to my husband as it is to me."

My father stayed by his friend and the child. The boy was plunged into a tub of water brought from the river, and after this icy bath he was put to bed, warmly wrapped in flannel. At the end of almost half an hour a heavy sweat broke out, and this saved his life.

I had heard my father tell of this extraordinary cure, and I suppose I must have felt the typhoid germ taking hold when I uttered the words, "If I were Dr. Oliva's little boy, I wouldn't die, even if I were very sick."

Dr. Oliva was now living in Quebec City. As soon as he arrived, he totally reversed the frater's treatment. It was the end of November, but nevertheless he had the fire in my room put out and all the windows opened. He then gave orders to change my clothing and bed linen, and to throw out everything that had been used for me.

"But he'll die in my arms while I'm changing him," protested my mother. "He's barely breathing."

"Fear nothing, madame," replied the doctor. "The fresh air is already giving him strength, and clean linen will do three times as much good."

And so he saved my life. The news flew around the parish that the doctor from Quebec had murdered me, and that instead of keeping me warm as his confrère had done, he was treating me with ice. It was not until after my convalescence that the parishioners would admit I was still alive. This admission was usually accompanied, however, by a shake of the head and the shrewd comment, "Just the same, the doctor did his best to kill him; the little mosquito must have body and soul bolted together, and as many lives as a cat!"

My mother, who had witnessed the unbelievable change resulting from the doctor's treatment, now told him that she had another anxiety: there was whooping cough in the house. She feared that in my weakened state an attack of this cruel malady would carry me off.

"The chances are a hundred to one against his catching it," said the doctor, "and if he does, the attack will be so slight as to be hardly noticeable."

For the next ten years I lived in fear of whooping cough, as my mother often pointed out that I had never had it.

"Bah!" I said to myself at the end of this time. "I don't care about Dame Whooping Cough now."

For a further sixty years I continued to live free from anxiety on this score, at the end of which I came down with a dreadful cold, accompanied by a raging fever and fits of choking. For three months I was so ill that my life wasn't worth tuppence. I maintained that it was whooping cough, since I had never had it and now exhibited all the symptoms. No one would believe me. The coughing was so violent that I frequently went several seconds without breathing. I hopped about, wheezing, while my daughters slapped me on the back like a small child, frightened that I would suffocate. Often during the night they would rush to my aid.

I have always considered a change of scene as beneficial as a visit to a doctor. At the beginning of my illness I had taken refuge in the country. When I felt strong enough, I went out in the carriage for a league or two every day. The habitants of Saint-Jean Port-Joli and L'Islet shook their heads ominously when they saw me pass by, which doleful sign I interpreted to my companions thus: "We'll soon be saying 'the late Monsieur de Gaspé.'"

Back in Quebec toward autumn, completely recovered despite the predictions of my well-meaning censitaires,^o among others, I recounted my symptoms to Dr. Morrin, a skilled physician as well as an honourable and respected citizen.^P

"Have you ever had whooping cough?" asked the doctor.

"Never, as far as I know. My mother always said that I never had."

"Well!" replied the doctor, "you can rest easy: you've just had it."

"And about time, too," I said. "At the age of seventy, one shouldn't have to worry about whooping cough like a mother with young children."

Dr. Morrin told me that in all his long experience as a doctor, he had only encountered one case similar to mine, although several instances were known.

I would give a great deal to have studied medicine in order to be enlightened on the following important question: Are all the ills to which man is heir, such as measles, scarlet fever, whooping cough, and even smallpox, necessary in order to purge the human body of all impurities? Do they clear the blood, fortify the constitution, and increase a man's strength and health once he has had them? The fact is that since surviving whooping cough at seventy, I have gained new vigour and strength. My health, which had been indifferent during the previous five or six years, suddenly improved. Since that time I have enjoyed perfect health. It is not given to everyone to make the experiment, however.

In the old days, smallpox caused frightful ravages in Canada. Heat and copious liquids comprised the treatment for those afflicted with this dangerous disease. Dr. Oliva was the first to introduce a diametrically opposed treatment. The use of cowpox vaccine against smallpox had not been discovered at the time, but each spring and fall he made a point of inoculating his patients with smallpox whenever possible, prescribing a daily outing as well. He inoculated me when I was five years old. It was October, and I was taken out in the carriage for more than a league each day. It was Dr. Oliva who said, when smallpox became epidemic throughout the countryside, "Anyone afflicted with this malady would be fortunate if he fell ill beside a stream in the forest, beneath a shelter of fir. Ninety percent would probably recover."[5] Dr. Oliva died about 1797 of a sudden stroke. When it happened I was actually playing in the street with the same child whose life he had saved in so singular a manner. His death was an irreparable loss to the city of Quebec, where good doctors were then a rarity, to say the very least.

I was but lately recounting the cure of Frederick Oliva by an ice-water bath to three friends, all members of the medical fraternity. To my great astonishment they showed no surprise.

"Why don't you apply this remedy in desperate cases?" I asked.

"Ah, well, you see. . . ." They shook their heads.

"I do indeed see," said I. "The parents! Public opinion! But why bother about them? I shouldn't have thought one little insinuation of homicide more or less would scare you."

My friends laughed heartily. "Poor physicians! How many witticisms have been aimed at them since Molière!"

Nevertheless, the routine treatment continued as usual.

To these same doctors I told how one of my children had become dangerously ill following scarlet fever. Dr. Holmes, an excellent doctor from the city of Quebec, was treating the case. Unable to get his patient to sweat, he had a bottle of spruce beer brought up from my cellar. It was winter at the time. The sick shild was given a goblet of this, and almost immediately began to sweat.

"We believe you," said my friends. "A highly appropriate procedure."

"Well, why isn't such a simple remedy used generally?"

The reply was the inevitable, "Ah, well, you see. . . . The parents! Public opinion!"

As for myself—to return to a subject dear to my heart—that unfortunate attack of typhoid was the source of much misery. My mother, believing she had brought a little prodigy into the world but

48

subsequently perceiving her mistake, was forever railing against the wretched fever. This in itself was not such a trial to me; but the message was not lost upon one of my young cousins who, whenever we fought, never missed a chance of pulling a long face and saying in her childish voice, "Of course, you know that my cousin would have been quite bright if it weren't for that horrid fever."

Those who knew Mrs. William Selby, née Marguerite Baby, who died in New York four years ago, were well aware that she was one of Canada's wittiest women. Although she suffered for many years from the dread disease that brought about her premature death, her natural gaiety was undiminished. When I saw her for the last time, we were discussing men and manners. She remarked, with the delightful smile that was habitual to her, "You know, Philippe, in our day we were just as clever as the young people of today, even though they think such a lot of themselves."

"You're perfectly right so far as you're concerned, dear cousin," I responded, "but as for me, you've no doubt forgotten that unfortunate putrid fever. Are you flattering me? Or is this a somewhat belated atonement for your early misdeeds?"

"What!" she cried. "Are you still thinking about that blessed fever? My, what fun I used to have with you! And how furious you used to get in our little quarrels!"

"Well, you may say so now, but all the same I rather liked being the butt of your jokes when it pleased you."

We laughed together for the last time, with the frank, unaffected laughter of our youth. A few months after this conversation, my cousin, who for over fifty years had been the delight of whatever society she graced, died on foreign soil where the vain hope of a cure had led her. Few women were endowed with such amiable qualities as Mrs. Selby. Lovely, good, witty, and charitable, her death left a great void in the community.

Before leaving the subject of my cousin, I will recount a little anecdote of her childhood.

One day, when all the members of our family were gathered, my younger brother was being reproached for being lazy at school by my father, mother, uncles, and aunts. It reduced him to tears. Marguerite Baby, then six years old, came up to comfort him, saying in a low but audible voice, "Don't cry, cousin. When you're grown up you won't find it hard to be as smart as they are."

49

Her mother wanted to punish her for this disrespectful sally, despite the shouts of laughter from the rest of the family. However, my mother took her little niece into her arms, crying, "No, no, Adé (Adélaïde). You shan't punish her. It's really too good a joke on us that a child of her age should perceive that our share of wit is rather limited."

My Aunt Baby was unmoved by this remark. To my way of thinking, she should have gently scolded the little monkey and laughed it off, as my mother did.

If it were not for fear of offending the modesty of Madame de Montenach, daughter of the late Baronne de Longueuil, I would say that the palm for wit was divided between Mrs. Selby and her young cousin of the same age. It was generally said that the sparkling repartee of the one would eclipse that of her absent rival, depending on who had the last word.

It is with some trepidation that I allude to a lady in these memoirs. However, as I have crossed the Rubicon, she may permit me to add that, although she treated her best friends somewhat roundly to their faces, she never allowed the slightest criticism of them in their absence. This is so rare and fine a quality that it pleases me to record it, as well as the even more precious virtue of always keeping her door open with undiminished cordiality to those friends and relations who had met with reverses, and who had been dropped by the wealthy members of society. Often I have seen her four-wheeled coach (of which there were then only three in Quebec) before the door of some modest little shop run by a poor woman, *déclassée* and consequently abandoned not only by her former friends, but by her very family. To those who expressed surprise at such visits, Madame de Montenach would reply simply, "She was my friend in happier times."

Is not this fine, generous, and noble, as well as being exceptional?

I would also name a very dear connection of Madame de Montenach, but I am not sure she would show such forbearance in the matter as my old friend. Nevertheless, she must forgive me if I say a word about her. She knows why gratitude should be the better part of discretion in this case. In deference to her modesty, I will say nothing about her more brilliant qualities, but only the grave can efface from my soul the memory of her generous and compassionate heart.⁶

In passing, let me shed a tear of regret at the untimely death of my friend, Monsieur de Montenach, one of the most accomplished gentlemen of my acquaintance. I shall then end this chapter wherein,

50

to the astonishment of my readers, I have made a prodigious leap of some fifty or sixty years. There are a great many more such leaps in store, and my dear reader will no doubt get used to them.

CHAPTER TWO

The Duke of Kent, hearing of a centenarian living on the Ile d'Orléans, one day paid her a visit. After chatting with the old woman, whose mind was as clear as a bell, he asked if she'd like him to do anything for her.

"Oh yes, Your Royal Highness!" replied the grandam. "Dance a minuet with me, so I may say before I die that I've had the honour of dancing with my sovereign's son."

The prince, acceding gallantly to this request, danced the minuet, bowed graciously, and led her back to her chair. She returned the compliment with a deep curtsey.

This anecdote quite equals any that went the rounds during the visit of the Prince of Wales, the Duke of Kent's grandson. [A]

The duke had a high opinion of a certain soldier in his regiment named Rose or La Rose, a Frenchman known for his unfailing courage. Master La Rose had little taste for the German style of discipline to which he was subjected, however, and so decamped. It was the Duke of Kent himself who arrested the man at Pointe-aux-Trembles. [B] The deserter was sitting at table when the prince and his escort surprised him.

"You're lucky I'm unarmed, milord," said La Rose, "for I swear to heaven that if I had a pistol I'd blow your brains out."

La Rose was condemned to nine hundred and ninety-nine lashes, the maximum allowed under the Mutiny Act. He underwent this terrible punishment without flinching, disdainfully pushing away those who tried to help him dress after the ordeal. Turning to the prince,

52

he tapped his forehead and said, "It takes lead, milord, not the lash, to break a French soldier!"

La Rose certainly deserved the death penalty, but it is reported that the Duke of Kent could never bring himself to apply it.

In days gone by, British soldiers were subjected to a cruel and barbaric discipline. Few Fridays passed during which visitors to the Upper Town market in Quebec were not distressed to hear cries of pain issuing from the barracks courtyard. There were apparently some soldiers capable of withstanding up to five hundred stripes of the lash without a murmur. Many a time have I discussed this subject with British army officers; they all agreed that only twenty-five or thirty miscreants in each regiment received this cruel punishment. Most of them had become almost impervious to pain as a result of frequent lashings. Their hide was so toughened that the cat-o'-nine-tails struck a surface resembling parchment clinging to bones. The officers added that, whenever possible, judges of courts-martial avoided inflicting the lash for the first time, as the men then became hardened offenders.

It seems to me that if English officers could make such an admission, it is blind folly not to remove such a degrading punishment from the Mutiny Act. People are often astonished that the English soldier, ruled as he is by so harsh a military code, shows such courage and perseverance on the battlefield. The reason is evidently that only a very small proportion have been debased by the lash.

It was during this period that the Duke of Clarence,[C] later William IV, visited the British possessions in North America.[1] He was received in Quebec with all the pomp and ceremony due the son of our sovereign. Only one anecdote concerning this visit need be related, I feel. Those who would like to know more about his voyage may consult the Halifax newspaper,[D] and I promise they will be amply rewarded for their trouble.

As was the custom, a grand ball was given at the Château Saint-Louis. Dinner was at four o'clock, and the ball commenced between six and seven. The young prince danced with a few of the more important ladies, be they beautiful, ugly, or merely plain, then kicked up his heels a little and chose his own partners from among the prettiest girls in the room. Lady Dorchester was greatly displeased with this departure from the etiquette laid down for him, and could be heard to exclaim from time to time, "That young man has no regard for the proprieties!"

The young sailor was having such a good time that it wasn't until somewhere between eleven o'clock and midnight that a peculiar circumstance struck him. He then asked my uncle, Charles de Lanaudière,[E] aide-de-camp to Lord Dorchester, whether it was usual in Quebec for ladies and gentlemen to stand during their meals.

"It is out of respect for Your Royal Highness that everyone remains standing in your presence," replied the aide-de-camp.

"Then," said the prince, "tell them my Royal Highness permits them to dispense with this etiquette."

After consulting Lord and Lady Dorchester, the aide-de-camp proclaimed that His Royal Highness, the Duke of Clarence, would allow the ladies to be seated. Not a few of the said ladies, particularly the old ones, were badly in need of this dispensation.

As Fanchette's corner has room for anything, perhaps even events that happened before I was born, I will recount a little story that greatly amused the idlers of the good city of Quebec.

Colonel Murray, nephew of Canada's first English governor, bought a little cottage on the banks of the Saint Charles River, to which he gave the name "Sans Bruit."[F] Once installed, he wrote in the following vein to Messis. F——, peddlers living in Quebec's Lower Town:

Gentlemen,

Kindly send me the following items as soon as possible: (herewith a long list of the colonel's needs).

I am, etc.

(signed) Murray

Sans Bruit, June 1, 17—.

"Now here's a fine thing!" said one of the partners upon reading the letter. "Does the colonel take us for smugglers, wanting us to deliver the goods he needs *sans bruit*, on the sly, like this?"

"Bah!" said the other, after looking over the letter. "These English are so eccentric that nothing they do would surprise me. In winter we wear our woolen stockings inside our shoes: they wear them outside. We wear our waistcoats underneath our jackets: they wear them on top.[2] In any case, it's no business of ours; the colonel is a good customer and we must oblige him. Fortunately, there's no moon tonight. I'll undertake to deliver his things without anyone being the wiser."

It must have been about an hour after midnight when Monsieur F—— entered the courtyard of "Sans Bruit," followed by tow carts laden with merchandise. Not a sound could be heard. At first he knocked softly on the butler's door, then a little harder, without success. Perhaps that worthy functionary had been inspecting the contents of his cellar too thoroughly and was enjoying a sound sleep. Another servant, possibly confined to imbiding the dregs of glasses and bottles, finally opened a door and asked what was wanted.

"I have the things the colonel ordered," said Monsieur F—— "Come quickly and show me where to unload the carts."

"Go to the devil!" said the servant, shutting the door and going back to bed.

Monsieur F—— began knocking again, this time making such a racket that Colonel Murray himself opened a window to ask if the town was on fire or the French rioting.

"Here I am, Colonel. I've brought the goods you ordered," said Monsieur F——.

"Well," said the colonel, "it seems to me you've chosen a very odd time to deliver them, coming here in the middle of the night like this."

"I'm only carrying out your orders, Colonel. I couldn't very well deliver them in secret during the day. But thanks to this dark night and my precautions, I can assure you that no one knows a thing about it."

Either he's mad or else this is his idea of a practical joke, thought the colonel.

"What, me?" he said aloud, beginning to lose patience. "You say I sent you a list and told you to deliver the goods in secret? You'd better go home to your bed, my dear sir; you seem to be badly in need of it."

"Go home to bed!" gasped Monsieur F——. "It's a good thing I've got your letter here in my pocket. These are your exact words: 'Send me the following items, etc., etc., *sans bruit*, June 1.' And if that doesn't mean secretly and on the sly, then I don't understand my mother tongue."

Murray burst out laughing at this, and all was then explained to the satisfaction of the peddler and his customer.

When visiting Quebec, my mother often stayed with her Aunt Desplaines,[G] a rich widow who had taken rooms in the hospice run by the nuns of the Hôpital-Général in order to have a quiet refuge in her old age. These rooms gave on to the church by way of a screened gallery. One morning my mother took me with her to mass. I heard the nuns' choir chanting the service and joined in, piping in my childish, rather off-key voice. My mother tried unsuccessfully to hush me up, then decided that her best course was to remove her unruly child from the sacred precincts. She was very annoyed at having been a party to this little disturbance, however, and after mass went to apologize to the elderly convent chaplain, Abbé de Rigaudville.

"You should have let him continue, Madame," answered the old priest with a reply that was at once gallant, witty, and imbued with religious philosophy. "He sang God's praises in his own way, as do the little birds."

The hospice of the Hôpital-Général was outside the city walls of Quebec. During the siege of 1775 it was protected by the black flag, with the consent of Lord Dorchester, and served as a shelter for the sick and wounded of the American army commanded by General Montgomery.[H] The Abbé de Rigaudville was passing through the rooms on the morning of January 1 when he heard mysterious lamentations—mysterious, because he couldn't understand a word of English. The Americans lifted their hands to heaven, crying, "Montgomery is dead!" The priest knew perfectly well that "Montgomery" must mean their general, but his knowledge stopped there. Presuming, and rightly so, that the news just imparted to the Americans was hardly to their liking and therefore favourable to our side, he hastened to repeat the words he had just heard to the mother superior and nuns of the convent. But the poor nuns were as mystified as the magicians at Belshazzar's feast confronted with the writing on the wall. "Montgomery is dead!" said everybody, trying a variety of inflections without being any the wiser. Finally Mademoiselle Desgoutins, a young Acadian from Louisburg who lived in the hospice, helped them out of their difficulty by informing them of the meaning of "dead," and that, applied to Montgomery, it heralded the good news of the American general's departure from this life. But as the sisters were at that moment surrounded by our foes, they were very careful not to show their joy; on the contrary, everyone pretended to be most affected by the loss, and joined the enemy in repeating lugubriously, "Poor Montgomery is dead!"

Engraved by E. Mackenzie, from the Painting by C.W. Peale in the Philadelphia Museum.

RICHARD MONTGOMERY.

General Richard Montgomery, leader of the American attack on Quebec City, was killed before the walls on December 31, 1775. ("Engraved by E. MacKenzie from the painting by C. W. Peale in the Philadelphia Museum.") Public Archives Canada. C-21122

Assistant Commissary General James Thompson wears the military dress of an earlier day in this 1867 photograph taken by Ellisson & Co. of Quebec. Thompson and de Gaspé were fellow members of the Club des Anciens, an informal group interested in the history and archaeology of old Quebec. Public Archives Canada. C-52167.

Those wishing to see where Montgomery's body was carried after being mortally wounded in the assault on Quebec, December 31, 1775, should go to the Rue Saint-Louis. There, in a tiny house then owned by the Widow Gobert, now No. 44, the body was laid. If the visitor continues his walk as far as the city gate, and is curious to find Montgomery's burial place, let him count one hundred steps in the direction of the citadel, then turn to face the city walls. He will now be a few feet away from the place where Montgomery was buried until about 1825, when his body was handed over to his family by the authorities of the time. Canada has nothing left today but the memory of his defeat and his sword, now in the possession of Assistant Commissioner-General Thompson.[1] It was left to him by his father, one of the defenders of Quebec.

The demise of the rebel Montgomery was not much regretted by the English whom he had betrayed, and even less by the French Canadians whose peaceful settlements he had burned in 1759 while serving under General Wolfe.[J] He had been three days in his grave, perhaps already forgotten by his erstwhile friends, when it was noticed that a last, solitary companion—the most faithful of friends, although not endowed with the faculty of reason—had not abandoned him.

Someone informed my uncle, Charles de Lanaudière, Lord Dorchester's aide-de-camp, that a magnificent dog of the great spaniel breed had lain on Montgomery's grave for three days, scratching the earth and howling mournfully whenever anyone approached.

Was this faithful guardian of the tomb imploring passers-by to bring his master back to life and help him clear away the suffocating earth? What was in that faithful and loving heart? His anguish must have been cruel indeed for him to seek the commiseration of his master's murderers!

When Monsieur de Lanaudière arrived at the graveside, the dog was crouched on the ground watching those present with calm defiance. My uncle said a few words in English, speaking in an affectionate tone and saying the name Montgomery. The poor animal leapt to his feet and let out a wail accompanied by a doleful look. Monsieur de Lanaudière came closer, coaxing the dog and offering him bread and water. The animal hurriedly lapped up a few mouthfuls of water and then sat down on his master's grave again, without taking any other nourishment. To make a long story short, a week passed before my uncle was able to drag him from his master's resting place, after much care and caressing, and giving the dog food and water with his own hands.

Montgomery, as he was now christened, soon became the favourite of his benefactor's family, to which he finally transferred his affections. Six or seven months later, my uncle left Quebec for the seigneurie of Saint-Anne de la Pérade. He ordered his servants to keep the dog confined for a day or two; but that very evening Montgomery escaped, either by using his wits or because of the servants' negligence. Almost twelve hours had elapsed since his master's departure. Early next morning my aunt, wakened by the sound of barking, said to her husband, "I hear Montgomery's voice."

"You're dreaming, Babet (Elizabeth)!"[3] said her husband. "The dog has never been here with us, and he couldn't possibly have guessed what road we took."

It was indeed Montgomery. His master's horses had left at six in the morning, and he had followed their trail during the subsequent night for a distance of twenty-two leagues.

It is my belief that children are generally born truthful and do not acquire the habit of lying except when pushed to do it. First the parents, then the masters to whom their education is entrusted, end by forcing them to hide the truth to escape the usual punishments for what, most often, are mere peccadilloes.

I was born truthful by nature, and don't believe I ever told my parents a single lie, mainly because of the way in which they brought me up, and a seemingly trivial incident. One day my father came in from his garden looking very annoyed indeed and holding a truncated young cucumber.

"Who could've cut this cucumber?" he said to my mother. "My friend Couillard[4] is coming over soon. He prides himself on being a first-rate gardener, and I had hopes of beating him this spring for the early garden prize. Your little devils wreck everything! It's just pure cussedness, too, as they haven't even taken away the piece that was bitten off. It's lying on the hotbed, and you can still see the teeth marks. I'm determined to find out who's responsible."

"What a fuss over a wretched cucumber!" retorted my mother. "You don't have far to look. Ask Philippe. You know he never lies and if he committed this dreadful deed he'll tell you."

I overheard this conversation from a nextdoor room, and learned with surprise and pride that I was not a liar. I didn't really see any merit in this, as it seemed perfectly natural to me. I was very young then. This childhood scene is my earliest memory, and yet the impression left by these words has never faded.

"Did you bite my cucumber?" asked my father, looking at me with his great black eyes.

"Yes I did," I answered. "I put it in my mouth just for fun, and clenched my teeth without meaning to bite through it, but the piece came off in my mouth."

I recount this story, not for the glory, but to point a useful moral. Some children are born with a natural aversion to lying, and parents should encourage such fortunate tendencies. They ought to accept everything the child says as true until they find him out in a lie.

When a child ingenuously admits a fault, he should be pardoned. If it is serious enough to warrant punishment, the child should be made to understand that such punishment has been made lighter because he has confessed.

My father often said, "Once a man has lied to me, I'll never believe another word he says, even if he tells the truth for the rest of his life."

The reader must realize that this pronouncement referred to serious matters only, not the harmless embroideries with which story-tellers enliven their narrative.

A liar constrained to tell the truth is an amusing sight. I had often wondered what M—— would do if summoned as a witness in a court of law. My question was answered most satisfactorily one day. Court was in session, and there he was on the stand, right hand on the Gospel, that declared enemy of all liars. He glanced uneasily back and forth from the Bible to the clerk and judges—those merciless judges who condemn perjurers to the stocks. If he didn't fear God, he certainly feared the stocks, an instrument of punishment that was a permanent fixture in Quebec's Upper Town market place.

Good heavens, how naïve men were in those days! They took everything seriously, even perjury. A poor devil who perjured himself of his own accord got no more sympathy than one of those straw men we put in gardens to scare the crows. Fortunately, all that has changed in our progressive century. A witness commits perjury that brings a family to ruin or condemns an innocent man, and today he is fined a dozen piastres[K] and told nonchalantly by the judge, "Run along, my friend, and mind you don't do it again!" What a vast field for exploitation by those tall, gaunt men Racine speaks of, who are summoned by plaintiffs to swear whatever necessary on their behalf![l] In days gone by, a perjurer was perforce a gaunt man: the continual spectre of the stocks tended to take away his appetite. At present, litigants enter court followed by hired witnesses, whose wide girth testifies to an epicurean existence! Let us join hands, dear friends, and chant the revolutionary "ça ira!" loud enough to demolish the city of Quebec!

But my liar awaits me with uneasy glance, his hand upon the Bible.

The case was a straightforward one of disturbing the peace and assault. The man had witnessed it, but was not otherwise involved. In answer to each of the lawyer's questions he began with a denial, only to revert to a fair approximation of the truth. He managed to get through his testimony somehow, having sweated blood and tears in the effort.

I mentioned that the stocks were a permanent feature of Quebec at that time. It would have been a costly business to build a set for each new malefactor destined to be pinioned therein, as they never remained empty for long. During my childhood and even my youth, few months passed without the city of Quebec being treated to a variety of degrading spectacles: either some unfortunate hanged for grand larceny, or a lesser thief bound to a post, yet a further permanent feature. A man guilty of petty larceny received thirty-nine strokes of the lash. Sometimes an incorrigible offender was tied by the hands to the back of a tumbril and paraded through the town's main thoroughfares, stopping at certain corners to receive a portion of the said thirty-nine lashes until the sentence was completed. On occasion a criminal might be exposed in the stocks for perjury or some other heinous crime. The wooden collar of the stocks formed a horizontal beam atop the gibbet, about three or four feet above the platform. This, in turn, was some eight feet above the ground. The offender had his head and hands imprisoned in the crossbeam, leaving him small chance of dodging the rotten eggs and other projectiles thrown by the rabble.

If the stocks were less than delightful during the warm weather, imagine the sufferings of an offender exposed for an hour on this raised platform, unable to move, in cold weather of twenty to twenty-

Quebec's Upper Town market was a lively meeting ground for all classes of men and beasts, dogs not excepted, as seen in this 1830 watercolour by James Pattison Cockburn. Musée du Québec, photo: Patrick Altman. 44.110

five degrees Réaumur.[M] Of course, this was no concern of the judges. Let the criminal worry about it. After all, he wasn't there for his good deeds. Nevertheless, as custom inevitably tends toward clemency, a certain sheriff took compassion on these poor creatures and in 1816 substituted a set of stocks turning on a pivot for the old-fashioned instrument then in use. (I forbear to name the sheriff in question. Louis Plamondon, one of his lawyer friends with a sardonic turn of mind, called him soft-hearted, although he might just as easily have said soft-headed.)[N]

The criminal could now take a certain amount of exercise, circling rather like the horses in a distillery. He thus avoided being hit in the face by some of the missiles thrown by the populace, who always stood on the same side as the spectators. Alas! the offender, taking advantage of his freedom of movement, began to circle round and round the post. The riff-raff, cheated of the pleasure of pelting their victim in the face, circled with him, still throwing their projectiles, many of which now landed on innocent bystanders. The crowd retreated pell-mell, heartily abusing the overly solicitous official who had given them an unexpected share in the prisoner's sentence.

One Friday in the year 1806, a criminal was pilloried for an odious crime. The enraged crowd was attacking him with increasing fury when soldiers from the barracks joined in. The rioters first hurled themselves on the farmers' carts standing in the marketplace, snatching everything they could lay hands on—eggs, vegetables, calves' heads, feet, entrails, and various organs—despite the cries of the women trying to protect their goods. Having bombarded the criminal, they then set upon the executioner, pursuing him under the farmers' carts where he had taken refuge. In vain did the poor blackamoor slither under the vehicles and between the very horses' feet. He was soundly beaten by both the rabble and the farmers whose goods had been looted.

The rioters next turned on the constables who were trying to maintain order. Attacked from all sides, some took sanctuary in the cathedral or the seminary while others fled down the Côte de Léry[5] where they were pursued as far as the Hope Gate.

The confusion was at its height when Colonel Brock arrived on the scene.[o] Being on horseback he could easily detect the main cause of the riot, and in a thunderous voice ordered the soldiers back to barracks. They hastened to obey the voice of their commander, a man they loved and feared equally. The colonel appeared to reprimand the officer on duty, who immediately ordered the barracks gate shut. The crowd subsided, no doubt fearing the guard would come to the sheriff's aid, and the scene dissolved into burlesque.

The constables had now recovered from their panic. Before they could resume their posts, however, a sailor, waving a brace of partridge, mounted the scaffold and began to harangue the onlookers. With one hand he ruffled the felon's hair, already somewhat tousled, and with the other rubbed the partridge over the criminal's face. This Irish sailor's speechifying must have been exceptionally funny, for spectators who were too far away to hear laughed as hard as those who understood every word.

This reminds me of an anecdote told me by my cousin, Monsieur de Montenach, who had served in the De Meuron regiment.[p] Every company of the Swiss army possesses a wag called a *loustic*.

One day an entire regiment began to laugh while on parade.

"What's so amusing?" said an officer to several nearby soldiers.

"I don't know," said one in heavily accented French, "but the loustic over there said something funny."

But I'm running somewhat ahead of my story and had better get back to the good old days, if only to report a decision that people would find extraordinary now, when judgments are only made with Code in hand. This doesn't prevent judges from frequently being wrong, considering the number of decisions overturned at each session of the appeal courts.

Madame B——, wife of a respectable and law-abiding citizen of Quebec, had one of those malicious tongues that cause the most reputable individuals to tremble. She cared not how outrageous the slander might be. Had it not been for the consideration accorded her husband, generally liked and respected, she would have been sued repeatedly for defamation of character. He disarmed those who laid complaints or threatened court action by saying, "Have mercy, gentlemen; spare me this! I'm already unhappy enough with a spiteful wife who is the bane of my existence!"

There lived in the same city a witty and facetious old man named Liard, who amused everyone with his sallies. He laughed in the faces of those whose reputations had been tarnished by B——'s wife, saying that if she had the audacity to slander him, he knew the recipe for a special plaster that would shut her mouth forever. B——'s wife, getting wind of this threat, immediately gave vent to the most defamatory statements. Monsieur Liard let her go on for some time, despite the raillery of his friends. But one market day, when he judged the time was ripe, he lay in wait for her, prepared to wreak vengeance. As she approached a farmers' cart where he had mounted his battery, he greeted her with these words:

"Hail to thee, fair lady of the viper's tongue!"

"You're a fine one to dare speak to me," cried the termagant. "You old drunkard! Disgusting roué! Thief. . . ."

She was about to continue in this vein when her voice was silenced by an indescribably revolting "plaster" that Monsieur Liard had kept hidden in the cart and now slapped across her mouth.

The affair came before the courts, making a celebrated and highly diverting case for the citizens of Quebec. The accused pleaded guilty, alleging that he had inflicted the punishment to revenge all the respectable people who had suffered so long at the hands of this slanderer.

65

Far from being blameworthy, he considered he had served his country well.

In handing down the sentence of the court, the judge openly regretted being unable to absolve the accused of the offense to which he had pleaded guilty, as the plaintiff well deserved what she got. Furthermore, the court hoped that in future she would profit by this lesson. Following this preamble, Monsieur Liard was condemned to pay the plaintiff the sum of eight piastres (the value of the silk mantle spoiled by him), with each party to pay costs.

Monsieur Liard paid the money and took possession of the mantle produced in evidence. He gave it to a prostitute who went by the soubriquet of "Pock-nose," owing to the loss of part of her nose. The said Pock-nose made a point of showing her appreciation for this fine gift by passing in front of Madame B——'s home at least once a day for the space of six months.

I don't know whether the judgment of this old-time court was strictly legal, but it had the desired effect, for never again did this evil tongue dare speak calumny of anyone. Possibly, so as not to lose the use of this precious organ, she contented herself with mere gossip-mongering.

In days gone by, people in rural areas seldom locked or bolted their houses at night. A lock was as great an object of curiosity for our good and peaceful habitants as iron stoves, of which the first examples made their appearance in the parish of Saint-Jean Port-Joli during my childhood. People would travel a good league of a Sunday to visit the happy owner of such a valuable piece of equipment and so grand a household ornament.

One morning a servant rapped on my father's bedroom door, shouting that during the night a strange man had taken possession of one of the guest rooms. My father donned a dressing gown and duly discovered his friend, Colonel Malcolm Fraser,[◊] who had just awakened.

"Well, Colonel! This isn't 1759!" cried my father.[◊] "Nowadays, when one occupies a Frenchman's house in the night, one at least has the grace to ask him for some supper."

"As for supper," replied the colonel, "I had an excellent one at the home of my friend, Monsieur Verrault, curé of Saint-Roch. He wanted me to sleep there as well, but I refused in order to get nearer Quebec where I want to be by this evening, so you may rest easy on that score.

"As a matter of fact I had difficulty capturing your fortress, defended as it is by your dog Niger.[7] Although I tried to explain that I was a peace-loving Scot as well as a friend of the family, and that he and I were more or less compatriots, I couldn't mollify him. But as one usually comes to some agreement when both sides are willing, your Cerberus finally capitulated on the following conditions, to wit: I was free to enter the house, take possession of a bedroom, and even get into bed, provided the said Niger didn't lose sight of me for an instant and stood sentinel outside my chamber door until daybreak. I suppose he feared my slumbers would be disturbed. Upon my honour, as each of us strictly respected the articles of capitulation, I slept right through the night under the watchful eye of Sir Niger."

To round off this chapter, here is an account of an English eccentricity with which my uncle Charles de Lanaudière, who lived in England for some years, used to amuse his Canadian friends.

A nobleman whose name I have forgotten pushed self-indulgence to the point of becoming addicted to a band of highwaymen. This wasn't in order to rob others, like certain lords of the manor when knighthood was in flower, but to be robbed himself.

Each time the worthy lord returned from London to his country seat, either after Parliament had risen, or after a dinner or an evening at the theatre, his carriage was sure to be stopped at the same place by the same band of thieves. His lordship lowered the carriage window himself, and the leader of the band said courteously, "Your purse, if you please, my lord."

An English lord always has a well-filled purse; but as the strain imposed on it would eventually have been too heavy, he carried a separate wallet for this purpose containing five guineas, no more, no less. This he tossed at the night prowler's head, saying, "Take that, you scoundrel!" The thief bowed low and with the utmost politeness replied, "Thank you, my lord; God grant you long life!"

He then told the coachman to continue on his way.

When friends of the philanthropic nobleman tackled him on the subject, he declared that, all things considered, he preferred to be robbed by this daring rascal who bravely risked his life for five miserable guineas, than to be fleeced by a bunch of cowardly lackeys who plundered his possessions with impunity. "After all," he added, "it's a taste like any other. As I'm so accustomed to it, I think I'd feel something was missing if I went to bed without the thrill of having a loaded pistol pointed at my chest from two feet away!"

Those of my readers who consider this not worth five guineas are certainly hard to please!

CHAPTER THREE

There are a hundred reasons why
I like the Recollets:
A band of jolly fellows they,
Who never stand on ceremony.

Canadian Folksong

THE RECOLLETS

The Recollets were always favourites of mine.[A] I was ten years old when their community was disbanded, after the fire that destroyed their monastery and church on September 6, 1796. The government took immediate possession of the site and outbuildings. A few days after the disaster, stalls selling all sorts of liquor were set up in their lovely orchard.

As the Recollets were universally liked, there was no hesitation in attributing the burning of their possessions to the malevolence of the British government. This slander circulated for quite some time, all the more readily because of the considerable distance between their convent and the place where the fire started. No one could explain why the Recollet church, which stood near the present court house, burned at almost the same time as the house of Judge Monk[B] in the Rue Saint-Louis, where the officers' quarters of the garrison now stand. It was here that the fire began.

During the great conflagration of the suburb of Saint-Roch, I witnessed a scene that explains this phenomenon.

I was in school at the old bishop's palace near the Lower Town gate when the tocsin sounded from the cathedral belfry, followed instantly by the drums raising the general alarm. It was then the custom to beat the drums through all the streets for as long as the drummers had the strength to hold their sticks. Sometimes the "drum! dum! dum!" could be heard ages after the fire had been put out.

I had just received a caning. The number of strokes equalled my mistakes in reciting a French verb of the first conjugation with the endings of the second (I leave the task of calculating the quantum to the grammarians). Suddenly I heard the sound of the great bell. At the first peal I grabbed my hat and raced toward the scene of disaster. It was September, and not a drop of rain had fallen for six weeks, so it was said. The roofs were as dry as tinder, and that of the Recollets' church had the added attraction of being covered with tufts of green moss in several places.

As I passed by this building I heard a noise and looked up to see a cowl emerging from a trap door in the roof, followed by an entire Recollet, pail in hand. He was putting out a live cinder carried onto the roof by the wind, which was blowing hard. This monk was probably the last person left in this tranquil retreat, as all the others were at that moment working desperately to save the Ursuline convent, which had already caught fire two or three times. The clergy, led by the bishop, had rushed to the aid of the worthy nuns, and it was their energetic action that saved this valuable building, devoted to the education of rich and poor alike.

I stayed nearly a quarter of an hour watching Judge Monk's house burn. It was it first time I had seen a fire. I thought the men rather stupid to be throwing mirrors and trays of glassware and precious china out of first and second storey windows. It was all right for the mahogany chairs and the sofas, I thought, for a cabinetmaker could set them back on their feet.

I knew very little of the ways of the world in those days. Had it been ten years later, I could have echoed the comment of a sailor, newly arrived from India, about some stupid act or other: "I've seen the same in Macaï and Macao."

Still eager for new thrills, I took my way toward the Ursulines where I heard a great deal of noise. I couldn't enter the courtyard, however, for the gateway was blocked by a group of jabbering busybodies. I asked for news, and they told me that the fire had been

De Gaspé was at school in the old bishop's palace (right) "near the Lower Town gate" when the great fire of September 6, 1796 broke out. "Prescott Gate, Quebec," W. H. Bartlett, engr. J. Tingle. Musée du Québec, photo: Patrick Altman. 66.133

extinguished for a second time, Monseigneur having blessed it. It seemed odd for the bishop to bless the fire, when it was already doing so much damage. Ah well, I like this naïve confidence. May our good Canadians always preserve the strong faith of their ancestors, source of so much consolation in this vale of bitter tears!

I was still standing listening to the women talk when someone shouted, "The Recollets' church is on fire!"

Off to the church I rushed, but by the time I arrived the roof was a mass of flames. The monastery and nearby buildings were also quickly reduced to ashes.

For a few days after the disaster the poor monks were seen hovering near the ruins of the monastery in which they had found a haven from the vicissitudes of life. Sad and pensive, they wandered close to the arches where they had hoped their ashes would mingle with those of their predecessors, who had served New France so well.[D]

A month later, scarcely three cowls were to be seen in the whole of Quebec. The sons of Saint Francis were dispersed throughout the colony, quietly earning a living like any other citizen. The educated ones such as Brother Lyonnais took orders and became priests. Those with sufficient instruction taught school, and the others took up a trade or farming. Wonder of wonders! the poisoned tongue of slander never attempted to tarnish the reputation of these virtuous men.

I began this chapter by mentioning that I always liked the Recollets. They are among the first things I remember, although the memory is mingled with other trifling details, such as a lone chimney, the only remnant of a house either burned or destroyed somehow, which then stood in the parish of L'Islet.

The old fellow's sawing away like a senile old fiddler, thinks my reader. What possible connection can there be between a Recollet and a lone chimney?

Not so fast if you please, kind reader. We're in no hurry. I may be inordinately fond of music, but I've never managed to play the violin, my favourite instrument. At the age of seventy-nine I ought to give up trying, as you'll no doubt agree, and break my bow.

But to come back to my Recollets and the chimney bereft of a house, it's hardly worth making an issue of which memory was the earliest. The reader—who no doubt has all his wits about him—will surely be able to solve the problem.

One day my father was on his way to dine at Cap Saint-Ignace with an old friend, Seigneur Vincelot. He held me either on his lap or seated close beside him in his cabriolet, one leg across the seat to keep me from falling, for I was quite little at the time. On coming to the little hills of L'Islet to the southwest of the large bay, I spied a chimney such as I have described. To me it seemed disproportionately tall, and its isolation gave it a melancholy air.

I had always seen chimneys attached to houses, and asked my father what that big machine was.

"It's a Recollet's hut," he answered.

As the weather was glorious, I felt that the Recollet must be quite comfortable in his hut, protected from the sun. On our return journey at nightfall through pelting rain I thought I glimpsed something stirring in the same chimney as we passed, and cried, "Oh, Papa! A poor Recollet in his hut. He'll be miserable during the night!"

"I'm sorry to hear it," said my father. "I suppose he hasn't found anywhere to stay."

Was my father giving me a lesson in charity? Did he want to make me understand that without the hospitality of charitable souls the poor Recollets had no other protection than the hovels encountered on their road?

The rain kept up all night. I lay awake for a long time, my heart heavy at the thought of the poor monk whom I fancied having seen, exposed to the fury of the storm in his tumbledown shelter. It was then that my affection for the sons of Saint Francis was born.

Dear reader, you need no longer rack your brains for the solution to my problem, for I must have known the Recollets before I saw their hut, as my father called it.

What a nonsensical penchant for a band of great idlers who lived off the sweat of the Canadian settlers! thinks the reader. I might reply that fools are created and put into the world for the amusement of wise men, and that a tiny minority of unscrupulous men grow fat on the labours of the majority of their fellow citizens, or sundry other stale maxims, but I feel too strongly on the subject to pass it off thus lightly.

The Recollets were cherished and loved by the whole French-Canadian population. The abundant alms they gathered, especially in rural areas, were proof of this. The habitants of the Saint Lawrence North Shore did not stop at giving generously, they also transported the goods donated in relays from one parish to another as far as the monastery. The people of the South Shore did the same, depositing their offerings at Pointe-Lévis, where the boatmen carried them across the river without payment to Quebec's Lower Town.

Just as I thought, muses the reader. Everything you say merely confirms my initial opinion of these useless monks who lived so well off their harvest, no doubt saying, like the fool of Holy Scripture, "Eat, drink, for tomorrow we die!"[E]

The Recollets distributed generous alms to the poor out of the donations of the rich. How many opulent people can in all conscience say as much of the fruits of their own wealth, often amassed by hounding poor debtors?

The Recollets returned hospitality given, not only to well-to-do habitants from the country whose welcome had been the most generous, but also to those who would have been hard put to pay for a night's lodging at an inn. They even took in the horses. How many wealthy city dwellers, who have received unstinting hospitality from country folk, avoid them or turn their backs if they meet in town!

The Recollets would sit by the sick, not only in affluent houses where they were sure of a good midnight meal, but in the homes of the poor, to whom they themselves brought supper.

They laid out the dead, watched and prayed by the body, and threw the last handful of earth onto the coffin.

The Recollets heard the little ones recite catechism and taught school for the children of the poor.

All the foregoing applies only to the brothers of the order, and not to the Recollet fathers, of whom I knew only one, their superior, Father de Bérey,[F] who received a pension of five hundred louis from the British government, the equivalent of fifteen hundred today. He had separate apartments where he received his friends, entertaining governors and even the Duke of Kent at dinner—or so I often heard said, and the following anecdote seems to confirm it.

The Duke of Kent had received an invitation from the reverend father for noon, when parade was over. This was held opposite the Recollet monastery on the site of the present small fountain square. Father de Bérey had been a regimental chaplain and had even been wounded while ministering to the dying on the battlefield. Consequently, there was something of the barrackroom about his tastes and demeanour. He rather resembled that worthy French officer who, taking a dislike to the army after several years' service, exchanged his uniform for a cassock. Whenever he swore he would invariably lower his eyes and add, "As I would have said when a colonel in the dragoons." I don't mean to say that Father de Bérey did this, merely that his manner and preferences were distinctly military.

Wishing to give a fitting reception to the son of his sovereign on the appointed day, he had arranged a model artillery battery, a me- chanical masterpiece designed to fire at the stroke of noon as the prince and his aides-de-camp arrived. These tiny cannon of pewter or lead, mounted on pretty gun carriages, were the work of one of the monastery brothers, and were set to go off all at once.

Now the prince was what the English call a great "martinet." In summer he would often "raise Cain," as the men of his regiment put it, coming into the barracks at three in the morning and laying about him vehemently with his stick to rouse slackers. Whether because he had disciplined his regiment enough for that day, or for some other reason, he ended the parade twenty minutes earlier than usual, and slipped into the monastery with his aides-de-camp. Father de Bérey, taken unawares, was very put out at being unable to salute the prince with a salvo of artillery as he entered the main door of the monastery. With his usual fiery temper, the priest snapped, "Your Royal Highness, one only takes one's enemies by surprise. I thought Your Royal Highness too strict on points of discipline to cut short a parade in order to assault a peaceable monastery!"

The Duke of Kent could not help laughing heartily, once the reason for the bad humour of this son of Saint Francis had been explained. Father de Bérey, loth to have gone to the trouble of preparing his courtly gesture for nothing, asked leave to drink the prince's health after dessert. As he uttered the words, "Gentlemen, His Royal Highness the Duke of Kent," a tremendous salvo shook the windows of the room. It came from the artillery battery, drawn up near the refectory door.

The Recollet superior was criticized for being too much of a courtier. His detractors forgot that, as the descendant of a noble French family, he was at ease in a level of society that he had frequented since childhood. Although his monk's habit and cowl laid him open to raillery in English drawing rooms, his manners, wide knowledge, and ready wit, at once subtle and biting, made him a formidable adversary. He even dined at the English army officers' mess, where his sallies, witticisms, and lively sense of repartee were highly appreciated.

This seems an appropriate place for a short anecdote about another member of the Catholic clergy descended from French nobility. Around 1809, the Abbé de Calonne, brother of the minister of the ill-fated Louis XVI, received an invitation to dine with Sir James Craig, then governor of Canada. Someone pointed out that it was Lent, and that there would probably be no fish on the table.

Said the abbé, "If your governor isn't well-bred enough to respect the religious principles of a gentleman whom he invites to his table, I will give him a lesson in savoir-vivre, first by eating only bread, and then by explaining the reason for my abstinence, should he ask."

This threat proved totally unnecessary, for the entire first course consisted of a meatless soup, and fish with various sauces prepared by the governor's French chef, Monsieur Petit. The dishes were thoroughly appreciated by the British palates—so much so that there was no room in the British stomachs for the second course, composed uniquely of meat. Some guests declared they would willingly be Catholics—once a week—if they were served such a dinner at their own tables.

Before taking leave of Father de Bérey I cannot resist telling two of his countless witty sayings. He was quite old at the time of the capture of our Holy Father, Pope Pius VII, when rumour had it that Napoleon wished to obtain a dispensation from His Holiness permitting the Catholic clergy to marry. Some said it had even been decided. A practical joker, coming up to Father de Bérey at a large gathering, said, "Good news! Rejoice, Reverend Father! Napoleon has obtained a dispensation from the Pope allowing all Catholic priests to marry."

"You know very well, blockhead, it's like serving the mustard after the dinner," retorted the old monk.

A priest living near Quebec had the reputation of being miserly and inhospitable, preferring to dine at someone else's table rather than receive guests at his own. He frequently came to Quebec, where he was generously accommodated wherever he presented himself, particularly at the seminary, the Quebec rectory, or the Jesuit and Recollet houses. Someone came up to Father de Bérey in the street and asked him if he had seen the curé in question. "Yes," said the monk. "He reminded me of the lion of Scripture: *circuit quaerens quem devoret.*"G

This quip has since been attributed to others, but I grew up with this anecdote about Father de Bérey.

However, let us return to my good Recollet brothers, to whom a dish of *oeufs à la tripe* eaten today quite naturally leads me.H

OEUFS À LA TRIPE

My family lived in the country where they found but little society. The arrival of Recollet brothers (they always travelled in pairs) at the Saint-Jean Port-Joli manor house was considered a great stroke of luck. Whether at my father's invitation, or because the sons of Saint Francis were assured of a good supper and a comfortable bed, they always arrived toward nightfall. I only mention the bed as a reminder that these monks, who slept fully dressed, must have cared little whether the sheets were white; it was the down bedding they appreciated.

At the time there were no post offices in the parishes along the Lower Saint Lawrence. My father received Nelson's *Gazette*,[1] the sole newspaper published in the District of Quebec, two or three weeks and sometimes a month after publication. Consequently the news was not always very fresh. The monks were often living newspapers, more truthful than those of the present day.

A Recollet, being a friend of all the world and welcomed into the homes of the whole population, constituted a living and walking chronicle of everything that happened in the colony. Their arrival was a gala event in my father's house. A bottle of old wine used to appear at dessert, and the brothers would declare it far superior to what they drank at the monastery.

It was October at dusk, the hour when spoiled children and kittens make the most racket. I leave it to the naturalists to explain why, but in the light of experience, having raised a family of thirteen, I can vouch for the authenticity of this remark. As for cats, that carnivorous tribe that hunts more by night than by day, like their great tiger brothers, I suppose they instinctively prepare themselves for battle by flexing their sinews as much as possible beforehand. Buffon forgot to treat this subject in his chapter on the feline species.[1]

It was as night was falling, therefore, that, having run out of the house to escape some maternal chastisement, no doubt well deserved, I pursued my reprehensible antics by making faces through the window at my little brother, still inside. After a fairly prolonged exchange of these brotherly amenities, I managed to squash my nose so that both forehead and chin were pressed hard against the windowpane. This tour de force came quite easily to me, given my extremely flexible nose. My brother, stimulated by the noble example set by his suzerain, began to press from his side of the window. Unfortunately, his nose being of an aquiline cast and hard as wood, he made little progress in this joust until, after a furious push, the wretched window shattered—not without exacting a gory toll from the weapons used by the two knights.

"The monsters!" cried my mother. "They've broken a windowpane just as night is coming on. There isn't a single one in the house, and our nearest tradesmen live a league and a half away."

My mother always referred to "our tradesmen" either through habit, being city bred, or to do honour to the parish of Saint-Jean Port-Joli, which in reality boasted only one shopkeeper. This lone merchant, who at the time supplied almost all the parish needs, was the worthy Monsieur Verrault, grandfather of Abbé Verrault, principal of the

An 1810 sketch of children by Wilhelm Von Moll Berczy shows a typical group, with the child on the left taking somewhat skeptical stock of his playmates' poses. Musée du Québec, photo: Patrick Altman. A-69 43-d

Jacques Cartier Normal School. I cannot help relating a little story about him.

He was a high-spirited man, given to a quick retort. A thick-witted fellow (as are to be found everywhere, let it be said in defense of my parish) came into the shop.

"Monsieur Verrault, do you have one of those clever little combs that we had in the time of the French—the kind that kill fifty, sixty, eighty, or a hundred lice at one blow?"

"Indeed I do, my friend," said Monsieur Verrault, "always provided the lice are there!"

I should point out that there are probably few people more clean in their habits than our Canadians of today. The poorest of housewives scrubs her floor each Saturday, and the whole family puts on fresh linen at least once a week. I know of poor women who put their children to bed all Saturday in order to wash their one and only shirt. In my childhood things were different in the country. The habitants, although not in need of the wonderful comb just mentioned, were not very nice as to the cleanliness either of their persons or the inside of their houses. The floors got washed only twice a year, for Easter and the parish feast day. It is true that the women swept every morning, after sprinkling the floor with a tinware contraption called a watering can, from which the water trickled out through a tube one quarter of an inch wide. This was considered a sufficient ablution for the six months between scrubbings.

But to return to the misdeeds of my brother and myself—he hid under a sofa, where he withstood a glorious siege of several minutes' duration mounted by my mother, not a difficult feat for a miscreant sheltered by a fortification seven feet long. My mother, giving up the attempt, called through the frame of the broken pane. "You're to come inside and go to bed without supper, and I'll tell your father!"

I retorted that I hadn't broken the pane, as my nose was too soft, and that the culprit was my brother with his aquiline nose—she being proud of this feature in her second son, whereas she called me, her oldest child, "snub-nose." Then, as I strode around the courtyard, I began to think seriously about my mother's threats. First, "You're to come inside." This was perfectly clear, and meant, "You'll get a spanking." It was more than likely she would think no more about it when I did go in, and even if she did, I could always duck or find safe harbour under the sofa. Second, "You're to go to bed without supper." I admit this was a punishment of the utmost gravity for a child with a voracious appetite, who had earned the family nickname of "tapeworm." However, this punishment was often threatened but never inflicted, and I was quite easy in my mind about it. True, after certain major crimes my mother would order me to bed without supper; but shortly after, my aunt or one of the maids would come into my room carrying a tray, warning me to keep very quite for fear my mother would find out that I was eating supper like the rest of the family. I wasn't fooled by this manoeuvre for long. A little cogitation soon convinced me that my mother, who loved to feed people and always offered refreshment immediately to any visitor, rich or poor, would never have the heart to send one of her children to bed without supper. I therefore had nothing to fear on that score either. There remained the third: "I'll tell your father." Aye, there was the rub, the thing I feared most. Although my father had never slapped me, I was mortally afraid of his doing so, even when I grew up. How could one look him in the eye when he was angry, or feigned anger?

Few could withstand the sight of those great black orbs afire with rage; I was so terrified that I longed to creep into the nearest mousehole.

Back and forth I paced, abstracted and miserable like Napoleon on the rock of Saint Helena, when suddenly I spied two enormous black shadows coming along the highroad, harbingers of two Recollets who entered the courtyard a minute later. I was saved. With a bound I leapt into the house, shouting, "Mother, the Recollet brothers!"

"Ah! Just as well," replied my mother. "Now we can have some peace and quiet!"

As soon as I heard this I rushed out again and a second later made a triumphal entry in the arms of one of the sons of Saint Francis.

"How nice to see you, brothers," said my mother. "You must be very tired and cold; sit down by the fire and have a little glass of raspberry cordial to warm you while waiting. My husband is just coming—he's in the stable making sure that the servants see to the animals properly, as they're apt to be careless. He says he can't enjoy himself until he's sure that all about him—men and beasts— are comfortable, which is my feeling too; not like some of the habitants, who leave their animals out in the fields on cold autumn nights. He can't eat a hearty supper or sleep in peace if he knows that those in his care are suffering from the cold. We like all those about us to be happy."

After this paean of praise in favour of herself and her husband, my mother disappeared to busy herself with household matters, and the Recollets settled into the two corners of the fireplace, where an armful of fragrant cedar chips blazed. Each of them took one of my mother's monsters on his knee. As she predicted, she was now sure of peace and quiet. The two enemies of domestic tranquillity listened with placid delight to the tales and stories told by the two monks.

My mother reappeared about half an hour later, holding a bowl in one hand and in the other a silver spoon, with which she was energetically beating a delicious-looking liquid. "Don't be uneasy, brothers," said she. "Although this is a meatless day, you'll have a good supper just the same." She counted off the dishes on her fingers: "To begin with, a cream soup with rice, turnips, carrots, and herbs, a pâté of dried cod in olive oil, a dish of our delicious trout from Lac Trois-Saumons in a spicy brown gravy, and to top it off—can you guess?—a dish of *oeufs à la tripe* prepared by my own hands; for you know, Brother Alexis, I'm the only one who knows how to give

CATHERINE TARIEU DE LA NAUDIÈRE

Épouse de l'Honorable Ignace Aubert de Gaspé, décédée en 1843 agée de 7 ans.

De Gaspé's mother, née Catherine Tarieu de Lanaudière, a descendant of the legendary Madeleine de Verchères. Lively, affectionate, and resourceful, she was the mainstay of her son through good times and bad. Charcoal drawing by P.N. Hamel, 1879, from an unknown portrait. Musée du Québec, photo Patrick Altman. A54.205D

Pierre-Ignace Aubert de Gaspé, the author's father, was a formidable figure in the family setting. "Few could withstand the sight of those great black orbs afire with rage," writes de Gaspé. Charcoal drawing by P.N. Hamel, 1879, from an unknown portrait. Musée du Québec, photo Patrick Altman. A54.204D.

the perfect touch to this excellent dish, just as with the sauce, Brother Marc, for a chicken fricassee."

Like many people, my mother had a tendency to think she did everything better than others, forgetting that she owed the culinary knowledge on which she prided herself to our mulatto, Lisette, who was a perfect cook.

A humble satisfaction showed in the eyes of the Recollets as the first three dishes were enumerated; but their expression darkened when my mother mentioned the dish made of hard-boiled eggs. She mistook their reaction and said, "I understand, brothers; you feel there are too many dishes for a fast day; but then you do enough penance in the monastery to allow for a good supper now and then." She laughed. "And remember, I am the mother superior in my own house, and you owe me obedience under my own roof."

My father's arrival brought a change of subject, and he asked a stream of questions until it was time to sit down to supper. The monks had already done justice to the soup, pâté, and trout, when the much-vaunted dish of *oeufs à la tripe* made its appearance. The two Recollets exchanged anxious glances.

My mother, jubilant in the anticipated praises of her culinary chef d'oeuvre, told the servant to change the plates.

"With your permission, Madame," said Brother Marc, "I will have some more of your excellent trout. I do not eat eggs now."

"Well," said my mother, somewhat put out, "some stomachs cannot digest eggs, it is true. But at least you, Brother Alexis, have not the same excuse?"

"My sincere apologies, Madame," said the latter. "I cannot eat them either. They have been forbidden me and our entire community for a certain period by the monastery doctor."

"But that's unheard of!" exclaimed my mother. "Prohibit eggs to a whole community of poor monks? How dreadful!"

"Ah! Madame, it is a most lamentable tale," said Brother Alexis.

"A tale that we'll have for dessert," interjected my father. "And if it is *very* lamentable, we'll add some cheer by drinking an extra glass of wine."

"As you no doubt know," continued Brother Alexis, "we observe two Lents."

"Two Lents!" cried my mother. "You'll surely go straight to heaven. We only observe one, and even so my husband complains as though he were being flayed alive."

"You're a fine one, my dear," said the lord of the manor, roaring with laughter, "wanting to pass me off to the brothers as a recalcitrant Catholic—I, who never tire of eating fish. You're the one who won't eat anything but salmon and fresh bass. I don't know which of us complains the most."

"Madame has all the more credit for observing Lent without liking fish," said Brother Marc.

Brother Alexis, bowed his head approvingly and continued. "As we eat only salt fish in winter, since fresh fish is too dear, it is the rule to serve eggs during the last two weeks of Lent. During the Lent just past, being heartily sick of salt rations, we looked forward eagerly to the delightful prospect of eggs. On Sunday we were served *oeufs à la tripe*; on Monday, a sorrel and egg stuffing; and on Tuesday, plain boiled eggs, but cooked as hard as those in the first two dishes. In short, we saw nothing on the table but eggs as hard as rocks for seven days. Some of us began to feel the unfortunate effects of such fare, and it was agreed that I would speak to the cook. I went to Brother Ambroise, the most cantankerous cook in the order of Saint Francis, and explained that we were all suffering as a result of this indigestible diet. I asked him most politely to damp down the fire in future, when cooking eggs for our table.

"'What a bunch of cowards, afraid of a little penance!' snapped Brother Ambroise. 'Has anyone ever heard a son of Saint Francis complain about the food in his monastery until today?'

"'But dear brother,' said I, 'we're all so feverish that we're beginning to lose sleep.'

"'All the better to chant matins, then," retorted Brother Ambroise. 'You'll be so wide awake, they won't have to shake you to find your place in the prayerbook. . . . Anyway, if you're feeling sick, perform a miracle.'

"I took these consoling words back to the others," Brother Alexis went on, "and for the next four days hard-boiled eggs, with or without a variety of sauces, rained down on our table. We were as feverish as plague victims; our faces took on the bright hue of the winebibber, our eyes shone like carbuncles, and our bellies were stretched tight as tambourines. There was nothing for it but to go in a body and complain to the superior, Father de Bérey, although we greatly feared his sarcastic jibes.

"'Well now!' said Father de Bérey, examining us with a jaundiced eye. 'What is it!? What do you want? You're walking bent over double as though you'd just had a beating—a form of discipline you cowards seldom use. And you're holding your bellies with both hands, writhing around as though you had the colic.'

"'The trouble is we feel unwell, Reverend Father, very unwell,' said I, speaking for the others. 'The cook has served nothing but hard-boiled eggs for the last eleven days. In answer to our repeated complaints we're told to perform a miracle.'

"'You certainly seem in a bad way,' said the superior. 'Follow me. I'll give a good dressing down to that great oaf of a poisoner who regularly serves his superior such disgusting food.'

"'What's this I hear, you lazy lout?' said Father de Bérey, going up to Brother Ambroise. 'I'm told you've been feeding the Recollets nothing but eggs as hard as diamonds for the last eleven days. Typical laziness! You needn't watch them boil, as an hour more or less can hardly spoil them!'

"'You'll have to perform a miracle, then, Reverend Father,' replied the cook. 'When the brothers bring back nothing but hard-boiled eggs for alms, I can't made them as liquid as they were in the henhouse.'

"'What do you mean, insolent fellow!' roared Father de Bérey in his parade-ground manner. 'Perform miracles for you, double-dyed idiot? Miracles for a sluggard like you? It would need a miracle to make you step lively!'

"'But Reverend Father," said the unfortunate Brother Ambroise, 'I mean it. The two brothers who collect eggs only brought in two quart-barrels,^{K} with the contents boiled hard as iron. Come and see for yourself.'

"After examining what was left of the two barrels," added the narrator, "we were convinced they had in fact been boiled.

"'This is beyond me,' said the superior. 'I can understand someone giving the brothers a few, rather than seem uncharitable; but it surely isn't possible that everybody would agree beforehand to give the Recollets hard-boiled eggs.' Father de Bérey turned to Brother Ambroise. 'It's more likely that you, lazybones, boiled them ahead of time to save yourself work.'

"In vain did the unhappy cook protest his innocence. The superior's immediate concern was to get treatment for his monks, sweltering in their habits. The frater was sent for, and he purged the whole monastery. I don't know how many *demiards*[1] of royal purgative we had to swallow before we were better. We've felt sick at the sight of eggs ever since."

Let me digress briefly on the subject of royal purgative, a remedy much in vogue during my childhood. I imagine it was the thought of this unspeakable medicine with its pompous name, rather than the hard-boiled eggs, that turned the stomachs of the sons of Saint Francis. As far as I can remember, it was a decoction of julep, rhubarb, manna, senna, and Glauber's salts,[M] a demiard of which one had to down in a single draught. I only took it once, and after more than sixty years the memory still sends shivers down my spine—although truth to tell my stomach soon rejected it. I choked on the last mouthful and threw up the whole dose in the face of the old frater, who was sitting by my bed coaxing me in oily, honeyed tones. "Take it, take it, young master. It's very mild and strengthening. Don't lose a drop of this precious beverage, for I've taken a lot of trouble to prepare it."

Neither my mother's pleading nor the threats of the frater, who wanted to make me take another potion once he'd emptied his coat pockets and boots of the precious beverage, could persuade me to swallow a single drop. All I can say is that there was enough left in my stomach to act powerfully on that organ for the remainder of the night, and I believe that body and soul would have parted company if I had kept down the whole dose.

My father had a good laugh at the trick played on the sons of Saint Francis, and asked for an explanation.

"We think we've solved the mystery," said Brother Marc. "As you know, the habitants are kind enough to carry the goods donated from one parish to another by cart. The two barrels of eggs were left with an innkeeper in the parish of —— at nightfall. There lodged at this inn a stranger who feared neither God nor the devil. He was a real atheist, forever jeering at the monks as good-for-nothings who grew fat on the labour of the poor. We suppose that, with the help of some scoundrels, he spent part of the night boiling our eggs, with no regard for the exhausted stomachs of those who had to eat them at the end of a strictly-kept Lent."

The family burst into laughter at this bitter diatribe, the brothers joining in.

"My poor brothers, you may be sure that never again will a hard-boiled egg be offered in my house to a son of Saint Francis from the Quebec monastery," said my mother, who had been obliged to get up from the table two or three times to give freer vent to her mirth during the Recollet's account. "And I forgive you with all my heart for turning up your noses at a dish that my artistic vanity had rated so highly."

I don't know where the saying, "I would rather be a Recollet's dog," originated. If it was in Canada, I believe I know why. The duties of a dog in the Quebec Recollet community were no sinecure. He couldn't complain about having to patrol the monastery meadow in order to scare off burglars, or having to bark at the mischievous urchins who rang the visitors' bell a hundred times a day, to the utter despair of the old porter. This was but the duty of a faithful dog in a well-run household, and he fulfilled it without a whimper. But added to these two chores was that of turning the spit in the kitchen twice a day, often in a heat of forty to fifty degrees Réaumur.

"What's this?" says the reader, shaking his head like Diderot when reading the Church Fathers. "A dog turning a spit![N] A tall story indeed! One must be pretty well past it to tell *that* to the present generation."

Today we have the steam oven, a fairly recent innovation. And for the past fifty years have we not had the tinware stove, in which the most succulent viands simmer gently without the cook's boy having to do a thing?

In my young days I was familiar with three kinds of spit. The office of turnspit was generally performed by a child seated comfortably by the fire, holding a long rod with a hole at one end. It was used as a crank to turn the spit, loaded with meats exposed to the scorching heat of the chimney fire. He kept this instrument continually in motion, while he alternately sang and wiped his brow, his homespun cuff doing duty for a sponge.

The mechanical roasting-jack in my father's house was wound up like a clock. When the cook had arranged the meat by the fire, she ran up to the attic and cranked a winding-lever that was part of the mechanism, raising a weight of some twenty-five to thirty pounds to

Cooking was a difficult art in the days before stoves. De Gaspé describes the duties of a young turnspit, seated beside a hearth similar to this one in "the old Philippe Aubert de Gaspé Museum" at Saint-Jean Port-Joli. Les Éditions Marquis Ltée/Public Archives Canada. PA 51704.

the roof. When the spit—or spits, as there were often two or three—stopped, up she ran again to repeat the operation.

The sons of Saint Francis had simplified the task immensely by installing all the necessary machinery on the hearth, and substituting a dog for a cook's boy.

"But," says the reader, "were dogs in your day so prodigiously intelligent?"

They were not much cleverer than a squirrel from the relatively uncivilized life of the forest. When shut up in a revolving wire cage, the obliging animal immediately begins to make it turn round and round in order to escape as fast as it can, yet it doesn't advance a step from morning till night, despite covering a considerable distance. Now do you understand? The dog was put in a similar round cage, but unlike the squirrel had no perch to rest on. He was obliged to run without stopping, stimulated by the heat, the smell of the meat, and the hope of freedom. By the end his tongue would be hanging half a foot out of his mouth. The poor beast received no pity, however. "Turn, Capuchon," (this was the customary name for a Recollet dog), "turn, boy; you'll have your dinner when you've earned it, and some water every now and then."

But Capuchon was often smart enough to disappear toward the hour when his presence was most desired, either because a gardener was negligent, or by ducking between the porter's legs when he opened the monastery door.

The problem then arose of finding a substitute—not nearly so difficult as one might suppose. Any dog of suitable size passing down the street was enticed with a piece of meat. As soon as he entered the monastery precincts, a wiry arm grabbed him by the scruff of the neck, pushed him into a cage, and secured the latch. The new conscript made desperate efforts to regain the sweet air of liberty, while Brother Ambroise, quite delighted, cried, "Go to it, old fellow! You're doing just fine! There'll be a nice bit of roast for you as a reward!" Sometimes a little boy, going by with his dog, agreed to lend it for a couple of hours in return for some fruit or a slice of bread and jam.

The Recollets esteemed the dogs of the neighbourhood highly. The latter did not return the compliment, to judge by the wide berth most of them gave the monastery, keeping an apprehensive eye on it and barking furiously if they saw a cowl. This was a sure sign that the dog had turned the spit for the good brothers.

Before closing this chapter on the Recollets, I feel I must recount an anecdote about one of the monks, dead these twenty years. Although they resumed a layman's life after the monastery fire, the Recollets continued to observe the conventual rules as much as their new circumstances would allow. According to one of the rules of their order, a Franciscan must die in his coffin. The Recollet of whom I speak, seeing his final hour approach, placed himself in his coffin, there to reflect seriously no doubt on the nothingness of life. The man who nursed him was an odd character, seemingly without a sense of humour, although one couldn't help being diverted by the comic aspect of his stories. I shall let him speak.

"I felt very unhappy about this poor Recollet. He was a good fellow, and had been in high spirits only the night before. Now he was stretched out full-length in that box, never to emerge, his hands folded across his breast as though already dead. Then I had an idea. The saintly brother liked a little nip now and then, although he never abused it. He was old, and told us that it comforted him. I said to myself, let's see whether my remedy will bring him out of his box. I took the bottle of *jean-marie* (Jamaica) rum, filled half a tumbler, added boiling water with lots of sugar and nutmeg to hide the strength of the rum, and presented it to the poor monk, saying, 'Drink this medicine. It's good for you; the doctor told me to make you take it.' Barely five minutes later the poor Recollet was out of his coffin, dancing about the floor and declaring himself cured. Never have I seen a Recollet in such high spirits. But, alas! he was obliged to return to his coffin on the morrow, there to live for two days more, never to leave it until Judgment Day."

CHAPTER FOUR

> We heard the boatswain's whistle and the
> cries of the sailors shouting, "Long live
> the King." This is the cry of Frenchmen in
> both extreme peril and great joy, as
> though they called on their prince to save
> them from danger, or wished to show their
> readiness to die for him.
>
> Bernardin de Saint-Pierre [1]

Long after the Conquest, Canadians retained an affectionate memory
of the French royal family. When my father received his newspaper
in the country, the old habitants would ask him for news of the king
of France, the queen, and their children—the ill-fated family struck
down by the hand of the executioner during the Revolution. My father,
and more especially my mother, often told the old countryfolk the
tale of their torment, and of the sufferings of the young dauphin under
the iron rod of the notorious Simon; yet each time they would shake
their heads, maintaining that it was all a fiction invented by the
English.

It is quite remarkable that I have never heard a man of the people
blame Louis XV for the disasters that befell the Canadians after the
colony was left to its own resources. If anyone accused the monarch,
Jean-Baptiste would retort, "Bah! It was La Pompadour who sold the
country to the English!" And he would launch into abuse of the lady.

It was the year 1793, and I was but seven years old. A circumstance that I will shortly relate reminds me that it was winter. I can picture the scene as vividly as though it had occurred this morning. My mother and aunt, her sister Marie Louise de Lanaudière, were sitting near a table talking. My father had just received his newspaper and their eyes were turned toward him in anxious questioning, for the news from France had long been of the most harrowing nature. Suddenly my father leapt from his chair, his great black eyes aflame and a dreadful pallor spreading over his countenance, usually so ruddy. Clapping his hands to his head he cried, "Infamous beasts! They have guillotined their king!"

My mother and her sister burst into sobs, and I saw their tears melt the thick frost on the panes of the two windows against which they leant their heads for many a minute. From that day on, I understood the horrors of the French Revolution.

A profound melancholy took hold of all people of finer feeling in Lower Canada at this news, and with the exception of a few hardened democrats, sorrow was general.

A few months after this catastrophe there was a large gathering at my father's home in Saint-Jean Port-Joli. Among the guests were three priests: Messrs. Péras, our curé, Verrault, curé of Saint-Roch, and Panet, curé of L'Islet. The latter was the uncle of the Honourable Louis Panet, today a member of the legislative council, and brother of the great patriot who was for several years speaker of our provincial parliament. [B] During dessert these gentlemen talked a great deal of politics, which was of course Greek to me. I began to understand the conversation when they deplored the cruel and untimely death of that good prince guillotined by the French.

"And to think that there were forty thousand priests in France!" exclaimed Monsieur Panet.

"What could they have done?" said Monsieur Péras.

"What could they have done!" protested Monsieur Panet, opening his cassock above his heart. "Cover the king with their bodies and die at his feet! That's where they should have been, instead of leaving the country."

My father, somewhat vindictive by nature, had been rather cool toward the L'Islet curé for the past few years, following some small difference that arose between them; but these noble words, which my father was still recounting thirty years later, brought about a cordial reconciliation.

Despite my long experience of men in all their perversity, I have never been able to understand how a people as loyal as the French could murder this good and virtuous prince, or how so chivalrous a nation had the cowardice to strike down those noble female heads, borne to the scaffold with such dignity and sublime heroism.

What a great and moving spectacle: the beautiful queen, who never bowed her head except to the executioner's blade, standing in the tumbril and crushing with scorn the craven beings who accompanied her to the place of execution! But I cannot believe that the French nation as a whole was responsible for this infamy!

A Canadian gentleman, Monsieur de Belêtre, was in Paris at the time of Louis XVI's execution. Knowing the sentiments of his landlord, he was surprised to see him ready to go out in the morning, wearing the tricolour cockade. Said he, "Where are you going, my friend?"

"I'm on my way to where the guillotine stands, to preserve my head and that of my wife and children, as well as your own, sir."

On his return to Canada, Monsieur de Belêtre told how, when the man returned home, he threw himself into his wife's arms, crying out amid his sobs, "It has been my sorrow to see the king's head fall at my feet!"

Anyone traveling down to Rivière-du-Loup will find it well worth his while to visit Monsieur Louis, a veteran of the French army who was decorated with the medal of Saint Helena. Our friend Monsieur Louis (for he is the friend of all who know him) is a fine old man with a rosy face and simple manners, quiet-spoken but articulate, who will give you a straightforward and unassuming account of the events he has witnessed. This Nestor of the French army, through the kind offices of a sacristan who knew his father, saw Louis XVI and his family attend low mass in a chapel whose name escapes me. From his father's farm, two leagues from Paris, he heard the cannon roar at the taking of the Bastille. "All respectable people trembled with sorrow at the sound and sight of the horrors being perpetrated in France!" said he. "But the entire population was petrified, and dared not say a word."

Monsieur Louis[1] took part in the first Italian campaign under the great Napoleon, and only laid down his arms after the disaster of Waterloo. He had been in General Grouchy's division, and was anxious to clear his commander's name. Grouchy was accused of failing to arrive at the battlefield where the fate of France was decided.

"The roads were so bad," he said, "that the Prussians abandoned their artillery and heavy baggage. Grouchy must have thought that Blücher would be unable to reach the field before nightfall."

It is not surprising that the Canadians of old kept their ties of affection with France before the Revolution of '89. Communication with their former countrymen had continued virtually uninterrupted since the Conquest. Several Canadian gentlemen—de Salaberry, de Saint-Luc, de Léry, Baby, de Saint-Ours, my two de Lanaudière uncles,[C] and others—spoke enthusiastically of France, extolling the wonders of the court, the king's generosity, the queen's beauty, and the affability of all the royal family. Monsieur de Salaberry[D] had seen the dauphin in the Tuilleries Gardens in the arms of a lady-in-waiting, when the Montgolfier brothers launched a balloon. Said he, "This fair and gracious child lifted his little hands towards heaven, where he was soon to fly himself after dreadful tortures!" Everyone was moved to pity by the calamities that befell the royal family, and cursed their executioners.

Monsieur Louis-René Chaussegros de Léry[E] belonged to Louis XVI's bodyguard, and was lucky enough to escape the massacre of August 10 because he was on furlough. When he returned to Canada, he sang a lament that made all who heard it weep. I can't remember it perfectly, being very young at the time. Nevertheless I think it worth setting down; let the poets correct it if my version doesn't satisfy them. Lady Milnes,[F] the governor's wife, requested him to sing it at a dinner in the Château Saint-Louis. She burst into tears after the first couplet and left the table for about ten minutes, begging Monsieur de Léry to continue on her return.

Here is the lament. Perhaps circumstances have made it more appreciated than it deserves, although it must be said that the sad and plaintive melody contributed much to its moving effect on responsive hearts.

> A troubador of Béarn,[2]
> Sang to his mountain kin,
> As his eyes filled with tears,
> This verse that roused their fears:
> The grandson of Henri
> Is a prisoner in *Paris*!

He had seen the rush of blood
From that faithful bodyguard
Who, dying, gave then
An example to Frenchmen
By fighting for Louis
The grandson of Henri.

He who was our dauphin,
Future hope and cherished son,
Now is nursed with tears!
And the cradle that is his—
A French prison in *Paris*
For the grandson of Henri.

Where Henri's monument stands alone
The brazen blade thunders down.
Why this sad necessity?
Do they then want his complicity
In condemning his posterity:
The prisoners of *Paris*?

Frenchmen! You have ungrateful been!
Release Louis and his queen.
He belongs to the Béarnais
Son of the mountainside is he;
The prisoner of *Paris*
Is yet the child of Henri.

Before relating a few short anecdotes told by my two uncles when they returned from France, I would like to publish a letter written about one of them, the Honourable Charles de Lanaudière, who died in Quebec in the autumn of 1811. This has been made possible through the kindness of the learned Abbé Ferland, whose untimely death was a loss to Canadian letters.[c]

London, September 5, 1786.

I have known Monsieur de La N——, whose note to me of this morning I enclose, for twenty years. We became friends in Paris in 1766, when he was assistant medical officer in the Sarre regiment. He joined this regiment in Canada, where in fact he was born!

He returned to the land of his birth and married the daughter of Monsier de Saint-Luc, settling in Montreal. . . . It was Monsieur de L—— [i.e., de La N——] who, at a decisive moment (the arrival of the Americans under Arnold) got General Carleton away from Montreal

95

and escorted him with three hundred Canadians as far as Quebec. The general made him his aide-de-camp at this time. He already held a position in the civil service that brought him between five and six hundred pounds sterling per annum. As a reward for his great service, Monsieur de la N—— found himself dispossessed of his post by the Act for the reduction of places passed by the efforts of Mr. Bourk during one of the short-lived governments of which he was a member.[3]

The Marquis de Lévis knows Monsieur de L——.

The Duchesse de Mortemart sees him frequently at Manneville, her country seat in Normandy, when he stays with his uncle, Monsieur de Boishébert, who lives in the Château de Rastot. He is related to Monsieur de Montet of Bois-le-Clerc, and to the Comte de Maleuvrier, minister at Cologne.

Backed up by so respectable a source as the Abbé Ferland, I will enlarge somewhat on the life of my uncle, who died in my arms in the year 1811.

The brave soldier is always modest. I knew that he had been wounded at sixteen in the battle of April 28, 1760, while assistant medical officer with the Sarre regiment, and that his bleeding body was carried to the Hôpital-Général, where a great many French and English wounded received the most charitable care. Two elderly nuns, my aunt Mother Catherine, and my cousin Mother Saint-Alexis, often told me, when speaking of this time, "That great baby de Lanaudière gave us more trouble during his illness than all the other wounded men in our hospital put together."

It seems that my dear uncle, finding himself among relatives, made liberal use of this privilege to tease his nurses.

I often walked with him over the battlefield that was the scene of our last victory before the Conquest. Strange to say, he never mentioned the glorious part he played there at sixteen. How much useful information for the present generation I could have gleaned from these men of olden times, if only I had been better versed in the history of my country! But the truth is that, at the time, these things were only spoken of in whispers, for fear of appearing "French and bad subjects," as the English put it.

One day, however, when I was driving by the Dumont mill with my Uncle Baby,[H] he stopped the carriage and said, "Do you see that stream running northward? During the battle of 1760, which took

The Chevalier Charles-Louis Tarieu de Lanaudière, de Gaspé's "English" uncle, friend of the Duc d'Orléans and the Prince of Wales, and aide-de-camp to Lord Dorchester. Musée du Château Ramezay, Montreal. CRX 979.27.1

L'HON. FRANÇOIS BABY

The Hon. François Baby, from a prominent Upper Canadian family, married de Gaspé's maternal aunt, Marie-Anne Tarieu de Lanaudière, in 1786, when he was 52 and she 15. They had a large family, and were popular and hospitable members of Quebec City society. From Benjamin Sulte, *Histoire de la milice canadienne-française* (1897). Lt.-Col. A.-D. Aubry/Public Archives Canada. C-8852 place on these fields, Monsieur de La Ronde, a brave officer, lay there mortally wounded. We were carrying out a retreat at great speed under the rapid fire of English guns, hard pressed by the swords of the Scottish Highlanders. As I passed by, this officer said, 'Water, my dear young sir, I beg of you.' I pretended not to hear, as the enemy guns were deafening. If I'd stopped to give him a drink I might well have needed the same service from my comrades the next instant.

"It was the second time we had been driven from this vital position. But we formed ranks again behind a small wood, part of which you can still see. Charging the position with fixed bayonets for the third time, we routed the enemy and only abandoned the mill to pursue the fleeing English and prevent them from entering the city by toppling them into the Saint Charles River. This was a terrible blunder, as the gates of the city remained open for at least two hours, and we could have entered pell-mell with the enemy. Several Canadians present at the battle have stated this for a fact."

I was relating the episode about Monsieur de La Ronde to my Uncle de Lanaudière when he remarked (the only time he ever alluded to the battle of 1760), "That's right. Our poor cousin de La Ronde was mortally wounded near the Dumont mill, reportedly uttering the following words, which were frequently on his lips, even in the midst of the carnage: 'Ah! How mad men are!' He was a kind and sensitive man, and a very brave one. He only fought because in honour bound."

As I have mentioned, my Uncle de Lanaudière never alluded to his military career. I knew he had fought on the Continent where he was again grievously wounded, and one day, when he was in a particularly good humour, I questioned him about these campaigns.

He laughed and replied, "My glorious exploits in France were directed against the gentlemen of the smuggling trade! The young officers were always assigned to this thankless task. However, we agreed among ourselves that whenever we knew them to be hiding in one direction, we would go in the other. We didn't feel like running ourselves ragged for the love and profit of the Farmers General, with no hope of glory. They were just as great rogues as the brigands whom they ordered us to fight."

King George III was always said to have a prodigious memory for faces. Apparently he only needed to see a man once (and sovereigns see a great many men) to recall him for the rest of his life. The following anecdote seems to confirm this observation.

Monsieur Charles de Lanaudière, while still serving in France, had accompanied his uncle, the Comte de Boishébert, on a diplomatic mission to the English court. Here he was presented to George III. Fifteen years after this first interview with the monarch of Great Britain, he was again presented, this time as a British subject. The king recognized him immediately and said in French, "You were formerly introduced to me as a French subject, but I am happy that today you're presented as one of mine." He then added in English, "But I forget that you speak English fluently," and continued the conversation in this language.

My uncle lived in England for many years after the Conquest, and spoke the best English of all the Canadians of old whom I knew. We used to call him our English uncle, for while most men of his age had retained the manners of their French ancestors, he had adopted the colder, less demonstrative style of the true English gentleman—although, to tell the truth, they were not so very different from the manners of the French gentilhomme of the period.

Scottish blood ran in the veins of Charles de Lanaudière. His grandfather, the Comte de Boishébert, last French governor of Louisburg, had married a Ramsay—hence the connection with the Saint-Ours family. He was the only child of my grandfather's first marriage to a Demoiselle de Boishébert. The society that he frequented in France and England caused him to spend enormous sums of money, and this led his father to remark, "My son has cost me his weight in gold and more, even before he's had his legitimate portion."[1]

My dear uncle was unlikely to have saved money in the company of the Duc d'Orléans (Egalité) or the Prince of Wales, later George IV. He consoled himself for the loss of part of his fortune by saying, "My youthful follies were many, but always in good company."

When he died tragically at the age of seventy, Monsieur de Lanaudière was still vigorous and could ride with the ease of a young man. Invited to dine with a certain Mr. Ritchie in Notre-Dame de Foie, he offered a seat in his gig to his friend George Brown, whose son, a colonel in the British army, later figured in the trial of Queen Caroline, wife of George IV. A young groom followed the gig on horseback.

During the meal Dr. Buchanan, a friend of Monsieur de Lanaudière, pointed out that he was eating undercooked fish, which was highly indigestible.

"Nonsense! I'm hungry," said my uncle. "I've never had indigestion in my life and I'm certainly not going to begin at my age."

When they left around midnight, Monsieur de Lanaudière told his servant to drive Mr. Brown home, as he would return on horseback. "The night is so fine that it will be a very pleasant ride," he said. The young groom, once home, unharnessed the horse and went indoors to wait for his master. Unfortunately, he fell asleep.

Between five and six in the morning, a servant of Lord Bishop Jacob Mountain[4] on the way to one of his master's farms noticed a horse grazing quietly beside the inanimate form of a man covered with hoarfrost—for by a cruel twist of fate there had been a hard frost during the night, even though it was only early September. Great was the man's surprise to find Monsieur de Lanaudière in such a place, and at such an hour.

There was no mistake, however. He lay unconscious on the very battlefield where he had fought half a century earlier, perhaps in the selfsame spot from which his blood-drenched body had been lifted and carried to the Hôpital-Général.

The man, seeing that there was still a sign of life, hastened to undo my uncle's neckcloth. Monsieur de Lanaudière, after several efforts, vomited profusely and quickly regained consciousness. Recognizing the servant, he said in English, "John, you give me life!"

He lived for three weeks after the accident, but said little. He had the young groom whom I mentioned brought to his bedside. "Why did you abandon me?" he said. "I wouldn't have been so cruel, had it been you."

My uncle was a man of sober habits, although he lived in an era when the pleasures of the table were indulged in freely. He remarked bitterly several times, "That I, a de Lanaudière, should be picked up off the Plains like a drunkard after a night of debauchery!"

Such was his strength of will that the doctors believed he would have recovered after throwing up the indigestible food that was choking him, had he not suffered almost six hours' exposure to the intense cold.

A word now about his brother, Charles Gaspard de Lanaudière, issue of my grandfather's second marriage to the daughter of the Baron de Longueuil, in order to record a few of his travel impressions.

His elder brother had sent him to school in London, and during his holidays he was taken to see the land of his ancestors.[J]

There was a large company gathered on the evening that they entered the drawing room of my great-uncle, the Baron de Germain. "Now go and find your aunt," said the elder brother.

The youngster looked carefully at the circle of ladies seated all around the room, then went straight up to the Baroness de Germain and said,"You're my aunt." He had recognized her likeness to his mother.

Everyone crowded around the little "Englishman." The French ladies exclaimed enthusiastically over his costume, so different from that worn by French children, who were dressed like little lords: coat trailing down to the ankles, short breeches buckled above the knee, silk hose, shoes with large gold or silver buckles, and hair powdered and tied with a ribbon in an enormous queue.

By contrast, the little Englishman was fitted out like a sailor in the British Royal Navy: blue jacket, waistcoat, and trousers, white cotton stockings, pumps tied at the instep with a black ribbon, a Byronesque open-necked shirt, hair close-cropped and unpowdered. It must have been the first child dressed in the English style that these ladies had seen, for they burst out:

"That's how our French children ought to be dressed! See how comfortable he is in his clothes, how freely he moves, while our children are as stiff as the starched coifs of the burgher's wives in the Faubourg Saint-Denis!"

This little sketch of manners is all that I recall of my Uncle Gaspard de Lanadière's first journey to France.

Great was his surprise, during a second trip to the French provinces some years later, at the appearance of the shepherds and shepherdesses, so different from those he had seen in the theatres of Paris. "It was impossible to imagine more repulsive-looking creatures!" said my uncle. "And as for the shepherdesses," he added, permitting himself a mild oath in the bosom of his family, "if they and I were the only ones left in the world, the world would come to an end pretty quickly!"

Just one more scene, characteristic of English manners, and I will close this account of my dear Uncle Gaspard. He was at the theatre one evening—Covent Garden, I think it was[k]. Queen Charlotte, wife of George III, entered her box and made a curtsey that the all-powerful commoners appeared to find insufficiently low, for they shouted from the pit and especially from the gods, "Lower, Charlotte!" Thereupon the queen most unwillingly executed a dip to the ground, supported by her lame leg. The gallant English, in return for this gracious royal gesture, burst into thunderous applaude that rocked the building!

At the outset of this chapter I mentioned the Honourable Louis-René Chaussegros de Léry, whose lucky star allowed him to escape the massacre of Louis XVI's bodyguard. I think a note about him and his four brothers, all Canadian-born, would be appreciated by my readers.[L] Only one, the Honourable Charles-Etienne Chaussegros de Léry, did not serve on the Continent. He and his brother, the former member of Louis XVI's guard, both died on their native soil. They served with honour during the last American war and occupied important posts in the colony.

One need only open a history of France to learn of the brilliant career of Vicomte François-Joseph Chaussegros de Léry, general in the engineers, present at seventy memorable battles, skirmishes, and sieges. The high praise given him by Napoleon on Saint Helena shows how much the former emperor appreciated the outstanding qualities of this general of Canadian origin.

I must mention a very odd coincidence in this celebrated man's career. He was called upon to demolish part of the fortifications at Toulon, built in 1681 by his great-grandfather, Gaspard Chaussegros de Léry, engineer-in-chief of that place under Louis XIV.[M]

Let those of our compatriots who visit the land of their fathers stop before the Arc de Triomphe in the Place de l'Etoile, and look up at the western face of this monument devoted to the most famous warriors of the Republic and the Empire. There they will read with pride the name of a French Canadian: Général Vicomte de Léry.

Having thus summarily disposed of the republican general, I must now turn to his brother, Gaspard-Roch-George Chaussegros de Léry, who remained faithful to the royalist cause until death. He was a lieutenant in the engineers, taking part in the campaigns of 1793 and 1797 under the Prince de Condé. By a further coincidence, the two brothers of Canadian birth, both educated in Quebec and each serving in the same branch of the army—the engineers—met on the shores of the Rhine under opposing flags.

The nature of the present work prevents me from following Monsieur George de Léry's military career. However, for the edification of those who have seen fit to criticize the Canadian nobility for their lack of

103

education, let me point out that this French Canadian, after emigrating to Russia when his sword could no longer serve the royal cause in France, was named tutor and governor to two imperial Russian princes. It was he who supervised the education of these princes, and in their company he visited almost all the courts of Europe, where he was accorded marks of esteem by the majority of reigning monarchs. Proof of this is found in letters and correspondence still in my possession, far too numerous to be quoted here.

The reader will forgive me if I close this chapter with an anecdote that my uncle, the Honourable François Baby whom I mentioned earlier, used to recount in other days.

A young man, arriving from France a few years after the Conquest, opened a wigmaking shop in Quebec. As he proved very skilful at his trade, he quickly became a fashionable hairdresser. After a sojourn of four or five years in the colony, he suddenly disappeared with a young woman whom he had married. About a year later Monsieur Baby was in Paris, when he was informed that a man awaited him in a sitting room of the hotel where he was lodged. To his surprise he found himself in the presence of an elegantly-mannered gentleman whom he nevertheless recognized as his former hairdresser. Since he was afraid of wounding the man's pride, he welcomed him with the same polite ceremony that he would have accorded a stranger.

"Don't you recognize me, Monsieur Baby?" asked the visitor.

"I'm afraid not," said Monsieur Baby, "although I *have* seen someone who resembled you."

"Well! That someone who resembled me was your erstwhile barber," stated the young man.

"Since you say so, Monsieur, I must believe you."

The mystery was forthwith explained.

"I am the Chevalier B——" said he. "Six years ago I had a small difference with my father. He wished me to marry an heiress, no doubt very noble and rich, but also old and ugly. As I have a marked aversion to rich heiresses when they are old and ugly, I preferred to leave the country and earn my living working with my hands rather than marry the old dowager. I had to choose a trade upon arriving in Canada. Since I am as nimble as a monkey, and the barber's trade is not a demanding one, I bravely took up shaving-bag, razor-strop, powder-puff, basin, soap-ball, and other tools of my new station. Here is how I began.

104

"I had never wielded a razor. If I were to skin my first client alive, thought I, he'd hurl the shaving-bowl and its contents at my head. I needed a man patient by nature for my debut. My wish was granted, for my lucky star brought me an old Recollet friar sporting two weeks' growth of beard. It's always easy to befriend a monk, since he has nothing to lose and everything to gain. We therefore engaged in a long conversation during which my whole attention was fondly fixed on the long whiskers of this son of Saint Francis.

"'Is it the rule for an old Recollet to let his beard grow like a Capuchin father?' I asked.

"'Oh, no, dear brother,' he exclaimed. 'I haven't been able to use a razor these last few days because of rheumatism in my right hand, and now I'm looking for a charitable barber to shave me.'

"'You're in luck, friar,' said I. 'This is my day for being charitable to those afflicted with long beards. Kindly step this way.'

"The monk accepted my offer gratefully, and was quickly installed in a chair, holding beneath his chin a shaving dish filled with boiling water in which floated an immense ball of sweet-smelling soap. I covered his face with a mask of lather from eyebrows to Adam's apple in order to keep him from seeing how nervous I was. Then I set to work. The old monk's stubble was as tough as a scrubbing-brush, and unluckily I began shaving him in the wrong direction. He grimaced like a demon doused with holy water and finally cried out in anguish:

"'Brother, it's plain to see you're shaving me for love, not money!'

"'Not at all, reverend friar,' I replied. 'I'm doing my best, I assure you, but I think you must have a naturally tender skin.'

"'Tender skin! Holy Saint Francis!' cried the monk. 'Thirty years ago I was captured by a band of Iroquois. I underwent the *bâtonnade*—that's their laudable custom of cudgeling prisoners—as we passed through three of their villages, without uttering a single cry.'

"'You were young then," I told him, 'and used to hardship. I fear the comfortable life of the monastery has made you soft.'

"'Perhaps,' answered the poor Recollet with all mildness. 'But would it be possible for you to do exactly the opposite of what you've just been doing? Shave me in the direction in which my beard offers the least resistance, please, and hold the razor by the blade instead of wielding it like a carpenter's plane.'

"Light dawned. I changed tactics, and—except for one or two gashes—the monk's face was as smooth as a fine lady-apple when

I'd finished. To make a long story short, after shaving all the sons of Saint Francis for nothing one Saturday—their day for shaving—I looked around for more profitable customers. You yourself have witnessed my success in the city of Quebec, Monsieur Baby.

"Now that you know my history, and even seem amused by it, I dare to hope that you will render me a service on which hangs my whole future happiness. I have been taken back into the good graces of my father, but he obstinately refuses to see my wife (who is yet worth more, I flatter myself, than his rich old heiress) unless a Canadian gentleman vouches for her belonging to an honourable and respectable family."

Having nothing but good to say of the young woman's family, my uncle was more than pleased to comply. He subsequently had the pleasure of seeing her installed in the home of her father-in-law, a highly affable old gentleman who showed my uncle the greatest courtesy during his stay in Paris.

> Ah, what bores
> These old men are!

cries my reader, along with the famous French chansonnier.

CHAPTER FIVE

Injustice revolts and enrages me: my voice
trembles when I speak or think of it. I
would rather not have been born.

Mémoires of the Marquis d'Argenson [A]

I am a dog that gnaws its bone,
I couch and gnaw it all alone—
A time will come which is not yet,
When I'll bite him by whom I'm bit.

(1736)
Inscription on the "Golden Dog" [B]

When, as a child, I saw this inscription, the tablet on the Rue Buade
did not gleam as it does today. The dog and lettering were of stone,
since gilded; hence the modern name, "Golden Dog."

A great many stories, some more ingenious than others, have been
woven about the tragic death of Philibert, fatally wounded by Monsieur
de Repentigny. Many were the jibes directed at the old Canadian
nobility, the more indulgent critics asserting that de Repentigny was
an arrogant nobleman who, because of his rank and certain attached
privileges, firmly believed he had a right to spill plebeian blood with
impunity. If it had been a commoner who had spilt the blood of a
nobleman, they added, the king would never have issued a pardon. [C]
There were sundry other remarks in the same vein.

Yet daggers and "revolvers" are now very much the fashion in this country as well as with our neighbours. Murderers are frequently acquitted on evidence of great provocation or even in the case of wrongs demanding redress. No longer is it men of gentle birth who arrogantly believe they can safely shed common blood; it is the commoners themselves who do the shedding in a fit of anger. Nowadays, instead of a king or tyrant always ready to pardon a murderer of noble birth, we have juries that acquit their peers.

Our English friends are always prepared to applaud aspersions cast upon the Canadian nobility, forgetting that their own wealthy upstarts are far more haughty and overbearing than the nobility of France or even their own nation ever were. I don't flatter myself on being particularly clever, merely on my common sense—a rare enough commodity these days. I swallow as few rumours as possible, never believe scandal, and listen to ill-natured gossip only when liberally supported by proof. But, above all, I consult plain common sense.

The following account will show that before the Conquest not only did French monarchs reprieve noble offenders guilty of homicide, but the populace took it upon itself to save murderers.

A few years before the Conquest, a soldier in Quebec killed one of his fellows, a known scoundrel whom he suspected of having an affair with his wife, if memory serves me aright. The soldier was condemned to be hanged in consequence. The murderer was by nature an unassuming, peaceable man whose conduct before the crime had been blameless, and who was well liked by all the citizens of Quebec, whereas the victim, a debauched, gross, and violent individual, was heartily detested by all. It was said that he got what was coming to him.

The guilty man's rescue was planned so carefully that the authorities suspected nothing. Everything was in readiness, and the criminal himself apprised of the plan. Here is what happened.

The place of common execution was then the Butte-à-Nepveu on the Saint-Louis road. On the journey from the prison to this spot, the Recollet father accompanying the criminal appeared to feel considerable affection for the penitent, hugging him firmly about the shoulders with one arm. The hand at the end of this arm was not idle, however; for while appearing to clasp the neck tenderly, it was dripping nitric acid from a phial onto the cord destined to hang the prisoner.

Once at his destination, the condemned man climbed the gallows ladder with halting step; the executioner swung the ladder aside, and the corroded rope snapped. Immediately the crowd opened its ranks. With a furious bound, knocking down one or two soldiers blocking the way, the prisoner raced toward the Lower Town. The crowd closed ranks in a trice, and the soldiers standing picket around the gibbet took some time to make an opening through the compact mass of men who were little disposed to let them pass. Presumably the soldiers were not very willing to recapture a comrade who had all their sympathy. Nevertheless, having pushed through the crowd they set off in pursuit of the fugitive, only losing sight of him after he had taken refuge with a cooper in the Rue Sault-au-Matelot.

On entering the house they found the cooper with a hoop in one hand and a mallet in the other. Behind him, right in the centre of the shop, stood a barrel that he had just finished making.

"Where is the prisoner?" said the officer in command.

"What prisoner?" asked the cooper, looking at them with mingled coolness and surprise—a marvellous piece of acting.

Seeing the open door to the courtyard, the soldiers thought the fugitive must have escaped in this direction. The cooper accompanied them in their fruitless search; he even went to the trouble of fetching a candle to visit the cellar, and appeared to do everything possible to find the criminal.

The whole thing had been concerted in advance: the cooper expected the fugitive and had his staves and mallet ready. A few days later the condemned man, whose previous history was known to the captain and crew of a vessel bound for Europe, went aboard in broad daylight inside a barrel as part of the ship's water supply.

A few years later my grandfather, traveling somewhere in France, found himself face to face with the fugitive.

"Captain de Gaspé," cried he, "I am lost if you denounce me!"

"I'm no informer," replied my grandfather. "Like everyone else, I felt sorry for you at the time of your sad misadventure; but I hope at least that you have profited by this terrible lesson."

"Ask about me in the village, by my adopted name of ——, and you will see that I lead a respectable and blameless life." He spoke the truth.

Thus it was that a commoner's life was saved for the second time, by a gentleman inspired by feelings of humanity that were not strictly in accord with the duty of a French officer. Oh, no! The French nobility was not as greedy for the blood of the people as the populace itself was to become for the blood of the nobles! Witness the horrors of the French Revolution.

Let us return to Monsieur de Repentigny, however. I have known a great many old men, gentlemen as well as men of the people, who lived in Quebec at the time of Philibert's death, and their versions coincide. The very motto of the man testifies to his vindictive, ill-tempered nature, for false rumour cannot change history carved in granite. The threat inscribed on the stone is dated 1736; it cannot therefore be a notice of vengeance for the blood of Philibert, which was shed in 1748. It is surprising that this circumstance didn't strike those writing about this unhappy event, which was nothing more than justifiable homicide committed in a fit of anger, a phenomenon far more terrible in mild and patient people than in others, as I have often had occasion to observe.

Here is the unembroidered account of this catastrophe, as told me by men of humble circumstances. Philibert was a quarrelsome, violent man. He was arguing one day with a French officer when a woman, coming away from the marketplace with a basket on her arm, stopped in front of the doorway where this scene was being enacted. From threats, Philibert progressed to blows, hitting the officer with a cane. The officer, a quiet and forbearing man, was parrying the blows as best he might, when the woman said to him, "What, sir! Would you let a scoundrel like Philibert give you a beating—and you with a sword?" The officer, overcome with rage, drew the sword and ran him through. Philibert died a few days later. Those who recounted this scene seemed to think that Monsieur de Repentigny would never have dreamed of drawing his sword had it not been for the woman's jeer.

What is most remarkable is that everyone appeared to sympathize with the officer, even the ordinary people. Those of gentle birth told the same tale, adding that Monsieur de Repentigny often averred that this catastrophe poisoned his life.

If my version is correct (and I have no reason to doubt it), then I ask men of good faith whether Monsieur de Repentigny deserves the stain that has sullied his memory. How many equally deplorable incidents would happen now if we always went about armed as in the old days? Look at what is happening in our own land and among our neighbours in recent years. Intendant Bigot's name has been brought into the story in order, I suppose, to throw further odium on Monsieur de Repentigny. However, I fail to see how a billeting order issued by Bigot or any other authority makes any difference in this sad business. Yet in an English brochure entitled *Reminiscences of Quebec derived from reliable sources for The use of Travellers, by an old inhabitant*, published at the *Mercury* office in the year 1858,[D] the author purports to say that, as Philibert had a bone to pick with Intendant Bigot, the latter had him assassinated by an officer of the garrison. Furthermore, this officer, supposedly proud to serve as executioner, ran his sword through Philibert's back as he was going down the hill to the Lower Town. What next! Now the officer is a coward, without even the courage to attack an unarmed man face to face—a distinguished officer in the colony, too, according to his service record appended to this chapter.

It is really credible that a French officer, the most chivalrous of men, would murder an unarmed man from behind in cold blood? There is no deed more vile, cowardly, or low that could be imputed to him. And this officer was a brave Canadian gentleman, enjoying the esteem of all the world, who retained the confidence of his superiors after this unfortunate affair and rendered a great many services to the colony, as his military record proves. Why, he would have spit in Bigot's face had the latter dared propose such an infamous deed! Do people not realize that Monsieur de Repentigny's comrades in arms would have turned away in disgust from an officer bearing such a stigma! Had such a one dared enter a drawing room, ladies both French and Canadian would have cried out, "Away with this man whose hands reek of blood!"

As it is no longer considered good form by certain Englishmen to apply the epithet "cowardly" when speaking of a Frenchman, as was the fashion only some thirty years ago, I will put an end to this calumny very simply. I appeal to every officer in the British army: if, after reading the note at the end of this chapter, there is but one who maintains that such a cowardly murder could possibly have been perpetrated by so brave an officer, then I will take back all I have written in justification of Monsieur de Repentigny.

As for the late Mr. Alfred Hawkins, author of the above-mentioned pamphlet, I have always known him to be an honourable man. He must have been acting in good faith when he included one of the countless slanders which his countrymen were inclined to spread concerning the Canadians. Let me here do him the justice to say that, had he known Monsieur de Repentigny's previous history, he would never have published anything so damaging to his memory.

While on the subject of Intendant Bigot and his method of revenging himself on his enemies by using French officers as executioners, here is an unlikely story that I believe was published some twenty years ago, noteworthy chiefly for its highly inventive style. [*]

Monsieur Bigot owned a château called the Hermitage, of which a few vestiges remain at the foot of the Charlesbourg hills. One day while hunting in the forest, he became separated from his entourage and lost his way. A beautiful young Indian girl, making a highly opportune appearance in order to help him out of his predicament, acted as guide. Bigot was inclined to gallantry, and took it upon himself to reward her by making her his mistress. However, as she was encroaching on the rights of Madame Bigot, the intendant's legitimate spouse, the latter, jealous as a tigress, surprised the young girl alone one night at the Hermitage and stabbed her. In another version she poisoned her victim.

I have no objection to allowing Sieur Bigot an Indian mistress. His conquests must have been few, however, since tradition has it that he was afflicted with ozena, a foul-smelling nasal condition that sickened those who came too near, despite the perfumes in which he drenched his clothes and person. Still, he was rich and powerful; the ladies doted on him, and I will therefore grant him as many mistresses as you like, for it must be confessed that Sieur Bigot was not a man of irreproachable conduct. As for Madame Bigot's vengeance, there is one small difficulty—a mere nothing, mind you, but it should be mentioned: it appears there never was a Madame Bigot!

Other spinners of legend have asserted that the young Indian's family, scandalized by her unedifying behaviour, probably killed her. I suppose they doubted the existence of Madame Bigot. In the old days I knew many young and pretty savages. It was said they were not above reproach on the score of chastity, although their parents viewed their lapses indulgently. One day a missionary called together the chiefs of a tribe that I will forbear to name, and scolded them severely for closing their eyes to the licentious conduct of their children. His hearers looked most contrite and repentant, drooping their shoulders and moaning "hoa!" at the most affecting points in his sermon. Convinced of their remorse, the missionary was about to leave when an old chief who had been consulting the others rose to his feet and said, "What can you expect, Father? It was so before our time and will be hereafter." That Indian must have been a fatalist.

The author of the English pamphlet, in telling how the wife of Monsieur Bigot poisoned her faithless husband's mistress, places the tragic scene much further back in history and attributes it to one of the early governors of New France, regretfully making it impossible for me personally to assume the chivalrous task of defending the honour of our Canadian ladies of old.

Quite seriously, however, if a murder had taken place in such circumstances I would surely be aware of it, for I knew several of Bigot's contemporaries.

In this connection, here are a few incidents that I remember.

An old lady by the name of Descarrières had a store of lively anecdotes from the old days. Despite her eighty years, she was subject to that vanity which even old women cling to, and loved to tell a story that proved she had been pretty in her youth, although one would never have guessed it when I knew her. Knowing her weakness, all her friends made a point of saying often, "Madame Descarrières, you must have known Intendant Bigot?" The old dowager would preen herself and tell her tale, always in the same words.

"The intendant, Monsieur Bigot, was a most courtly man. When I was presented to him at the age of eighteen, he kissed me as was the custom for coming-out presentations, both at the intendant's palace and the Château Saint-Louis. Then he clasped me around the waist with four fingers (I was so slim then that the fingers met) and exclaimed, 'What a gorgeous handful of brunette!' I had light brown hair, you see."

She told how, during the siege of Quebec, the same intendant had a dish of roast horse served at his table, which was always sumptuously laid in spite of the lack of food. Everyone agreed that this was to give an encouraging example to the rest, although he didn't eat it himself.

I was strolling one day with my Aunt Bailly de Messein[F] on the shore of the Saint Charles River, opposite the ruins of the intendant's palace.[G]

"Let's stop here," she said, "and see whether I can recognize the spot I often visited in my childhood." Her eyes wandered over the ruins.

"Over there—that was the drawing room where those with an entrée to the palace used to dance. Around it ran a gallery, which the populace could enter by a staircase from the public ballroom, for Bigot in his munificence also entertained the common people, with whom he was very popular. Our mothers used to send us to see this spectacle with our maids, who took advantage of the opportunity to spell one another in the gallery while the others danced. Although I was only twelve years old when this colony was invaded by the English, I had watched a ball in this palace two years before, chaperoned by my maid."

Apart from these two ladies, I knew a great many people from Bigot's time. Not one ever mentioned the Hermitage tragedy; yet they would surely have known about it and had no reason to suppress the story—quite the contrary, as in other respects they didn't spare the reputation of this last inmate of the intendant's palace. Such a murder would be too recent to be forgotten; even the English version that I mentioned would not have faded completely from the memory of the old colonists. It seems a shame to discourage such flights of fancy, but I feel bound to set the record straight.

English tourists, and others of their nation who have lived in Canada a fairly long time, have always amused themselves at the expense of Jean-Baptiste. Many are the tales fabricated in their writings, many the slanders spread concerning us. One shouldn't take umbrage, however, for this innocent diversion was quite the fashion in bygone days, and still is, although of a somewhat less caustic nature. But enough! We will get to know one another better, I hope, and with a little effort on either side will finally become good friends. [1]

Sixty years ago, an English tourist announced that French-Canadian ladies spent entire days sitting with their sewing at an open window in the summertime, in order to be admired and flirt with passers-by. There were, in truth, two seamstresses in Quebec who could be justifiably reproached for this little weakness. Although innocent, all the rest fell under the same disapprobation, and were obliged to swallow the insult.

At one time rumour had it that three officers of the British army, brothers and French Canadians by birth, had been cashiered, whereupon the English gazettes remarked that this was not surprising, given the manner in which our race reared its children. This barb also had to be swallowed, but it didn't prevent one of the officers, Daniel Baby,[2] from rising to the rank of general, which he retained until his recent death in London. Nor did it prevent another, Louis, from getting himself killed in a duel in the East Indies, still in uniform, several years after his supposed expulsion from the regiment. The third, Dupéron, only left the army when peace was declared.[H]

The following extract, which I shall translate, is taken from a work published in London in 1809, entitled *Occasional Essays on various subjects, chiefly Political and Historical, &c., &c., &c.* This is but one of the thousands of slanders about Canadians that were then circulated. It concerns Bishop Jean-Olivier Briand of Quebec, and purports to be "extracted from a letter written by a person of credit in the said Province to his friend at London, about the end of September, 1775." Incidentally, this person of credit, Attorney-General Masères, was no papist, in spite of the French origin that his name indicates, as may be seen from his pious horror of Roman Catholics. Here is the extract:

"Another and a much stronger instance of this bishop's violence of temper happened about four months after the former. A man that lived in the parish of St. John, of which Monsieur Gaspé is the Seignior, wanted to marry a woman who was his cousin, though in a pretty distant degree. In order to do this he applied to the bishop for a dispensation to enable him to do so. As Mr. Briand is rather fond of money, he required of this poor man, for the dispensation he wanted, a sum of money which was greater than the whole value of the land he held in the parish. This threw the poor man into despair; and he went to the protestant minister of Quebeck, and desired him to marry him. But the minister refused to do so. . . . Upon this the man. . . . invites his relations and friends to . . . a feast; and, before they sit-down to table, . . . in the presence of the girl's father and of all the company there assembled, the two parties declare their consent to take each other for man and wife. Now this proceeding was undoubtedly blameable. . . . But the punishment of the guilty parties was not sufficient to satisfy the bishop's vengeance. Besides the man and the woman who had been thus married, he excommunicated all the company who had been present on the occasion, and all the inhabitants of the parish without exception; so that Monsieur Gaspé,[3]

Seignior of the parish, and his Wife, who lived at a distance of four miles and a half from the place where this offence was committed, were involved in this excommunication. The Curate of Islette, who does the duty of the parish of St. John, was sent thither . . . to carry this sentence of excommunication into execution. He . . . comes to the parish-church, and extinguishes the lamp of the principal altar, throws-down the wax-tapers upon the ground, orders the bell to ring, burns the consecrated bread, and carries away the box that contained it, . . . and the Sun [monstrance], and reads the sentence of excommunication, and declares that it is to continue in force so long as the parish shall harbour within it those two rebels. . . . Alarmed at this terrible threat, the inhabitants of this unfortunate parish depute their church-wardens to the bishop to implore his mercy. The church-wardens repair to Quebeck, and on their knees intreat the bishop to take-off the excommunication. But they could make no impression on him. On the contrary he behaved to them with the greatest rudeness and contempt, saying, '*No! I will by no means take-off this excommunication. I will teach you to dread the power of a bishop: and the rest of the province will, in consequence of your example, become more obedient to the church. I therefore command you to drive those two wretches from among you: and, if you obey . . . I will then consider what it may be proper for me to do. . . .*' The poor church-wardens, still on their knees, fell into tears at those harsh words, and said in answer to them, '*that, as those persons were upon their own land, they . . . had no authority to drive them out of the parish . . . but that this could only be done by the Judges.*' [']Get you gone, you blackguards, get out of the room this moment;' replied the bishop, and at the same time opened them the door. Upon this they rose from their kneeling posture, to go out of the room. But one of them, growing bolder than the rest, stayed behind . . . for a short space of [t]ime after the rest had quitted it, and said to the bishop in a steady tone of voice, in the hearing of Mr. Mabane,[4] (one of the Judges of the court of common pleas,) who happened to be with the bishop at the time, '*My Lord, if this man had given you the 150 Dollars which you asked of him for a dispensation . . . you would have granted him the dispensation; and then he would not have been guilty of this offence. And, now, my Lord, that he has been guilty of it, you ought to have confined your punishment to him alone, and not have extended it to the inhabitants of a whole parish, who are entirely innocent.*' Mr. Mabane was struck

116

L'HONORABLE JUGE ADAM MABANE

Judge Adam Mabane, a Scottish surgeon, became a controversial politician and judge in the early days of British rule, often defending the rights of the French Canadian majority over the interests of the English merchants. From P.-G. Roy, *Les Juges de la Province de Québec* (1933).

"The governor's nose was quite a handful!" in the opinion of a habitant who noticed that Lord Dorchester's nose was frozen, and applied a handful of snow to thaw it out. Musée du Château Ramezay, Montreal. CR 438

with the justness of the observation, and could not refrain from laughing when the man delivered it; and he earnestly interceded. . . . But he did not succeed. For the bishop thought fit to continue it for two months longer, and then at last took it off at the humble and urgent request of Monsieur and Madame Gaspé. This story was related to me by Francis Le Clerc, one of the church-wardens above-mentioned, who waited on the bishop . . . on the occasion above-recited."[1]

A most touching account of the bishop's despotism is this tale of his refusal to grant dispensation for the marriage of two hapless lovers, too poor to pay the hundred and fifty dollars to fatten the opulent prelate's purse. Unfortunately for the veracity of the author, as well as Judge Mabane *et alii*, in Canada there never was a dispensation for marriage for which the alms (always given to the poor) amounted to one hundred and fifty dollars. The most, for first cousins, is only a hundred, and the author himself admits that the cousinship was distant. How, then, could the churchwarden have talked of one hundred and fifty dollars when he must have known that the bishop could demand ten at most?

This took place twelve years before my birth. I was virtually rocked in the cradle with this story, and I even knew the individual who celebrated the marriage. The habitants, who have inherited a ribald sense of humour that always strikes home, immediately dubbed him "Pope." He had indeed appropriated the prerogatives of the head of the Church of Rome, for he had accomplished what neither priest nor bishop were empowered to do. When he passed by on the road, the habitants would say, "Look! There goes the Pope," or if he drew near a house would exclaim, "Here comes the Pope: get ready to ask for indulgences!"

I have before me the bishop's pastoral letter of veto, stating that he has no power to marry the couple. Here is the passage, in paragraph seven: "We declare that the persons who have thus endeavored to marry while an impediment exists for which we have not granted dispensation, *because we are not empowered to do so and because it would require papal intercession, are*. . . ."

So much for the hundred and fifty piastres required for dispensation, as well as the prelate's tyrannous tendencies!

My grandfather and grandmother appealed several times to their friend, Monseigneur Briand, for dispensation to marry on behalf of these two censitaires whom they pitied; but they invariably received the same answer: "We are not empowered to do so."

Here is how the mock marriage was celebrated. A sham altar surmounted by a crucifix was erected; the improvised high priest, a habitant of the parish of Saint-Jean Port-Joli, after aping the customary Catholic ceremonies, declared the couple well and truly married. Much merrymaking followed, as was then the custom at country weddings. Since marriage has been elevated to the dignity of a sacrament by the Catholic church, I ask even the most prejudiced persons: was this not a shameful profanation of our faith's most holy rites?

I know, without being a theologian, that even bishops cannot grant dispensation to marry in certain cases. Here is one: a married woman conspires with her lover to murder her husband and kills him for the purpose of marrying the lover, or vice versa. The bishop has not the right to grant dispensation.

Our Canadians are a fundamentally religious people. They had let themselves be taken in by the fine words of a glib talker, such as are still busy undermining their natural good judgment. Great was their dismay when the bishop pronounced his sentence shutting them out of their house of worship, source of so much consolation in times of suffering.

The entire parish of Saint-Jean Port-Joli, led by their seigneur, made such frequent appeals to the prelate that he relented, and at the end of two months the sentence was lifted. They promised to be good children in future, and have kept their word. Under the guidance of their worthy and beloved curé, Monsieur Parent, successor to my old friend, the venerable Monsieur Boissonnault, they may pride themselves on giving place to no parish in the matter of morals and Christian virtue.

In a lighter vein, and for the sake of variety after this unedifying tale, here is a little scene that probably took place at about the same time. Captain Gouin, an old and respectable farmer of Saint-Anne de la Pérade, tells the tale.

"I was driving Lord Dorchester in my cariole, in January weather as cold as charity, when I noticed that his nose was as white as rich cream. What a fine protuberance was the governor's nose! I can say it without disrespect to his memory, for he was a good sort, and treated a habitant as politely as he would a bigwig. Chatting with him was a real pleasure; he spoke French like a Canadian and was always asking questions.

"'Excellency,' says I, 'with all respect, your nose is as frozen as a piece of pig's crackling.'⁵

"'What should one do, then?' says the general, lifting his hand to the afflicted part, which he could no more feel between his fingers than the nose of his neighbour.

"'Ah! *Dam*! You see, General, I've only handled Canadian noses. English noses may be quite another kettle of fish.'

"'In that case, what does one do for a Canadian nose?' asks the governor.

"'A Canadian nose, Excellency, is used to roughing it, and so gets pretty unceremonious treatment.'

"'Suppose mine were a Canadian nose instead of English?' says he.

"'Yes, Excellency; but there's still one small difficulty. Not all Englishmen have the honour to possess a governor's nose, and out of respect and consideration, as you must appreciate. . . .'

"'G----m!' cries Lord Dorchester, losing patience. 'Will you leave off being so considerate of my poor nose, which is already as hard as a block of wood? Apply the remedy, I tell you, if you have it with you.'

"'Oh, that's no problem, Excellency. It's not necessary to make special provision; I have three good feet of this medicine under my cariole, and it's cheaper than the surgeon's remedy.'

"'What! Snow?' cries the nobleman.

"'Certainly.'

"'Well, get on with it then, before my nose falls into the cariole.'

"'I daren't,' says I. 'The respect, the consideration that I owe Your Excellency. . . .'

"'Will you hurry up, you infernal chatterbox!'

"When I saw him getting angry—a man always so mild and good-natured—I set to work with a will and unceremoniously thawed him out with several helpings of snow, just as if he were one of my own, although it must be admitted that the governor's nose was quite a handful!"ᴶ

I don't remember Lord Dorchester myself, but I recall his wife perfectly, because one day she placed me back to back with one of her children to see how tall we were. A distinguished personage

Lady Dorchester was born the Lady Maria Howard, daughter of the Earl of Effingham. Educated in France, she was known as a stickler for etiquette. From an old photograph of a portrait, artist unknown. Archives nationales du Québec (Initial collection). N79-1-130

leaves no more impression on the mind of a child than any other individual, unless some circumstantial details prod his memory. In about the year 1810, I came to know his son, Colonel Carleton, well. My mother used to say he was the spitting image of his father, in which case I can well see that Captain Gouin was right in saying "the governor's nose was quite a handful."

Hysterics were practically unknown among the Canadians of old, as the ensuing scene would seem to prove. My maternal grandmother tells the tale.

"One evening I was at Lady Dorchester's. Her sister, Lady Anne,[k] seemed very disturbed by the absence of her husband, who had gone hunting that morning and was four or five hours late. We tried to reassure her as best we could, giving all the usual reasons to explain his absence. Around eleven o'clock, Lady Anne burst into peals of laughter, which seemed to us most strange. Lady Dorchester looked very uncomfortable and whispered in my ear, 'Pay no attention; my sister is having an attack of hysterics.'

"'I've never heard of that ailment,' I answered.

"'It's frightfully dangerous,' said Lady Dorchester. 'I'm very uneasy, for this is the most alarming phase of the nervous disorder. If she could cry, the danger wouldn't be so great.'

"I stared, and was fairly unable to take in what I saw and heard. After some ten minutes had passed thus, Lady Anne began to emit howls that would have made a timberwolf jealous, and then burst into a flood of tears. Her husband came in shortly afterward and put an end to her wifely fears.'

"'Don't you know about this cruel malady?' asked Lady Dorchester, once her sister had left the drawing room with her husband.

"'No, my lady,' said I. 'But I can assure you that if Canadian girls took it into their heads to have what you call hysterics, their mothers would quickly cure them with a sound box on the ears.'

"Lady Dorchester laughed. 'You're all the same: you call everything that's foreign to your race "English ways," and you even want to deprive us of our cherished hysterics.'"

It has been said that the use of tea produces these nervous disorders in Englishwomen. However that may be, our Canadian ladies are now almost as much attached to their precious hysterics as to their infusions of tea-leaves.

General Prescott,[L] governor of Canada around the year 1796, was much liked by the French Canadians. He didn't always rely on the advice of his executive council, but consulted those citizens whom he considered most reputable. As a result he left Canada on bad terms with all his councillors. I knew him in my childhood: he was a tiny old man who didn't stand on ceremony. In winter especially, he always dressed as though he were trying to look like Haroun al Raschid of *A Thousand and One Nights*.

A Beauport habitant, carrying wood to Quebec over the ice bridge on the Petite-Rivière, met an old fellow clothed in a shabby frock coat, his head covered by a mangy cap of marten fur. A few tears fell from his reddened eyes. Jean-Baptiste, moved to pity at the sight of this old man apparently weeping with fatigue, said to him:

"You seem worn out, old gaffer; my cart isn't very comfortable, but you'd be a lot better off on top of my wood-load than walking in the snowy ruts."

The pedestrian thankfully accepted his offer and climbed up on the wood. A lengthy conversation ensued between the passenger and the farmer, so conspicuous for his kindness to old gaffers. Arriving at the foot of Palace Hill, the farmer felt some surprise at seeing him remain on top of the load instead of easing the horse's burden. "Well," he thought, "the poor old boy must be pretty tired; he's quite skinny, and my nag is stout-hearted; she'll never notice."

"Guard! Turn out!" bellowed a sergeant as soon as they passed through the city gates. The old man lifted his hand to his cap. Jean-Baptiste looked along the street. He saw no officer, but doffed his cap too, thinking that such courtesy demanded a response. The habitant continued his way to the wood market, situated where the butcher stalls in the Upper Town now stand, by taking the Rue Saint-Jean and coming out on the Rue de la Fabrique. The stranger, looking very much like the old wretch in *A Thousand and One Nights* who clung to the back of Sinbad the Sailor, kept his perch atop the wood load. "Guard! Turn out!" bawled the sentinel at the Jesuit barracks. The guard presented arms, and again the old man lifted his hand to his moth-eaten cap, including in his salute some passers-by who uncovered their heads on seeing him. Again Jean-Baptiste doffed his own hat, bowing first to the guard and then to all the citizens who had shown them such polite attention. He was quite amazed to see how civilization had progressed—or rather, regressed by fifty years—

since his last visit. At last he stopped his cart. The old man jumped briskly down, thanked him for his kindness, dropped some money in his mitten, and was already far away when a few curious bystanders asked the habitant what the governor had given him.

"What governor?" snapped Jean-Baptiste. "I'm not one to be made a fool of, as you'll find out. If my cart isn't good enough for governors, it's good enough to bring you wood. You'd freeze to death and die of hunger, you lazy good-for-nothings, if we habitants didn't provide you with warmth and food! I'll have you know that I own a handsome and sturdy cariole for when I want to turn out properly of a Sunday, which is more than a good many of you can say."

As the old Canadian saying does, "A Beauport habitant is nobody's fool."

"Well, look in your mitten," said someone.

The habitant took his advice, and drew forth a fine gold piece, a bit worn at the edges as were most foreign coins then, but worth at least eight piastres. It was a Portuguese half-ducat.

"But . . . but!" said Jean-Baptiste joyfully. "And I thought I was giving him a ride out of charity! You can't judge by appearances these days!"

The following scene will give some idea of General Prescott's plain manner of life at home. A carpenter was doing some work in the kitchen of the Château Saint-Louis when he heard the bell ringing. He looked all about him, but the servants were nowhere to be seen. The bell rang a second time, and he went on with his work. Clang! Clang! The din was earsplitting, but the carpenter continued unperturbed. Then he heard footsteps storming downstairs, and an irritable voice demanding to know why he hadn't answered the summons. It was the governor in person. The carpenter excused himself, saying he wasn't a servant of the château.

General Prescott, all the while expostulating about his domestics, opened an armoire where food was kept, took out a beet salad, and cut himself a slice of bread and cheese; then, armed with this provender, he went upstairs again, still grumbling.

"It was the first time I had spoken to a governor," the workman told me, "and his red eyes scared me like the devil." (Prescott was blear-eyed.)

The officers of His Britannic Majesty's 6th regiment of foot, stationed in Quebec at that period, were the most unruly body of men to grace

125

the colony since the Conquest. The number and variety of pranks played by them on the unsuspecting citizenry were legion. One morning a habitant, sporting a brilliant scarlet tuque or stocking cap two feet long, had delivered his load of hay and was standing in his parked sleigh opposite the Jesuit barracks, chatting peaceably with a friend. Some officers were gathered at a short distance, pointing and laughing loudly, to the accompaniment of a barrage of uncomplimentary remarks directed at the flaming red bonnet adorning the habitant's head. The acknowledged wag of this jeering group separated himself from the rest, and came up to Jean-Baptiste.

"That's a fine bonnet you have there, just like a Catholic bishop," said the officer in broken French. "Want to sell it? Where did you buy this magnificent ornament? I'd like to get one for big parades."

Jean-Baptiste shrugged his shoulders and scowled. He knew perfectly well what was going on.

"Your wife must kiss you a lot when she sees you with that sugarloaf on your head," continued the officer. "She must think you a fine buck (dandy)."

"No more of a *bouc* [billy-goat] than you!" retorted the habitant, stung to the quick. "When my wife kisses me, she kisses a white man, not a d----d nigger like you, d'ye hear?"

Ed----, having been born in India, was very dark.

"Take it easy!" said the officer. "I'll pay you many pounds sterling for your pudding-bag."

"Go to the devil, bag and baggage!" snapped Jean-Baptiste by way of ripost.

"Softly, softly," admonished the officer. "I want to make a friendly offer of a little exchange. What about my fur hat for your cheese-sack?"

So saying, the officer snatched off the red tuque and donned it himself, putting his own cap on Jean-Baptiste's head. The spectators roared with laughter, particularly the officer's military friends. But suddenly the tables were turned, for Jean-Baptiste, keeping his wits about him, drew out a whip tucked in his belt and gave his high-spirited horse a sharp slap on the rump. It shot forward like greased lightning. Down the Rue de la Fabrique and the Rue Saint-Jean he went. Coming out on the Palace road, he sped through the city gate and launched his horse at a gallop onto the ice bridge over the Saint Charles River—in a hurry, no doubt, to show his wife the fine trade

126

he'd made: his tuque for a marten cap worth at least six or seven guineas.

Need I add that the hurrahs and bravos of the populace could be heard long after Jean Baptiste had disappeared from sight?

NOTES

I would have liked to cite in full the service record of Captain Pierre de Repentigny, following the homicide mentioned in these memoirs. However, the nature of the present work permits me to give only brief extracts from the military diary of the Chevalier de Lévis.

"July 30, 1754, Captain de Repentigny took command of the forts of Presqu'île and Rivière au Boeuf.

"October 7, 1755, Captain de Repentigny commanded a party of 600 Canadians in the engagement led by Baron Dieskau at Lac Saint-Sacrament [Lake George].

"September 12, 1758, the Chevalier de Lévis formed a detachment of 300 men—marines [i.e. regulars of the Compagnies franches de la marine], Canadians, and Indians—under Captain de Repentigny, on the said Lac Saint-Sacrament, etc.

"On September 13, 1759, Captain de Repentigny was before Quebec. On the 20th, he was put in charge of a detachment of 100 men west of the Cap Rouge River, etc. On November 17, 1759, he commanded a detachment of 300 men at Pointe-aux-Trembles. From December 1, 1759 to June 1, 1760, he held advanced posts as far as Saint-Augustin, as well as leading frequent offensives in the field. On the occasion of the battle of April 20, 1760, Monsieur de Lévis noted: 'The battalion of the city of Montreal, under the orders of Captain de Repentigny, served as bravely as the regulars.'"

EXTRACT FROM FRENCH ADMIRALTY ARCHIVES

Being the service record of Philippe-Ignace Aubert de Gaspé, Infantry Captain, Chevalier of the Royal and Military Order of Saint-Louis.[M]

COLONIAL SERVICE RECORD

"In 1727 he entered the troops as a cadet, satisfactorily performing garrison duty until 1735, when he served in the campaign against the Indians (Foxes) under Monsieur de Noyelle.

"In 1739 he was promoted second ensign and took part, under the Baron de Longueuil, in the campaign to subdue the Natchez and Chickasaw Indians.

"In 1742 he was detached from his unit in order to join the garrison at Michilimackinac, serving there for three years under Monsieur de Verchères.

"In 1745 he was promoted full ensign and took part in the Acadian campaign in this capacity under the command of Monsieur de Ramezay. He remained there during the summer. The following winter he and Monsieur de Coulombier [sic] de Villiers were detached to Les Mines, from which they drove the English. In 1750, he was sent to construct a fort on the St. John River, where he was in command for two and a half years.

"In the winter of 1753 he traveled to the settlement at Belle Rivière, and was with Monsieur de Villiers[N] at the taking of Fort Necessity from the English.

"In 1755 he was sent on detachment with Monsieur de Villiers for five months to protect Fort Niagara against English attack.

"In 1756 he was made a captain and spent six months at the Carillon portage under orders to Monsieur de La Corne. The following winter he commanded Fort Saint-Frédéric, where he remained until the spring of 1757. Here he received orders to proceed to the Carillon portage to assume command; and from here he took part, under Monsieur de Montcalm, in the campaign against Fort George.

"In 1758 he was ordered to Carillon where he remained for the summer under orders to Monsieur de Montcalm, and was present at the engagement of July 8, at which the enemy was repulsed with severe losses.

"In the spring of 1759 he received orders to proceed to Carillon and stay there until this fort was evacuated, there to assume command of two pickets of marines. From there he went to Ile-aux-Noix, where he remained until winter came on.

"In 1760 he was present at the battle of April 28 in which the English were beaten. He accepted the post of captain of the grenadier company that had been formed. He replaced Monsieur de La Ronde Denis, who had been killed in the fighting, and kept this command throughout the siege and during the digging of a trench for eighteen days after the siege was lifted.

"He returned to Deschambault to continue serving with the grenadiers, under the orders of Monsieur Dumas.

"According to the testimonials of Messrs. Ramesay [sic] and de Noyelle, he performed his duties with valor, zeal, and distinction.

GASPE

Expectative second ensign, Canada, March 25, 1738
Second ensign, Canada April 1, 1739
Full ensign 1745
Lieutenant 1749
Captain 1756
Chevalier de Saint-Louis, March 24, 1761

I feel I must add an anecdote to my grandfather's service record, if only to show that a man's life or death often depends on the most trivial incidents.

During the siege of Quebec in 1760, Captain de Gaspé was having a quiet pipe with two comrades in arms, Captains Vassal and de Bonne, in a crater made by an enemy bomb the previous day. This retreat sheltered them from an icy northeast wind accompanied by torrential rain, and seemed a safe haven from enemy bombs and cannon balls.

"If another bomb blows us out of this hole on such a dark night, it'll be the devil's own doing," laughed Captain Vassal. "Let's smoke and talk in peace."

They had been there several minutes, chatting with the cheerful ease of the French, when Captain de Gaspé thought he heard someone calling him.

"Apparently they think our legs are swollen for lack of exercise," he said as he climbed out of the crater.

He had barely taken a few steps when a second bomb fell into the shelter he had just left, killing his two friends.

The late Judge de Bonne[o] and the late Colonel Vassal,[p] adjutant-general of the Canadian militia during the War of 1812, often discussed with my father the twist of fate that made them both orphans, while a lucky accident preserved the life of their friend's father.

CHAPTER SIX

It is the voice of years that are gone!
They roll before me with all their deeds.

Ossian

In the year 1795, after shedding a few tears on separating from my good mother, I found myself in a boarding house presided over by two spinsters named Chôlette. It would be a great mistake to reproach myself for teasing them unmercifully during my three years there, for in spite of my pranks I was the golden-haired boy of the house. Even their brother Ives, an old man of crabbed and mournful aspect who was the long-suffering butt of my jokes, never smiled except when I pestered him or jumped up on his shoulders as he returned from work. My antics seemed to amuse him, and he used to screw up his face in a satisfied grimace that, in his case, passed for a laugh.

Old Chôlette smacked me only once, very lightly at that, and this was also the only time I saw him laugh heartily. One evening I was working, or pretending to work, at my lessons for the next day, seated at a table where Ives had installed himself in order to keep an eye on me while he mended one of his shoes. "I'm going to look up roly-poly pig's fat in the dictionary," said I, winking at two of my comrades. This was the nickname with which I had graced him, most ingeniously I felt. Not only was he short and fat; he was bald, and I had caught him in the act of rubbing his scalp with a piece of pig's fat in the absence of some more fragrant pommade. Hardly had I uttered the offending phrase than he smacked me on the chops with his shoe, saying, "Look up shoe!" The laugh was clearly on me, and next morning, "look up shoe" was the joke of the whole class.

If Ives Chôlette was fond of me, he certainly couldn't complain of neglect. Monkey-fashion, I would take a running jump onto his shoulders as he went downstairs to his work. Like the tenacious old man who clung so stubbornly to Sinbad the Sailor, I would go for a long ride through the streets on this new-fangled steed. Chôlette, I think, enjoyed giving me the ride, although he kept shouting, "Get down, you little devil, or I'll chuck you off!" Yet while he scowled on one side of his face, he smiled on the other.

The memory of affection bestowed by even the humblest individual is sweet. Poor Ives, ugly, dull-witted, probably never having had any signs of affection from his family, naturally became attached to the mischievous child who gave him constant attention, even if only to tease him. One day I received a proof of his attachment that I have never forgotten. It was evening, and I was playing in the street when I threw a ball that hit one Poussart, who immediately gave chase. This Poussart, whose strength was prodigious, was the terror of all the bullies of Quebec. Ives Chôlette, usually so slow-moving, leapt from his doorway in a single bound, throwing himself in my enemy's path.

"Stop, Poussart! Don't you touch that child. I love him like my own."

"And who's going to stop me?" glowered the other.

"I am, Poussart. I know I'm not strong enough to fight you," he added, seizing his adversary by the arm, "but I'll hang onto you like a bulldog and chew you to bits."

On this day I realized how Ives loved me, although I ought to have known it before, as he never allowed anyone else to take the slightest liberty with him—neither his sisters nor the other boarders. Poor Chôlette! After I was launched in my profession some years later, his face would light up whenever we met in the street.

One Sunday morning Chôlette said to me, "Don't say anything to the other two boarders, and this afternoon I'll take you to see a strange animal that arrived the day before yesterday in an English ship."

The two boarders, Paschal Taché and Gaspard Couillard, were the most lovable, good-natured children in the city of Quebec. Perhaps

"We went by way of l'Anse-des-Mères," wrote de Gaspé of his childhood walk beneath the bluffs to Sillery, to see a donkey—a great novelty. Maurice Cullen, "L'Anse-des-Mères." Musée du Québec, photo: Patrick Altman. 49.75

it was because of these very qualities that Chôlette wasn't as fond of them as of me.

On setting out from the house that afternoon, we met an old German who was the husband of one of my companion's cousins.

"Vere are you goink?" said the Hanoverian.

"We're going to see a strange beast that landed at Sillery yesterday," said Chôlette. "Won't you come along?"

"Vell, vell! Dis must be a fery stranch beast inteet for to valk zo far! Idz hot as hell!"

We were having a typical July heat wave, hot enough to melt an Ethiopian. Ives assured his cousin that he wouldn't be sorry, as this animal was said to be the most extraordinary ever to appear in Canada. The cousin agreed to come along.

We went by way of l'Anse-des-Mères, a good league from Sillery. We kept stopping to let our old German rest as we followed the shoreline, for he had a raging thirst, despite frequent libations of fresh water from the Saint Lawrence River.

"Could we see the strange beast you have here?" asked Chôlette of a servant in a pretty cottage at the foot of a Sillery bluff.

"Behind the house," replied the stout female, energetically fanning her face with her apron.

At the sight of the animal, the *schlinderlitche* burst out in wrathful scorn, "*Der esel!* A jackass! *Un âne!*" The *donner wetter* that he let fly must have been a terrible oath, for it shook the foundations of the bluff under which the German was seated in the shade.

As for me, I quickly struck up an acquaintance with this new friend, who submitted to my petting with the best will in the world. It was the first four-footed ass I'd ever seen, and I was filled with wonder. Had I possessed a macaroon I would have fed it to him far more willingly than that egoist Sterne, who offered a similar biscuit to a poor donkey. As a naturalist, he wanted to see how much an ass would enjoy a macaroon after rejecting a rotten and bitter artichoke root, which the animal hadn't the courage to swallow. Not having a macaroon, I gave him what was left of some gingerbread I'd been nibbling, and he ate it with a satisfied expression that went straight to my heart. "How do you like Canada?" I asked him. He let drop one ear and lifted the other in reply. I understood this dumb language to mean, "Canada is a fine country, but I'll be very lonely without animals of my own kind." I gave him a pat on the rump and said by way of consolation, "Don't give up hope, dear friend. Canada's population is increasing rapidly, and in fifty years when you're in your prime, you'll have lots of friends of your breed." This seemed to comfort him, so I bid a fond farewell and set off down the road to Quebec. The German kept up a stream of rude remarks to his dear cousin throughout the journey, then slunk off home. Whenever we met in the street after this, I would shout, keeping at a respectful distance, "Let's go to Sillery to see *der esel donner wetter!*" and he would grind his teeth and shake his fist.

The reader will easily appreciate that, living in a household that spoiled me so, I quickly became absolute master of all my actions and was not slow to take full advantage of this state of affairs. First, however, I had to pay the price of my own inexperience.

I began by getting to know all the young scapegraces of the neighbourhood, in particular one Joseph Bezeau, otherwise known as Coq

Bezeau because, I suppose, he was cock of the walk among the street urchins. He then introduced me as a most promising subject to a wide acquaintance, both inside the city walls and in the suburbs. I doubt if Beau Brummel were more proud of his pupil, the Prince of Wales, than the said Coq Bezeau was of me. But like the English adventurer, who occasionally took liberties with his royal pupil, my tutor was in the habit of bullying me, to the point where one day I lost all patience and "called him out," as the urchins used to say.

"You won't get *me* in the eye!" said Bezeau, drawing himself up on his spurs like the winged creature whose name he bore.

In my innocence I took this quite literally, thinking it was agreed among the boys not to hit in the face, for fear their parents would see the black eyes and punish them. I was unaware that "you won't get me in the eye!" was the most insulting taunt that a street urchin could hurl at a despised adversary. It was, to paraphrase Sam Waller in Dyckens [*sic*], to add insult to injury. I told him not to worry, but he mustn't hit me in the eye either.

"Agreed," he sniggered.

Battle was joined: a fist closed one eye at first blow, leaving me half blind.

"But you promised not to hit in the face!" I yelled, rubbing the afflicted organ.

Pow! was all the answer I got, as another blow closed the other eye, and there I was, totally blinded.

Once Coq Bezeau had "creamed" both eyes, as the current expression was, the combat became very one-sided. In boxing the great art is to give and not receive; and since I was receiving ten blows for every one I gave in hitting out blindly, I admitted defeat.

A child who has been thrashed quite naturally acquires an enduring fear of his adversary. My gorge rose, nevertheless, not so much because of the licking itself as of the jeers of the other little ruffians, Coq Bezeau in particular, with their eternal, "Gaspé, when you fight, make sure to aim for the eyes!"

Finding that I lost my nerve each time I was tempted to ask for a return bout, I took desperate measures that left me no retreat from battle. One evening, while looking out of a second-floor window, I spied my enemy seated on the doorstep below. A maid had just come upstairs with a bucket of icy water from the well in the courtyard; I grabbed it out of her hands and poured it over the naked head of the urchin-chief. Had he possessed the wings of a rooster, he couldn't have leapt higher. There was no going back now. When we met next morning Bezeau commenced settling accounts with a clout on the head, which I returned with interest, after which we were the best of friends.

I must take leave of Coq Bezeau, who has been gathered to his fathers these twenty-five years, to deal with his younger brother Charles, whom we used to call "Little Red" because of his fiery mane. He was a veritable Tom Thumb, a devilish little imp. A hundred times a day his mother wished him in the company of all the evil genies he so resembled. I should deal with him, as I said, if only to offer some comfort to parents whose children drive them to distraction.

The mother was at the end of her tether, or perhaps, since mothers are proverbially long-suffering, she lacked the strength to mete out suitable punishment. In any case, she sent him to the Hudson's Bay Company to be broken in. At the end of three years, an agent of this powerful trading company entered the house of Mother Bezeau, or rather Mother Chôlette, as she had long since celebrated her second nuptials.

"Madame, I bring you back your son," said the agent.

"I well knew that such a scamp would soon be turned away by the Company's bourgeois!"[1] cried the tender mother. "Whatever will I do now that he is three years older? Since he was seven, it's been almost more than I could do to give him a whipping!"

The mother armed herself with switches to beat the little devil, and at the end of a long combat, when all further resistance seemed useless, he himself offered the besieged part to his attacker, shouting for as long as the whipping lasted, "Hit! Hit!" accompanied by oaths and bloodcurdling insults directed at his parent.

"Yes, yes!" said Dame Bezeau. "I knew the scoundrel would be thrown out, to end up getting himself hanged somewhere!"

"How's that, Madame!" said the Company man. "Get himself hanged? A scoundrel? But this child alone is worth ten of our best men! He's the most valuable interpreter imaginable and has been incredibly quick to learn the tongues of the Indians we trade with. Get himself hanged? What an idea! I brought him here as a reward for services well rendered. Here is a purse filled with cash to buy clothes, so that

135

he can cut a dash during his three weeks in Quebec; and I want him to have money in his pocket at all times to treat his young friends."

At this, Mother Chôlette fell upon the neck of her precious offspring, who scolded her in excellent Eskimo by way of thanks.

Let the Fate who holds the distaff spin away some thirty years of Charles Bezeau's life. I was standing on the ramparts of Quebec, admiring the beauties of nature, when a well-dressed gentleman came up beside me. He was a compatriot, so I was sure he would respond to my proffered remarks. Also, as I have a surprising memory for faces once seen, it seemed to me that I had known this stranger in times past, and after a few moments' conversation this led me to inquire whether he was from the city of Quebec.

"I was born here," said he, "but left around the age of eleven. Since then I've visited the city occasionally, but not often."

"I knew I couldn't be mistaken," I told him. "You were born and raised on the Côte à Moreau[2] and your name is Charles Bezeau."

We renewed our acquaintance with mutual satisfaction; he told me his life story, ending with these remarkable words:

"My mother often wished me dead during my childhood. It would have been a great misfortune for her, my stepfather, and my sisters. I rescued them from poverty, and they now live happily beneath my roof."

Not only had Charles Bezeau made a handsome fortune; he was well-liked and respected in the parish of Lotbinière, I believe it was, where he was a magistrate.

Lachesis, the Fate who spins the thread of life, continued her task uninterrupted. Some twenty years later, my son, the curé of Saint-Apollinaire, told me that a respectable old man by the name of Charles Bezeau, of the parish of Saint-Antoine, often spoke of me and had made him promise to bring me to his home on my next visit. I accepted the invitation and was agreeably surprised, five years ago, to be received by my acquaintance of old in a well-appointed, comfortable house. Indeed, he was one of the wealthiest citizens of Saint-Antoine. But when I again visited my son eighteen months later, the respectable Monsieur Bezeau had died, leaving a considerable fortune to some young girls, of whose upbringing he had taken charge. This worthy man, although twice married, left no descendants.

O Mothers! With such an example before you, never despair of your children, no matter how incorrigible they may be in their childhood.

A letter concerning this period in our lives, sent to me by Assistant Commissary-General Thompson[B] following the publication of *Les Anciens Canadiens*, deserves a place in this chapter. I believe Mr. Thompson, a most respectable octagenarian, is the oldest living resident born in the city of Quebec, irrespective of race. After a short introductory paragraph in English, the letter is written in good French Canadian, which he spoke from childhood like all children of British origin at that time.

My dear sir, and old acquaintance, I venture to address you in French although at the risk of exposing myself *aux rigueurs de la critique* [*sic*].

I have read your story of *Les Anciens Canadiens*, and more especially the "Notes and Clarifications." Although I found a great many anecdotes, I did not encounter the incident that occurred in the Upper Town marketplace, then laid out in a straight line between the Jesuit barracks and the cathedral.

The matter is not one of historical significance, although interesting enough to you and me. Here it is. You were then a pupil at the seminary, wearing the regulation blue tunic and sash,[c] whereas I was a scholar with Mr. Tanswell, a former Jesuit,[3] who had a school in the old Bishop's palace near the Prescott Gate. One fine spring day we met in the aforementioned marketplace. You were armed with a little bag of brand-new marbles, and I had some as well. You issued a challenge that I readily accepted, and we settled down to a game of *snoque* (in English, "the last knock"). The contest went on for some time, and I eventually stripped you of all your marbles. Thereupon, moved by jealousy, the desire for revenge, or some other motive, you administered such a hard and well-aimed punch to my left eye that for a moment I thought you'd annihilated it. I nevertheless found the courage to give as good as I got, when my school friend John Ross entered the fray on my side, and between the two of us we gave you an awful drubbing. Surely you must remember it? I certainly can't forget it, for my left eye still bears the scar where my eyebrow was so battered that I could hardly see. But no matter; although we may have been desperate enemies at the time, it didn't prevent the exchange of civilities between myself and the Honourable George [*sic*] Saveuse

137

de Beaujeu, your son-in-law, during my whole time (fourteen years) as one of his censitaires at Soulanges.

Kindly accept my visiting card.

I remain yours truly,

Your obedient servant,

(signed) Js. Thompson,

A.C.G.

I feel Mr. Thompson must be pulling my leg when he says he still bears the marks of my fist, so readily applied some seventy years ago. All the same, it is true that the Canadian children of those days hit hard and often, aping the men. The latter were formidable athletes, ever ready to indulge in a round of boxing, an art that they no doubt learned from the English. Their brawls in town weren't nearly so bloody as those in the country, however. There the vanquished one was indeed luckless if he lost his balance; the winner would bend over and beat him mercilessly until some charitable souls dragged the victim out of range. In the towns, by contrast, the combattants observed the rules of British boxers fairly strictly.

Be that as it may, a letter from a gentleman of such sound judgment as Assistant Commissary-General Thompson gave me distinct pleasure, and encouraged me to include several anecdotes that I would otherwise have omitted as too trivial. I thought that if a man of different background to our own enjoyed reminiscences of times past, my countrymen would welcome them with equal favour.

After receiving this letter, I met Colonel John Sewell, another figure from former days, albeit somewhat younger than we. I asked him the origin of the game of marbles we called *la snoke*.

"It's a French game," said he. "I don't know its origin."

"Well, Colonel," said I, "thanks to our friend Mr. Thompson, I have just learned that what we call *la snoke* is an English game, and that one ought to say 'the last knock.'"

The colonel laughed. "I spent ten years playing *la snoke* without the faintest idea of its being a British game."

This supports my note published in *Les Anciens Canadiens* regarding the ruthless way we used to massacre the English language.

During the first six months of my sojourn in Quebec, I was the butt of many a practical joke. I was exceedingly gullible, a trait of which the local urchins took full advantage.

On the second Sunday after my arrival I betook myself to high mass. Four young scamps were watching for me, and suggested we sit in their own pew in the cathedral. They sang the praises of the excellent holy bread given out in city churches and then inquired whether I had any money in my pocket. I answered in the affirmative; all was well, they declared, because holy bread was only given to those who gave money for the collection taken up at high mass. This custom seemed strangely different from that of our country churches, where the holy bread was distributed without charge; but they probably did things otherwise in the city.

Instead of taking me to their pew, these gentlemen led me into the chapel of Our Lady of Mercy. They made me sit on the steps of the small altar, averring that we would be like princes and more comfortable than in their own pew.

"Now," said one of them, "give me five pennies for the collection. Holy bread costs a penny a piece in Quebec."

I pointed out that the verger's assistant, who handed out the holy bread, wouldn't know what had been given to the head verger, who took up the collection.

"That may be the case with your imbecile country vergers," retorted the urchin, "but I'll have you know that our vergers are much smarter."

His three companions nodded their heads in approbation.

After a fairly long wait, the rascal returned with three pieces of holy bread the size of an egg-yolk, stating that the basket was empty, a thing that had never happened before. The others made signs of deepest sympathy at this misfortune. Great was my surprise when the verger appeared fifteen minutes later in our chapel, his basket still half filled with bread.

It was about this time that I was introduced to Justin McCarthy,[1] who in time might have become one of our most eminent men, but whose brief career was so lamentable. Although we were the same age, he was infinitely more worldly-wise. His father, a surveyor as well as Canada's foremost geometrician, was a family friend, and we quickly became inseparable companions. The wiliest of youngsters, he attached himself to me like a leech. No doubt he took my measure at our first meeting. I will have a great deal to say about him in these memoirs, for he later became my constant companion at school. He had a biting and caustic nature, and I think I was the only person to whom he ever said anything civil.

"I like you," said he, "because you've the heart of an Irishman."

Justin knew just how to turn this easy-going organ to his advantage. He was fond of money, not to use as other children his age did, but to indulge in a penchant that prematurely killed one of Canada's brightest talents.

As of our first interview I was his dupe. "Gaspé has two shillings," said one of my comrades, "but he won't treat us because he owes them to old man Maillet, the pastrycook, and he's promised to pay him tomorrow."

"Monsieur de Gaspé is right," said McCarthy. "A gentleman must never go back on his word."

During this preamble the other urchins stood around me sticking out their tongues.

"It's really too bad," continued McCarthy, "that it isn't tomorrow, as that's when my father gives me my pocket money. To tell the truth, it's not much: only four and a half shillings a week."

A less astute child would have given a round figure; but how could one doubt so precise a sum: four and a half shillings, no more, no less?

"When do you have to pay old Maillet?" asked McCarthy.

"Tomorrow morning," I replied.

"Well that's that, I guess," said McCarthy. "My father's in the country and won't be back until one o'clock sharp for dinner. He's very punctual at meals, and scolds us roundly if we're late. If it weren't for that, I would've offered to treat you today and pay you back tomorrow. But it'll be too late to pay back old Maillet at one o'clock, so let's forget about it."

I immediately fell into the trap by saying that a couple of hours would make no difference, and off we ran to the Lower Town market where the vendors quickly emptied my purse. I'm still waiting for my two shillings: that was Justin McCarthy all over.

One day McCarthy took me to his father's office and proudly showed me a costume representing a full-dress outfit for a bishop celebrating mass. The mitre was particularly splendid, glowing with leaves of gold paper and ornamented with numerous hieroglyphics by the artist, who prided himself on being a great painter. To my eyes, the mitre was a masterpiece fit to adorn the high priest Aaron, whom I'd seen in biblical engravings. Before such marvels I was ecstatic.

"You know that next Sunday is the great Corpus Christi procession," said Justin. "All the children of wealthy families will accompany the procession dressed as priests, bishops, or Recollets. Just think how envious they'll be when I appear among them on Sunday!"

"Oh, dear Justin," I begged, "sell me your fine costume!"

"I can't," he answered. "There's not enough time left. Even if I worked nights I couldn't make one as beautiful."

And he spread out all the pieces of the costume before me. Tears stood in my eyes.

"On second thought," said Justin, "you're the son of a seigneur. I'm very fond of you, and if you *are* in the procession I'd feel badly if anyone had a better costume. Of course, all this cost me an awful lot: seven shillings and eighteen pence in cash, not counting my labour, but as it's between friends I won't charge for that."

Seventeen shillings and eighteen sols! There was no gainsaying so exact a figure. Nor could I sufficiently express my gratitude to Citizen McCarthy, as he insisted on being called during the French Revolution despite his tender years.

"But I'm afraid I only have thirty sols," I told him, "and I never ask my parents for money. I just couldn't."

"You're wrong there," retorted the Citizen. "I'm always asking mine, and they almost always refuse. But listen, Aubert de Gaspé," he added grandly, "your word is as good as a king's. Take this magnificent costume and pay me the balance at your leisure."

I bounded out of the office into the street, carrying my treasures with me.

Those who are disposed to consider me a perfect little simpleton for a child of nine should read Goldsmith's life, where he recounts how his last guinea was extracted from him by a good-for-nothing friend. The pretext was that the friend had sent to the East Indies at great cost for a pair of white mice, male and female, which he wished to give to some duchess or other who adored them. He lacked only a guinea for the proper cage in which to present these charming little animals and thus make his fortune. Let those who have read this anecdote judge me less harshly, for I was then but a child, whereas Goldsmith was already a great poet; yet he was as confiding and gullible as I.

Barely had I stepped into the street Sunday morning, clad in the bishop's costume, when seven or eight urchins who had got wind of my good fortune clustered around me with a chorus of exaggerated compliments. Suddenly the scene changed. One of them gave an exploratory tug at my stole, which came away in pieces in his hands. From behind, another pulled at my chasuble. It ripped along both shoulders and fell to the ground. A third, making a prodigious leap, brought his fist down with a crash on my mitre, which skinned my ears as it tumbled to my shoulders, cleft from top to bottom.

At the end of six or seven months I had learned enough about the way of the world to run with the pack and render blow for blow. In a word, I became a thorough little ruffian. Citizen McCarthy alone continued to victimize me, and great was my desire to throw off his irksome yoke. He forced me to buy all the gewgaws of his making; all my money passed from my pockets to his, and I was forever in debt to him. Young as he was, he had guessed the userer's secret for keeping the borrower beneath his heel. McCarthy may have lacked muscle power, but he ruled the other children through sheer force of personality. They feared him and were never able to have the last word.

Like the bat in the fable,[E] Justin was fortunate in having dual status. Born of an Irish father, he would make use of an English youngster to punish a French-Canadian child who had given him a beating. As the son of a French-Canadian mother, he would call on the young French boys to get even with his British foe. The ease with which he spoke both languages, a rare thing for the period, gave him a considerable advantage in assuming either role. His sympathies were all with our race, but when it came to getting his own back he was not overscrupulous.

McCarthy was therefore a formidable enemy; but I was determined to escape his tyranny, and he himself supplied the opportunity. One day as I made my way to school, carrying my books, scribblers, and inkbottle in a satchel, he asked for the money owed him. I replied that I had none, upon which he grabbed the satchel, saying he would sell everything and get his money.

It was a bluff. I took it seriously, however, and landed a punch that laid him out on the pavement. Up he came, and never did a young tiger leap upon his prey with as fierce and furious a temper as he did, so unexpected was my abrupt attack. The struggle was violent; he ripped my clothes, but was obliged to plead for mercy. Knowing his vindictive nature, I went about in trepidation for several

142

days; but whenever I met him he turned his head away, pretending not to see me. One day I accosted him in order to repay what I owed him.

"Are you still angry with me?" said he.

"No."

"Well, then! Let's be friends again."

And with the exception of a few minor skirmishes, we remained the best of friends.

It was during the summer of the following year, towards five in the afternoon, that my boarding-house was besieged by a gang of sailors. We were looking out the window when Coq Bezeau arrived on the scene in tears, shouting that his father had killed a man.

This father, or rather stepfather, Hyacinthe Chôlette, was the brother of my old Ives, as well as being one of Quebec's rowdiest bullies. He had been in a brawl with a sailor and had left him unconscious at the foot of the Côte à Moreau, now known as Côte de la Prison. Why this hill was thus named, I don't know. Perhaps because one Moreau lived there—or was it because this hill and its surroundings were infested with hemlock, then commonly called "carotte à Moreau"?[F] Whatever the reason, it was a fact that the city of Quebec, especially in that quarter, was overrun with this poisonous plant. The smell was unbearable, particularly when it was drying out in the autumn. At this time of year young boys used to cut the thickest stems to make fifes and flutes, although I never heard of their suffering any ill effects. I had the honour of commanding a regiment of young scamps, and these musical instruments were a significant addition to the intensely martial air of this illustrious corps. Without them, our band would have consisted of a single drum—or to be exact, a tin kettle turned upside down.

To return to my story: following hard upon the son's cry of alarm we saw the stepfather, pursued by a mob of sailors. He took cover in our house (he lived on one side of the lower half), barred the street door, slipped out a back way, climbed over the walls of the Jesuits' courtyard, and ran for help to the guard stationed at the barracks near the Upper Town market.[1]

Upon arrival of the said guard led by a sergeant nodding his head sympathetically, the sailors fled, but not before kicking in two of the doorpanels and breaking innumerable windowpanes. That night I was highly diverted by the spectacle of the old Chôlette sisters scurrying about, trying to keep the wind from blowing out the candles. They managed quite cleverly by using their wardrobe as a barricade against the largest holes in the windows. Children are indeed easily amused.

It was the custom among small boys to torment the poor Recollet monks by yanking the heavy chain that rang the convent bell. My companions told me many a piteous tale of how the monks seized children as they indulged in this innocent pastime and imprisoned them for months on end in the monastery dungeons. There the children were subjected to the most severe penance, not to mention regular beatings morning and night. In vain did I tell them that I knew several Recollets who frequently came to my father's house for charity, and that they were gentle, peaceful men. My friends paid not the slightest attention. The monks were hypocrites, they insisted, who assumed a docile mien while going about the countryside, like the donkey who wants his oats. One boy even asserted that he had actually been taken prisoner and had only escaped by jumping out of a second-storey window into the street. He showed me the pavement where he had broken his leg, and even limped for the occasion.

Despite my terror, my comrades succeeded one day in dragging me to the convent door, on the pretext that one of them had been given a message by his father for the superior. They swung on the chain, the bell clashed wildly, the door opened, and one of the urchins, by pre-arrangement, gave me a hard shove. I lost my balance and shot between the porter's legs. Even his long robe didn't stop me, and I fell onto the stone-paved corridor floor, giving myself an enormous lump on the head in the process. Needless to say, the mischief-makers had fled.

To my utter horror, the Recollet asked me severely what I wanted. Dismayed though I was, my presence of mind didn't desert me and I answered, trembling, that I wished to speak to Brother Juniper.

"He's not here, my child," said the porter. "But what is your name?"

"I'm young Gaspé," I replied very humbly.

"I know your family," he said, "and it pains me to see you running around with a bunch of little hooligans like those you were with just now. What would your good mother say if she knew?"

Tears filled my eyes at this reproach.

"There, there!" said the monk. "Let's not talk about it any more. Come along with me."

144

Shaking in my boots, I followed him, believing he was about to throw me into the dark dungeon. To my surprise, he led me into the convent orchard, situated where the Anglican cathedral and its attendant offices now stand.

"Eat all the plums you want, and then fill your pockets," said he.

I accepted this light penance with alacrity, but, alas, quickly forgot the first of the good Recollet's injunctions.

Shortly after my arrival in Quebec, Cog Bezeau introduced me with all due ceremony to his first cousin, Lafleur. This Lafleur was an amphibious little animal of my own age who passed as much of the summer playing in the waters of the Saint Lawrence as in his mother's house, which stood on a quay in the Lower Town beside the Cul-de-Sac.[G] When not in his natural element he became the most feared young scamp in the old part of town; quarrelsome and pugnacious, he terrorized his peers and even the older children. Nevertheless, I owe him a debt of gratitude which I now hasten to pay his departed shade.

At the outset this little devil had conceived a singular affection for me, and woe betide anyone who dared maltreat me in his presence! Then great and small were sure to bear the trademark of Master Lafleur somewhere or other. He never lacked for weapons: stones, pebbles, anything suited his purpose. But for all his tender solicitude he twice nearly drowned me.

One morning I went down to the Lower Town to get a fine little sailboat, his own handiwork, which he had promised me. Lafleur was at his usual post on the quay, ready to jump into the water. He gave a joyful shout at seeing me and asked me to come along with him on a little call he wished to pay a vessel anchored offshore.

"But the tide is going out as fast as can be, and there's a real sou'wester blowing," I protested.

"That's what makes it fun," answered Lafleur. "We'll rest in the chaloupe moored behind the ship and annoy the *goddams* on board."

This last consideration decided me, and several minutes later we neared the ship; but whether because Lafleur was a stronger swimmer, or because he judged the force of the current more accurately than I, he managed to catch hold of the chaloupe while I was swept away by a current moving at the speed of a racehorse. After desperate efforts to get back to the safety of the boat, I had made up my mind to swim for shore as my only hope, when a sailor—a sort of philanthropic

145

Hercules—saw my danger. Taking a cabin boy, he jumped into the boat where Lafleur was making faces, and quickly overtook me. Jack was a man of action, but few words. He grabbed me by the scruff of the neck, slung me stomach-side-down on the edge of the chaloupe, and whacked me mightily on the back twice for good measure. Then, with as little respect for my bones as if I were a small spaniel whose life he'd saved, he tossed me onto the bottom of the boat where I crouched, shivering, like a cat just out of the water. While all this was going on my friend Lafleur, seated on the edge of the chaloupe with the aplomb of a real seaman, such as he was forever mimicking, kept up a highly animated dialogue with the sailor, sticking out his tonque, making monkey-faces, and giving *goddam* for *goddam* while Jack threatened us each in turn with his enormous fist.

I didn't understand English in those days, whereas my companion spoke the purest British sailors' lingo. I asked him what Master Jack was saying.

Said Lafleur, "As soon as we pull alongside the quay, this animal proposes to double the number of whacks you've already had, just to teach you to swim better in future. As he can't accuse *me* of not swimming well, he's going to give me the same treatment on the excuse that last year, when the ship was tied up at the wharf, I threw his drawers into the ship's soup pot."

"What'll we do?" said I, rubbing the afflicted parts. They stung like fury.

"Well," mused Lafleur, "a gentleman's son like you is pretty thin-skinned. But, as I'm your friend and have a hide as tough as leather, I've suggesting taking a beating for both of us to pay for his stupid drawers. I told him that they slipped out of my hands when I was hanging them up to dry above the cook's soup pot. But," he added, "if one of us is going to be beaten anyway, I don't see why we both should. I stood by you like a real friend, as you might expect; but I've one more trick up my sleeve. As soon as we get close to shore, jump into the water on the port side of the chaloupe, and I'll dive over starboard. That way, he can only catch one of us, and the other will have time to get ashore and make fun of Jack Tar."

I thought this a marvelous idea, and a few minutes later we flopped into the water like a couple of startled frogs. As I was on the port side, the current quickly carried me a fair distance, so close to shore that I felt it safe to turn and look at the chaloupe. To my intense surprise, I saw the good sailor, his hands on his hips, laughing heartily at the clever trick played on him by us rascals. Then I spied Master Lafleur standing on a quay throwing stones at the chaloupe as hard as he could, no doubt to thank Jack for his forbearance.

When Lafleur wasn't in the water, one could be sure to find him perched like a little monkey on the highest part of some ship's rigging, for which he knew all the correct nautical terms. From here he would taunt the crew, leaping about the cordage like a squirrel to escape pursuit by the most agile sailors, and nearly always getting off without too much rough handling. I should imagine that being a ship's apprentice came easily to him.

The city of Quebec had been relieved of Lafleur's presence for eight years, when early one winter I met a young mariner in the Lower Town decked out in the spruce Sunday best of a sailor. He accosted me with the easy manner of a man of his calling, although with the utmost politeness.

"I liked you so well as a child," said he, "that I couldn't resist speaking to you, though you be a gentleman and I a poor sailor."

With his tar-blackened hand he wrung the one I proffered, visibly moved.

"Lafleur," said I, "to prove how genuinely glad I am to see you, let's go to your mother's house where we can chat more comfortably."

"My dear mother has taken a second husband to console herself for the absence of her most amiable son," said Lafleur. "I can only congratulate myself on her choice of a rich and indulgent old man, Sieur Labadie, who married her for love—she's still a handsome woman, even if she *is* nearing forty—whereas she married him for love of his money, some of which is rubbing off on me. He's a capital stepfather, let me tell you, always ready to help me out at my mother's bidding. My dear mother may not be able to boss her good-for-nothing son, but she leads her old husband around by the nose, as you shall see.

"Three days ago I got into an argument with a Portuguese sailor, or perhaps Spanish. As I detest quarreling for nothing, I hit out in the hope that he'd punch back like an English sailor. You know, Monsieur, it's a pleasure to do business with a British Jack Tar. Right away you put up your fists, and in five minutes settle an affair that would drag on for days if it were just a matter of slinging insults. Well, to get back to the Portuguese sailor, he told me that people in his country only fought with daggers or swords, and if I really felt like it, he'd give me a lesson with these weapons.

"I saw he'd missed the point entirely. I retorted that he hadn't even the courage of the ladies of Liverpool, who could punch as hard as any man, and that he didn't deserve those gold earrings he was so proud of. Then I promptly relieved him of these ornaments."

"What!" I exclaimed. "He let you do it without saying a word?"

"By heaven! I didn't wait for his permission," answered Lafleur. "I gave them a bit of a tug and they came right off. The wretch bellowed like a bull and the bystanders backed him up. I was taken before a magistrate.

"'Well, back again, Master Lafleur, stirring up trouble in the Lower Town,' said this landlubber. 'It's been quite peaceful since you left. You'll pay now for all your old pranks as well as my broken windows, you worthless rascal!'

"Luckily, my stepfather arrived while all this was going on. He's a great friend of the judge, and my mother, who had learned of my plight, had him in tow. He looked like a cur being prodded along with a big stick. I got off with a fine of thirty piastres, which the decent old boy paid to the Portuguese dog."

Lafleur forthwith gave me a lengthy account of his journeyings over the years. He spoke enthusiastically of a sailor's life and of the two shipwrecks he had already experienced, although only twenty years old, cursing meanwhile the last of these, which forced him to spend six months on land.

"But it's an ill wind that blows no good," added Lafleur. "While keeping my good stepfather's money in circulation, despite the fact that he'd rather see me in hell, I'm going to look for recruits. Don't you think this country should be ashamed of having hundreds of strong and alert young men among our Canadians who've never swallowed a breath of sea air? It's a disgrace to see them loafing about here like land turtles on the shores of the Leeward Isles, submitting like sheep to their mothers and fathers, judges and justices, when they might be free as the ocean wave once they set foot on a good ship!"

"You don't mention the cat-o'-nine'tails?" I queried.

"The cat! The cat! I don't give a damn about the cat! The only time I got a taste was when I really itched for it, and then only because of my pranks, never for neglecting or being unfit for a sailor's duties. I've always been proud to show what a Canadian can do, and I've always been well liked by my captains.

"Eight years ago, on the very day I took ship as a cabin boy on a vessel bound for England, a young sailor said to me while we were still in the roadstead, 'Hey, you little French shrimp! Get my shoes from between-decks.'

"'Go to hell, you lazy dog!' was my answer.

"English sailors are first-rate seamen, but usually pretty heavy. Before he could grab me I was already at the topsail. Then I led him a merry chase, to the great delight of the crew and even Captain Patterson. The captain almost split his sides laughing, and shouted to the sailor not to harm me. I saw they found the whole thing very funny, and I took refuge at the far end of yardarm where Jack thought he could easily get hold of me. But at the very moment he reached for his prey, the frog jumped into the Saint Lawrence, and Jack came tumbling after. Here began a new comedy. He was a grown man, while I was barely twelve years old, and he would have caught up with me quickly enough, but as he was about to lunge I did a duckdive and swam under him. He didn't even realize it. While he waited for me to surface, I swam with the current to the ship and clambered on deck with the help of a rope thrown to me by a sailor.

"Don't you remember the good times we used to have with an overturned chaloupe between the Quai de la Reine and the Cul-de-Sac?" Lafleur went on.

"Perfectly," said I. "Thanks to you, I nearly drowned."

"Pooh!" said my interlocutor. "Could you drown with Lafleur for a friend? Anyway, you would've deserved it for taking me on in my own element. You know, I was the one who first thought of diving off the keel of the boat, swimming under it, and coming up on the other side. After a week all the other swimmers could do it too. I was humiliated! All night long I thought about it, and next day I had a new trick in mind. I told them, 'Diving frontwards with your arms above your head and then swimming under the boat is a stunt worthy of those lobsters from the Upper Town; but the really difficult thing is to do it backwards.' And with this I somersaulted backwards and in a few seconds was hanging onto the other side of the boat. This was child's play for me, as I was used to leaping about the rigging and dangling by my feet like a monkey. Everyone had given up when you arrived.

149

"'Here's Gaspé who does such splendid *acrobatatics*, like those he saw at the circus!'[5] I shouted. 'Just watch him slip under the boat like a piece of lard!'

"'Phooey,' said LeBlond. 'He's just a landlubber from the Upper Town. We'll have to dig him out of the mud!'

"You were full of self-confidence and were bound to uphold the honour of the Upper Town swimmers, so in you plunged as soon as I'd explained the trick to you. You took off beautifully, going straight down into the water head first; but when you didn't reappear I began to get worried and dived over starboard in case you needed rescuing. At that moment you surfaced, spouting like a baby whale, but unharmed except for a shoulder scrape from the oarlocks. If it had mischanced to be your head instead of your shoulder, Lafleur would have been very upset, and wouldn't now have the honour of welcoming you into his mother's house."

"Well, you needn't reproach yourself for not doing your best to drown me at least four or five times, my dear Lafleur," I countered.

"It was out of pure friendship," replied Lafleur. "I wanted you to develop a taste for the sailor's trade. Take my advice: throw paper, pen, and ink at your employer's head. Your father's rich; let him buy you a little boat, and hurrah! for the ocean wave! Lafleur will be petty officer. What with me coaching you in our spare time, may a shark eat me if you're not a real seadog at the end of three years."

I thanked my friend Lafleur for his good advice, although I didn't follow it. I don't know whether he had better luck with other young men, or whether my youthful compatriots were suddenly seized with travel fever; but the following year seventeen Canadian youths, some from well-off families, left Quebec to seek their fortune at sea. Of this number, only two have seen their homeland once again, while a third returned to settle and die in the town of his birth, after several voyages all over the world. As for Lafleur, two years after the conversation just recorded, his mother learned that he and two other sailors had been swept into the sea by a wave.

When memory turns to the happy days of childhood, I am often carried in spirit to the Château de Belle-Vue in the parish of Saint-Joachim.[H] This château, the property of the Quebec Seminary, stood upon a promontory dominating a wide valley, washed by the pure, clear waters of the Saint Lawrence. In summer this valley is covered by the richest of crops and lush meadows. It affords one of the most beautiful sights in Canada, quite apart from the imposing scenic grandeur that surrounds it on every side. To the west is the Ile d'Orléans, seemingly afloat upon the majestic river; opposite lies the green countryside of the South Shore, dotted with white-washed dwellings that give the effect of a continuous village stretching as far as the eye can see. To the northeast unfurls the Laurentian chain, an immense green serpent whose gigantic head, Cap Tourmente, throws huge evening shadows across the fine meadows spreading from its base to the bluff atop which stands the château.

If the reverend gentlemen of the Quebec Seminary had wished to choose the one site in all Canada best suited to give their pupils a refreshing break from study, they could not have found a country retreat where everything united more happily to serve this object. Those who liked hunting had only to step outside with a gun. Game was always plentiful. Pigeons were so abundant that we killed them at the château door. We found partridge within fifteen arpents, and the shores were covered with wildfowl of all kinds.

For those who were more peacefully inclined and preferred to fish, the clear waters of a little river running through the property provided a daily supply of trout in quantity. But the fishermen's favourite spot was atop Cap Tourmente. A stranger, viewing this Laurentian giant from afar, would never guess that its superb head is graced by a picturesque lake about half a league around.

At the thought of this lake, all the delights of youth rise up before my imagination, awakened suddenly from the torpor imposed by the weight of years. It is a Thursday; some twenty pupils set out at dawn for the lake, each with rod in hand and a pack on his back, in order that their fellows may feast next day on excellent trout. The novices among them also carry a little gift for the old woman, known as *la bonne femme du cabaret*, who runs a canteen on the mountain. After a scramble up one flank of Cap Tourmente and a lengthy walk through the forest, we arrive dead tired in a little clearing covered with brown moss, where a spring of ice-cold water jets forth, clean and limpid. "The canteen! The canteen!" everyone shouts. "Get out your presents for the canteen lady!" The mystified neophytes look for her everywhere, much to the hilarity of their companions.

We rest for a time, drinking deeply of the hospitality offered by the generous naiad of the spring, and then go on our way. Half an hour later we come to the enchanted shores of a lovely stretch of

"La Chasse aux tourtes" (1853) by Antoine Plamondon (1804-1895). A scene reminiscent of de Gaspé's schoolday holidays at Saint-Joachim, although painted somewhat later. Art Gallery of Ontario, Toronto. 2601

water, where our attention is immediately caught by a tall, black-painted cross. All kneel silently before this symbol of the Redemption raised in the wilderness, and the priest or seminarian who always accompanies pupils on such outings intones *O Crux Ave!* This devout observance completed, everyone gives themselves up to the most madcap antics.

Some break off fir branches to repair the bed of boughs in the sleeping-cabin; others cut wood to keep the pot boiling and give us light and warmth during the night. Five or six of us take possession of the canoe to fish and paddle about the lake, while those who dislike such peaceful pursuits create enough uproar to scare the fish away.

After the evening catch, always plentiful when the weather is right, we gather in the cabin for a first-rate supper washed down with a few glasses of wine. The master doles it out with care and circumspection, according to age, this being a not inconsiderable addition to one of the most agreeable evenings in memory.

Little Seminary uniform, circa 1806, from John Lambert's *Travels*. De Gaspé notes that Quebec urchins used to call pupils "blue sheep" because of their distinctive outfit. Department of Rare Books and Special Collections of the McGill University Libraries, photo: Robert Rohonczy

CHAPTER SEVEN

To roam, close by the lovely lake where
plays the swan,
The once-green meadows of his dear
Mantua.

L'abbé Delille [1]

Today is the twentieth of August, 1865, yet I seem to see before me
the nine friends of my childhood, gathered at the manor of Saint-
Jean Port-Joli. It is six in the morning on August the twentieth, 1801,
and we are preparing to set out for Lac Trois-Saumons after a hearty
breakfast. Have the shades of the departed souls that came to me
one stormy night stamped their features, their image, so firmly on
my mind, that I can picture them as vividly now as I saw them then?
Answer my call, O my friends! as you did those sixty-four years ago,
when I led your merry band to the lake of my ancestors. Answer the
roll call, my friends: Louis LeBourdais, Pierre LeBourdais, Joseph
Painchaud, Paschal Taché, Joseph Fortin, James Maguire, Jean Marie
Bélanger, François Verrault, and you, my only brother, Thomas Aubert
de Gaspé! One alone, Dr. Painchaud, replies with a quizzical air,
"Present!" The silence of the tomb is all the answer vouchsafed by
the rest.

To a man we refused my father's offer of a ride in the carriage as
far as the home of old Laurent Caron, who was to be our guide to

the lake. A guide was necessary in those days, otherwise one would soon be lost in the maze of paths through the sugarbush of the third and fourth ranges of the seigneurie. Only the land on the first range and part of the second had been cleared. Well, we refused my father's offer, being in too much of a hurry to set off, each shouldering a knapsack, with rod or gun in hand and a hatchet stuck through the belt. There was a good league to be covered between the manor house and old Laurent's dwelling, but we insisted that by taking our way through field and forest we would cut the journey in half. Off we went, singing thus—in honour, I suppose, of the woollen caps we had donned for the occasion:

> Go, go, go, little bonnet, big bonnet,
> Go, go, go, little bonnet so round.
>
> My father had a house built,
> Go, go, go little bonnet so round.
>
> Shoemakers[1] three 'twas built it,
> Go, go, go little bonnet so round.

Laurent Caron, who was what we Canadians call an old pensioner, came forward to greet us at the foot of his front steps, his red tuque tucked under his arm. With the consummate but unaffected politeness of the French Canadians of old, he begged us enter.

I can't help remarking, at the risk of being soundly beaten by our modern dandies, that most of them look like servants in their Sunday best compared to those old men of yesteryear.

After exchanging a few civilities, as was the country custom, I brought up the purpose of our visit and asked if he would be kind enough to guide us to the lake.

"Certainly, my young seigneur," said old Laurent, winking comically at my friends, "but it will cost you something."

"Oh, yes of course," I replied.

"Very well, then," said the old man, keeping up the same pantomime, "but we must begin by breakfasting."

As we had already come more than a league through field and forest, laden like mules, our refusal was a matter of pure form, the upshot being that we did full justice to the pig's cheek omelette[B] and the table covered with dishes of sweet cream sprinkled with maple sugar.

Fortified by a second breakfast, we quickly entered the forest, walking in single file after our guide, Indian-style. I prided myself on being the best walker for my age, and fell in close behind Laurent Caron. I had reckoned without my host, however. He was a tall old man with a youthful physique and limbs as strong as those of the moose he had hunted for thirty years. In vain did I lengthen my stride; in the end I was forced into a trot to keep up. At the summit of the first of the three mountains we were to climb, I saw that he was prepared to go on, and remarked that several of our companions had fallen behind.

"Are you tired?" asked our guide. "Have a rest then. Actually, before tackling the mountain, I hadn't planned to stop until the second knoll. It's not far, and much higher than this."

I thought that "knoll" was the name of the mountain where we already stood, but it was a term of scorn applied by old Laurent to what he judged to be an insignificant hillock. I was humiliated. I put down my pack and stretched out on the cool grass, as did all my friends. Old Laurent, however, with a pack on his back, a long rifle in one hand, and an iron kettle weighing at least fifteen pounds in the other, bawled out a verse of the following song, holding himself as straight as the maple against which he leaned, no doubt to rest.

> Oh, who will carry me through the wood,
> I who am so small?
> Let it be this gentleman here:
> He looks a healthy fellow.
> Are we in the wood still,
> Or have we reached the shore?

After a rest that seemed all too short, we set off at a trot behind old Caron, whose legs appeared to be growing with each step. As the path was fairly level for the next fifteen arpents,ᶜ we managed to keep up until we came to the second knoll. Our guide scaled it without changing his stride. As we dragged ourselves half-expiring up the mountainside, old Laurent consoled us from the top with the following ditty:

> When I was but little Jeanette, dinga-dan-dang,
> I left my lunch behind, dinga-dan-day,
> I left my lunch behind. (bis)

156

A fellow from my father's house, dinga-dan-dang,
Came to bring it to me, dinga-dan-day,
Came to bring it to me. (*bis*)

By way of thanks, Big Peter, dinga-dan-dang,
All I have to do is eat, dinga-dan-day,
The sheep have strayed away. (*bis*)

At the sound of his fiddle-dee-dee, dinga-dan-dang,
My sheep came gathering round, dinga-dan-day,
My sheep came gathering round. (*bis*)

Old Laurent's verses were not much to our taste: first, because the ragamuffins of Quebec used to call us "blue sheep" and shout "Ba-a-a, ba-a-a!" after us in the street; secondly, because the "fiddle-dee-dee" seemed to taunt our lack of strength. The reader who considers us puny weaklings is greatly mistaken. On the contrary, we were all very strong and energetic, but the oldest among us was barely sixteen. Despite our fatigue, after a long hike we began to climb the third mountain, twice as high as the two preceding ones that old Laurent had so scathingly described as knolls. Painchaud, Maguire, and I were the strongest walkers for our age, yet in spite of sweating blood and tears and straining every muscle, we had only climbed half way when we heard the sonorous voice of old Laurent serenading us from the summit thus—no doubt to spur us on:

My father had three hundred sheep,
'Twas I the shepherdess, (*bis*)
Dong-dinga-dong-dong,
'Twas I the shepherdess, dong.

One day while in the meadow,
Fifteen the wolf did steal, (*bis*)
Dong-dinga-dong-dong,
Fifteen the wolf did steal, dong.

A cavalier was passing,
Fifteen he brought me back, (*bis*)
Dong-dinga-dong-dong,
Fifteen he brought me back, dong.

Kind sir, I thank you greatly,
For coming to my aid, (*bis*)
Dong-dinga-dong-dong,
For coming to my aid, dong.

When we come to shear the sheep,
'Tis you will have the wool, (*bis*)
Dong-dinga-dong-dong,
"Tis you will have the wool, dong.

A merchant rich my father is,
My mother demoiselle,[2] (*bis*)
Dong-dinga-dong-dong,
My mother demoiselle, dong.

Finally, after repeatedly consigning old Laurent Caron to the devil,
we arrived atop the mountain overlooking the cleared trail down to
Lac Trois-Saumons. Below us lay one of the most magnificent views
in Canada. We were two leagues back from the shores of the Saint
Lawrence and nine leagues from the Laurentians, yet as though by
magic, the mountains to the north seemed to draw nearer to the
southern range where we stood, and the prince of rivers, seven leagues
broad, appeared to roll his silver waters at our very feet. I could write
for pages on the marvels of the panorama visible from our lofty perch.

Painchaud said to our guide, "How many more mountains must
we climb before coming to your blessed lake, that new Promised Land
that we never seem to reach?"

"What mountains?" queried old Caron. "You surely can't mean
those two knolls we've just been over!"

"Aha! Those were knolls!" exclaimed Painchaud. "It's just as well
you told us, for upon my honour we never would've guessed. But
never mind that. Are we still a long way from the lake?"

"We're almost there," answered Caron. "It's just a step or two
further."

We looked at our guide's formidable legs with as much misgiving
as if he had donned Tom Thumb's seven-league boots. Then we
thought of the dreadful knolls, and our hearts sank.

Old Laurent, seeing that we were not disposed to resume our march
without first resting a little, decided to throw down kettle, axe, and
rifle, although keeping on his enormous pack.

"Well then, let's have a pipe while waiting for you to catch your
breath."

The pipe was smoked, and we descended the far side of the mountain
by a rugged path. After we had trudged on for about fifteen arpents,
stumbling over stones and pebbles, the terrain changed. A damp

carpet of emerald-green moss soon cooled our burning feet, and all our fatigue vanished. Spruce, fir, and aspen became more scattered as we progressed southward. Ahead of us the gloom of the forest receded, a sign that a clearing was near. We pushed forward, and a gasp of admiration rose as from a single throat: there at our feet, a beautiful lake lay sleeping. At that moment, the cries of two loons,[1] our superb Canadian swans, seemed to bid us welcome to their watery domain. I am truly ashamed to confess that we responded to these hospitable advances with two blasts of the shotgun. A hail of lead seemed to cover them, but in fact merely hit the water where they were floating. We thought they must be mortally wounded. To our great surpise, they bobbed up five or six arpents further off, taunting us with their shrill, piercing call. It was rare in those days to kill a diving fowl with a flint gun, for the birds would see the spark of the primer and disappear beneath the water before the shot could reach them.

Lac Trois-Saumons, lying on the southern slope of a high mountain, is almost the width of the seigneurie of Saint-Jean Port-Joli. The seigneurial boundary actually passes through the middle of the lake, two and a half leagues back from the Saint Lawrence River. The breadth of this sheet of water varies between half a mile and a mile, depending on the contours of the land.

The profound and religious silence that reigns in this solitude is what first strikes the visitor. He experiences a feeling of well-being and security, much as a man who, prey to the persecutions of his fellow citizens, finds himself suddenly transported to some restful haven far from the malicious attacks of men. I didn't think of this at the time, for I was at an age when life is all rose-coloured, but I have often done so since in my frequent visits to this lonely place. We were young fellows then, freed from the constraints of college life and parental supervision, and like captives regaining their freedom after long seclusion, we felt a strong surge of independence. In this unpeopled retreat we could give full vent to all our youthful impulses. We were indeed transported to a new world, for apart from ourselves and the two waterfowl tracing a long, rippling wake on a surface otherwise as smooth as the most beautiful Venetian glass, no living thing appeared to break the solitude. The weather was so calm that fir and spruce were reflected without a quiver as they bent over this immense mirror. A few islands were scattered here and there on the translucent surface, like garlands of greenery dropped onto a looking-glass by some lady at her dressing table.

We had gathered at sunset on a small island a few feet from shore, all talking at once, when we heard the sound of many voices. It seemed as though a group of men were talking on the other side of the lake. We stopped speaking, the better to listen, but all was silent. We resumed our talk; our friends on the opposite shore resumed theirs. It was a confused murmur of voices such as one hears in a thronged assembly. We looked toward our guide for an explanation of this phenomenon.

"They are the groans and lamentations of poor Joseph Marie Aubé, who died more than a hundred years ago near Toussaint Cove,[3] or perhaps of Joseph Toussaint himself, drowned near the cabin of the unfortunate Aubé," said old Laurent Caron. "But it's time for supper. The tale is a long one, and I'll tell it while smoking my pipe by the fire."

One of us began shouting, "Come to supper!" as loudly as his lungs would permit. The finest echo repeated distinctly, "Come to supper!" and reverberated several times in diminishing tones. At last, only the word "supper" could be heard, as though someone had spoken quietly in your ear. This was the murmur of the seventh echo.

There followed a veritable fusillade of shouts, comments, and questions as silly as ever any echo was condemned to reproduce. In vain did old Caron tell us that supper was ready and the biscuit[4] burning; we paid not the slightest attention for a good half hour at least. Finding, I suppose, that we weren't making enough racket, I ventured to fire my shotgun. The effect of the detonation was so startling that we bowed our shoulders as though the mountains, shaken by some powerful earthquake, threatened to crush us.[5]

All pleasures must come to an end, even that of shouting oneself hoarse like a maniac, and so we acceded to old Caron's pressing invitation, resolved to resume our fun after listening to the legend of the strange sounds we had heard. From what this Nestor of the forest had said earlier, he was about to tell us the story.

OLD CARON'S TALE

"It was in the time of the French," said old Caron. "The Englishman had not yet set foot in the land, or if he occasionally did, he left quicker than he came—if he was lucky enough to escape with a whole skin. You know, some of our Canadians were husky fellows who'd stick at nothing."

"Ah!" said Maguire, whose French was then somewhat sketchy, "Irishmen have bullyboys too, but it hasn't stopped the English from taking over my country!"

"Begging your pardon, sir," replied old Caron, "but the English never took Canada. It was *la Pompadour* who sold it to the king of England. But you'll see: our own folk will come back!"

Fortified by this belief, very common at the time among the old habitants, Caron continued his tale.

"The story I'm about to tell you is absolutely true. A venerable priest, the late Monsieur Ingan, curé of L'Islet, used to tell it to my uncles.

"It was about ten o'clock of an October evening. The curé of L'Islet, who also served the parish of Saint-Jean Port-Joli, had gone to bed. He was woken up by his verger, who lived in the presbytery, saying that someone was knocking on the kitchen door.

"'Well, open the door,' said the curé. 'I suppose they've come to get me for some sick person. I'll get dressed right away.'

"'But it's a redskin,' protested the verger. 'I can tell by his voice. There's no trusting them; they're as treacherous as the devil!'

"The curé knew that his verger was far from brave, so he pulled on his trousers, wrapped himself in a blanket, and hurried to the kitchen door. 'Who's there?' he asked.

"'Me, Brother,' replied the stranger. 'I wish to speak with *patliasse*.[1] I bring him words of dead man.'

"'Don't open the door, for the love of God!' cried the verger. He had armed himself with an iron poker and stationed himself behind the curé. 'He's probably come straight from the redskin's hell, where every single dead Indian is sure to be found!'

"The curé paid no attention to his verger and opened the door immediately. In stepped a young Huron of proud yet benevolent mien. He leaned on the barrel of his gun, the butt resting on the ground, and looked all about. Not finding what he sought, he said, 'I wish to speak with patliasse. I bring him words of dead man.'

"The verger grabbed hold of the curé, who shrugged him off and said to the Indian, 'I'm the patliasse.'

"'You are not patliasse, you,' asserted the Huron. 'You have no black robe, you cover back like red man.'

161

"The curé, seeing that the Huron refused to recognize a priest without his black robe, took another tack. Turning his back he placed a finger on his tonsure and said, 'Look.'

"'Houa!' exclaimed the Indian. 'You real patliasse!' And he seated himself on the floor, holding his gun between his legs.

"'I was there—over there,' stated the Huron, stretching an arm toward the south, 'four days' march from the Saint Lawrence River. I was returning to my village after hunting, when I came on the trail and blaze of a Frenchman.[6] Good! I said to myself, there is a hunter here. I will go and sleep in his cabin. After walking for a long time, I saw from tracks of the Frenchman that he was very tired.'

"'How did you know it was the trail of a Frenchman, and that he was tired?' asked the priest.

'Not difficult,' replied the Indian. 'Red man always walks with feet pointing in, as if on snowshoes. White man walks with feet straight or pointing out. I saw that the Frenchman was tired because his steps got shorter all the time and his foot sank deeper into the soft earth.'

"As the curé was satisfied with this explanation, the savage continued his story.

"'I walked faster and faster to catch up with him, but it was night when I reached the cabin. It was empty: he had gone. I lit a fire, and I saw that my brother, the Frenchman, was sick.'

"'How did you know that?' asked the curé.

"'Need not be clever to know that,' retorted the Indian. 'He had slept on the old bed of fir without putting fresh branches on top; he had left his pelts behind without storing them up in a tree, safe from rodents; and he had left no wood in the cabin. You see, Father, Frenchman always leaves enough wood in the cabin for a good fire, to be used by himself or other hunters who come in the dark of night or during a storm. It is agreed among them.'

"'Yes,' snapped the verger, who was beginning to regain confidence, 'and when the red men sleep in the Canadians' cabins, they burn all their wood and don't chop any more to replace it. They're too lazy for that.'

"'The Great Spirit created palefaces and told them to till the soil,' replied the Indian. 'Our patliasse read us these fine words from a book. He also created redskins and said to them, "The forests, lakes, and rivers are yours: hunt, fish, and make your slaves work for you."'

"'Continue your tale,' said the curé, not much inclined to engage in theological discussion with this forest philosopher.

"'I took up the trail again next day, walking fast, for I wished to help my brother the Frenchman. I saw by the trail that he was getting still weaker, but when I reached the second cabin I found only his gun, which he had not strength to carry farther. I would have gone on at once, but it was so dark I feared to lose his trail, and I waited until next day. I began to run, but even so, I only arrived after the sun had gone down on Lac Trois-Saumons. It was dark in the cabin; the fire was out, and at first I saw no one. "Get me water," said the sick man, "I'm very thirsty. Take that birchbark bowl by your feet." After he had drunk some water, he said, "Stay close by the cabin door. There is a huge bear in here, at the back. He's been watching me since yesterday with enormous, fiery eyes."

"'"You are very sick, my brother," I said. "I see your sealskin bag, but no bear. I will light the fire to warm you." "Thank you. I'm very cold," he answered.

"'I lit the fire and made the whole cabin bright. "You see," I said, "there's no bear at all." "He's still there, ready to pounce," was the answer. "Put that from your mind, my brother," said I. "You are weak and the manitou⁷ sends you bad dreams. I will make you a broth to give you strength."

"'I plucked a partridge, skinned a hare, and made him a broth. He drank it and said he felt a little better, but that the great beast threatening him was still in the same place. I saw that it was useless to talk about it, and set about eating my supper. He told me to have a short sleep, and he would talk to me afterward. I was falling asleep when I was awakened by a cry from the sick man.

"'"I was terrified," he said. "The bear was so close that I felt his fiery breath burning my face. Promise me that you'll stay here as long as I'm alive, and that after I'm dead you'll go to the curé of L'Islet, my pastor, for me."

"'I promised him what he asked.

"'"My name is Joseph Marie Aubé," he continued.'

"'Joseph Marie Aubé is dead!' cried the curé. 'God have mercy on his soul! *Ah! Mon Dieu! Mon Dieu!* What dreadful news! But continue, my son.'

"'I will tell you his words,' the Indian went on. 'It is he who speaks. Listen, my father. "I have been a sinner since childhood. I

163

have drunk and eaten the family patrimony; my father died of a broken heart long ago, and instead of helping my poor mother in her poverty, I led the life of a vagabond. I never went to church and was forever mocking good Christians. My kindhearted mother shed buckets of tears over my wicked conduct, but my soul was so black that I laughed at her. She reproached me tearfully for abandoning her, old and infirm as she was, on the edge of the grave. I swore at her. But a mother's love is not rebuffed by ingratitude or maltreatment. She answered my insults only with tears, patience, tenderness, and resignation.

""'When I saw her for the last time, six weeks ago, she was kneeling near my bed as I awoke after a night's debauch. At first I wanted to send her away, but, at the sight of her tears mingling with her white hair, I hadn't the courage to do it, despite my usual brutality.

""'My mother spoke. 'I had an evil dream this night, and I sense that I am talking to my son for the last time. I'll no longer plague you with my reproaches, but I have a favour to ask, one so little that you won't refuse me,' said she with a sorrowful smile. 'You were baptized Joseph Marie; here is a small medal of the Blessed Virgin, your patron saint. Will you hang it around your neck and call on her if you think you have need? It is so small a thing to grant me.' I accepted the medal for the sake of peace, determined to get rid of it at the first opportunity, but I forgot about it and it remained around my neck.

""'When I fell ill four days ago, I felt dispirited and strangely sad. In the bitterness of my heart, I went over my sins. I recalled my father, always so kind and indulgent, despite my disorderly life and the ruin it had brought on him. I remembered my old mother, her prayers, and the constant tears shed for me. I knelt at the foot of a tree to pray, but sobs stifled my voice. I felt myself unworthy to pray to God, whom I had so offended, and wished for a priest as mediator between myself and the Deity.

""'When I arrived here yesterday after three days of weary trudging, I lay down exhausted. Scarcely was I on the bed when I saw an enormous bear seated on his hind paws, staring at me with burning red eyes. I thought it was Satan waiting to carry off my soul. My whole body trembled, but at the thought of my crimes and blasphemies, I feared to anger God further by imploring His aid. The animal prepared to leap. I cried, 'Mother! Mother!' as I did when I was a child and danger threatened. The medal of the Blessed Virgin appeared between my fingers as though she had heard me. I lifted it toward the bear and he shrank back, terrified, into the far end of the cabin. I realized then that God had not abandoned me, that He had heard the prayers of His holy mother, the mother of all Christians. My patron saint, who had shed so many tears for her divine son, had been touched by the despair of a Christian mother pleading for her child. It was clear to me that the Blessed Virgin had pleaded for divine mercy until Christ had granted her wish. At last I prayed— prayed with fervour and confidence. Unable to confess to a priest, I confessed to God. I acknowledged my sins amid tears of repentance, and peace and hope entered my soul. Tell all this to the curé of L'Islet. Beg him to console my mother and ask her forgiveness for all the heartbreak I've caused her.'"

"The Huron continued his story. 'My father, I have told you all that Aubé charged me to tell you. I spent two days and one night more beside his bed, and he died this evening at sunset. He told me he still saw the manitou in the depths of the cabin, and from time to time he raised his medal to keep it from coming nearer. He lost consciousness toward midday and died with his arms folded on his breast, holding the image of the Blessed Virgin. I have told you all. It is for you, my father, to do what remains to be done.'

"'Why didn't you come and get me?' said the curé. 'I would have administered the sacraments of our holy faith and strengthened him in the terrible battle that he, poor repentant sinner, had to wage with the forces of hell, resolved upon his damnation. I would have supported him against my breast, and with cross held high would have defied the infernal spirits and exorcised them! You are a bad Indian.'

"The Huron bowed his shoulders beneath this reproach and remained silent for some time. Then he said, 'You are very old, my father, to travel six leagues there and back through the forest in this season, with the cold rain that has been falling since yesterday. You would have died, my father.'

"'What does it matter?' said the old curé. 'As pastor of this parish, I am answerable before God for all my sheep. I would have come before the judgment seat with the soul of a great, repentant sinner. It would have been the most holy work of my ministry! But,' he added, seeing the Huron downcast, 'you acted for the best. Forgive me for what I said. On the contrary, you are a good Indian and I thank you for your kindness to the poor Canadian.'

"The following morning six charitable habitants went to fetch the body of Aubé," continued old Laurent Caron, "and he was buried without much ceremony. It was only fitting for a man who had set a bad example to the parish all his life.

"It was about a year after Aubé's death. He was practically forgotten. If he was mentioned now and then, the more generous gave him several hundred years in purgatory, and that was that. Then the L'Islet curé received a letter containing the following passage from a friend who was a priest in France. 'During October of last year, I was called upon, along with two other priests, to exorcise a possessed person who was creating a terrible uproar. He broke his bonds and spat out the most horrifying obscenities and blasphemies. After the customary forms of exorcism had been pronounced, he became calm, and we thought Satan had given up possession. To our great surprise, we were again called in three days later, and told that the possessed person was worse than ever. It was I who spoke, and the following dialogue took place between myself and the spirit of the shadows. "Why did you stop tormenting this Christian for three days?" "Because I went on a journey." "Where did you go?" "To the forests of Canada." "What had you to do in the forests of Canada?" "To be present at the death of Aubé." "How long did you remain with him?" "I stayed three days by his bed in order to carry away his soul when he died." "Did he die?" "Yes." "Did you carry off his soul?" "No." "Why?" "Because I found Mary there."'

"The curé read the letter during the sermon the following Sunday. Everyone in church wept, and the whole parish had a fine memorial service sung for poor Joseph Marie Aubé. He had earned it well and is in paradise these many years. But when you're talking on this side of the lake in calm weather, you can hear voices on the other shore as though he were still calling on good souls to help him. You see," added the old man, "he had wretched company."

We were all very young and imbued from the cradle with tales of ghostly visitants, particularly those among us with a country upbringing. Throughout old Caron's recital we felt a certain tingling of the spine, and each of us edged closer to his neighbour. This didn't stop us from going back to our little island and taxing the mountain echo to its utmost until we were nearly asleep on our feet, at which point we sought shelter in our guide's cabin.

Once back among the homesteads I offered to pay old Caron.

"Why, my young seigneur," said he, "didn't you get my little joke? I'm amply repaid by the agreeable time I've passed with all you gentlemen. I only ask in return that you always come to me when you feel like making up a party for hunting or fishing in our forests."

Laurent Caron continued to guide me to this same lake until death took him from us, carrying off one of the most respected habitants of the parish of Saint-Jean Port-Joli. His numerous descendants have inherited the virtues of their grandfather and great-grandfather.

If the reader has already forgiven me my lack of method in these memoirs, I can without apology speak of a subject outside the scope of this chapter. If he has not, it will be but one fault more in this work, after all. In a note to chapter thirteen of *Les Anciens Canadiens*, I related how a young Indian, an Abenaki, I believe, had killed two Englishmen some years after the Conquest, and was handed over by his tribe to the government. This was only done on the express condition that he not be hanged. He was convicted of the murder and executed by a firing squad. I then observed that the country must have been under military law at the time, for a regular criminal court could not have legally substituted lead for the rope in a case of murder. I was mistaken, however, in supposing the Indian had been condemned to the firing squad by a military tribunal. My friend Major Lafleur assures me that he had it from his uncle, who was an eyewitness to the execution, and it was indeed a legally constituted criminal court that substituted shooting for hanging. What led me into error was that I had tried several avenues of fruitless research on this subject in the criminal court archives with the help of my friend, the late Mr. Gilbert Ainslie, clerk of this court, and was obliged to conclude that this Indian had been sentenced by a military tribunal.

Those who wish to see where he was shot should follow the main street of the Saint-Jean ward as far as Sutherland Street. There, on turning their backs to this street, they will face a recess in the small cliff that runs along the entire south side of the Rue Saint-Jean. It was here that the execution took place. The curé of Quebec, Monsieur Lefebvre, and a Jesuit, Father Glapion, I believe, exhorted him in the face of death, assisted by Monsieur Launière, the government Indian interpreter. As the two priests spoke he reported their words to the Indian. At the ultimate moment, the eyes of the condemned man were covered with a bandage. In giving the criminal the final exhortations, 'the two priests held him as they spoke, one on each hand, for some time, then with slow steps drew away. They did not stop speaking until they were some distance off. Monsieur Launière, translating their words without interruption while also moving away from the condemned man, gave the agreed signal. The soldiers fired; the Indian, who was standing upright, jerked several feet forward and fell face down on the earth. He was stone dead: two bullets had pierced his heart.

The two chiefs of the Indian tribe, who had delivered him to the authorities of the day, were standing beside the officer in charge of the execution. A large number of savages from the Huron and other nations attended the execution of their brother redskin. When he fell down dead the men emitted their usual "Hua!" and the women hid their heads for a moment beneath their blankets. This constituted the dead man's funeral oration.

This Indian, who I believe was eighteen years old, died with the greatest courage—I might almost say unconcern. On his way to the place of execution one would never have thought him the victim, but rather the indifferent observer of all the lugubrious preparations. He maintained the same indifference when the chiefs of his tribe brought him to Quebec. I had it from a mulatto girl, our servant, that they stopped at the house of my grandfather in Saint-Jean Port-Joli, where they breakfasted. He was not bound, she said, and wandered about rummaging in all the rooms of the manor house in an inquisitive and unabashed manner.

During my childhood I often visited the spot where this Indian had been executed. It was there that we used to gather strawberries in the grasslands and thickets that covered the cape.

CHAPTER EIGHT

Love me in spite of my follies;
I'm a good enough fellow at heart.

Benjamin Constant

We Britons had at a time settled that it
was treasonable to doubt our having and
our being the best of everything.

Dickens

I look about me, listen with my one good ear, read the newspapers with my two good eyes, and it all strikes me as astonishing. How times have changed since I was young! Today each man states his opinion quite openly, discusses the most sensitive political issues without fear, criticizes England, and praises France, all with impunity. Anyone who had dared take such liberties in times gone by would have been considered "French and bad subject," that is to say, a Frenchman and a disloyal subject. We spoke in whispers then. Yet at present the newspapers are carrying on a controversy as to the advantages or disadvantages of annexing the Province of Canada to the Republic of the United States, and their publishers are "British and loyal subjects"! Or so, as least, we must believe, since our indulgent government appears to look kindly on these shenanigans. The authorities of another day would have taken things more seriously: publishers, editors, contributors, all would have danced at the end of a rope, and in order to make sure they were well and truly dead, their hearts would have been burned on a brazier and their heads severed from their shoulders. Ah, the good old days!

Nowadays one can publish the most atrocious calumny about men of the greatest respectability. The epithets of thief, assassin, or murderer skip merrily through the sententious prose of our newspapers. But since it is political differences that are at the root of these amiable libels, the slandered one is careful not to take his grievance before a court of law, knowing full well that, a hundred to one, half the jurors, being of a different political persuasion, will support the slanderers. Oh, what happy times we live in!

I mentioned that certain things used to be spoken of in whispers only. The English papers, and even some French news sheets published in England with the financial backing of the British government and French émigrés, as well as pamphlets from the same sources, used to spread the most outrageous slander about the great Napoleon. He was represented as a sort of vicious animal who struck his wife and her ladies-in-waiting, beat his aides-de-camp and tore their ears off— a bloodthirsty tiger who, mounted on his chariot, swept over the battlefield after victory, crushing wounded soldiers and the dead or dying of his army beneath his horses' hoofs. The most odious incest was among the least of his many crimes. At the precocious age of eleven, the young Bonaparte had reputedly violated a respectable woman. The very names of his accomplices and victims were given, thus nailing these innocent women to the pillory of public opinion. Nothing was spared: places, circumstances, every detail was related with revolting cynicism. We were meant to credit that, like that impudent dog Absolom of unfortunate memory, Napoleon was in the habit of committing his most shameful crimes in the face of all France.

Sensible people felt there was something highly improbable about these accusations, but we were obliged to feign belief for fear of passing for "French and bad subject." We weren't even allowed to admire the brilliant exploits of this prodigious man who had no rivals beyond Caesar and Alexander, if indeed he did not surpass them. Ah, the good old days!

The scene I'm about to describe may not amuse my reader, although my mother and I found it highly diverting.

My father was a true-blue Tory, an unswerving royalist. Although he grudgingly recognized Napoleon's powerful military genius, he

170

had no love for the emperor and considered him a usurper. He called me a republican and a democrat whenever I dared to differ. I was an enthusiast by nature, and sometimes praised my hero in his presence more than he liked. My friends, on the other hand, reproached me for being a borderline Tory. I suppose that I must have been steering a middle course, and, as the English proverb has it, was prepared to give the devil his due.

In the year 1805 we were on the eve of Austerlitz. The Old and New World expectantly awaited events that could change the face of Europe. Everywhere one saw engravings displayed of fierce Cossacks mounted on tiny horses and armed with lances capable of spitting ten Frenchmen at a single thrust. The Russian and Austrian armies, commanded by their two emperors, were to crush the audacious conqueror who had dared penetrate as far as Moravia.

My family was spending the winter in Quebec. I was sitting up with my mother waiting for my father, who was dining at the Château Saint-Louis. He returned at about ten o'clock, coming into the drawing room with his thick, jet-black brows drawn into a frown. Up and down the room he paced, not saying a word. Those with a bad conscience are always on tenterhooks. Had my father found out about one or several of my escapades? I wasn't exactly a saint, and I was scared to death of my father, who was as severe as the devil about my peccadilloes. The suspense was more painful than the reality, and in order to end it I faltered out a few words. His eyes softened immediately as he answered my question. I was saved for the moment, which to a nineteen-year-old is an eternity.

"Well now!" said my mother. "Did you have a good dinner? Was it very lively, in spite of the ladies' absence?"

My father mumbled some reply and continued walking up and down in silence. My mother signaled to me with a smile that meant the bomb was about to go off. What disagreeable incident had occurred? We hadn't long to wait.

"Would you believe, Catherine," snapped my father, stopping suddenly, "that tonight I passed for a disloyal subject? What *Messieurs les anglais* call a 'bad subject'?"

"How very provoking," laughed my mother, "especially since I've just prepared a memorandum for our good King George III, informing him that if he knew your boundless loyalty he would grant you a generous pension."

My father was in no mood for joking, however, and continued with increasing excitement. "Yes, I passed for a disloyal subject! I have more loyalty in my soul, even though the government doesn't pay me a penny, than two-thirds of those gentlemen who are so well rewarded for it!"

"Come, come, my dear," said my mother merrily, "tell us your tribulations so we can sympathize."

"You know," he said, "or rather you probably don't know, as women busy themselves with frills and furbelows instead of attending to politics, that the French are now face to face with the Austrian and Russian armies. We are anxiously awaiting the outcome of a great battle that could settle the fate of Europe. Nothing else was talked of this evening. All the Englishmen declared that Alexander and his terrible Cossacks would crush the usurper's army. I hazarded the opinion that there was every reason to fear a different result, that thus far Bonaparte's genius had been enough to vanquish the Austrian armies, which I considered the best troops in Europe, and that Emperor Alexander's host of undisciplined barbarians would be of little help to the Allies. The better-mannered among them protested loudly, and the others simply laughed in my face. It made my blood boil."

"I can just imagine your expression," observed my mother, making a valiant effort not to laugh. "But what on earth possessed you? You always make short work of anyone who says something flattering about the Emperor Napoleon. How could you stick your head into such a hornets' nest?"

"Hornets' nest indeed!" cried my father, clenching his teeth. "You know I don't mince words and I'm not a complete imbecile! It was maddening to see military men blinded by their preconceived notions and deceiving themselves. They behaved as if they were unaware that great battles are won by strategy, or that the Emperor Alexander and his Cossacks are no match for Napoleon. Why, with only thirty thousand men in the first Italian campaign, he successively defeated four Austrian armies twice the size. I was merely expressing a modest doubt, after all, in spite of my inner convictions. Even if events should prove me wrong, I didn't deserve to be considered a disloyal subject and. . . ."

My father left the sentence incomplete and continued to walk to and fro, muttering unintelligibly. I moved closer to my mother, who said to me in a low voice, "There's more to come."

My father stopped in front of us. "You're no doubt familiar with that agreeable way English gentlemen have of mocking someone with the utmost gravity? They don't have to expend much mental energy in the process, but the victim's blood boils just the same. Languid baiting is far more infuriating than spirited raillery. According to the English system, the baiter merely has to repeat the words of his victim and enlarge upon them as though he agreed. Colonel Pye, damn his eyes, speaks our language as well as any Parisian, and took it upon himself to answer me.

"'Monsieur is undoubtedly correct,' said he. 'The redoubtable sword of the formidable French will quickly get the better of those little Cossacks with their tiny lances. Are not the French invincible, as proven by their Egyptian campaign?'

"I had difficulty preserving the self-control of a well-bred man," added my father. "I replied that irony didn't constitute an argument and that I was as anxious as he to see the Allied cause triumph."

"'Who would dare dispute it?' sneered the imperturbable colonel, devil take him! 'It's only natural that Monsieur (he pronounced this *Monsoor*, which the English consider extremely witty), being of French origin although a British subject, would rejoice at the defeat of his former countrymen!' At this I flew into a rage. All eyes were upon me. Then the governor, taking pity on my torment, I suppose, gave the signal to rise."

My father began striding about the room. Purple with rage, he shouted, "May God forgive me! I'd laugh my head off if Napoleon gave them a thundering good licking!"

Seeing me smile he added, "And as for you, you young democrat, I suppose you'd be delighted."

"For this time only, my dear father, in order to see you avenged on that insolent colonel."

My mother rose and with an air of mystery closed the drawing room doors. "Sh-h-h!" she said. "If anyone should hear us, I'd have to burn my famous memorandum to His Majesty George III."

As my father remained unmoved by this bit of roguishness, my mother ordered up some light refreshment, saying that if he wouldn't take any supper he could at least have a glass of wine.

"No," he snapped, "for fear you might say afterward that it was to help me swallow the pill stuck in my throat." And so saying, he bid us goodnight.

The bomb of Austerlitz had exploded and the fragments had fallen in our hemisphere, when my father came home wearing an expression less satisfied than his friend Pye might have supposed. "I knew it!" he cried. "Bonaparte has crushed the Allied armies!"

A German gentleman recounted to me an anecdote about this frightful battle. I have read it nowhere else. He had it from one of his cousins with whom he corresponded, who was an officer in the Prussian army. Here it is.

At the rout of the Allied armies, the French artillery was battering the unfortunate fugitives huddled on the banks of Lake Sokolnitz. Meanwhile, the cavalry was in hot pursuit of the vanquished, cutting them down mercilessly with sabres. An Austrian general who had been taken prisoner threw himself at Napoleon's feet, crying, "For God's sake, Sire, stop this carnage!"

It was a rather singular characteristic of the English in those days that, while boasting of having always conquered the French, they refused to recognize the courage of their enemies. "Cowardly" was the epithet usually applied to the name of Frenchman, and we were all thus defiled. It seems to me, as a man of common sense, that there was little glory in their doing battle with cowards and poltroons, let alone being beaten from time to time by men of such pusillanimity! No matter: we were nobly avenged, and by an Englishman, as it turned out.

It happened a short time before the War of 1812. Preparations to resist attack by our powerful neighbours were going forward, when some officer declared that it would be well-nigh useless to give arms to the Canadians, as they probably wouldn't have the courage to use them.

"Why not, sir?" demanded General Brock. "Have they not French blood in their veins? (And he might have added, 'As I have in mine.') Gentlemen, I have found myself face to face with Frenchmen on the field of battle several times, and I can testify to their bravery under all circumstances. Good blood always tells."

All the world knows of this man's brilliant abilities and of his grievous death at the head of his brave regiment, the 49th Infantry, while leading a charge against the American army at Queenston Heights, [B] where a monument to him has been erected. I shall therefore speak only of his social qualities. The officers and soldiers under his command adored him. He made a point of introducing his officers

"De Gaspé is a very foolish boy," said Colonel Isaac Brock of the 49th when stationed in Quebec. Watercolour of Sir Isaac Brock, hero of Queenston Heights, by an unknown artist. Public Archives Canada. C-11222

into the social milieux to which his rank gave him entrée. As he put it, "I answer for them as for myself." I can in all truthfulness assert that never did a body of gentlemen merit the praise accorded by its colonel more than did the 49th.

I was unlucky enough to offend him, although quite unintentionally, at a supper given at my Uncle Baby's house. He never held it against, me, however. In those days it was the fashion to sing at dessert. I had an immense repertoire of drinking songs. I don't know what came over me, but when my turn came I took it into my head to choose one with this refrain:

> Mon père était pot,
> Ma mère était *broc*
> Ma grand-mère était pinte.
>
> [My father was a pot
> My mother a pitcher (i.e., "Brock")
> My grandmother a quart jug.]

No sooner had this disastrous refrain escaped my lips than I turned red, like the turkey cock that I was. Not knowing how to retrieve the situation, I decided to continue, abridging the dreadful song as best I could. I was ready to sink beneath the ground, if only such a thing had been possible.

My friend, the Honourable Lieutenant Butler of the 49th, was at this supper. The next day he asked me, "What the devil prompted you to pick such a song? Do you realize that the colonel felt very uncomfortable?"

"That's nothing to what I felt," was my reply. "I'd rather have been a hundred miles away. I was in a terrible sweat. I'll go and apologize immediately."

"No, no," Butler countered. "He found it amusing in the end and said, 'De Gaspé is a very foolish boy.'"

This verdict appeared perfectly just to me, and I accepted it in all humility.

This scene, and another that I will describe, may be of some use to young and inexperienced men who are making their first appearance in the great world. It will put them on their guard, for one is not always dealing with true gentlemen inclined to be indulgent toward youth.

We were dancing a quadrille at an assembly ball. Neither the tune nor the steps appealed to me, and I said to my dancing partner, my cousin, "Damn the dance!"

Major Lloyd, a brave officer covered with wounds, came toward me and said, "Monsieur, one doesn't damn a dance chosen by a gentleman."

I replied that my outburst had been against the dance itself, not the gentleman who'd requested it and whom I didn't even know.

"In that case," said he, "withdraw your offensive words."

This is what a young man of twenty ought to have done without hesitating, but I, believing my honour to be in question, particularly as the ladies were looking on, refused outright.

"Very well, young man," said the major, "I will force you to retract."

He walked off.

I must admit that I felt somewhat uneasy after this. I reflected that my entry into the great world would be pretty dismal if I were to begin by quarreling with a man of Major Lloyd's age and respectability. I will confess, with my usual frankness, that each knock on the door next day seemed to signify the arrival of a hostile message from the terrible major. Fortunately, I was dealing with a true gentleman. That evening I received a note from Colonel Carleton inviting me to dine at his house the next day. Prior to his coming to Canada, his mother, Lady Dorchester, had asked him to call on the families she had known during her long sojourn in this colony. He himself would hardly remember them, having left Canada while still a child. The first families he called on were the Hales, the Smiths, the Sewells, the de Gaspés, the Babys, and the de Lanaudières.

Imagine my surprise, on entering Colonel Carleton's drawing room next day, to find the dreadful major!

"Allow me to introduce my young friend, Monsieur de Gaspé," said the colonel.

"Delighted to make his acquaintance," said the major, shaking me cordially by the hand.

Gaiety reigned during dinner, in spite of a certain constraint on my part. I was anxious to be alone with the major in order to apologize. Once we were out in the street I expressed my deep mortification at having offended him, even unintentionally, and explained that a fit of self-consciousness had prevented me from making my apologies earlier.

"Think no more about it, young sir," he replied, pressing my hand. "I probably would've done the same thing at your age."

He invited me to dinner at his mess the following day.

I have since learned that, knowing I was a friend of Colonel Carleton, he told him about our little quarrel, and the two of them arranged this reconciliation after the colonel had given a favourable account of me. I was by no means conceited or a hothead. I think I may even say that I was more than ordinarily polite in my social relations, particularly with my superiors. It had been an act of misplaced pride by an inexperienced young man.

My friend Mr. Hamond Gowan,[1] one of the oldest and most respected citizens of Quebec, reminded me yesterday of the anecdote that I am about to recount. I would not have mentioned it in these memoirs otherwise. Although the circumstances are a testimony of my youthful follies, they may be of some use to the young men of the present.

One day I met my college friend William Philips.[2] "Are you coming to the race tomorrow?" he asked. "What race?" I queried. "Where've you been?" "I've been to lunch, and I'm about to return to the treadmill," said I, nodding toward the office where I was studying law.

"Well," said William. "As you appear to have dropped from the skies, when usually you're the first to turn up at any of our contests, I herewith inform you that tomorrow, on the Plains, there'll be a race open to anyone with a good pair of legs. The reason for this marathon is the following. A young Cockney named Bowes, recently arrived from London, is giving himself airs that we English Canadians find highly displeasing. He's scornful of everything here, and keeps repeating that it's not like old England! To hear him talk, you'd think he did everything to perfection. He says he's a great hunter, a consummate fisherman, and a stupendous runner, and he undertakes to beat any young man of Quebec at this last sport. We accepted the challenge. Tomorrow is the great day, at six in the morning. The lists are open to all comers. The stake is one piastre per head, with the winner being obliged to give a breakfast for all the entrants at the O'Hara Hotel. I'll count on your being there. You were the best runner in the seminary, with the single exception of big Vincent, the Indian.

He was at least six years older than you, but you were always at his heels."

"But you've got Grant of Montreal here, who reputedly runs like a deer," I countered.

"Unluckily he left the day before yesterday. He couldn't stay longer. We're very keen to take this Cockney down a peg," added Philips.

"I know you all too well, my English-Canadian friends," was my reply. "I'm convinced you'll choose the lesser of two evils, preferring to be beaten by an upstart of your own race than by a Canadian of French origin."

William laughed. "In that case you can just imagine our triumph when we tell him that we didn't make too much of an effort, knowing very well that a French Canadian was enough for him."

"Pretty sharp, aren't you? But just to even the score, I'll say I'm a full-blooded Indian whom you hired for the occasion because you knew you couldn't run against the Cockney yourselves."

"He won't believe it when he sees your delicate white skin."

"Well, I'll tell him I'm a member of the albino Indian tribe. He's never heard of such a thing, so he'll believe it."

After exchanging this sort of banter for a while, I promised to be on time for the race.

Next morning eighteen of us presented ourselves. The course was a mile, and the Cockney and I soon took the lead. The others, convinced they couldn't win, dropped out of the race. It was almost as if, in the light of Philips' prediction, they'd agreed beforehand to let the Frenchman run alone against the English thoroughbred. To make a long story short, his boast of being a great runner was without foundation. I won a fairly easy victory, to the thunderous applause of all my friends, both English and French-Canadian.

A Cockney rarely admits defeat. During breakfast my antagonist said to me solemnly, "I could've won that race easily."

"Why didn't you then?" I replied.

"Because you have a way of running that is so . . . so ridiculous that I was more inclined to laugh than to get ahead."

"Thank you, Monsieur. But that's my way, you see, and so far I've found it works very well."

My antagonist's jibe didn't have quite the effect he intended, for the young men laughed outright in his face.

My little triumph nearly cost me very dear about six weeks later. Let a young man get a swelled head, and if he isn't already a perfect idiot he'll soon become one.

I received an invitation from the members of a military club to take part in a game of cricket the Plains of Abraham. I replied that this game was unknown to us French Canadians.[3C] "Never mind," said my friend Captain Day. "If you don't play, you can always hold your own at a good dinner to be held on the spot after the game."

Once we were at the playing field, the two best players took turns choosing their team. One of them picked me to make up the full number. During dinner, and especially at dessert, the talk was entirely given over to this closely played game of cricket, the winners declaring that my fast running had done much to clinch the match. I would never have suspected it. However, this was all I needed to turn my head, already in an exalted state from the Madeira that flowed like water, as was the custom in those days. As a result, I made the most idiotic, thoroughly senseless bet that ever a young man did. I wagered ten guineas to one that I could run the mile and beat any officer garrisoned in Quebec. Every single man took me up on this without hesitation, but I still had enough gumption left to limit it to four. Captain Skynner immediately offered to uphold the army's honour.

It was after dark when we returned to Quebec, some on foot, others in vehicles. At the Saint-Louis Gate a balking horse refused to go through and had to be unharnessed. A bright idea entered my head. Why not make a triumphal entry into the city pulling the calèche ourselves, with the best cricketers inside? The vehicle was full in an instant, three of the passengers even standing upright on the back of the calèche, like footmen.[4D] As a just reward for my folly, the honour of acting as cart horse fell to me, while the others helped by pulling the shafts on the outside, with three more pushing the calèche from behind. We swept along the Rue Saint-Louis like an avalanche, shouting "Hurrah!" as we went and bringing people to their windows, although the night was so dark that no one could recognize us.

So far so good: the ground was flat and I ran no risk. This wasn't the case once we came into the Place d'Armes, now the Parade. In vain did I shout, "Stop! Stop!" My friends only pulled and pushed all the harder, and we rushed down the slope at lightning speed. I calculated my chances of survival. There were three choices for my prospective demise. Either I could smash my head on the houses

180

The site of "Gaspé's furrow," Quebec's Place d'Armes circa 1818, showing the Anglican (left) and Catholic (centre) cathedrals. On the right is the Union Hotel, according to Joseph Bouchette's contemporary map of Quebec. Anon. watercolour. National Gallery of Canada, photo: Hans Blohm. 16683

opposite and decide once and for all the burning question of whether that head contained a brain. Or I could let go of both shafts and have my back broken by the chassis. Then again, I could throw myself on the ground and possibly be crushed by one of the wheels. Happily, the survival instinct came to my aid in a flash, for the scene I have just described lasted barely half a minute. With a tremendous effort, which made the men who were helping to pull the carriage lose their grip, I hurled myself on the ground without letting go of the shafts, this being my only chance of survival. The sudden jerk dislodged some of the calèche's occupants, and two of them fell right on top of me. The extra load was no help, nor did it stop me from plowing the ground with my poor body for a distance of seventeen feet of hard earth mixed with rubble, stones, and pebbles, as proven a week after the incident by an inspection of the site, dubbed "Gaspé's furrow"

181

by certain wags. Jacket, shirt, and trousers were all torn to shreds, along with a generous portion of flesh from my chin to my kneecaps. I had been skinned like an eel dressed for the grill. A borrowed dressing gown made it possible for me to make a decent entrance at the supper that terminated this field day, held at the O'Hara Hotel.[5]

A crestfallen youth was Master Philippe Aubert de Gaspé next morning. His skull felt as though a bell-clapper were suspended from the top of its now vacant interior, beating furiously on his shriveled brain. A burning thirst racked him, and he tried to move his tongue to moisten his mouth—but, O horror! like his brain, the tongue seemed to have abandoned its post. He raised his hand to make sure, then snatched it back. His tongue was so dry that he was afraid it might snap like tinder between his fingers. He saw a jug of fresh water on a table near his bed and tried to sit up, whereupon a cry of agony escaped him, and his head fell back upon the pillow.

Having spoken of this worthy personage in the third person, in view of the respect in which I hold him, I must now acquaint the reader with the following dialogue:

Conscience: You were drunk last night, Philippe my son?

Myself: I deny your basic premise. Overexcited, yes. Drunk, no. A young man of twenty-one who was drunk could never have run the distance from the Saint-Louis Gate to the Rue Sainte-Anne at such a brisk pace, harnessed to a vehicle containing six or seven people: nor could he have executed the tour de force that saved his life.

Conscience: We won't quibble over trifles, my boy. But at least you can't deny that you're a thoroughgoing fool?

Myself (very humbly): Agreed, Madame. The sad condition to which I'm reduced offers abundant proof. It'll take me at least a month to grow a new skin and resume my place among the human race. Unfortunately I lack the enviable capacity of that vile reptile that sheds its old covering only to find itself immediately provided with another skin, far more supple.

Conscience: A mere detail, my boy. Let's talk of more serious things.

Myself: You make very light of the matter, Madame. It's clear you don't feel the pain I'm suffering. To begin with. . . .

Conscience: Stuff and nonsense! Let's get down to business. You made an even sillier bet than the one proposed by that Cockney you jeered at. You've thrown down the gauntlet to the whole Quebec garrison. If you lose you'll have to appeal to your father and confess all your misdeeds, and he'll fly into a terrible rage. He makes you a generous allowance—more than he ought. It should cover the expenses of a young man your age, and yet you're always down to the last penny because of your prodigal ways.

Myself: It's a debt of honour, and he'll lose no time in paying it.

Conscience: Yes. He's too honourable to do otherwise. But he'll be even more furious at the thought of paying for your follies simply to let others laugh at your expense. He has a high opinion of his dear son Philippe.

Myself: To mollify him, I'll tell him to deduct forty guineas from my allowance.

Conscience: Your heart is in the right place, my boy. I forgive you: may your dear father do likewise!

At this juncture, my friend Pierre de Sales Laterrière,[E] a medical student, interrupted this interesting dialogue. I gave him a faithful account of my adventure, but he only laughed and said, "Not bad for a start. I couldn't have done better myself." My only reply to this ill-timed remark was a long shudder.

"Now then, m'lad, seeing as how you aren't in your usual good humour this morning, let's have a look at the damage. No fractures, at any rate. Your bones are in their normal state."

"Very consoling," I sighed heavily. "A multiple fracture would be all I'd need."

"Of course, you've been skinned alive. But a few rolls of sticking plaster, judiciously applied, plus a little help to nature in the form of a diaphoretic will have you right in no time."

"That's just fine!" I retorted. "As far as my injuries go, I'm being let off easily, am I? A few rolls of sticking plaster! Nothing at all, of course!"

"Not so fast," resumed my friend. "One of your knees is very swollen. I fear a tubercular inflamation. Very dangerous. You'll be lame for life at the very least, if indeed we're not forced to amputate. What a pity: you make such good use of the legs God gave you."

Thereupon he embarked on a long speech, no doubt very scientific, explaining my symptoms and the successive stages of this cruel malady, adding that it could bring on anchylosis.

"What the devil! Speak like a Christian or get out of here with your barbarous names, and leave me in peace!"

Laterrière laughed and said he was only trying to scare me a little.

"Now, my dear Aesculapius," said I, "when can I go out?"

"In a week, I hope."

"But I've made up my mind to go out tomorrow."

"I forbid it in the name of the Faculty," declared my friend, who was well up on his Molière. "I forbid it on pain of being plagued with all the ailments we keep in reserve for recalcitrant and fractious patients."

"Go to hell, you pitiless joker!" I shouted. "I don't give a damn for you or the whole medical faculty. I'm going out the day after tomorrow."

"You'll die of bradypepsia, then!" countered Laterrière, keeping up the joke.

"You damned executioner! Can't you see I'm in no mood for your humbug. Keep your facetious remarks to cheer the parents of the people you've already killed off. I absolutely must talk to the men with whom I made that insane bet. I hope they'll consider it cancelled under the circumstances."

"I'm more experienced than you in these matters," said my friend, becoming serious. "Believe me, it would be better not to speak to them; or if you insist, make light of it, so as to let them think you don't care about the outcome."

I went out on the third day anyway, as planned, and told Captain Kerr, one of Governor Craig's aides-de-camp who had accepted my wager, about my sad state of health, adding that it would be impossible to race in five days, as I was limping painfully.

"My dear fellow," he replied, "when a person makes a ten to one bet, one must suppose he is sure of winning. One only accepts the wager in the hope that he'll have an accident such as spraining his ankle in the race, or better still, skinning himself alive like you!"

"Pardon my ignorance," I answered, blushing to the eyeballs. "In a similar situation. I would have suggested cancelling a silly bet made under the sole influence of your excellent Madeira. However, let's say no more. I'll just have to pay my idiotic bet, as there's not much chance I'll have the strength to run next Tuesday."

"*Et tu videris*," said the gentleman, saluting me with the utmost civility.

That *et tu videris* stung me as though he had applied a hot iron to my flayed skin. Gritting my teeth, I retorted, "Oh, I quite understand.

184

That's my affair. It's also my business not to let myself be plucked like a sparrow. I'll give you a run for your money if it kills me."

The great day arrived. I climbed awkwardly down from my carriage onto the racecourse, where my adversary was waiting in company with a fair number of curiosity seekers. My whole body ached, and I was running a low fever. Without consulting me, three of my close friends, Lieutenants LeBreton, Angouville, and Captain Day, told my opponents that in all justice the race should be put off to another day. But they refused, alleging the same reasons as my acquaintance of the *et tu videris*.

Suddenly an extraordinary agitation shot through my whole system. I had only one need: to avenge myself for what, in my ignorance of the rules of the turf, I believed to be an injustice.

No doubt my lucky star influenced their choice of a champion. Skynner had the wind of an Indian, but not much speed. After half a mile, surprised that he was not running faster, I couldn't help saying, "If we keep going like this we won't be through until sundown."

"Go ahead then, if you're in such a hurry," he said.

I thought he was joking, but just to make sure I replied, "In that case, goodbye!" and off I went as fast as I could, finishing in the same style. Skynner had neither increased nor decreased his speed. He was far from rivaling my Cockney in a similar distance. After his defeat he suggested running a course of six miles against me in a week or two. I thanked him, but remarked that some misfortune might overtake me in the meantime, and I would have to race just the same or pay up.

"That needn't be an objection," returned the captain. "We could make it a condition that if you catch typhus or break your neck going down to the Lower Town harnessed to a calèche containing six people, not counting the two or three pushing from behind, the bet will be canceled."

"Thank you, Captain, you're too kind," I laughed, "but I'm unable to take advantage of the offer."

Skynner had previously won a six mile race and was an indefatigable runner. Had my opponents chosen a young artillery officer named Collins, Dr. Holmes' son-in-law, whose agility I had remarked on the day of the cricket match, I would probably have had to suffer the consequences of my mad wager.

185

On the following morning, nine days after my escapade, I returned to work in the office of the Honourable Jonathan Sewell,[1] at that time attorney-general. Here my two fellow students, Green and Cartwright, told me my employer had learned all and was waiting to give me a good dressing down. The bell rang. I entered my employer's office with a contrite and shamefaced air. He looked at me and said:

"I thought you had run away from us?"

This was an adroit allusion to my escapade and subsequent absence from the office, as the English expression "run away" is applied to horses that get the bit between their teeth.

Mr. Sewell was not only very indulgent toward his clerks, but treated them as he would his own children. Apart from frequent invitations to his table when he gave large dinner parties, we were continually asked to evening parties. In spite of the criticism to which his political views have exposed him, Mr. Sewell was nonetheless, in his social and private life, one of the most estimable men I have known. Leaving aside his charity to the poor and other sterling qualities, he possessed the courtesy of an Englishman born of an old family. Upon joining his office, I signed the usual articles of indenture and my father placed a roll of one hundred guineas on his table, the attorney-general's fee for five years' articling. Mr. Sewell signed a waiver for this sum at the bottom of the form, and said to my father, "To accept your money, sir, would be to deprive myself of the pleasure of taking into my office a young gentleman such as your son."

The expression of gratitude has never been a burden to me, and it is with pleasure that I take this opportunity, the only one afforded me, to do justice to the eminent qualities of my former employer.

The young James Cartwright, an Upper Canadian of whom I have already spoken, died three or four years after returning to his family. I have rarely known a more amiable young man. We became fast friends immediately, and remained so throughout his three years in Quebec. Some time after his departure, a lively correspondence developed, which, to my great surprise, suddenly ceased. Receiving no reply to my last two letters, I knew not how to explain a silence that distressed me. I was standing near the Quebec Cathedral one day when I saw an English merchant, whom I knew only by sight, coming toward me. He was with a young stranger who, after exchanging a few words with his companion, approached me, held out his hand, and said with great feeling, "Poor Cartwright is dead!" Having thus

186

spoken, he went on his way. These brief words, uttered with such profound melancholy by a stranger who immediately withdrew, made so unhappy an impression on me that I went into the deserted church to hide my sorrow.

Dear Cartwright had not forgotten me. He had often talked of me to his friends in Upper Canada, and must have said, "If ever you go to Quebec, I'll give you a letter of introduction to Gaspé, my most sincere friend. He'll be glad to honour it." The young stranger, whose appearance had been so sudden and brief, would no doubt have profited by the introduction had Cartwright been alive. But the link that would have brought us together was now broken; I was henceforth a stranger on whom, with typical British reserve, he was afraid of imposing without sufficient introduction. I tried to get in touch with him the next day, but he had set sail that evening for England. It seems to me his name was Baldwin.

I was in Kamouraska three or four years after the death of this fine young man, when my friend John Ross[6G] told me that Councillor Cartwright[H] of Upper Canada, knowing that I was in the region, wanted very much to meet me. I hastened to pay him a visit. He was a tall, handsome old man, whose every feature recalled his son, especially that mild and candid expression that I have so rarely seen imprinted on the face of even a young man. As soon as Ross mentioned my name, he rose from his chair, held out two hands trembling with emotion, and said as he held mine firmly, "Poor James loved you well." He talked to me of his loss for a long time, but with the greatest resignation to the decrees of providence, repeating often, "I have lost a good son!" He added, "Your last two letters have been sealed in an envelope with those that you wrote my son while he lived. It would have been indelicate to violate the secrets of two young people who were close friends."

What I am about to recount must have taken place during the summer of 1807. Insignificant as this little adventure may appear, it will perhaps cause some wide-eyed stares among the younger generation who are familiar with the Quebec of today.

About ten in the evening we were coming back from a charming picnic at Ancienne Lorette. The other carriages had already passed within the walls of our good city when we arrived at the Saint-Jean Gate. Too late! The gate was irrevocably closed. I had a lady in my gig, and one of my friends was behind me with two ladies in his calèche. Knowing that one of the city gates was always left open at night, we hastily turned our horses' heads toward the Palace Gate, hoping to have better luck; but our welcome there was equally ungracious.

"Let's try the Hope Gate," we said, somewhat uneasy about our precious cargo.

We came out into the Rue Saint-Charles, but at the old McCallum brewery (the ruins of which are still visible) another obstacle lay in our way.

"Hah!" says the reader. "We can easily guess what it was. A rockfall from the cape had probably blocked the street. In that case you could simply have taken Rue Saint-Paul to the Hope Gate or to the Lower Town Gate."

There was one small difficulty, however: the Rue Saint-Paul didn't exist in those days. The beach on which the quays have since been constructed, and over which this street now runs, was at the moment under twelve feet of water.

"But," you say, "do you mean that communication between the Saint-Roch ward and the Lower Town was cut off at high tide?"

It was so for vehicles, certainly. The carters used to wait, swearing like pagans, until it pleased Dame Tide to grant them passage. Pedestrians had an alternative, thanks to the accommodating nature of our good Canadians. Their houses were built on the edge of a quay at the foot of the cape, with communicating galleries all the way along that offered those on foot a means of getting through.

As the most pressing need was to deliver our ladies to their homes, I went along the galleries to get news of the Hope Gate. It was shut tight. Much dismayed, we proposed to our amiable young ladies that, while one of us remained to guard the carriages, the other would accompany them home, going through the gate in the Lower Town, which would surely be open. All we had to do was pass along the galleries, go down La Côte aux Chiens or the Rue Dambourgès running into the Rue Saut-au-Matelot. Shrill cries greeted this suggestion: it was very dark; they might have a disagreeable encounter with a drunken sailor; a frigate was in port and if they met the press gang they would die of terror.

We assured them that the officers of the British navy were too gallant to *press* the fair sex.

The ladies replied that they were monsters who respected nothing and were accustomed to slaughter.

We laughed heartily at their fears but were obliged to yield, waiting two mortal hours before being delivered. Our subsequent welcome by the anxious papas and mamas of our young ladies was anything but pleasant, and despite our innocence we were roundly told off.

I was recounting this scene recently to Major Lafleur, one of our older inhabitants, adding that today I would never be able to recognize the spot that I wished to describe exactly.

"I'm just the person to help you remember," said he. "I've gone back and forth in that part of town since childhood."

The next morning found us on the spot.

"Here is the portion of the Rue Saint-Charles and of the Canoterie landing that the water covered at high tide," he told me.

"There, at the foot of the cape, stood the houses with galleries that enabled pedestrians to pass over. Ten feet to the north, where that grocery now stands, I saw a ship unloading a cargo of bottles fifty years ago."

As he spoke, light glimmered. I was carried back to the happy days of my youth, and everything passed before my eyes like the shadows from a magic lantern.

"All the Canadians knew each other in those days," resumed the major, "and the passers-by used to sit down quite familiarly at the windows of the people who owned the galleries. They'd chat with the inmates, making themselves completely at home."

And the two old men sighed at this recollection of an earlier, kindlier age.

In view of the scene decribed between myself and Doctor Laterrière, I can think of no better way to end this chapter than by telling the reader about this friend of my childhood.

DOCTOR PIERRE DE SALES LATERRIERE

It is with painful feelings that I write this description of one of my friends whose death, in breaking the ties that had united us since childhood, afflicted me most. Two children with the same tastes, penchants, and passions are almost always drawn to one another. Thus it was that, as soon as I met Pierre de Sales Laterrière, we became inseparable. Like me, he had been an intrepid little rascal since early childhood. His father, like mine, found it necessary to

189

send him as a boarder to the Quebec Seminary, in order to terminate a career that, while perhaps not without honour, held very little promise for a budding Aesculapius destined to inherit his papa's large practice.

If we didn't actually burn down the seminary, it is because providence was watching over this house, which has rendered such eminent service to the youth of Canada. Pipe smoking was strictly forbidden to pupils, which naturally made us want to do it all the more. There used to be an immense woodpile where the present handball court now stands. All we had to do was hollow out a small space in the very centre to make a safe hideaway. As we were very closely watched, the work took a long time; but we persevered, and a pipe committee was at last formed.

Rumour had it that an unhappy member of our legislature—a real Jean-Baptiste, as farmers were nicknamed—had found an ingenious way to circumvent the ban which that august body had issued against pipe smoking in all rooms occupied by the Canadian conclave. Lying flat on his stomach, Jean-Baptiste blew the puffs of tobacco smoke that would otherwise have choked him into the small door of the stove heating the parliament lobby.

O tempora! Had he lived in our day, he would have had plenty of elbowroom, and would have smoked sitting at his ease in a comfortable armchair, in an elegantly furnished apartment called the pipe committee room, where the best tobacco is smoked. Uncharitable souls say this takes place at the public's expense. They are scandalmongers.

You must have been a pretty poor lawmaker, my dear Jean-Baptiste, for you certainly didn't suffer from a surfeit of bright ideas! If Painchaud, Laterrière, Maguire, and Philippe de Gaspé, children though they were, had been members of parliament, they would have smoked under the speaker's chair if they'd felt like it, and no one would have been the wiser.

Let us draw a veil over our youthful follies once we had entered the great world. Suffice it to say that the feverish desire to have a good time shared by Laterrière and myself was not laid aside with the schoolboy's uniform. If two powder trails run side by side, it only needs one to burst into flame for the other to explode.

While I was doing law, my friend was applying himself seriously to the study of medicine in Quebec. He then went to England, where he studied successfully under Sir Ashley Cooper.[1] After three years, he returned to practise in Canada, where he gained distinction as one of our most capable surgeons.

He told me a story that may surprise those unfamiliar with my friend's manly, sincere, and open countenance.

"We were leaving London in a hurry," he said, "to bring help to a great many wounded men in the British army who had landed at Ramsgate. The most advanced students in surgery, of whom I was one, had been commandeered. So hasty was my departure that I set off before drawing on my banker, although I did so as soon as I arrived. At the end of three days I had but a single guinea left in my pocket; but as it is always better to be the object of envy rather than pity, I spent it with my friends that very evening. The next morning I went to the post office, but there found neither letter nor money. This put me in some embarrassment, but I quickly resolved to extricate myself by going to a banker, recounting my mortifying circumstances, and resolutely asking for ten louis in exchange for my note of hand.

"The person to whom I spoke shook his head, probably surprised at such boldness on the part of a stranger. At that moment a manager, who had overheard the whole story, looked at me narrowly and said to the teller, 'Give this gentleman the ten louis he wants.'

"I returned the following day with a draft on the selfsame bank from my London bankers. After making the withdrawal, less the ten louis received the day before, I asked the manager who had so graciously obliged me why he had trusted the word of an unknown.

"'My dear sir,' said he, 'in this world of ours everyone has his weakness. Mine is to consider myself an expert physiognomist, having studied Lavater. In applying the principles of my mentor, I decided that if your face weren't sufficient security for ten louis, I'd have to give up my favourite hobby.'

"'Then, sir, it is you are are now in my debt,' I replied jokingly.

"'Indeed I am,' he answered. "And to begin discharging it, I invite you to dine at home with my family today, an invitation that I trust you'll accept.'

"I accepted this first invitation, which was followed by several others, and the evenings spent with this amiable family and their friends kept me from numerous other follies."

The most light-hearted of men, Laterrière said to me in this regard, "You can't imagine how I was taken up by my young English friends, who had no idea of the high spirits of the French. As soon as I came into a gathering where I was expected, the young men would shout, 'Here he is! Now we'll have an enjoyable evening.'"

Laterrière told me of an amusing episode that occurred during one of his trips to England.

After we had stopped boarding at the seminary, Laterrière and I became friendly with a young Englishman called Walker, under the following circumstances. One day we were admiring a magnificent ship anchored alongside the Quai de la Reine, when a well-dressed young stranger with engaging manners invited us to visit his vessel, after which he had some excellent refreshments served. Young men of the same age get to know one another easily, and although Walker was not introduced to our families, we and our friends took him up nonetheless.

Some years later, Laterrière was visiting a town in England—I forget which—supplied with excellent letters of introduction to the gentlemen of the place. One Sunday afternoon he met our old acquaintance, Walker, taking the air in a popular spot with two friends. They met with mutual enthusiasm, and Walker introduced him to his companions. Laterrière was walking arm in arm with them, when, in the middle of a conversation, he was taken aside by two of the gentlemen who had responded to the letters of introduction from their London friends.

"My dear sir," said one of these gentlemen, "your society has given us much pleasure, but we shall have to stop seeing you if you continue to frequent the persons you have just left."

"The only one I know is Mr. Walker, a young gentleman whom we used to know in Canada," said Laterrière. "Is there something against his character?"

"Nothing," replied the other. "On the contrary, he's a perfectly respectable man. The thing is, my friends and I move in different circles from our barbers."

Laterrière then told them the circumstances of his acquaintance with Walker. He had been amply supplied with money, and had spent it generously among his friends in Quebec.

"I have it now," said one of the gentlemen. "I remember that Walker received a small legacy from one of his aunts. He left his father's barbershop, where he had wielded scissors and razor with great deftness. When he had spent it all he returned bravely to finish his apprenticeship, and I suppose he had played the gentleman in foreign lands."

That very evening, Laterrière told Walker of this revelation. The barber took it in good part, as does a man of sense who recognizes the social distinctions, and accepted with pleasure Laterrière's invitation to visit him privately from time to time at his hotel in the evening, when they could talk of his old acquaintances in Canada.

If Goldsmith's old Parson Primrose was taken in for one whole evening by a butler acting the gentleman, it's not surprising that two young men like ourselves took Walker for a fashionable London man about town.

At the start of the War of 1812, Doctor Laterrière was named medical officer of the Voltigeurs, the crack light infantry batallion of the incorporated militia commanded by Colonel de Salaberry. He served with distincton throughout the struggle with our neighbours, and then went to England, where he married a rich heiress, the daughter of Sir Fenwick Bulmer. Regarding his marriage, he recounted an incident typical of a London businessman.

"My dear father-in-law put forward two powerful reasons for refusing me his daughter's hand," said he. "First of all, I was a Catholic. Secondly, he considered me a dissipated and even prodigal young man (he was very much mistaken), more inclined to spend money than make it grow. But when a woman makes up her mind to something, even heaven must yield, and Sir F. Bulmer finally gave in grudgingly to our union. On the eve of the day set for the wedding, he said to me:

"'I should imagine, with your style of living, you haven't much money. Here's a draft for one hundred louis on my banker, but you owe me a shilling for the stamp.'

"I put his cheque in one pocket and, drawing out a shilling from the other, presented it to my future father-in-law, who coolly put it in his. It was his intention to give me a present of one hundred louis, not a penny more. As for me, I'd gladly make the same exchange every day of my life."

My friend subsequently returned to Canada with his young English bride, whose lively, sweet, and amiable nature quickly made friends for her in the new society to which she was introduced. After a short stay in Quebec, she spent a year at Les Eboulements while her husband had one of his houses in the Lower Town put in order for the following year.

Madame Laterrière, after returning from this temporary exile, amused us greatly by recounting how frightened she was of the Laurentian habitants.

"I'd read a great many books about the North American aborigines, and it was with some misgiving that I set foot on Canadian soil. My fears were quickly allayed at the sight of your city folk; but not so once I arrived in your mountains. Apart from the fact that the primitive costume of the Eboulois differed from any I'd seen, even in Quebec, these mountain people were naturally very brown. So convinced was I of being surrounded by savages that for a long time I didn't dare venture far from the manor house alone. I thought they were cannibals, and supposed that if they hadn't already eaten me it was because they found me too skinny to be worth cooking. And yet our Eboulois are good, stout-hearted people whom I later came to appreciate."

After living in Quebec for several years, Monsieur and Madame Laterrière returned to London, where they were called by the advancing years of Sir Fenwick Bulmer. He died two years later, leaving a handsome fortune to his daughter. My good friend Madame Laterrière never returned to Canada, and still lives in England,[7] but the friend of my childhood, youth, and middle age has lain for thirty years beneath the soil of Canada, where he had always said he would come back to die.

About two years before his death, he paid me a visit at Saint-Jean Port-Joli, and this was the last time I pressed the hand of one of the men who loved me most.

We went fishing together at my beautiful Trois-Saumons lake. Laterrière climbed the three mountains that we had to scale with as much vigour as I, and we sat down to rest on the peak of the third. After admiring the superb panorama that unrolled before our eyes, including the parish of Les Eboulements where he was to sleep his last sleep, he took a lancet from his pocket and said to me:

"Here, my dear Gaspé, look at this instrument. You know, I'd be willing to start life at twenty-five again, with no other worldly goods than the clothes I stand up in and my lancet in hand."

"Leave that kind of talk for others!" I said. "You're only forty. You have a charming family. You've always liked money and you're rolling in it, with a fortune of at least one hundred thousand louis.

Yet you want me to believe that you'd give it all up for a few more years of life? Come now, you're not serious!"

"What good are riches to me, when I have one foot in the grave!" he retorted.

"You must be joking," I answered. "You have the vigour of a mature man. You climbed those mountains with as light a stride as I and your colour is as good as it was at twenty. Everything about you bespeaks unusual muscular strength, and you talk of dying! You must be teasing!"

"Death is too serious a subject to speak about lightly," he answered. "I have diabetes, and this cruel malady will soon put an end to my life."

He explained the symptoms of this disease, about which I then knew nothing. I told him that the strength of his constitution would triumph, and that doctors were even more likely to be alarmed than their patients. I continued to joke about the supposed cowardice of surgeons who cut and snip human flesh without blinking an eye, and cry loudly at the least little hurt of their own.

My friend resumed his usual gay spirits, which lasted throughout his visit.

Some eighteen months after this, a member of my family, arriving from Quebec, said to me:

"I saw your friend Laterrière. He's come back to Canada where he plans to spend the winter. I was struck, as was everyone, by the change in him. I shouldn't be surprised if he's dead within six months.

"What! Already!" I cried. "He's come back already to fulfil his vow to die on his native soil! Impossible! There was too much vitality in his ardent soul! In his iron muscles!"

Five months later, a Quebec newspaper announced the death of my friend. I dropped the sheet and locked myself in a room from where I could see the parish of Les Eboulements. Over there, I reflected painfully, lay the lifeless body of the man whose gaiety had brought such animation to his wide circle of friends, whose face would break into a smile of pleasure each time we met, like an affectionate friend after a long absence. "O nothingness of life!" I burst out. "If I could cross this icebound river to kneel before the tomb of my friend, I would meet there but the cold welcome of the grave!"

Sleep in peace, O my friend, upon the right bank of the majestic Saint Lawrence! He whom you so loved will soon find his rest on the other side of this same river. The storms that stir its waves will not trouble your rest, any more than the far more terrible tempests of human life. These your friend must face until the day when he, too, will find peace and tranquillity in the silence of a grave looking toward your tomb![8]

CHAPTER NINE

I feel somewhat ill at ease in commmencing this chapter, for, like myself, three of my contemporaries who were pupils at the Quebec Seminary still bask in the sweet light of day. It is sixty-seven years since we began our studies together. Will the Honourable Louis-Joseph Papineau and Doctor Joseph Painchaud read these pages with pleasure? This is what concerns me. As for the third and most exalted, his Grace Monseigneur Flavien Turgeon, Archbishop of Quebec, the recollection of these scenes from childhood will not lighten his infirmities, for he is now insensible to anything but pain.

THE HONOURABLE LOUIS-JOSEPH PAPINEAU

The political life of this great man is carved in indelible letters by the chisel of history. His struggle to keep the constitution granted by Great Britain intact, in the face of longstanding efforts by the Canadian oligarchy to strip it away, piece by piece, is inscribed in letters of fire on the hearts of his countrymen. I would not presume to attempt a subject to which I could not do justice, despite my admiration for this powerful orator.

Young Papineau's renown preceded his entry into the Quebec Seminary. [A] Even then, all things foretold a brilliant career for this precocious child who loved to read, and whose mind was already more cultivated than that of most graduating students.

Papineau rarely played with children his own age. He used to read during part of the recreation period, play checkers or chess, or discuss literature with either the masters or students in the classes ahead of him. It was generally agreed that he would always have led his class if he hadn't preferred reading to studying Latin.

As he had special permission to read without asking leave of the class teacher, even during study hour, he used to hurry through his homework in order to indulge in his favorite pastime. This dispensation may have been in recognition of signal services rendered the Quebec Seminary by his father, or perhaps it was because his superiors believed, and rightly so, that it wouldn't prevent him from being an outstanding student.

From time to time the masters would take boarders from the Little Seminary[B] to sessions of the provincial parliament. As children love to ape everything they see, it was decided that we too would have our house of assembly. We began with elections. What intrigues! What corruption, even, to get our candidate elected!

The Conservative party, fearing its candidate's failure, proposed that the theology students in the Grand Seminary should vote. The opposition, led by Papineau, fought might and main against the introduction of this clause to our charter. Long debates and heated discussion ensued, but the Tories triumphed.

On the great day of the election, the two candidates made the usual speeches, promising, as is done today, more butter than bread to the credulous simpletons, of which I was probably one. A second dawning of the Golden Age awaited the scholars! No more lines to write out, no more canings, but jam with every meal. Nothing was easier: all we had to do was present the superior with a demand backed by our august parliament.

Papineau, then about thirteen or fourteen, mounted the hustings and demolished our hapless candidate in a speech lasting almost half an hour. Often since have I heard him thunder in our provincial assembly against abuse, corruption, and oligarchy, but I can certify that never was he as eloquent as on that day. The priests of the seminary cried, "Just like his father! Exactly like his father! What a champion for the rights of Canadians when once he has studied the laws that govern us!" And indeed, Fathers Demers, Lionnais, Bedard, and Robert, who made this observation, were competent to judge.

There was a striking contrast between the two Papineau men. The father, Joseph Papineau,[C] a short, thickset man, appeared quite ordinary except for his immense head. His clothes were out of keeping with the rank he occupied in society. The son, on the contrary, cut a

Louis-Joseph Papineau as a young man, from an engraving by W. Holl, taken from "an Authentic Portrait under the superintendence of a gentleman personally acquainted with M. Papineau." Papineau and de Gaspé were schoolfellows. Public Archives Canada. C-20761

JOSEPH PAPINEAU.

"Never have I forgotten my first impression of the eloquence of Monsieur Joseph Papineau," writes de Gaspé of the father of the great Patriot party leader. Engr. "by the Burland Desbarats Co. of Montreal" in L.-O. David, *Biographies et portraits* (1876) handsome figure and was immaculately turned out, although no fop. His elegance of dress and manner was slightly affected in the eyes of those who, in daily contact with English society, had contracted a stiffer mode of behaviour.

In conversation and especially when speaking in public, the son would hesitate, if necessary, to find the most felicitous expression. The father, on the other hand, would not substitute a more polished word for the one already on his lips the moment he expressed a thought.

Never have I forgotten my first impression of the eloquence of Monsieur Joseph Papineau. As a youngster I was visiting our parliament when I saw a member, very plain in his manner, rise slowly. In his right hand he held a paper that he had probably just finished reading. He wore a thick pigtail that fell below his shoulders, although the style was out of fashion in the towns. This, taken together with his clothes, gave me the idea that he was one of those worthies sent by country ridings to represent them in the provincial assembly. He spoke for half an hour, and his words rolled forth as easily and abundantly as the calm waters of a great river, yet all the while he stood as immobile as the shores on either side. I found myself under an inexpressibly binding spell. At each moment I feared he might stop speaking, and yet the surprising thing is that I only half understood the speech. Absolute silence reigned in the house. I dared not breathe. Restless though I was at that age, I felt I could listen forever.

I didn't really understand the nature of my experience until some six or seven years later, when I read Book III of Pope's translation of the *Iliad*.

The aged King Priam is on the walls of Troy, and by his side Helen is listing the most famous leaders of the Greek army, whose numberless batallions cover the plain. She names Ulysses. Antenor then speaks, saying:

> Myself, O king! have seen that wondrous man:
> When, trusting Jove and hospitable laws,
> To Troy he came, to plead the Grecian cause.

I cannot resist the pleasure of quoting the English poet's magnificent lines, at the risk of following them with a very pale translation. Antenor, after deservedly praising the eloquence of Menelaus, continues thus:

201

But when Ulysses rose, in thought profound,
His modest eyes he fix'd upon the ground,
As one unskill'd or dumb, he seemed to stand,
Nor rais'd his head, nor stretch'd his sceptr'd hand.
But when he speaks, what elocution flows!
Soft as the fleeces of descending snows,
The copious accents fall, with easy art!
Wondering we hear, and fix'd in deep surprise:
Our ears refute the censure of our eyes.[1]

TRANSLATION BY THE AUTHOR

"Mais lorsque Ulysse, absorbé dans des méditations profondes, se lève de son siège, lorsqu'il abaisse avec modestie les yeux vers la terre sans les en détacher, et sans même étendre la main dans laquelle il tient le sceptre royal, on le croirait alors muet ou sans intelligence, mais dès qu'il parle, quels flots d'éloquence coulent de sa bouche! éloquence aussi douce que les flocons de neige qui descendent dans une vallon par un jour de calme. Ses paroles abondantes s'échappent avec un art si facile qu'on l'écoute avec surprise! et saisis [sic] d'un profond étonnement nos oreilles repoussent la censure de nos yeux."

The schooldays of a child and young man as poised, studious, and precociously reasonable as young Papineau do not give the biographer much material. It is the fun-loving, turbulent ones who offer a rich mine for exploitation.

Nonetheless, here is a little scene that afforded us much amusement, after which I take leave of my subject with regret.

Papineau, then in the second to last year, I believe, was playing chess with our director, Monsieur Lionnais, during the midday break on a fine summer's day. They were seated on the steep steps of the perron in the seminary's main courtyard.

An Indian—I don't know to what tribe he belonged—finding the gate open, approached the chess players and followed the movement of the pieces with absorbed interest until the game was over. He pursed his lips whenever he saw the rook move, emitted a "Ho!" at the queen's forays, and a "Hoa!" each time the knight made a leap.

At last the victor pronounced the fatal "Checkmate!" and Monsieur Lionnais asked the Indian whether he knew how to play chess.

"Not know how," grunted the Indian, tracing little circles on the palm of his left hand with the index finger of his right and adding, "Good! Good! Play like that!"

"Oh! You know how to play checkers," said the director. "Papineau, just for the novelty of the thing, go and fetch a set of checkers, and let's give this *canouah* a good trouncing."

At the sight of the checkerboard and men that Papineau was setting out while inviting the Indian to play, the latter gave a joyful shout. "Me play with little patliasse!"

The Indians often used this name for students of the Quebec Seminary, whom they looked upon as small priests.

Papineau, sure of victory, began to play quite negligently. The Indian took one piece in forfeit, captured three others, and exclaimed, "Not well played, little patliasse!" Papineau, piqued by the massacre of his men, and even more by the triumphal cries of his adversary, asked for a return match. He was again forced to give up, to the accompaniment of roars of laughter from the students and even the director, all of whom had taken a lively interest in the game.

"For heaven's sake, Monsieur Lionnais, take my place," said Papineau, "and for the honour of the seminary, teach this forest animal a good lesson."

The director didn't have to be asked twice to uphold pale-face honour. Having been a Recollet monk before being ordained, he had played checkers frequently in his monastery and had reason to pride himself on being an adept. He took the loser's seat and motioned to the Indian, who had risen, to sit down.

"Cannot play against big patliasse," stated the savage.

However, after some apparent hesitation, he finally resumed play. But I fear it must be told that our director fared as badly as Papineau, whom he was meant to avenge.

"I'm hungry," announced the Indian after two more games.

"I'd have thought you were replete, considering the large number of men you've devoured!" retorted Monsieur Lionnais. He turned to me and said, "Gaspé, be good enough to take this glutton to the kitchen and tell Joseph to stuff him with bread and meat until he doubles up with pain."

We laughed heartily at our director's scheme of revenge after the beating he had taken.

I have since learned that Indians are generally formidable opponents at checkers. Being naturally indolent, they often pass whole winter days lying in their cabins indulging in this white man's game.

JOSEPH PAINCHAUD

Doctor Painchaud began and ended his studies in the same class as myself. What he was as a child, he still is today: light-hearted and lovable, intelligent and witty, making a joke of everything, even the most serious. Occasionally he has been criticized for being slightly eccentric,[E] if he will pardon my saying so—although, old friends as we are after a comradely and unclouded intercourse of sixty-six years, we aren't likely to quarrel for so little. I wouldn't for the world have him take it in bad part, and indeed, knowing Doctor Painchaud's considerable athletic prowess, I would be sure to come off somewhat the worse for wear. However, I have nothing to fear. Although Painchaud, the eternal tease, dealt out satire left and right, he was the first to laugh at the shafts hurled at him by others. I never once saw him bad-tempered during all our schooldays, or after.

If we wore the cross of honour on the right side, Painchaud would wear it on the left; if we wore it on the left to imitate him, he'd pin it to the flap of his cap in winter or his hat in summer.[F] If we were caned on our right hands, he would hold out his left, although more sensitive, and if we wore our sashes high, his was down around his hips. Yet despite our hoots of derision, those who laughed were always on his side.

Painchaud rarely missed introducing some word or phrase to make us laugh, no matter how serious the assignment. The class teacher one day gave us an essay to do on Horace's *nemo suâ contentus.* Painchaud dealt with the subject in his own particular style, presenting a picture in which many of our classmates had the pleasure of recognizing themselves, although they dared not take offense. He requested those who were cross-eyed to look straight ahead, and those whose noses were overly long to exchange them for a more acceptable article. For one he desired fine weather when it rained, for another heat when it was cold, or snow to slide in when it was late in coming. Unlike the inimitable Berquin's[G] little Fleury, he wished for everyone the season or weather they weren't at present enjoying, and wound up with this comical sentence: "And even if God sent us the four seasons at once, we'd never be satisfied."

L'HONORABLE JUGE JOHN GAWLER THOMPSON

As young men, Judge John Gawler Thompson and de Gaspé were among "the bon vivants of this friendly city," notes the author in a description of a 1820 dinner, adding that "our Canadian-born English friends all spoke French as easily as ourselves." From P.-G. Roy, *Les Juges de la Province de Québec* (1933)

L'HONORABLE JUGE JOSEPH-RÉMI VALLIÈRES DE SAINT-RÉAL

Judge Joseph-Rémi Vallières de Saint-Réal, son of a blacksmith. De Gaspé admired his friend's sense of fun and compassionate heart as well as his formidable intellect. From P.-G. Roy, *Les Juges de la Province de Québec* (1933)

The teacher thought this was nonsense. Painchaud, winking at us, gravely argued that it had deep philosophical meaning, amid shrieks of laughter from the whole class. He had got what he wanted.

This didn't prevent Doctor Painchaud from doing brilliantly at his studies and becoming one of Quebec's distinguished citizens of the present day. His talent and assiduity as a physician have brought him a fine and independent fortune. Thus by personal worth has he repaired the injustice of fate, which caused him to be born of poor parents.

HONOURABLE CHIEF JUSTICE RÉMI VALLIÈRE DE ST. RÉAL

I think I am right in asserting that the subject of this biographical sketch was the most naturally talented man Canada has produced. Orphaned at the most tender age, his genius shone forth in spite of all obstacles. At first merely one of the children who attended catechism at the Quebec cathedral, he attracted notice as soon as the vicar who was preparing the youngsters for their first communion questioned him.

The vicar spoke to Monseigneur Plessis, then coadjutor and curé of Quebec. "This morning I saw an amazing youngster in the catechism class. I was surprised by his answers, and asked him questions far beyond the understanding of a child his age. He replied just as confidently as before."

Monseigneur Plessis was not one to let such a pearl be lost, and had the young Vallière brought to him. The child told him that he had been born in Quebec, but that his father had left this city for Upper Canada, I believe it was, where he had been brought up. His mother had married again after his father's death, and his uncle M——, a citizen of the Lower Town, had given him a home.[H] The eminent prelate asked the child the same sort of questions as the vicar, and was equally astonished. The child frequently answered by saying, "I read this in such and such an author."

"You like reading, then?" asked the prelate.

"I read everything that comes my way," was the reply.

"But you're quoting me English writers as well as French. What was your early schooling?"

"I went to a little school in Upper Canada, where I learned to read English."

"And French?"

"I learned it all by myself. It was easy for anyone whose mother tonque was French."

"What are you going to do now?"

"My uncle isn't rich and has a big family. He's going to get me a job as grocer's clerk if he can find me a place."

"Would you like to be educated?"

"Oh, yes, Monseigneur! That's my greatest ambition."

"I'll speak to your uncle this very day, and tomorrow I'll give you your first lessons in Latin."

Eighteen months later Vallière knew Latin thoroughly! Yes, Latin! Not only did he read classical authors with the greatest facility, he also spoke the language of Cicero with elegance and ease, as the following anecdote proves.

Vallière, endowed with the most noble heart that it has pleased God to create, never forgot the debt of gratitude that he owed his generous patron. Contrary to the majority of young men, who avoid, if they do no worse, the society of those who have opened to them the road to fame and fortune, he made it a point of honour to visit his benefactor often, and only the death of the distinguished prelate ended their friendship.

"You've come at just the right moment," Monseigneur Plessis told him one day. He was holding a volume of Horace. "I've turned this line every which way, and I can't believe that this is what the author means. It doesn't make sense."

Vallière read the passage and said that yes, it was nonsense. But after a minute's thought, he picked up a pencil, inserted a colon or a semicolon, and said, "Read it now, Monseigneur." He had changed the sentence entirely, and the author's meaning was perfectly clear. Monseigneur Plessis loved to tell this anecdote about his young protégé.

Vallière always had some Latin author in his pocket, and neither his many occupations nor his somewhat frivolous life—like ours— as a young man prevented him from reading a page or two every day.

But let us go back a few years.

Great was the consternation and excitement among the ever suspicious authorities of Quebec, who had just learned that one of Napoleon's generals was not only within the walls, but had had the temerity to recruit a regiment. The executive council met, and required the Catholic prelate's immediate presence. The council made it uncomfortably clear that it was surprised to find he knew nothing about this vital bit of information, and, in particular, that he hadn't informed the authorities. Thus challenged, the bishop replied that the whole thing seemed ridiculous. It was, of course, possible that a French general might be hidden in the city of Quebec, but he would never have the audacity to raise a regiment there. The attorney-general drew a paper from his pocket and passed it to the prelate. It was a captain's commission, made out with all the proper formalities. The captain belonged to a regiment commanded by a general bearing a French name.

"What do you say to that, Monseigneur?" demanded the attorney-general.

"I undertake to produce the general in question tomorrow at the opening of the council meeting," replied the bishop. "Until then it is useless to look further."

The council was gathered in its formidable entirety next morning when Monseigneur Plessis walked into the council chamber unattended. Anxious glances were exchanged, and the bishop was charged to keep his promise.

"I'm about to bring him in," said the bishop. "He's waiting for me at the door." He came back into the room a minute later, leading a child of eleven or twelve by the hand.

"Gentlemen, may I present General Vallière."

A few members of the council, sworn enemies of all French Canadians, thought some trickery was afoot and turned pale with anger, but sensible men who knew the bishop's probity of character burst out laughing. All was clear: Vallière was raising a children's regiment and had appointed himself general.

Interrogated about the document that had been so like the real thing, the child stated that he had chanced read an officer's commission two year's previously, and had remembered the form.

We must have been in the second to last year when Monseigneur Plessis, holding a notebook two inches thick and bristling with chronological tables, entered our classroom with his pupil. He handed the notebook to our teacher and asked him to test Vallière, turning the pages frequently. Vallière answered correctly and without hesitation for at least a quarter of an hour, yet he was no parrot, for each reply was obviously well thought out.

The following feat of his prodigious memory seems to me even more surprising. Vallière only attended the seminary to study philosophy. We were in the same class and boarding out. A friend one day remarked, "I met Vallière with a young foreigner, and they were both speaking some strange language."

I made a point of mentioning this to Vallière.

"It was a young Portuguese, newly arrived in Quebec, who'd been recommended to the firm of Lester and Morrough," he said. "He only speaks his mother tongue. As we're neighbours in the Lower Town and he seemed very bored, I lost no time in learning his language so as to be able to talk to him. Come to Plamondon's tonight. We're meeting there, and I'll introduce you to everybody."

We spent a very agreeable evening asking the young stranger a thousand questions about Portugal, its manners, and its customs. Vallière, as our interpreter, transmitted his answers without a moment's hesitation. According to Vallière, the Portuguese had only been in Quebec for twenty-two days, and subsequent information confirmed this.

Vallière, LeBlond, Plamondon, and myself were all admitted to the legal profession at about the same period and underwent our baptismal fire on the Kamouraska circuit. One of the clients who fell to Vallière's lot for his sins was a compulsive litigant, like Racine's Chicaneau. This man talked and dreamed of nothing else but his suit for five sols, and thought that every one else must be intensely interested in it. He importuned his unhappy lawyer from morning to night. It was July, and he would start pounding on the door at three o'clock in the morning. This attentive suitor's vehicle was parked in front of our hotel all day long, ready to carry the hapless practitioner on his errands while the client discussed his case. The tenacity of the plaintiff was such that if we were out to supper at Seigneur Taché's home, where we often stayed past midnight, the first thing Vallière saw on coming out was his client waiting for him in his calèche.

We were forever teasing Vallière about his wretched client.

"And to think I shan't even have the consolation of losing his case in revenge," he remarked one day.

"How so?" inquired Plamondon.

"Because it's a hopeless case and you're pleading against me," retorted Vallière.

"My dear fellow, lawyers bandy such banal pleasantries as that every day. It would've been more modest on your part, and more witty, to have said, 'The case is hopeless, but even so I shan't have the consolation of losing it because Judge B—— will decide it.'"

Vallière, in spite of his wit, rarely came off best in this sort of encounter. Here Plamondon was on his own ground, like Crébillon in hell,[1] and the only duelist he feared was Justin McCarthy, about whom I will have occasion to speak later.

Liquor flowed freely on the Kamouraska circuit. The parish inns were supplemented by tents set up near the court, where anyone could quench his thirst at will—the successful plaintiff to celebrate, and the loser to drown his sorrows.

The last day of court was over and I was returning with my three friends to our boarding house. As we passed a shed we saw a man sleeping face down on the ground. He wore a long couette or pigtail of formidable proportions, bound with eelskin.[1J] There was no mistaking this outmoded embellishment: it was Vallière's client. Our friend gave him a push to make sure he was really asleep. Satisfied on this point, he pulled out his pocket-knife, lopped off the pigtail close to the head, and placed the trophy in the man's hand. Then he fetched a long pole that was propped on a fence, and began to poke the man in the ribs. We all hid behind a door and waited for him to wake up. Vallière's vigorous jabs made the man turn on his side. He waved the object that his lawyer had placed in his hand, and, with his eyes still shut, shouted:

"Devil take them all!"

"Courage, my friend!" exclaimed Vallière. "You've twenty-four hours in which to curse your judges."

"And twenty-four years to curse your precious lawyer!" cried Plamondon.

The habitant opened his eyes and caught sight of the knout in his hand. "Damnation!" he burst out. "It was twenty-two inches long! How can I show myself in public? I'll have to wait until after dark to go home! How can I face my wife after such an insult?"

"I'm revenged," crowed Vallière. "I've lost your case and cut off your pigtail!"

With his friends Vallière displayed a boisterous gaiety. It seemed that his Maker had given this privileged individual everything. He had both the most brilliant mind and the most feeling heart. No unfortunate ever sought his help in vain.

O my friend! How many times have I seen you weep at the misfortunes of others! Cold-hearted men reproached you, as a judge, for often obeying the dictates of your kind heart and departing from the strict letter of the law in handing down sentences. The ermine[2] you wore was never sullied! It was as pure and as white when you came to face God's judgment, preceded by the prayers of widow and orphan, as on the day your sovereign queen decorated you to the acclaim of all your countrymen.

Like all men of high heart and hot blood, you were not exempt from the grand passions in your youth. Men of cold temperament may choose to remember it, but the angel of mercy, in recording your errors on the black page of your life's record, will wash them away with his tears! Would you, whose life was consecrated to the defense of humanity in distress, have lacked an advocate at the foot of the great tribunal?

LOUIS PLAMONDON

> Monsieur de Feletz could never hold his
> tongue once a cutting remark was on it.
>
> Sainte-Beuve

Monsieur Louis Plamondon,[k] distinguished lawyer and member of the Quebec bar, was the first of my contemporaries from the seminary to be carried off by death from his many friends. Rarely have I known a man of greater intellect and wit. Plamondon was a formidable opponent, and everyone feared his incisive and biting repartee. Only Justin McCarthy could stand up to him and get away with it. It must be admitted, I'm sorry to say, that the laugh was often on Plamondon's side because McCarthy's reprehensible behaviour constantly laid him open to his adversary's jibes.

Plamondon's precocious wit earned him a powerful patron. Monsieur Deschenaux, curé of Ancienne Lorette, one day called on Plamondon's father, who lived in Saint-Ambroise. He made much of little Louis, whom he singled out from the rest of the family for his brightness. The child responded to this affectionate treatment, and the curé took him for a ride in his carriage. Monsieur Deschenaux found the six-year-old an agreeable companion, and little Louis was so satisfied with his new acquaintance that he refused to get down from the carriage when they returned to his parents' home. His mother's admonitions and threats were of no avail: he fought like a young demon.

"Oho! So that's the way it is!" said Monsieur Deschenaux. "You don't want to part with me? Well then, stay, if your parents will consent."

Plamondon's father, burdened with a large family, was only too ready to accept this offer, and Plamondon was forthwith installed in the wealthy cleric's dwelling.

Monsieur Deschenaux, although a very rich man in his own right, nevertheless served the parish of Ancienne Lorette until he was extremely old. The tithes he received were distributed about the parish as alms.

"I don't want to stop receiving my parishioners' tithes," he used to say, "as it would be selfish to lay my successor open to unfavorable comparisons between my conduct and his."

During the War of 1812 a rich habitant, who had a payment to make Monsieur Deschenaux, drew from his purse an army-bill for a hundred piastres, bearing six percent interest and redeemable by the government after the war.

Meanwhile, the cook had taken a frying pan from the fire and placed it on the hearth. It contained a delicious fricassee that the curé's old dog was eagerly sniffing. The army-bill slipped from Jean-Baptist's hands right into the middle of this excellent dish, and the owner of the bill bent over and snatched his treasure out, plunging his hand into the fricassee at the risk of burning it to a crisp. But the dog was quicker still. Before the habitant had time to straighten up, the animal snapped up the bill dripping in rich and succulent sauce. Monsieur Deschenaux was in his bedroom when he heard a terrible· uproar coming from the kitchen. He rushed in to find our man armed with an axe and the cook brandishing a broomstick, like one of Macbeth's witches, with the dog barking furiously behind her. The curé was convinced a murder was about to take place in his presbytery.

"The brute!" cried the cook, her eyes alight with anger. "He wants to kill our dog because it swallowed his dirty bit of paper."

"Dirty bit yourself, you old trollop!" vociferated Jean-Baptiste. "A fine bill worth one hundred piastres, plus interest, that I'd kept safe in my strong-box like my most precious possession until your starving cur swallowed it up in his devil's maw."

"Well may you talk of starving dogs, you tight-fisted miser!" retorted the cook. "You feed yours so little that he has to lean against the stove to bark."

The long and short of it was that Jean-Baptiste didn't want to lose his bill, preferring to kill the dog and get the pieces from the gluttonous animal's stomach. Monsieur Deschenaux, on the other hand, was much attached to his old dependents, and he agreed, after laughing heartily at the adventure, to reimburse the hundred piastres with interest, as demanded.

It was Plamondon who recounted this comic scene for us, having witnessed it himself. Of course it lost nothing in the telling, coming from a clever man with such a flair for the humorous.

The Abbé Deschenaux raised the child he had adopted with as much affection as the tenderest of fathers, and the boy quickly acquired the style and manners of the best English and French society frequented by his patron.

LOUIS MOQUIN

> The honest man is an anomaly of his kind,
> as is the man of wit.
>
> Chamfort[1.]

Monsieur Louis Moquin,[M] a celebrated member of the Quebec bar, was almost always undemonstrative, morose, and taciturn as a child. Already he carried in his breast the seed of the cruel malady that brought him to an early grave. Yet he had the occasional day of good-humoured gaiety when he would be the most popular boarder in the seminary. We used to gather round him, and often he would keep us laughing during the whole recreation period. What amused us most were the songs, improvised in the quaint habitant style, with which he teased the young country boys. I feel I must give one of them here, for it reminds me of my happy young days. Moquin had been entertaining us for about half an hour when a farmer's son came on the scene. He was a new boy, all ears, his mouth agape.

"Your father," demanded Moquin, lengthening his jaw, "did he go to war in the time of the French?"

"No," said Leclerc, "but my late grandfather was at Carillon."

"Aha! Your late grandfather was at Carillon! Then he must have known General *Macalm* (Montcalm), and you must be familiar with the fine lament the soldiers sang when he died."

214

"No," said Leclerc, "but I'd like to hear it."

Moquin began to laugh and said, "So would I."

We all shouted, "The lament! The lament! General Macalm's lament!"

"Are you crazy?" said Moquin. "You know very well there's no such thing and that I just made it up."

But we only shouted all the louder, "The lament! The lament!"

"Well, if you absolutely insist, all right," said Moquin.

Even as a youth, Moquin had the visage of an old man, but to suit the role he pulled an especially long face and intoned in a cracked and quavering voice:

> 'Twas the late, great General Macalm, of course,
> Who, mounted upon his fine, high horse,
> Licked the poor English at Carillon,
> Canada's fort on the way to Baston. [N]

"That's all," he concluded.

"No! No! More! More!" yelled the schoolboys amid roars of laughter.

Looking about he spied a pupil whom we nicknamed "the black" (the poor fellow was as dark as a mulberry) and another whose soubriquet was "ram," probably because it rhymed with his name. This was enough for the bard, who went on thus:

> The battle being joined in the murk,
> His black and his ram went berserk:
> The ram missed the black
> And went on to attack
> The defenses, which fell with a jerk.

The black and the ram slunk away behind the crowd, and we kept on shouting, "More! More!" Five young Englishmen from Halifax, Richard Clery, —— Comyns, Andrew Bulger, Henry Bulger, and James Macguire shouted, "More!" along with the others.

"So! I thought you'd had your fill, *Messieurs les anglais*, but it seems you're rather demanding. In that case I'll go on:

> The English, besieged on each side,
> To the Iroquois injuns did ride,
> To urge them to arm
> Against our Macalm,
> Who'd dealt the Brits a broadside.

215

The young foreigners were about to retire as well, when Moquin called to them, "Wait, I'll try another verse." But the bell announced the end of recess and cut short his comic vein.

The five young Englishmen whom I named had as many friends as there were pupils at the Quebec Seminary. They were all about the same age as myself. Except for James Macguire, who died in the West Indies, the others may still be living, and I'm sure they would be ready to testify to our fair treatment.

Some twelve or fifteen years later I was dining at an English officers' mess. Across the table I noticed a veritable giant: six-foot-four, bony of frame, and strong of feature. The giant was looking slily at me and laughing to himself. I felt my colour rising but thought I must be mistaken and continued talking to my neighbour. When I looked again at this Goliath of Geth, I perceived the same mocking smile. I was extremely ill at ease but too well-bred to mar the distinctive harmony of an English mess, where guests are treated with the utmost consideration, not only by all the officers of their acquaintance, but generally by all the members. I was therefore about to look elsewhere, putting off until the morrow the explanation that I deemed necessary, when the giant spoke in a voice that shook the glasses on the table.

"De Gaspé, a glass of wine for the sake of old acquaintance."

"With pleasure, sir," said I. "And if, on my part, it isn't in memory of our former friendship, I'm nonetheless happy to make your acquaintance today."

"What!" said he. "Have you forgotten your old friends the Bulgers from the Quebec Seminary?"

"My friend Henry Bulger!" I cried.

"No," he retorted, "your friend Andrew Bulger."⁰

Now of the two Bulgers, Andrew, a child of unusual beauty, had been very small for his age when he left the seminary at thirteen. Henry, the elder, was much taller, with features already formed that were far from Adonis-like.

"I understand your mistake," said Bulger. "My brother Henry is now a handsome man of ordinary size, while I, delicate-featured pigmy that I used to be, have become the giant you see before you. We've switched roles, and I've lost much in the exchange." Hoots of laughter greeted this remark.

Richard Clery also went in for a military career, and I had the pleasure of seeing him in Quebec again when he returned from the

216

Spanish peninsula after the twenty years' struggle that embroiled all Europe. These are the only two of my English friends from the seminary who returned to Canada. I have never heard since of Fairbanks or McWater, who were also my schoolfriends. I think only Clery finished his studies with us. The others generally left the seminary once they knew enough French.

This digression hasn't made me lose sight of my friend Moquin, removed by death from the Quebec bar almost at the beginning of his career. The few words that the late Chief Justice Sewell spoke over his grave in the name of his confrères are, I believe the finest funeral oration ever made for a lawyer

"It is the opinion of us all," stated the eminent chief justice, "that the late Monsieur Moquin never undertook a case unless he was thoroughly and conscientiously convinced that it was just and legally sound."

Moquin had in fact stated, when called to the bar, that he would only take on worthy cases. Two or three instances were cited in which he had unceremoniously shown clients the door of his office, because they pressed him to take on cases that he had told them were unjust and could not be upheld in law. Moquin was not eloquent, saying only what was necessary to support his case, but on the other hand he had the satisfaction of seeing judges take frequent notes during his pleading.

The portrait of this conscientious advocate is in the office of the superior court of the District of Quebec. Each time I contemplate his pale and uncompromising face, I am moved to speak these words: "Patience, my friend! The bar is fast increasing. We may justifiably hope a chief justice will soon be able to give some future paragon lawyer an equally deserved eulogy at his funeral, and you will no longer be alone."

A propos Leclerc, that excellent child to whom Moquin chanted General Montcalm's lament, here is one of the many examples of my somewhat unusual ability to remember details.

I was at Beauport, staying with my son-in-law, Mr. Andrew Stuart, now a judge of the superior court, when an old farmer came driving by in a haycart. After a moment's conversation (for I never deprive myself of the pleasure of talking to an old Canadian when opportunity offers), I said to him, "Were you a boarder at the Quebec Seminary as a child?"

217

"Yes indeed," he answered, looking at me with surprise. "Would God I'd stayed longer. I left at fifteen, to my great regret. But fifty long years have passed over my head since then."

"You're nonetheless my old schoolmate Leclerc, whom we used to call little Alexis. Think back: which boarders did you like, even though they teased you the most?"

"Ah! *Dam!*" exclaimed the old man. "My best friends were Gaspé, Painchaud, and Maguire—fine young fellows, all right, but mischievous little devils."

We renewed our acquaintance with mutual pleasure, and after a fairly long conversation I concluded that he was wrong to regret not having continued his studies. I saw before me the happy and unclouded face of the little Alexis of yesteryear. The passions had left no mark on the features of this elderly and respectable Canadian farmer.

After this thirty years' leap, let us now return to my friend Plamondon.

Plamondon, the pupil of the Abbé Deschenaux, had certainly acquired the tone and manners of good society, but we found his excessive politeness old-fashioned. We who had come into contact with English manners used to twit him about his somewhat clerical mien.

I think it must have been about the year 1820 when a young English gentleman, recently arrived in Quebec, desired to meet some of the *bon vivants* of this friendly city. He invited the leader of this class of worthy young men, Monsieur François-Xavier Perrault, to dine at his Lower Town hotel. With typical British generosity, he asked him to bring along his friends, and friends of friends.

We were gathered in full force and seated at table when the door of our diningroom opened to admit an officer of the 60th, who had arrived the previous evening. He was about to withdraw when our host, who knew him, called, "Take some dinner, O'Gorman." The gentleman thus summoned was not one to refuse so hospitable an invitation and sat down without further ado. We were all French Canadians, with the exception of the late Mr. John Ross and Mr. John Gawler Thompson, who has since been named a judge in the Gaspé. As our Canadian-born English friends all spoke French as easily as ourselves, the conversation was carried on in this language. Our new military acquaintance would have been less than gracious had he appeared ill at ease, for he spoke the most refined Parisian French. The first use he made of it, after the soup, was to address Plamondon, who was sitting opposite him.

"Monsieur l'abbé will perhaps do me the honour of drinking a glass of wine with me?"

This sally sent us into gales of laughter.

"I don't think I'm mistaken, however," said O'Gorman. "Monsieur is without doubt the curé of the city of Quebec?"

We found this even more hilarious, and assured O'Gorman that he had guessed rightly.

Plamondon rose to the occasion. He told O'Gorman that he was correct, and said, "Allow me, Monsieur, to introduce a confrère, Canon Aubert de Gaspé."

Plamondon could hardly have fixed on a more typical individual. At the time I was very corpulent and in blooming health—enough to make the canon in Boileau's *Lutrin* look pale in comparison.[1] The laughter increased, this time at my expense, but O'Gorman was not to be put off.

"A thousand pardons, Monsieur l'abbé," said he, "but surely no canon ever had your neighbour's piercing eye or mobile features?"

"He's got you there, my dear curé!" I cried. "The wolf is always visible beneath the lamb's clothing."

"That's nothing new," retorted Plamondon.

"No, but it's very much to the point."

For once in his life Plamondon admitted to being worsted, although to tell the truth, his audience had decided against him from the beginning.

O'Gorman was quickly initiated into our Canadian fellowship. Rarely have I met a man more friendly and downright sociable. He was an amalgam of French and Irish high spirits. One could even consider him a Frenchman. His family had been established in France long before his ancestor, Sir Thomas O'Gorman, married a Mademoiselle D'Eon de Beaumont in 1757. She was a member of one of the most ancient families of France, listed in the records of chevaliers of military and royal orders published in 1779.

O'Gorman probably emigrated with his family during the Revolution and returned to France after the Restoration, for when we met him he had just left the bodyguard of Louis XVIII. I can't explain why he left the service of France to enter the British army, but it leads me to suppose that he had powerful friends in both realms.

Occasionally, when talking of his father, he would give him the title of Comte O'Gorman, mentioning that he was a member of the family of that Chevalier D'Eon who had been considered a woman. It is only today that, moved by curiosity, I have done some research which convinces me that this was no idle tale.

As for the famous Chevalier D'Eon, quarrelsome swashbuckler and duellist, everyone now knows why he wore women's clothing for some years.

The chevalier had insulted the French ambassador in London. This dignitary could not take part in a duel because of his position, and as retribution Louis XV forbad the chevalier to return to France unless he wore female attire for the rest of his life.

If the good O'Gorman is still alive, I'm sure he has not forgotten his friends in Canada and will read this article with pleasure, although there is not much chance of its falling into his hands.

The members of the Quebec bar of forty-five years ago were as close as brothers. The dinner that they ate together on the last day of each term of the court of king's bench added much to preserving a spirit of perfect harmony. Nothing could be livelier than these dinners *en famille*, as we used to call them, which were also attended by the sheriff and the clerks of the court.

While waiting for the meal to be served, those who had lost what they felt were legally sound cases aired their grievances against the judges, taxing them with ignorance and thus whetting their appetites for the fun to come.

Vallière attributed his losses to his clerk Simon's lapses and blunders, which he humorously referred to as "simony."

By dessert a veritable running fire of wit, comic songs, and high spirits marked the proceedings. The dinner always lasted well into the night, and it was when we had reached the highest pitch of hilarity that Vallière used to sing the familiar ditty, "Londres qu'on m'a tant vantée," in order to bait Fletcher.⁰ It was usually our English-Canadian friends who egged Vallière on, having a good enough sense of humour to be tickled by this facetious song. I never knew anyone more prejudiced against French Canadians than Fletcher, although I should add that he disliked everything that wasn't English to the core.

Mr. Fletcher was a London attorney-at-law who had come to practise in Quebec and died a judge. He was certainly a man of the most distinguished talents and vast erudition, but, *Bon Dieu!* what a disagreeable voice he had when pleading! It would have grated on someone tone deaf. Imagine with what sort of music he regaled us when he took it into his head to sing!

Fletcher was stung almost to fury when Vallière sang the aforementioned satiric verses. His large, protruding eyes threatened to burst out of their sockets, and he revenged himself, or so he believed, by intoning "God Save the King." Lully would never have recognized his composition, and Louis XIV would have fled the room. The lyrics were written in the king's honour and sung by the pupils of Saint-Cyr when he visited the convent with Madame de Maintenon.

The lyrics, which the English translated practically word for word, were written by Madame Brinon.[R] Here they are:

> Grande Dieu! Sauvez le Roy, (*bis*)
> Vengez le Roy!
> Que toujours glorieux,
> Louis victorieux,
> Voye ses ennemis
> Toujours soumis!
> Grand Dieu! Sauvez le Roy!
> Grand Dieu! Vengez le Roy!
> Sauvez le Roy!

The learned Fletcher probably had no idea of the origin of the national anthem, which the English had the good taste to adopt and the French the bad taste not to appreciate. Had he realized that England owed this fine song to a Frenchman and that it had been composed for a French monarch, he would have sung "Rule Britannia" at the risk of forcing even the most tin-eared individuals to leave the room.

Mr. Fletcher went about his work with a will when he sat as stipendiary judge in the quarterly sessions of the magistrates' court, while also occupying the post of chief of police in Quebec. If he condemned a criminal to the lash, then a frequent punishment for petty larceny, the sentence stated that the guilty man was to be whipped until his back bled. Too bad for those whose hide was as tough as sharkskin: that was their problem. Why couldn't they be more thin-skinned?

One day he heard of a poor devil stationed near the Saint-Jean Gate with a roulette wheel. Passers-by would put a sol or two on the table and turn the wheel, sometimes winning a skein of thread, a paper of pins, or something of similar value. Occasionally they went away empty handed. Fletcher had the miscreant brought before him and sent for the executioner without even advising the sheriff. The delinquent was given thirty-nine strokes of the lash. The latter abandoned his roulette wheel in the magistrate's office and put the walls of this inhospitable city behind him as fast as his legs would go, crying, "I'm off to Montreal; here they beat you for nothing!"

Another time, Fletcher, while presiding over the quarter sessions court, wanted to try a man for a crime that carried the death penalty.

The two other judges sitting threatened to leave him alone on the bench, and he was forced to renounce, much to his regret.

Let no one think Fletcher behaved this way through ignorance. Oh, no! He always entrenched himself behind some old English statute that had fallen into disuse but never been revoked.

Most certainly he was a man of enormous knowledge—a walking encyclopedia, as we used to say then.

But let me come back to more congenial companions. Messrs. John Ross[3] and John Gawler Thompson,[4] born and brought up in Quebec City, had all the high spirits of French Canadians. Here is a little sketch of the first that amused us no end.

It must have been ten o'clock on a magnificient July night. Some friends, including myself, had dined at Ross's house in Palace Street opposite the wall of the Hôtel Dieu. It was about a hundred feet from the sentry post by the Palace Gate. Our host possessed a fine magic lantern. Finding the night favourable, he projected a magnificent ship under full sail on the recently white-washed wall opposite. The sentry, taken unawares by so marvellous a spectacle in the middle of town, shouted with all his might, "Guards!"

The entire watch was on the alert, thinking it must be an officer doing his evening rounds. "Come and look at the ship going down the hill under full sail," called the sentry.

They all came into the street, but the ship had disappeared. The sergeant, thinking it was a joke, severely reprimanded the poor sentry, who swore by all the gods that he'd seen a ship.

Hardly had the men returned to the guardroom than the same object reappeared. The sentry shouted even louder that he saw the ship again. To cut a long story short, the sergeant, roused to indignation after a third alert, thought the sentry must be moon-struck and removed him from his post.

A few minutes later we heard a voice from the top of Palace Hill. It was a carter, standing up in his vehicle and singing a joyous Canadian song at the top of his lungs. But scarcely had he reached the middle of the hill than he let out a fearful howl, jumped to the ground, and took to his heels yelling like a madman. What frightened him was nothing less than a gruesome devil, sporting horns and brandishing a fork.

We all ran out into the street and stopped the horse, calling to the carter to come back, although he was already far off. This he did when he saw how many we were.

"What's the matter, Flamand?" asked Ross, who knew the man. "Why lose your head and run off like that? Better watch out for your wife! I'm afraid you've had a drop too much."

"I saw the devil, Monsieur, that's what's wrong with me!" exclaimed Flamand. "You can't blame me for running away from him, can you?"

"Go to bed, my good Flamand," said I. "Try to slip in quietly beside your good woman; she won't stand for any nonsense once she finds you've had a glass too many."

"Oh! So I've had a glass too many?" retorted Flamand. "I guess you're going to tell me I didn't feel the devil's fork poke me in the behind as I jumped out of the cart!"

We laughed so hard at this that Flamand swore and climbed into his cart. Whipping his horse with all his might, he quickly disappeared through the Palace Gate.

Here is another scene that suddenly springs to mind.

There was an old bachelor, rich and very miserly. He promised his lawyers and a number of their friends a good dinner, over and above their fees, if he won a certain case about which he was extremely anxious. At first glance, the menu put us in excellent humour, as did our host's insistence on placing one of us at the head of the table instead of occupying it himself. None of the *bons vivants* objected to this departure from custom, for only the miser's cellar would be the loser if he weren't in charge of handing round the wine.

It would take a Horace or a Boileau to describe adequately the dishes offered at this dinner.[5] First course: at one end of the table a boiled calf's head, baring its teeth and sticking out its tongue; at the other end, a boiled shoulder of veal. In the centre of the table sat four dishes: creamed veal, a stew of sundry bits of the same animal, veal tripe, and slices of roast veal. The crowning feature of the first course was a rice soup for which the aforementioned head had furnished the broth.

"We'll be mooing in a minute," said Plamondon to his neighbour. As I saw that everyone was making superhuman efforts not to laugh, I came to the rescue by saying very loudly:

"Gentlemen of the bar, here is a tongue that has never lied."

This remark was greeted with shrieks of laughter, and the master of the feast declared in delighted tones that never had he heard such wit, particularly as applied to gentlemen of the bar. The guests set to with a will, nevertheless, in hopes of a little more variety in the meat offered for the next course.

Second course: a huge loin of veal at the head of the table, and a dish of braised veal at the other end. We thought the animal must surely be disposed of by now, but no: the maidservant returned with a calf's foot marinade and breaded veal cutlets. We contained ourselves with difficulty until Major LaForce brought us timely deliverance by telling a funny story, thus enabling us to split our sides with some semblance of propriety.

We were all under the impression that the master of the house had that morning made a clean sweep of all the calves in the market, when he remarked, with an air of evident satisfaction, "Veal, gentlemen, is at its delicate best at this time of year, and knowing the ability of my lawyers, I was sure my case would win on the twentieth of this month of June. My cow presented me with a fine calf two months ago, and I therefore had the happy notion of fattening it in order to feast you today."

"How very considerate of you," said I. "We're extremely grateful— all the more so, because I imagine the son must have drunk all his dear mother's milk and left you with none."

"You're absolutely right," returned the miser. "For the last two months I've had to drink my tea like a Chinaman!"

Then a ray of triumphant joy lit up his face as he cried, "Gentlemen, the plum pudding!"

This wonderful plum pudding formed a cone some eighteen inches high. It made us think—this was Ross's idea—that the cook couldn't find a suitable bag, and must have cut off the end of one of her master's old nightcaps to concoct this giant among Britannic desserts. Ross, noticing it was somewhat wobbly, gave the table a little push. The top of the pudding leaned toward him, and he cried, "How do you do?" Once set in motion, the pyramid saluted all the guests, who gaily shouted, "How do you do?"

"I knew you'd be delighted with this grand plum pudding," declared our host.

He was perfectly correct, and I'm sure that, like myself, my old friend Judge Thompson hasn't forgotten the famous plum pudding.

I will now turn to Justin McCarthy, whose story offers an inexhaustible mine of anecdote. We were on holiday at Saint-Joachim, and Justin kept begging our director, Monsieur Demers, to let him hunt. The answer was always no, however. McCarthy was only fourteen, and the use of firearms was forbidden him according to seminary rules. After repeated refusals, Monsieur Demers one day told him that if Moquin would lend him his gun, he would allow him to hunt, but for this one time only. Moquin, who was in on the secret, readily agreed.

Ever suspicious and fearing some practical joke, Justin waited until Moquin had gone, then checked the weapon. He blew down the barrel of the gun; the priming-hole was clean. He placed powder in the pan and pulled the trigger; the flint generated a few sparks, but the powder refused to light, and three or four times in a row the gun failed to go off. McCarthy put the supposed gunpowder in his mouth: it was onionseed.

He laughs best who laughs last, said the hunter to himself.

Off he went to the large seminary farm. Old Jean Guilbaut was away from home, but his wife was there.

"Good day, Madame Guilbaut," called McCarthy. "I bring great news. Our people are coming back soon, and to prove it one of our cousins in Normandy has sent my mother a fine present of onionseed."

"But what an extraordinary idea to send onionseed to your mother, instead of making her a present of ribbons, laces, or silks," said Mother Guilbaut.

"Mother, have you ever heard tell of General Bonaparte?"

"Indeed I have," said the old woman. "They say he's as great a warrior as the late General Montcalm."

"Pooh!" snorted McCarthy. "Your General Montcalm could only spit two Englishmen with one sword-thrust. Bonaparte can skewer ten; and since he's always at war with the English, he's seized all the ribbons, laces, and silks to stuff his cannons. That's why my dear cousin couldn't send any to my mother."

"What a droll little fellow you are, Monsieur McCarthy!" exclaimed the old woman.

"Well, one must laugh sometimes," said Justin, unfolding the handkerchief containing the onionseed. "Bonaparte is coming back with our own good folk pretty soon, and you know how the French like onions. My cousin was afraid we might have run out of seed, and that's why she sent us some."

Opening the handkerchief, McCarthy spread out the contents before the old woman.

"Oh, what fine seed!" said Mother Guilbaut.

"You're not hard to please, Mother," said Justin. "It's pure French seed, nothing foreign mixed in."

"The French are right to like onions," said the good woman. "You can't make anything taste good without them."

"It shows your discernment, Madame. What a delicious lunch a raw onion on a slice of bread with a pinch of salt makes, of a Friday!"

"You're so right, Monsieur McCarthy, but there should be butter on the bread. In the meantime, give me a good thimbleful of your fine French seed."

"One good turn deserves another, Mother. I'll give it all to you, but give me a few charges of gunpowder in return, as I've no ammunition left."

"With all my heart," said the old woman, and from her husband's store—he being a great hunter—she gave Justin all the powder he wanted.

Justin hurried down to the shore, where the horned larks were so plentiful that he quickly bagged as many as he wanted. We were all waiting impatiently for his return, eager to tease him. Great was our surprise to see such a well-stocked gamebag.

"Where did you get this?" asked Monsieur Demers.

"I killed it with your onionseed," retorted McCarthy. "I did a little trading with the habitants, and exchanged your onionseed for powder. McCarthy outwits others," he added, wagging his head, "but you have to be pretty smart to trick *him!*"

"What, you wretch!" cried Monsieur Demers. "You traded our gardener's onionseed for a few charges of powder? Do you realize there was at least twenty-five to thirty shillings' worth?"

"What can you expect, gentlemen?" riposted McCarthy. "I'm fairly new at the game, having just started in business this morning. Next time I'll do better."

Monsieur Demers resigned himself to the loss of the onionseed and laughed heartily at McCarthy's turning the tables. As well as I can remember, a thimbleful of this seed used to sell for thirty sols. As for McCarthy, he proceeded to entertain us enormously with the account of his interview with Mother Guilbaut.

Excellent Monsieur Demers! We all loved him like a father. How generous he was, and how indulgent of the faults and follies of youth! I owe him a debt of gratitude that I have never been able to express, but he knew that I felt it in my heart! May he forgive me, profane being that I am, for evoking the memory of so worthy a priest, a saint in heaven!

It's still a mystery to me how McCarthy ever managed to get a sound education, or how, without doing a stroke of work, he left the seminary knowing Latin as well as any of us. I know, because I asked, that he never did any homework as a matter of fixed principle.

"Why don't you learn your lessons like the others?" I asked him one day.

"Because I could be doing something I like instead."

"You're just asking to be caned, and yet you screech like a maniac when the teacher punishes you."

"Well, it's no skin off your nose."

I couldn't refute such a rational argument.

"Only numskulls waste their time studying," McCarthy continued. Either the teacher's going to ask me the lesson, or he isn't. If he does, and I'm second in line, at least I'll know enough to escape punishment. If I'm third or fourth in line, I'll know as much as those imbeciles who did their homework. If, on the other hand, he doesn't ask me, it'd be a terrible waste of time to study."

The ruthless logic of his reply was unanswerable. On the same principle, he never did his preparation for construing the Latin authors we studied. As for the exercises and translations we were supposed to produce in class, he supplied about three out of six. His fertile mind enabled him to find a thousand excuses that no other child could have imagined.

McCarthy may not have studied, but he led a very active existence, nevertheless. He attended the assembly sessions as well as the law courts, and showed his contempt for judges, lawyers, and members of parliament by imitating them to the life. He could quote legal lights like Blackstone, Cujas, and Pothier at will. He could slip in anywhere, knew everyone in the garrison, got into the barracks courtyard on days when the soldiers were being disciplined, and frequented the circuses and theatres without necessarily paying admission.

Having harassed all the peaceable citizens of Quebec, McCarthy entered the Quebec Seminary as a boarder, no doubt relishing this change of scene. One of his first exploits there occurred as follows. The tables in the dining hall of the Little Seminary were divided into teams of four students, one team serving the others during the meal and eating afterward. We looked forward eagerly to being servers, for once the dining hall was empty we were our own masters. I was on McCarthy's team. We had done our stint and were now free of all supervision and prepared to take full advantage of it while the teachers were gone. Justin immediately put this temporary emancipation to the test by opening the stove door and tossing in a mutton stew, the meagre and sole dish intended for our supper. We all protested loudly, being as hungry as wolves. All that was left to assuage our pangs was a fricassee of dried bread. The first fruits of liberty appeared bitter indeed, as they have to many of my fellow citizens in the present generation.

"My friends," said McCarthy, "moderate your lamentations. I'm as hungry as any of you. All we have to do is find a much better supper at someone else's expense."

"You're crazy! What happens if we don't?"

"That's the whole point," said McCarthy. "Necessity is the mother of invention. If hunger hadn't driven the young Spartans on, they would often have gone to bed without supper. Wait a bit and don't worry; you imbeciles are always out of ideas, but never Citizen McCarthy."

After a ten-minute wait that seemed like a century to us, this artful dodger reappeared with two magnificent roast chickens, which he held delicately by the drumsticks in each hand. True, there was no gravy, but this was a minor inconvenience to which we paid little attention.

"Let's be quick," said the Citizen, "because the fat'll be in the fire any moment now!"

Inner court of the Quebec Seminary. Charles Huot (1855-1930) captured the enduring French colonial flavor of the Seminary, where de Gaspé spent his schooldays. Musée du Québec, photo: Patrick Altman. 43.155

Barely had we devoured half these succulent fowl when a loud knocking was heard on the dining hall door, which was latched on the inside. Then we heard footsteps walking away.

"Hurry," said McCarthy. "He'll be back with a passkey. Let's put out the candles and get under the tables. Watch me, and do the same."

A few minutes later Monsieur Joseph, the lay superintendent who had been deprived of his choicest dish, came into our dining hall. It was now as dark as a tightly-closed oven. He stepped forward and said, "They can't have escaped. I heard them talking a moment ago." Having delivered himself of this monologue, he went out again.

"Come on," said McCarthy. "He'll be back with a candle. Don't forget to follow my lead."

Monsieur Joseph came back quickly with a light, but hardly had he reached the middle of the room when the candle was extinguished by a chicken carcass launched by the sure hand of McCarthy. Stimulated by so noble an example, we hurled whatever was left of the bones at the head of the unlucky superintendent.

It was recreation-time when Monsieur Joseph came to air his grievances to our director. Being as wise a man as he was worthy a priest, Monsieur Demers immediately had the accused brought before him. The culprit protested, feigning hot indignation.

"What, Monsieur? You dare accuse me—me!—of theft? I'll have you know that my father brought me up to respect others' property!"

"Then he should've brought you up to respect my chickens," retorted the superintendent.

"Would you have the kindness, Monsieur Joseph, to answer two or three questions?" asked McCarthy.

"Speak, Monsieur. I'm listening," snapped the superintendent.

"Did I not come into the main dining hall and greet you politely?"

"Yes."

"Did I not ask after your health and that of your respectable spouse?"

"Yes."

"Did I not ask after your children, and did you not reply, with a deep sigh, that you had none and that heaven had denied you this consolation?"

"Yes! Yes! But what's that got to do with my chickens?"

"Stick to the question, if you please, Monsieur Joseph. Argou says one must never stray from the point, and the judges always agree with him.

"Now, did I not express my deep compassion for you and your virtuous lady? And did I not add that it was a loss to the country, as your children would doubtless have followed in your footsteps on the path of virtue?"

"Oh, yes! You buttered me up just as you say!"

"Did I not tell you of the misfortune that befell our stew, which I overturned by accident, and plead with you to help the poor children, condemned to sup on dry bread? And did you not reply that you were very sorry, but you had nothing except two chickens simmering in the oven for your dinner, as well as that of the head refectioner, the baker, and the cook? And did I not then say, bowing myself out, that we would be none the worse friends for it?"

"Certainly, Monsieur. Then you made off with my chickens."

"Ah! I made off with your chickens. And you didn't stop me?"

"*Parbleu*! I would if I'd noticed them, in spite of your bowing and scraping all the way to the dining-hall door."

"I ask you to take note that Monsieur did not see me with the chickens in my hands," stated McCarthy.

"How could I see them when you had your hands behind your back!" expostulated Monsieur Joseph.

"Have you not admitted that I was bowing low?" said McCarthy. "Well, Monsieur Joseph, when a well-bred person bows low he is obliged, in order to keep his balance, to hold his hands behind his back. What do you say to that?"

"That you were the only person to enter the dining hall, and that it was certainly you who stole my chickens while you hung around the stove."

"Monsieur Joseph, do you state categorically that no one other than myself entered the dining hall? Be careful! Until now you have answered my questions with a frankness that does you credit. Blackstone says that prevaricaton is a terrible crime!"

"Nobody but you came in," said Monsieur Joseph.

"Who brought you the soup, in that case?"

"Noël, the kitchenboy."

"Oh! Just now it was no one else but me who entered. You're contradicting yourself, Monsieur Joseph."

"Noël is a perfectly honest man who has served us for years," said Monsieur Joseph.

"Hah!" snorted McCarthy. "If I were lucky enough to have a well-lined purse in my waistcoat pocket, I'd be very uneasy about meeting that lean and hungry wretch in a dark alley, with his pock-marked face that seems to inspire you with such confidence. But never mind that: if he served the soup, he must also have served the chickens?"

"How could he serve them, since you'd carried them off? All he took out of the oven was the platter, the gravy, and a strip of bacon for basting, which you forgot."

"Do scullions usually feast on chicken?" asked McCarthy.

"No," replied Monsieur Joseph.

"Then, Monsieur, say thy *meâ culpâ*, for thou hast led thy neighbour into temptation. According to Buffon, tall, pock-marked men have a keen sense of smell, and the aroma of the fowl must have been too much for him. I'll wager he brought you the empty platter in one hand?"

"It's possible, but I didn't notice particularly," gasped Monsieur Joseph, wiping the perspiration from his fat face.

"Well! Monsieur, be persuaded and convinced that in the other hand he held your chickens wrapped in his greasy apron, which was rolled up over his hips to hide the theft. Master Noël isn't the cleanest kitchenboy in town. What's more, you have it on your conscience that you led him into temptation," added McCarthy with calculated sophistry. "That's the opinion of the great Bourdaloue."

The superintendent was floored. He saw that McCarthy was apparently exonerated, and he sweated under the laughter of the spectators to this amusing scene. McCarthy had achieved his goal, which was to entertain us; he lived for nothing else.

"The proof is," said Monsieur Joseph suddenly, plucking up courage, "that you ate my chickens and threw the bones at my head."

"Do you know anatomy?" demanded the Citizen.

"No, and I don't care a bit for your *atomy*."

"What! You don't know *tomy*?" cried Justin. "That wonderful science which teaches you about the bones of humans, birds, and ferocious beasts that howl and roar, and of all beings that have the good fortune to possess bones?"

"I know enough to prove you guilty; I'm going to fetch the bones."

"Go! Go!" retorted McCarthy with superb indifference. "Go! I'll wait for you here, and we shall see."

"Now we're for it," I said to Justin.

"You little innocent!" he scoffed. "Didn't you notice how he was sweating and red with indignation at the way everyone laughed at him? He won't come back, don't worry. He's had enough."

Even then, McCarthy understood the human heart. He had guessed aright. I have certainly not embroidered my account of this incident, which kept us laughing for three months afterward. In fact, it has lost much in the telling.

As for our director, he always had a soft spot for our mischief-making and was not one to take such childish pranks seriously. He made a supreme effort to keep a straight face and not to hurt Monsieur Joseph's feelings. In any case, Monsieur Demers was sure that this worthy functionary wouldn't go to bed on an empty stomach, as he had the keys to the pantry.

Poor McCarthy! Brilliant meteor diminishing in brightness as you approached the age of manhood, and totally extinguished by the time you came to the bar. Poor McCarthy! Great was the surprise of your friends and the general public, who had entertained such high expectations. Who would have thought that McCarthy would not become a distinguished member of the Quebec legal profession? He was a young man endowed with such intellect and natural eloquence; he had debated so successfully against Papineau, Vallière, and Plamondon in our little college parliament and in our literary society founded about 1809. Oh, the burning fever of a fateful addiction! The lamp gave not even a glimmer of that divine light, of those gifts of the Creator that he had abused! At first he felt the remonstrances and reproaches of his friends, and often made desperate efforts to conquer his unfortunate predilection and recapture his genius, all to no avail: alcohol ran in his veins before he was even born!

Poverty-stricken, McCarthy dragged out a wretched existence for nearly twenty years. The only one of his faculties that he retained until death was the spirit of bitter raillery and sarcasm that made all those he met fear him.

One of my aunts, Mademoiselle Marguerite de Lanaudière, unostentatious by nature, arrived one day at the Pointe Lévis landing stage in a modest cart drawn by an even more modest horse. It was autumn and the roads were very bad, so that either to spare her own horses or for some other reason, she was being driven by her farmer.

"Good day, Mademoiselle de Lanaudière. How's your Ladyship?" said Justin, who was watching everyone on the wharf to find an opening for some malicious remark.

My aunt, herself quick-witted and satirical, felt nettled but replied with a smile, "My Ladyship is quite well, Monsieur McCarthy."

Justin drew near the vehicle, slapped the rump of the old nag that passed for a horse, and said, "An old servant, Mademoiselle! One always remains fond of old friends!"

"They are the most sincere," replied my aunt, much amused.

McCarthy examined the patched old harness, shook his head now and again, and finally said, "Well, at least one can always tell the nobility by their livery!"

My aunt was still laughing at McCarthy's jibe when she got out of her cart in front of her home in the Rue Saint-Louis.

Let us shed a tear for those whose overweening appetites have ruined their future in their very youth! Shed a tear of regret for those men, already famous, whose genius has gradually faded until it has

233

become extinguished! But let us not judge them too harshly, for miserable human nature craves indulgence.

Very few people are natural drunkards; drunkenness is the result of a long habit of hard liquor. How, then, can one account for the physiological phenomenon that I am about to describe?

A drunkard stops suddenly on the brink of disaster, seeing hideous poverty rise in all its tatters. He regains his fortune, and for fifteen or twenty years never lets a drop of liquor pass his lips. He then reasons to himself: the abuse of spirits for a number of years rendered me a drunkard, after being a naturally sober man. It is therefore only habit that leads to this vice, and I have nothing to fear from my former enemy now, after fifteen sober years. I can do as others do; past experience will serve as my protector. He swallows a glass, a single glass, of eau-de-vie. The madness for drink instantly overpowers him, and he becomes a greater drunkard than ever. This is no isolated case. Indeed, I could cite numerous examples of drunkards as bad or even worse than in the past!

We in Quebec all used to know an English gentleman who had made a large fortune in Canada, where he lived for many years. He was considered a teetotaler, and often used to say when dining with friends, "As long as the Saint Lawrence still flows, I'll never lack something to drink." We were therefore surprised to learn he was a vagrant in the streets of London, where he had returned in his old age. We heard with equal surprise that, having been a drunkard in his youth, he had made a vow not to take spirits for twenty years. Thinking his fault corrected after so long a time, he thought he might take a glass of wine with impunity at a dinner with friends. Alas! The demon drink snared his prey that very moment.

Nothing remains of poor McCarthy but the sad remembrance of his misfortunes and a work that he published in the year 1809, entitled, *Dictionnaire de l'ancien droit du Canada ou compilation des Edits, Déclarations et arrêts du conseil d'Etat des Rois de France, concernant le Canada.*

I think it was in 1818 that I was returning one fine night from a hunting party at Château-Richer, gun in one hand, the reins of my horse in the other, and a gamebag well-stocked with snipe on my back. I was traveling the fine road lined with poplars that ran from the old Dorchester Bridge to the foot of the Côte d'Abraham. Suddenly my horse shied so violently that I thought I was about to be tossed.

Once settled back in the saddle, I drew near a black shape stretched out at the foot of a poplar.

"Who's there!" I cried.

"*Sub tegmine fagi*,"[T] replied a voice I recognized as that of the unfortunate McCarthy.

"Alas, poor McCarthy!" I exclaimed.

"Oh, it's you, Aubert!" he said. "You're perhaps the only one of my former friends who feels compassion for my misfortunes, for you see that McCarthy, like the Son of Man, has only a stone on which to rest his head."

Tears blurred my eyes, tears all the more bitter because I myself was then at the height of what men call happiness.

"Your partiality for me makes you unjust to your other friends," I replied. "Vallière, Plamondon, LeBlond, Faribault, Moquin—haven't they all worked hard for your rehabilitation, and hasn't it always failed because of your wicked penchant? Haven't English lawyers who barely know you done everything to help us make you change your way of life? Think of your sister, young, beautiful, and virtuous! Think of your old father! They reach out to you in supplication, they who have no other support in this world!"

"Get away, Philippe, get away!" cried McCarthy in a strangled voice. "You're tearing my heart out!" And he burst into sobs.

I dug my spurs into my horse's flanks to cover up my emotion.

Madame Desaulles, sister of the Honourable Louis-Joseph Papineau, offered the father of the luckless Justin McCarthy a refuge beneath her hospitable roof. There he died at a great age, surrounded by the care of this generous lady who was in every way worthy. It is but a crown of virtue added to the many others that this distinguished woman carried heavenward, where she received her reward for all the works of kindness and charity her name calls to mind.

CHAPTER TEN

> He (Talleyrand) is well aware that an
> honest man who can write is as useful as a
> rogue—indeed, preferable in certain
> cases, for he is more trustworthy and costs
> less.
>
> Fontanes

I do not dispute this aphorism of the witty Fontanes,[A] although I
believe it applies more to France than Canada. However, instead of
"the honest man who can write," I would put "the honest man who
can speak," and the judgment would be worthy of rumination by those
who govern this province. I infinitely regret that this chapter is not
written by a better pen than mine, for it might then be of great service.
Lacking style, I have to make do with the ever respectable logic of
common sense—less brilliant, but more comprehensible.

A young man entering the world after finishing his studies in our
colleges usually thinks himself a fine fellow, whereas, with all due
respect, he is often a conceited pedant. Those who are still at that
happy age when one's illusions are untarnished will take exception
to this and perhaps abuse me. I only ask, out of deference to my
white hair, that they postpone their anger for a few years. If they do
not then see that I am right, their faculties of reasoning will have
made but little progress. My departed spirit shall be undismayed,
however, as the opinion of sensible men will have done me justice.

Timeworn and pensive, de Gaspé posed for this photograph by Ellisson & Co. of Quebec around the time of publication of *Les Anciens Canadiens* (1863). Public Archives Canada. PA-74099

One day, while attending celebrations for the great national holiday of Saint-Jean-Baptiste, I saw a young man in the procession wearing the costume of the Canadian farmer: rawhide shoes, buttons cut from a piece of belt leather, and so on down to the last detail. I asked his name, and was told that this gentleman was a democrat despite his rank, and that he was wearing this getup to discourage foreign manufacturers and offer walking proof of his patriotism. I was all the more surprised because I knew he belonged to a family distinguished for its intellectual powers. That same evening he made a speech. I was struck not only by its style, profundity, and high-minded sentiments, but even more by the honest and deeply felt conviction it displayed. Hah! I said to myself. For all that, you won't be a democrat for long, my dear fellow. I give you five years at the outside to change your convictions.

Finding myself in his native parish several years later, and having assured myself that his democratic inclinations had undergone a radical cure, I obtained an introduction. Without preamble I told him of my earlier verdict. He burst out laughing and said, "Monsieur, with a modicum of honesty and a lot of common sense, such follies are soon put aside."[1]

Let those who, like myself, sincerely love their country—this dear Canada where we were born and hope to die—tremble to see that such men are not at the helm of public affairs. There are men of this calibre among us. Everyone admits their superior talents, unshakable honesty, and sincere, edifying piety. It seems that such virtues are of little merit when it comes to governing a people, however, as great care is taken to see that these men are kept from the high places where they might promote our best interests.

I am straying from my subject, however. When I emerged into the adult world, I was neither more stupid nor more intelligent than my contemporaries. Nevertheless, a certain innate shyness, which I still possess, saved me from ridiculous posturing, one of the dangers to which they were prone. I may have had a good opinion of myself, but I never dared play the great man, a common affectation of the time. This wasn't due to an excess of modesty on my part, but to a lack of confidence. Nevertheless, I shared all their other silly and irrational ideas.

Young men are apt to unjustly disparage the female sex, attributing to them all our faults and, it would seem, all our vices as well. From such youths I don't expect high-flown physiological theories, nor can they plumb the depths of the human heart, that labyrinth where so many philosophers have lost their way. I don't expect them to be discerning beyond their years, merely to reflect. Surely, witnessing as they do in their families the virtues of their mothers, sisters, and all the women to whom they are closely related, they ought to be convinced.

God did indeed create woman with a soul very different from ours. With rare exceptions, her very features bear the imprint of purity and virtue. Thousands of young women judged harshly by the opposite sex have souls as pure as the angels on which they are modeled. If it were otherwise, what numberless miseries would be added to those under which humanity already labours! What social disorder and upheaval would arise, should women be born with the same vices as men! God in His wisdom has foreseen such enormities and applied a brake by making women virtuous. The promiscuous woman is an exception, whereas the love of man for woman is as changeable as the colours of a chameleon's skin in response to the objects around it. A woman attaches herself with surprising tenacity to the unworthy object of her affection. Desertion and the cruelest treatment rarely sever the ties binding her to the man she loves. Slow death or even suicide are all too often the consequences for a woman betrayed in love.

Man cannot judge woman until he has reached the age of discretion, when the ardent warmth of youthful passions has passed, thereby allowing him to exercise his judgment objectively. I do not speak of those vile beings who, even in old age, go about spreading venom and calumny against women, although such despicable men are unfortunately too numerous in the human race.

In early days, ladies who moved in military circles were the particular target of young men's malicious remarks, and indeed I believe the same holds true today. A little thought on the matter would have shown them that the rank of these ladies naturally classed them with this level of society. Had I myself been more experienced, I would have responded as follows.

"I can well believe that military gentlemen don't always behave like Cato the Stoic. However, we ourselves scarcely fall into that category, as you must admit, and women run no greater risk in their relations with officers than with you, my dear friends!"

Even the wives and daughters of the military were subject to wholesale criticism.

Those who made such remarks were unaware that a fraternity exists among army men, and that he who does not respect the wife and daughter of a brother-at-arms exposes himself to relentless snubbing, of which being ostracized or "sent to Coventry" is the least terrible. An officer is rarely able to endure this torment for more than a year. All communication ceases between other officers and the man being punished. His name is struck from the mess list. No one speaks to him except on strictly military business, and even his closest relatives cannot talk to him without being involved in his disgrace. I knew a lieutenant who attracted all our sympathy. He supported his old mother and sisters with no other resource than his pay. For eighteen months he bore up, but his health began to deteriorate from one day to the next, and in the end he had to sell his commission.

He would only go for a walk at nightfall, always outside the city walls, not returning until late at night. Death was painted on his face, reflecting the death in his heart. What his offense was, I don't know.

I began the study of law under the late Chief Justice Sewell, then attorney-general. As a foretaste of the delights of my new profession, he handed me the *Coutume de Paris*.[B] I was leaving the office with my dry-as-dust tome tucked proudly under my arm when I met one of my young friends from the seminary. He was studying under Monsieur Borgia,[C] a well-known lawyer of the period. I acquainted him with my joy at possessing such a treasure, and told him how I had been advised to throw myself into the study of a profession that, although it might at first seem arid, would eventually yield me inestimable pleasure.

"As far as I'm concerned," said my friend, "I haven't opened a book since a certain conversation with my employer. As a matter of course I asked him what reading he would recommend. After walking up and down his office for a while, he answered me.

"'If you'll take my word for it, my dear fellow, you won't read a thing.'

"'That certainly simplifies my professional studies,' said I. 'But then why did you make me sign the articles tying me down here for five long years?'

"'Because,' he retorted, 'you can't be admitted to the bar[D] without this formality, as required by law.'

"'Then allow me to bid you good day,' I returned. 'I undertake to call on you at the end of my five years in order to collect the required certificates and complete any other formalities needed to practise as advocate, attorney-at-law, and counsel in all His Majesty's courts of the Province of Lower Canada.'

"'Not so fast, my boy,' said my employer. 'You may quite sensibly spare yourself the grind of studying legal theory, but without practical knowledge you run the risk of barking your shins at your first step in the profession—an inconvenience I'd gladly spare a man I like. I also have another powerful motive for being much attached to your kind and assiduous company for the next five years: my large and numerous clientele. How am I to get through all the necessary scribbling by myself? Actually, two thirds of it is useless, but we have to do it nevertheless, because, you know, content implies form.'

"'Very well,' I replied. 'That's plain speaking. But you're reputed, quite justifiably, to be one of the greatest legal experts in Canada. You surely weren't born that way?'

"'My dear child,' he said, 'it's just because I *have* studied much and grown pale with twenty years of poring over books, that I'm now convinced it's a sheer waste of time. There are so many anomalies and contradictions in the laws that govern us, that it's almost impossible to find your way through this inextricable maze of French and Roman codes, coutumes, English statutes, provincial statutes, and what have you. You see, a lawyer sometimes has a conscience, and he can be as sensitive as the next man. The case may be one that, if lost, would ruin the respectable father of a large family. He's plagued by doubt, and frets over it day and night. Or he may worry about widows and orphans whom he couldn't keep from ruin, although the case seemed sound enough after a thorough study of the points under litigation. You must admit, it's very aggravating, not to say humiliating, to think that the best lawyer in the whole province can't say to a client, "Sleep well, I'm sure of winning," even after the most careful consideration of his case.'

"'Well, Monsieur Borgia, if you with all your knowledge can't avoid such misery, what hope is there for me unless I study?'

"'You have sound judgment,' retorted my employer, 'and there's no danger of your going astray more often than I do. In any case, you can always solve your difficulties by the simple expedient of keeping a cup of dice on your desk. When you're in a quandary, you can let chance decide.'"

If these sarcastic and bitter words were true fifty years ago, I leave it to our present-day lawyers to decide whether jurisprudence sheds a more certain light nowadays.

Monsieur Borgia was a disinterested and generous man, possessed of remarkable tact and feeling. Honour his memory, and shed a tear for the misfortunes of his latter days!

He neglected his business to go into politics, and died in dire poverty, for politics was not then, as it is now, the road to fortune.

This conversation with my friend hardly stimulated my zeal for professional study, but even so I was obliged to get down to serious work. For several days I had been poring over my cherished *Coutume de Paris*, yawning until my jaw was well-nigh dislocated, when I made a singular discovery in our office. While ruffling through a pile of papers in a corner, I came upon a dust-covered book. As I was shaking the dust off before opening it, I asked my fellow articlers, Green and Cartwright, why it was there.

Said Green, "It's such a detestable work that Mr. Sewell threw it among those papers in our presence, to show his scorn and disgust."

I opened the book. *Horresco referens*! I nearly fell over, for in my hand I held Volney's *Ruines*.ᴱ Now Citizen Volney and his *Ruines* were hardly surrounded by an odour of sanctity at the Quebec Seminary, which I had just left. Among other precepts, our metaphysics teacher had inspired in us a holy terror of, first, the devil (honour to whom honour is due), then Messrs. Voltaire, J. J. Rousseau, D'Alembert, Diderot, and, in particular, Citizen Volney. However, then as now (I intend no slight on the present generation), young men all too often mistrusted the salutary advice proffered by their parents and other moral guardians. This being so, or perhaps at the prodding of some imp, I couldn't resist the temptation of reading at least a few pages of the proscribed book.

I opened the volume, to be confronted with an engraving of Palmyra, queen of desert cities. On a tomb sat a European, contemplating the desolate scene. One could almost hear the screech of an owl perched atop a temple, and the nocturnal silence seemed to be pierced by the lugubrious and discordant howls of some jackals, their mouths agape.

This desert scene, the meaning of which I fully grasped, impressed me deeply. In those days I was inclined to be wildly enthusiastic about things, a trait that probably only my friend Plamondon possessed to a greater degree.

I read aloud the first lines of the invocation, which I cite here from memory.

"I salute you, O solitary ruins, sacred tombs, silent walls!"

"Trash!" said Cartwright, who understood little French, whereas Green, who appreciated our classical authors, was all ears. I continued reading, and my friend cried, "What fine language!" At this point the door opened to admit our employer. With my right hand I stuffed the unfortunate volume into my coat, the tails of which came down to my heels as was the fashion then. Indeed, I could have concealed the weighty *Coutume* in these coat tails. Unluckily for me, my face has always been a mirror of my inner feelings, an infirmity I would wish upon all liars. My employer saw from my troubled expression that I was hiding some object which I was most anxious to prevent his seeing. Amused by my obvious discomfort, he handed me a paper on the right. Feeling quite properly that it would be rude to accept the paper with my left hand, I hastened to exchange it for the one trapped behind my back, thus restoring its freedom of action. Mr. Sewell, being a gentleman of the old school, was far too well-bred to wish to penetrate the little secrets of the young men in his office, and withdrew with a smile.

I will confess to my shame that I did not resume reading the *Coutume de Paris* until I had finished the *Ruines* of Citizen Volney. I am also constrained to admit, with the candour of a man making a full confession, that I occasionally experienced a certain thrill on reading doctrines that were so new to me and so boldly put forward. What a terrible leveler was Volney! He assembled the doctors, ministers, and priests of all the creeds in the universe, set them against each other, overturned their arguments and doctrines, and made mincemeat of all the religions of the known world. Only Jehovah, fortunately reinstated by Robespierre, found favour in his eyes.

You democratic philosophers are ungrateful wretches, always calumniating the nobility, unmindful of Monsieur *de* Volney, who made things easy for you by destroying all creeds that might have denied you freedom of conscience! You don't appreciate Monsieur *de* Robespierre, who reinstated the good Lord to prevent you from cutting each other's throats. Be it known that these two men were of noble extraction, if one may credit their own statements, and that you ought to respect the class from which they sprang. True, certain simpletons with pedigrees a mile long have repudiated them on the vain pretext that one sent their mothers, wives, and children to the guillotine, while the other, by sabotaging the foundations of all religion, could plunge France once again into the horrors of a new revolution. [2]

Napoleon I had the good taste to approve Chateaubriand's *Le Génie du christianisme*, which leads me to suppose that, had Volney not had claims to favour other than his *Ruines*, the great man would have passed him over.

As you know, Volney visited our hemisphere, and he even took a short trip on Lake Erie in the same boat as Madame Dupéron Baby, [3] my wife's grandmother. I regret to say that this good lady didn't find the French philosopher's company much to her liking, for although he hadn't yet published *Les Ruines*, he nonetheless tried to destroy the faith of his fellow travelers by his derisive remarks. He kept up a stream of biting sarcasm directed against the Catholic religion and all Christian denominations.

Coming up to Madame Baby, who was occupied in reading some spiritual work, he unabashedly offered her a book drawn from his pocket, telling her she would find it much more amusing than the one she was reading.

"I'm not reading this book to amuse myself," snapped the lady. "I'm praying God to preserve us from all perils during this often dangerous journey."

"You're afraid to die, no doubt," replied Volney with a snicker. "Such a fear is very natural to your sex."

During the night a fierce storm arose, the kind that the most intrepid sailor fears more on our lakes than on the ocean itself, the waves being much choppier. Madame Baby calmly set about saying her rosary, whereas Citizen Volney exhibited a terror that many shared without giving such manifest signs.

The storm only abated after twenty-four hours, spreading joy to the crew and passengers and calm to the soul of the philosopher. When Madame Baby saw Volney recovered from his terror, she said to him, "I'm surprised that a great philosopher like you should have shown more fear of death than the Christian woman whom you mocked."

A philosopher is never at a loss for an answer, and Volney replied emphatically, "Madame, I don't fear death at all personally. However, I have a great mission to accomplish: that of spreading the light to blind humans! Once this task has been completed, I shall be prepared to enter into a state of nothingness."

This scene was often repeated to me by Madame Baby and by one of her sons who was a passenger on the same ship, the late Honourable Jacques Dupéron Baby, father of Eliza-Anne Baby, widow of the late Honourable Charles E. Casgrain.[F]

A young man just out of school usually reads modern philosophers more out of curiosity than anything else, unaware of the dangers to which his faith is exposed. This was not the case with the man I'm about to describe, who went about it deliberately. This scene took place several years after I had left the seminary.

The Quebec library[G] contained a complete collection of the works of modern philosophers. A pupil from the seminary who had just finished his philosophy course went up to the librarian. This philosopher was a pale, thin young man with a rather dazed expression. His scalp was bald in spots as a result of various cruel maladies, and on his shoulders fell the few dead hairs that had managed to grow.

The librarian, wishing to make sure that this walking spectre possessed the precious gift of speech, asked if he might be of service.

"Aren't you the one, Monsieur, who lends books that corrupt youth?" said the young man, scratching his head.

"There are certainly books such as you desire here," replied the librarian. "But since every privilege has its price, even that of losing one's soul, you must first pay a guinea subscription in order to enjoy the inestimable advantage you seek."

The petitioner, no doubt already endowed with exalted notions of democracy, went out muttering against aristocrats and rich men, who alone had the privilege of perverting their minds, while the poor populace was obliged to vegetate in lifelong innocence.

I have already said that, when entering the great world, I was neither smarter nor more of an ass than other young men, although I must admit I made a very poor showing in the study of the English criminal code.[H] While my friends praised our jury system to the skies, I considered it absurd, and to my shame I will confess that I haven't altered my opinion at the age of seventy-nine—far from it.

"That's because you don't understand this magnificent system!" said my friends, to which I replied, "I admit in all humility that I'm quite in the dark."

They shook their heads pityingly, the meaning of which was that Master de Gaspé's understanding was deficient. I was piqued.

One day I said to them, "I know as well as you fellows do that twelve jurymen are put in a box and made to swear they'll give a verdict based on the evidence they're about to hear, and that this verdict isn't accepted unless the twelve jurymen are unanimous. If they aren't, the presiding judge, a man always well versed in the science of arithmetic and who knows that twelve minus one equals eleven, orders the court clerk to tell one of the jurors to leave the box. Exit the juror, as humiliated and embarrassed as if he'd committed a crime. After this expulsion, the judge orders the said clerk to count the said jurymen. This functionary does as he is asked, turns to face the court, throws wide his arms with an air of consternation, and says that there are, alas! only eleven left of those who answered the summons. At this the judge says, 'Send them away; the court is incomplete.'"

"Look at Gaspé trying to be witty," said Plamondon. "The young man promises well."

Plamondon's barbs spared his friends no less than his enemies. Having raised a laugh, he added seriously, "My friend, you'll never make me believe that you don't understand this admirable system. You frequently contradict us for the pleasure of argument."

"Yes," I replied, "for the pleasure of letting your wit shine forth, so that I can appropriate a few shreds for my own use if necessary."

"Oho!" cried Plamondon, "As to that. . . ."

Court went into session, putting an end to our banter. A man charged with grand larceny was in the dock. The jury was formed and the preliminary hearing began.

"What an admirable system!" exclaimed Vallière. "The accused won't be judged by these haughty men covered in ermine, but by his peers. He is a man of the people, and will be judged by his equals."

"Talk lower, my dear friend," I told him. "You might be overheard by the jurymen, who would scarcely appreciate the compliment. What! That miserable C——, who has already been condemned to the gallows four times, the peer of these respectable men who sit over him?"

246

I should point out that in the good old days petty jurors were as respectable as any other class of citizen in Quebec. Some of them were small landowners or property-holders, and all were master craftsmen or of a similar level.

Vallière shook his head without answering, so I continued.

"If this criminal and the five or six ragged scoundrels awaiting trial after him are not the jurymen's peers (and you must admit the latter are rarely found in the dock), then why can't they simply be tried before the three judges on the bench today? What's the use of a procedure whereby all power is taken from educated men and delegated to honest but ignorant ones?"

My English friends Green and Christie, who still hoped I might see the light, raised their eyes to heaven and exclaimed, "You'll understand this glorious system one day!" Their admiration prevented them from saying more on the subject.

"You know," interjected Plamondon, "or perhaps you don't, since you seem rather weak on the criminal code, my friend, that petty jurors decide only one very simple thing that anybody can grasp: whether the accused has or has not committed the offense with which he is charged, in accordance with the testimony heard by them. It's only a question of establishing the fact, and twelve men will do it with more certainty than the three judges who sit in criminal courts. As for legal questions, they fall exclusively within the competence of the bench."

"It's really too bad that points of law don't fall within the competence of petty jurors," I retorted. "No doubt it's an oversight on the part of the legislators. Never mind; much as I admire friend Plamondon's flashes of wit, my admiration knows no bounds when he begins to talk sense."

"It's always an advantage to talk sense occasionally—an advantage not shared by everybody, let it be noted," said Plamondon.

"Agreed," I said, "for the sake of novelty. But we're straying from the subject. What you've just said certainly seems more sensible than anything else I've heard in this respect. Let us suppose that fourteen entirely disinterested persons are eyewitnesses to some deed. Twelve of them report the facts one way and the other two give a different version. I would surely give more credit to twelve pairs of eyes than just two, provided all the witnesses were equally well placed. If this weren't the case, two witnesses might be right as against the other twelve. However, when it comes to moral qualities, judgment, or discernment, I humbly submit that I would rather rely on the decision of two judges regarding testimony given in their presence and written down word for word by them, than on the verdict of fifty jurors who are no doubt honest, but uneducated. Anyway, if you need twelve men to pass judgment on a fact, why not name twelve judges? You'd only need to make their bench longer, after all, and then these seventy-five worthy jurors could go about their business. You would have served your country well."

"I take everything back!" exclaimed Plamondon. "Gaspé speaks with angel tongue. Twelve judges on the Quebec bench! What a glorious prospect for the bar!"

Let us return, however, to Master C——, whom I have left in the clutches of judges and jurymen. He'll be condemned to death, but don't let that worry you. It's only the fifth time this minor inconvenience has befallen him. He'll have the pleasure of hearing three similar sentences pronounced over him without being any the less alive, and will finish his days peacefully in Botany Bay. How did it happen that, at a time when three or four people were hanged regularly each year for grand larceny, he escaped the gallows? I simply cannot understand. It was never C——'s turn. His confessor prepared him for death six or seven times, without curing him of his propensity for larceny. He cannot have repented of much, being under the impression that a man called Joseph could not die by the rope—a somewhat excessive show of confidence in his patron saint. C—— was not a bad man, and if he had been left alone would have led a happy, tranquil life in the midst of his fellow citizens, of whom he was only mildly critical.

Regularly every six months, he was tied to a post in the Upper Town marketplace in Quebec and whipped for stealing. But as the thief's skin had finally become as tough as a rhinoceros's hide, he underwent this punishment in a fairly stoic manner, although I did one day hear him complain somewhat bitterly of man's injustice to man.

Seeing that the whipping post had no effect, the court ventured to condemn him to being whipped on the corner of certain streets, his hands tied behind a horse-drawn cart.

It was cold. The unfortunate fellow was naked to the waist and the blows were doubly painful. When the cat-o'-nine-tails, as the English call it, came down harder than usual, he spoke with feeling eloquence.

248

"Why do they mistreat me like this, when I haven't harmed anyone?" C—— was already a communist!

A sad though slightly comic scene took place one day in criminal court, involving a poor young man who had been expelled from the British army and who subsequently fell into a deplorably degraded state. He had just been convicted of stealing a silver piece from the counter of an inn. The clerk, as was usual, asked him whether he had anything to say against the death sentence that the court was about to pronounce.

"Beg for benefit of clergy!" cried those present.

The criminal was about to kneel, as was customary when begging a privilege granted under the criminal code in certain cases of grand larceny. This privilege would save his life.

His lawyer, Justin McCarthy, cried, "You are a British subject! You have worn the uniform of an officer of His Britannic Majesty! It would be a disgrace to humble yourself like this!"

Heeding this wise counsel, the criminal declared that he claimed no privilege.

"Make proclamation!" said the chief justice.

The sheriff's officer thereupon pronounced in solemn tones, "Oyez! Oyez! Oyez! Silence in the court while His Honour the Chief Justice passes sentence of death upon the prisoner. God save the king."

"On your knees! On your knees!" shouted the people. "Ask for benefit of clergy!"

"No! No!" cried McCarthy. "Remember that you are a British subject!"

The criminal judged it advisable to take advantage of the privilege accorded him by law at this rather critical stage in the proceedings. He knelt and claimed benefit of clergy.

"Take it," said Chief Justice Sewell. "The law grants it because you claim it, and we have not the right to refuse you."

As he spoke these words, the eminent judge's voice held a note of scorn mingled with compassion that left a strong impression on those present.

There was something hideous in the sight of a young man, doubtless of good family, perhaps a brave soldier before vice had degraded him, groveling to implore a few days' grace for his dissolute and miserable life.

249

Judge Sewell often told me that he found sitting in civil courts diverting and relaxing, but that presiding over a criminal court was torment.

I was present when he pronounced his first death sentence shortly after being named to the bench. The criminal, convicted of murdering his wife, was called James Craig.

Dusk was falling, and deep silence reigned in court. The clerk, as was customary, asked the criminal if he had anything to say against the sentence of death. The unfortunate man said nothing.

"Make proclamation!" said the chief justice, in a voice trembling with emotion. The solemn words of the court officer, as he commanded total silence while the terrible sentence was delivered, sent a shiver through the audience. The criminal, as we shall soon see, deserved the sympathy accorded him.

The chief justice was only able to pronounce the two words "James Craig." Covering his face with his hands, he pressed his head against his desk and burst into tears. Everything conspired to affect the minds and hearts of those present: the semidarkness, making it difficult to distinguish the features of the murderer, as still as the statue of death; the judge's breakdown; and the half-stifled sighs of sensitive souls.

Craig was executed despite efforts to save him.

He was a soldier in the artillery, a respectable man of good character, sober and thrifty, whereas his wife was a drunkard and a spendthrift. One evening, when he had come home carrying a bag of money, his drunken wife began to shout abuse. On an angry impulse he threw the ill-fated bag of money at her head and killed her outright.

Nowadays the man would only have been found guilty of manslaughter, but so great was the respect for human life, to which men apparently clung more closely than than they do now, that the wretched fellow was found guilty of murder in the first degree.

This took place during Sir James Craig's administration, and some people thought he would be loth to allow a man bearing the same name to die on the gallows. But the governor did for his namesake what he would have done for any other criminal in similar circumstances: he submitted the condemned man's request and the trial dossier to all the judges in the province, and in view of their unfavourable report refused pardon.

Some lawyers criticized Chief Justice Sewell's conduct in certain criminal cases, but the more I think about it the more I approve it.

L'HONORABLE JUGE JONATHAN SEWELL

Chief Justice Jonathan Sewell, a Loyalist, was not popular with French Canadians as a public figure. In private, he was a generous host and indulgent master to articling law students like de Gaspé. From P.-G. Roy. *Les Juges de la Province de Québec (1933)*

I feel that a judge has as great a duty to prevent crime and keep it from spreading, as he has to punish the guilty.

The wife of a respectable workman was accused by her neighbour of having stolen a pair of shoes. I can still see this poor young woman exposed on the criminals' bench, her colour coming and going under the stares of the spectators. The proof against her was overwhelming. Before reading his notes on the testimony, the chief justice, in a most eloquent speech, made a point of warning the jurymen of the danger to public morals in allowing crime to escape from the class where it is customary into another class of society that is free of it.

"Gentlemen," he added, "let us leave crime in its disgusting abode, and let us not allow it to infect respectable classes."

He then read the testimony, and, availing himself of some minor contradiction, acquitted the prisoner, to the great satisfaction of the spectators. On the same principle, two young men must have been grateful to Judge Sewell for his indulgence, which allowed them to resume a rank in society that they had the good sense never to forsake again. If these young men had been judged according to the strict letter of the law, they would in all probability have gone to swell the number of incorrigible criminals instead of becoming respectable citizens.

A criminal trial that took place before this period only confirmed my opinion of the jury system. A cold-blooded murder had been committed without any provocation in broad daylight in front of fifty witnesses. The evidence for murder was so clear, so positive, and so overwhelming that everyone must have thought the jurymen would give their verdict without leaving the courtroom. Great was the surprise of all, therefore, when at the end of ten minutes they asked to retire to another room in order to deliberate. At that time the jury used to be put in a room deemed "comfortable," but without anything to eat or drink, and without fire or candle, until they had agreed on the verdict. It was only after three days, weakened by fasting, that they reappeared in court to declare that the man in the dock was not guilty of the crime of which he was accused.

I can certify that eleven of the twelve jurymen who gave this verdict were honest and respectable men, but it became known that the twelfth, having successfully deceived the sheriff by some manoeuvre, got his name on the list of jurymen with which this functionary supplied the court. When he reached the room where the jury was confined,

252

he lay down on a bench, telling his fellow jurors that he would take no part in the deliberations, as he had made up his mind to acquit the prisoner. It was even said that he had enough food with him to outlast the others, so that he suffered not at all.

I know that the present generation will find nothing extraordinary in what I have just recounted. Hardly a session of the criminal court passes without the public witnessing similar denials of justice, these being applauded by the friends and partisans of the wrongdoers. Such was not the case regarding the murder just cited. The majority of the public were vehement in their opinion that the eleven jurymen should have died of hunger rather than bring in a verdict that ran counter to their conscience.

In the last four or five years I have been too disgusted to attend the criminal assizes. I was filled wth indignation on detecting signs of intelligence pass between jurymen and criminals, and on seeing the guilty escape justice because of sympathy accorded race or religion.[1] Would such shameful scenes take place but for the infamous jury system? A remedy has been found for the former blatant abuse of justice in our appeal courts, where the chief justices of the District of Quebec used to overturn two thirds of the judgments handed down by the chief justices of the District of Montreal and vice versa. Yet the matters involved were petty compared to the protection of our citizens' lives! But who would dare touch our admirable jury system! When I have occasion to complain about this deplorable state of affairs in the presence of educated people, they cannot deny what they have seen with their own eyes, yet they still go into ecstasies about the glorious system that regulates us. Common sense is an even rarer commodity than I thought! Egoism isn't only the foible of misanthropes.

As little as twenty years ago, people were astonished to read of the crimes committed in New Orleans. They could hardly credit that it was dangerous for a law-abiding citizen to go about without a dagger, even in daylight. Today no one is in the least surprised. A great many people are knifed, but the assassin can trust the jury to absolve him! Perhaps within ten years the citizens of Canada's large cities will hang daggers around their necks like watch chains, and keep revolvers wrapped up in their pocket-handkerchiefs.[4]

Men are curious beings. Why don't naturalists carry out more intensive physiological studies of the human species, instead of in-

253

specting the manners and morals of insects? Let a robbery, killing, or murder take place, and everyone cries, "Where were the police?" Well, gentlemen, the police were where they would normally be: at the posts assigned them. A policeman on duty in the Rue Saint-Louis can hardly prevent a murder in the Rue Saint-George. Instead of placing the blame on these men, let it fall on your own heads. Say your *meâ culpâ* for not having obliged your aldermen to double or triple the police force. You all agree that the number of policemen is insufficient, and yet you continue to point the finger! What citizen would refuse to contribute the funds necessary to protect his life and property?

Forty years ago, watchmen looked after the citizens' security. What a feeling of well-being, comfort, and security was ours when the watchman announced the hour of night beneath our windows! We could hear him sing out, "Past one o'clock, and a starlight morning," and so on. With what snug ease did we slip back into a slumber momentarily broken by his voice! We could sleep in peace: a friend watched over us and our property. But this policing system was too perfect. Our magistrates and pious aldermen no doubt felt that man was not put on earth for his own pleasure and that a little tribulation was needed for the good of his soul, so they abolished the night watchmen.

An unprejudiced Englishman, one of those rare people who do not visit other countries for the sake of making comparisons to England's advantage, said to me one day, "After all, a man doesn't feel free, independent, and perfectly safe except when surrounded by policemen as he is on the Continent."

CHAPTER ELEVEN

Among the contemporaries of my youth I count Major Pierre LaForce. [A] Although older than myself and the others whom I have described, this likable gentleman seemed perennially young. The major's sense of fun enlivened our young bachelor parties, and the festivities would have been incomplete without him. He had a rare talent for perpetrating a variety of hoaxes, as well as the "knack"[1] of imitating German and various Indian dialects cleverly enough to fool either a German or an Indian.

I was in my office one day talking with my friends LaForce, Vallière, Plamondon, and LeBlond, when in came a German bailiff called Nupert. LaForce, who was seated near me, turned his back to the newcomer. The bailiff reported on a writ that I had given him to execute, and I began to take him to task for some of his blunders. He was attempting to excuse himself as best he could when LaForce turned slightly and started to mutter something ill-humoured in his bogus German. Nupert came to a dead stop, shot a malevolent glance at the major, and continued his defense. LaForce raised his voice as he talked, turned to face Nupert directly, and kept up the harangue while staring wrathfully at him. Nupert, the worst-tempered German I have ever known, flew into a rage and retorted in his native tongue. Both were talking at once, gesticulating like soap-box orators. No comic opera could have amused the spectators more. The fury, real on one side and simulated on the other, was at its height when I ordered my bailiff to be quiet. He obeyed grudgingly.

"Monsieur," he said, "*you* have the right to criticize me for not performing my duties, but I have no intention of being abused by all the gentlemen who pass through your office."

The bailiff's error cost me a few piastres, but I didn't regret it for a moment. I had a good laugh for my money, and so did my friends.

The Chevalier Robert Destimauville[B] spoke German fluently, as he had served in the Prussian armies. We told him one day that our friend the major, who was present, was equally fluent. The chevalier immediately opened fire, and LaForce responded with a long tirade, all the while maintaining an icy seriousness.

"You speak a very corrupt German, Monsieur, the language of Lower Saxony," said the chevalier. "Upon my word, you wouldn't be understood at the court of Berlin."

"I'm sure of it," replied the major humbly. "I studied this fine language a little in Lower Saxony, but in no other part of Germany."

The Chevalier Destimauville took a very dim view of this hoax, once he found out about it. As for the numerous other Germans who fell victim to the major's comic imitation of their language, the less said the better.

Of all those whom the late Mr. Andrew Stuart[C] invited to dine at his country place in Jeune Lorette forty-six years ago, only two remain: my worthy fellow citizen, Monsieur Barthélemy Faribault, and the author of these memoirs. Yet, even as they reflect on this delightful party where such witty and exuberant men gathered, they bow their heads sadly at the thought that today death has spared only them. Thirteen guests took their places at the hospitable board of our eminent friend: Messrs. Nelson, Planté, LaForce, Vallière, John Ross, Juchereau Duchesnay, Plamondon, Moquin, LeBlond, Faribault, two great chiefs of the Huron tribe, and myself. Mr. Stuart had invited these two Indians, the only pure-blooded savages in the village of Lorette, because he was an honorary chief of this tribe, a distinction only accorded those who had rendered great services.

For the occasion the chiefs had donned their magnificent Indian costume. It consisted of a short tunic of the finest blue woolen broadcloth, with silver bands decorating the sleeves from below the shoulder to the elbow, gaiters[D] of the brightest scarlet, deerskin shoes richly ornamented with porcupine quills, a varicoloured silk shirt open to show the chest and heavy with silver medals, one of which bore the likeness of King George III, and finally a beaver hat garnished with splendid plumes. To complete their costume, each had two silver circlets for earrings, four inches in diameter, hanging down to their shoulders. The bearing of the Hurons throughout the meal contrasted with our own as much as their dress. Amid our joyous revels they remained cold and impassive. Not a smile crossed their lips. Although it was not the custom then, as it is now, to make tedious speeches at dessert, our host requested Plamondon to deliver a parliamentary discourse. We were particularly fond of this type of fare from our witty, trenchant friend, and we knew beforehand all who were to be roasted.

Plamondon rose, and with a pronounced Gascon accent said, "Mr. Speaker, I'm going to talk to you this evening about the Constitution of and which we have the happiness to live under," and continued in this vein, delivering the most quaintly farcical oration ever to gladden the reveler's heart. After this tribute to the shade of a departed member of the provincial parliament, whose memory was still fresh among us, he requested permission to answer the learned discourse of the honorable member who had just spoken.

"God forbid, Mr. Speaker," Plamondon began in a nasal twang, "that, making the most of a classical education which many members of this honourable house have not been fortunate enough to receive, God forbid, say I, that, fortified by the extensive studies in which I have engaged since childhood, I should, by sophistical argumentation, undermine the religion of honourable members less favoured than I in this regard, etc., etc., etc."

Plamondon sat down amid the laughter and applause of all the guests.

LaForce got up next and asked leave to propose a toast that everyone, he was sure, would welcome with pleasure: to our two friends, the Huron chiefs. He began in French with a eulogy of this tribe's warriors, who had rendered so many services to their French and English allies before and after the Conquest. Then, addressing the great chief in Indian dialect, or so it seemed to us, he delivered a speech of some twenty minutes' length, resounding with consonants harsh enough to split the strongest ear-drums. The two chiefs listened attentively, only breaking the silence to utter their "Hoa!"—a sign of admiration and approval.

Mr. Stuart appeared uneasy when the major launched into the Indian tongue, although I was probably the only one to notice it. A fleeting shadow passed over his face, but he knew that his guests were true gentlemen, too well bred to lack the consideration due to those whom he had admitted to his table. We all listened to LaForce's speech without moving a muscle, and gave not the slightest indication of sharing the joke. Then we drank the redskins' health with "Hip, hip, hurrahs!" enthusiastic enough to satisfy their sense of dignity.

At this point one of the chiefs spoke in Huron, making what I suppose was a lengthy speech of thanks addressed to the major. One of us called on him to give his opinion of LaForce's contribution, to which he replied the major spoke great and beautiful words, but in a branch of their tongue—Iroquois, I think—that they, the Hurons of Lorette, barely understood.

One day we were visiting one of the waxworks collections that the Americans used to exhibit frequently in the towns of Lower Canada. Major LaForce, seeing three or four habitants come in, grabbed a nearby chair and sat down between Washington and some other personage who figured in the collection. There, immobile, with eyes staring fixedly like the automatons around him, he awaited the rustics. It must be admitted that his pale countenance lent itself admirably to the illusion. Little did we know what was to follow, thinking it just a bit of tomfoolery. We gathered around the new arrivals when they stopped in front of our friend, whom they contemplated in silence for quite some time.

"My, my!" said one. "Wouldn't you say he was a real Christian who'd just passed over?"

To verify this assertion, he reached out a hand to feel the face. But, O horror! as his hand came near the mummy's mouth, the latter snapped at his forefinger and almost bit the end off. Blood spurted, and Jean-Baptiste, his hair standing on end, shook his fingers frantically. The major, meanwhile, resumed his original position.

The objects on view in the museum were hardly calculated to calm the terrified rustics. In one corner of the room was a Goliath of Geth, armed to the teeth, his head touching the ceiling. He was indeed a hideous spectacle. Black blood gushed from a wound in the giant's forehead where a large pebble from David's sling had struck, and the eyes of the expiring monster registered a painted fury ghastly to behold.

In the middle of the room, General Hamilton fell mortally wounded in the arms of his friend, his chest pierced by a bullet and his mouth

258

bleeding. His adversary Burr, scowling fiercely, held the murder weapon.

Further on, old General Soworow[E] of Russia lay in state. At first he was prone, but, as the goggling spectators looked on, he slowly sat up. This was too much for the habitants.

"Let's get out of here, my friends!" cried one. "Can't you see that all these English inventions are just worked by springs?"

"Yes, yes!" said Gabriel as he staunched the blood from his well-nigh severed finger with a cotton handkerchief. "Yes indeed! Let's get out of here!"

Would that I possessed our friend Major LaForce's gift for comedy or "humour,"[2] in order to recount at least one of the many tales that kept us in stitches for a whole evening at a time. Even a faithful rendition of his exact words lacks something of the narrator's comic verve. Let him speak for himself, however.

"I used to spend a lot of time primping when I was young, being especially partial to the powder that men wore then, and on which I laid out a considerable amount of money. I never went out in the morning unless greased and pomaded like an Eskimo, with my head whitened and curled like a cauliflower. Add to my adornment a shirt-frill six inches wide, starched and pleated like Madame Nadeau's coifs, descending unchallenged from my chin to the bottom button of my jacket, and you will have a pretty fair idea of the appearance of an old-time dandy of sixteen named LaForce.

"Well, one morning on the way to my office I met young C——, who, being very dirty and untidy himself, never missed an opportunity of making a few sarcastic remarks about my toilet. I was not disposed to suffer his jibes that day. My father—who detested dandies and was himself always decently but simply dressed—had just compared me to Jupiter descending from Olympus as he spied me issuing forth from the house in all my glory.

"As I said, I was in no mood to endure the taunts of C——, the most insolent young man in Quebec, and I gave as good as I got and more on the subject of his unkempt appearance. He was distinctly lacking in forbearance, and punched me in the face by way of answer. I was sixteen, and he was at least nineteen. He was taller than I, and took advantage of his height to aim at my highly offensive and luckless head. In the sweltering July heat I was instantly covered

259

with powder and pomade from head to foot, looking very much like a rat that had jumped from an oil barrel into a flour bin.

"This took place on a busy street in the Lower Town, and a circle of onlookers gathered around us in no time, each one urging on the combattant of his choice. Only moral fortitude enabled me to hold out against an athlete older and taller than myself, while fighting off streams of powder and pomade that progressively blinded me at every blow received and returned. Sheer willpower, as I said, kept me on my feet until five or six sailors from a frigate came to my aid— perhaps because I was the smaller of the two, or, as is more likely, because they took me for a hairdresser with my powder-and-pomade coating, and were not loth to see me thrash a gentleman.

"The error was quite understandable, because in those days every gentleman was shaved and had his hair dressed by a *perruquier*. One saw them going about their business every morning, their clothes covered not only with powder, but with numerous pomade stains.

"'Well done, little barber!' shouted the sailors. 'Giv'im a proper thrashing!'

"My rage swelled at this misunderstanding, so humiliating to a dandy and a gentleman. At the same time, the sympathy of these brave sons of the sea gave me strength and courage, and after a desperate battle I was declared the winner. But, good God, in what condition!

"My first wish was to remove myself as speedily as possible from the public gaze, hoping to get home without my father seeing me. But I had reckoned without my allies from the frigate, who were too proud of my triumph to part with me so promptly. The wretches accompanied me to my doorstep with cries of 'Hurrah for the little barber!'

"Their infernal racket brought everyone to the windows, and one of the first people I saw was my father, seething with rage at the sight of his dear son's triumph. The ovation he gave me was somewhat different from that of my friendly tars, I can assure you."

The blood of heroes ran in the veins of Major LaForce. His paternal uncle had distinguished himself in many military exploits before the Conquest, as Canadian annals show. His father was one of the most heroic defenders of Quebec during the two seiges of 1759 and 1775. His mother, too, was a woman of fervent patriotic sentiment. If, during these two sieges, she heard the alarm sound when her husband had

260

been overcome by exhaustion, she would immediately rouse him, bringing him his weapons with the cry, "Hurry up, LaForce! We'd be disgraced if you weren't the first on the ramparts!"

This story was told me by two of my uncles who were also within the walls of Quebec during the two sieges.

Major LaForce was criticized for being a hothead, in the wake of several encounters in which he dealt roundly with his adversaries. It is my belief that he must have been provoked beyond measure, for I have never known anyone so easy to get along with.

Although as loyal to the British Crown as he was sincere and devoted in his love for his homeland, this light-hearted and witty man nearly perished under the tyranny of the government during the administration of Sir James Craig. While Bédard, Blanchette, Taschereau, and others,[F] loyal subjects as well as distinguished patriots, were jailed March 17, 1810 at Quebec, LaForce was imprisoned in Montreal for his political opinions, and almost died in his cell as a result of maltreatment. Yet he was among the first to rush to the border in aid of his country when the War of 1812 against the Americans broke out. [3]

His firm and indomitable character earned him more bad treatment during his detention than any of the other patriots persecuted by the oligarchy, with the exception of Corbeille, who died a victim of his tormentors' cruelty. Major LaForce himself was at death's door, and owed his life to his iron will and strength of soul.

"As long as I wasn't ill," he used to tell us, "I kept up my spirits in that frightful hole. Having no books, ink, pen, or paper, I amused myself by drawing with charcoal on the cell walls, depicting everything that came into my head. My only light came from a small, barred window. One day I was sketching two field guns facing one another, with two cannon-balls in their mouths ready for firing. Underneath I had written the motto, *La force contre la force*. The jailer informed the authorities immediately, the result being a visit next day by two magistrates. These gentlemen were horrorstruck at the sight of the bellicose emblems. They looked at each other, shaking their heads in silence. Finally, they asked me what was the meaning of this threat.

"'What threat?' said I. 'Surely one doesn't have to be endowed with any special wisdom to understand my motto? What better than two loaded cannon facing one another to show LaForce against *la force?'*

"My scribbling with its ingenious motto earned me the increased severity of my tormentors," added Major LaForce, laughing. "No doubt they were afraid my artillery would blow up the prison."

Of all the victims of the tyranny wielded by the government of the period, Judge Bédard, then a lawyer, endured his captivity with the greatest fortitude. This disciple of the Stoic Zeno was always deeply occupied in study, and in his solitary confinement he could do what he liked best without fear of interruption. A practical man, thoroughly familiar with the British Constitution, he only communicated with the authorities to ask of what crime he was accused, and to request them to bring him to judgment if there were grounds for a criminal indictment. Those in power carefully avoided bringing him to trial, however, for he was no more guilty of treason or seditious practices than I am of wishing to usurp the Pope's triple crown. I think it was after a year's imprisonment that he was told he was free to go.

"I'll not leave this place until a jury has declared me well and truly innocent," retorted Monsieur Bédard.

The authorities left him alone for some ten days, hoping to wear down his resistance, but at the end of this time the jailer informed him that he had orders to throw the prisoner out if he didn't leave of his own accord the next day. Monsieur Bédard shrugged and went back to his algebraic calculations. Like several members of his family, he was an accomplished mathematician.

The following day the jailer waited until one o'clock, but as his prisoner made no move to leave, he told him that if he didn't remove himself voluntarily, he would put him out with the help of the turnkeys. Monsieur Bédard realized the jailer meant what he said and that there was no resisting brute force. "Well, Monsieur, at least allow me to finish my problem," he said. Reid, the jailer, found this request so reasonable that he agreed without demur. At the end of an hour Monsieur Bédard, satisfied with the solution to his geometric problem, walked slowly home.

When Sir George Prevost took over the government of this colony before the War of 1812, his first concern was to see justice done to the victims of his predecessor's tyranny. Messrs. Panet, Bédard, Taschereau, Borgia, Blanchette, LaForce, and other officers of the Canadian militia who had been dismissed by Governor Craig, were restored to their rank. The new governor also made it his business to repair the injustices of the previous administration as far as possible.

Fully confident of the loyalty of French Canadians during this war, Sir George Prevost entrusted the local militia with the protection of Quebec, where very few regulars remained. Captain Bédard was one of the most zealous among us, and although military duty was a new experience for a man of his years and habits, he acquitted himself with geometric precision.

The security and defense of the citadel were always entrusted to a captain, this officer traditionally keeping a liberal table, well supplied with excellent drinks that the officers doing the rounds never missed a chance of sampling, especially on the night watch. I was on duty atop the cape one cold night when Captain Bédard came to visit my post. The thermometer stood at 36 degrees Réaumur, not uncommon for January at that period.

My visitor was chilled through, and I urged him to go into my room in the guardhouse to get warm with the help of stimulants, but to no avail. I pointed out that British army officers, even majors and colonels, didn't consider it a breach of military discipline to accept a similar invitation. He remained inflexible, however, keeping to the strict letter of his orders, which enjoined him to do the rounds and nothing more.

The British army officers were somewhat amused by Captain Bédard's reports following guard duty, and used to claim that they contained a little bit of everything—French, Latin, even algebra—everything, that is, except English. His minor eccentricities were passed over indulgently, however, as the most cordial understanding existed between the officers of the regular army and the militia.

It would be intriguing now to look back at the reasons which induced the government of that earlier period to persecute such thoroughly respectable citizens. It is no secret that the grievances which motivated the oligarchy's severity arose from *Le Canadien*, the newspaper published by the patriots of the time to defend themselves from the venomous and abusive attacks in the English gazettes. The press, type, and other material used to print this paper were seized and deposited in the courthouse vaults by a detachment of soldiers commanded by a justice of the peace who was, I am obliged to admit, my father-in-law, Captain Thomas Allison, retired, of the 5th regiment of foot.[G]

The early issues of *Le Canadien*, from its inception until March 17, 1810, when it was seized by the government, would make fascinating reading today. It was maintained that several articles in the paper were aimed at arousing the populace, thereby constituting grounds for an accusation of seditious practices and for imprisoning publishers, owners, and contributors. Those least guilty in the eyes of the authorities, such as officers in the militia or men occupying some government post, were dismissed. Ah, yes! It would require a very special kind of research to uncover the crimes committed by so many loyal and respectable citizens of French origin, which resulted in such cruel persecution by the British government. I challenge the most dyed-in-the-wool Tory, provided he have some inkling of the British Constitution, to show me a single sentence in this paper that could have justified the stringency of the oligarchy under the Craig administration. May I pass for the biggest fool in Canada if he can.

The following instance of disinterested generosity, which occurred during this reign of terror, is too honourable for me to let pass unremarked.

Monsieur Joseph Planté, a member of the provincial assembly, inspector of crown lands, and clerk of the register of landed property, was dismissed for the same grievances as those just mentioned. Smarting under this unjust treatment, Planté, a great and loyal patriot, asked for and obtained an audience with Sir James Craig himself. He pleaded his cause to such good effect that the governor, who was perhaps not such a devil as he was painted, agreed that he was innocent. However, he added, it was too late: he had appointed Monsieur Olivier Perrault. Nevertheless, in the unlikely event of the new clerk's agreeing to submit his resignation, the governor would be ready to restore Monsieur Planté to his post. Monsieur Perrault came to the governor after an interview with Monsieur Planté. "Your Excellency," said he, "I gratefully accepted the post you offered, but I am loth to profit by another's misfortune. I therefore ask that Your Excellency kindly accept my resignation."

Sir James Craig, touched by an act of generosity that enabled him to repair an injustice, gave Monsieur Perrault[4] the praise he deserved and promised to compensate him at the first opportunity.

Truth had pierced the shadows that clouded the governor's soul, and it is to be regretted that other Canadians persecuted by the oligarchy did not follow Monsieur Planté's example. Craig, guided by his sound judgment and wide knowledge of the British Constitution, would probably have rendered them full justice.

GOVERNOR SIR JAMES HENRY CRAIG

In physical appearance Sir James Craig was short and fat, in spite of being in ill-health from the time he arrived in Canada. He had a most expressive face and must have been handsome in his youth. His piercing, falcon-like glance seemed to penetrate the innermost thoughts of those to whom he spoke in his harsh voice. In England he was called "the little king Craig" because he loved pomp and circumstance. He was considered a vain man, and it is true he was proud and haughty, but he had too much intelligence to be vain, for vanity is the trait of a fool.

I am going to make a judgment that will seem extraordinary in relation to a man whose memory is still odious to French Canadians after a lapse of fifty-four years. Although I was a very young man, my position in society brought me into contact with his friends and foes. I was constantly hearing the pros and cons of his character, and concluded that far from being tyrannical and wicked, Sir James was a good-hearted man, as I will show. I have it from a reputable source. My uncle, Charles de Lanaudière, saw Sir James Craig frequently and had known him in England and in Canada during the 1775 war. As a member of the legislative council and a high Tory if every there was one, my uncle had approved almost all the arbitrary steps taken by the oligarchy. Yet he told me the governor had said to him, shortly before leaving for Europe, "that he had been basely misled, and that if he had the chance to begin administering the colony again, he would act differently." Such an admission is not that of a wicked man.

How could someone so perceptive allow himself to be misled? This is what I find difficult to understand. His friends maintained that, having an army background, he had sinned through ignorance of the British Constitution. Nothing could be further from the truth. Sir James Craig was a distinguished man of letters in the British Army and considered to be one of its best writers. Furthermore, as a young man he had filled the post of judge-advocate in the army, which requires a more than passing acquaintance with English law. I know for a fact that he often presided over the Quebec court of appeal, and his comments were those of a man who possessed a legal knowledge rarely met with outside the bar. Someone once observed to him that Monsieur Borgia, who had pleaded before him that morning, was not naturally eloquent. "True," he replied, "but I think there are few lawyers in this colony so well-versed in Roman law." Sir James was not mistaken.

The governor was acting in good faith when he sanctioned the tyrannous measures proposed by his council, as proved by his actions as commander of the garrison. When Bédard, Blanchette, and the others were incarcerated, he believed the French Canadians were about to rebel. As of four o'clock in the afternoon he had doubled the guard at all vital posts in the city of Quebec and installed a detachment of men opposite the arsenal. He sent for the adjutant-general of the Canadian militia, my late Uncle Baby, to tell him that it would be advisable to mount guard over a small supply of some fifty militia guns stored in a building beside the bishop's palace, near the Prescott Gate.

"If Your Excellency has the slightest qualm about this store of arms, I myself will sleep there alone tonight," replied Monsieur Baby, then over seventy.

The general paled at this stinging reply and turned his back on the old man without a word. For the historical record, I should add that my worthy uncle, despite his cutting remark, nonetheless sanctioned the cruel measures of the executive council that evening, both by his presence and his signature. In his defense, let me say that it was difficult for an old man with a superficial knowledge of the English criminal code to withstand the arguments of the eminent legal experts on the council and of the chief justice who presided over it.

I have said that Sir James Craig was not a wicked man, and the proof is to be found in his famous proclamation of March 23, 1810, containing the following passages:

> It is boldly told you, that I mean to oppress you. Base and daring fabricators of falsehood, on what part or what act of my life do you found such an assertion? What do you know of me or my intentions? Canadians, ask of those to whom you formerly looked. . . .
> For what purpose should I oppress you? Is it to serve the King? Will that Monarch, who during fifty years. . . . will he, contrary to the whole tenor of a life of honor and virtue, now give orders to his servants to oppress his Canadian subjects? . . .

Is it for myself, then, that I should oppress you? For what should I oppress you? Is it from ambition? What can you give me? Is it for power? Alas! my good friends! with a life ebbing not slowly from its period, under the pressure of disease acquired in the service of my country, I look only to pass, what it may please God to suffer to remain of it, in the comfort of retirement among my friends. I remain among you only in obedience to the commands of my King. . . . Is it then for wealth that I would oppress you? Enquire of those . . . to the value of your country laid at my feet, I would prefer the consciousness of having, in a single instance, contributed to your happiness and prosperity.

These personal allusions to myself—These details, in any other case might be unbecoming and beneath me; but nothing can be unbecoming or beneath me that can tend to save you from the gulf of crime and calamity, into which guilty men would plunge you.[11]

Those who had pushed Sir James to acts of tyranny must have laughed in their sleeves to hear this outburst of sublime but harsh logic from an old soldier labouring beneath his infirmities, soon to die.

No! A dying man does not express himself thus, in a manner that bears the very imprint of truth, without being sincere.

It is regrettable, I repeat, that those slandered by their enemies did not, like Monsieur Planté, request an audience with the governor himself, for it is probable they would have obtained full justice.

The following anecdote is evidence that Sir James Craig was not an evil man, for I am among those who firmly believe that anyone capable of one of the noblest and most admirable sentiments, that of gratitude, cannot be a monster. On the contrary, he must have an excellent heart.

Shortly after his arrival in this colony, the governor made it his business to find out whether a habitant called Léveillé, from a Montreal parish that he named, was still alive. Receiving an affirmative answer from those sent to enquire, he had the man brought to him. Jean-Baptiste was quite amazed at getting such a message from a governor, but nevertheless complied with the order, or invitation. So it was that two men, who in the vigour of their youth, thirty-two years earlier, had met by chance for a moment on the soil of Canada, found themselves face to face in old age.

"Do you remember in the year 1775," asked Sir James Craig, "ferrying a young English officer, pursued by American soldiers, across the Saint Lawrence in a small canoe?"

"Oh, yes!" replied the habitant. "He was a handsome little officer, too, and paid me a good sum."

"Well, now!" said the governor. "I was the man to whom you rendered this service. I've never forgotten it. But for you I would have been captured by the enemy."

"If it was you, Governor," blurted out Jean-Baptiste, "you've obviously made the most of it, for you were pretty skinny then."

Sir James Craig laughed heartily at this outspoken comment and asked kindly after the habitant's affairs, which were not going well. He gave the order to buy the man a good farm, with implements and livestock, and made him a generous present of money, sending the habitant home as rich as he was poor before. Such an act of gratitude and generosity could not come from a man of evil character. It was the late Colonel Vassal[5] who witnessed this scene and described it to me.

I am indebted to my friend Major Lafleur for another anecdote that tends to prove Sir James Craig was not such a fiend as claimed, but rather that, in spite of his reputed haughtiness, all classes of society could get to see him.

One Bellehumeur, whom I knew well, requested an audience with Governor Craig and was immediately admitted by the aide-de-camp on duty. Bellehumeur was a tall old man of dignified and confident bearing.

"What is your name?" Sir James asked him. "And what do you want of me?"

"My name is Bellehumeur. I'm very old and unable to earn a living. I am asking Your Excellency to please find me a place among the invalids of the Hôpital-Général's hospice."

Sir James was struck by his martial bearing, and asked if he had served in the army.

"Excellency, I was a grenadier in the de Berry regiment at the time of the Conquest, and a plucky regiment it was, I'm proud to say! We were husky fellows, not afraid of anything!"

"You must have killed a few Englishmen, in that case?" commented Sir James.

"As many as I could, Excellency. A poor devil of a soldier does his best. Thank God I've nothing to reproach myself with on that score."

"What?" exclaimed the general, who was enjoying the scene. "You come to ask a favour of me—me, an Englishman—and you boast of not having killed as many of my countrymen as you'd have liked?"

"That's exactly why I'm here," retorted Bellehumeur. "If we'd killed more Englishmen, they wouldn't now be masters of this country, and the king of France would see to it that I was comfortable in my old age. In his absence, I appeal to Your Excellency, since you're in command here."

Sir James, after a lengthy chat with this unconventional old character, whose forthright army manners he found highly diverting, said in a benevolent tone, "Go to the hospice tomorrow, old man. The order for admission will be sent this very day."

The governor probably made ample provision for the old veteran, for he was very generous.

GOVERNOR CRAIG'S GARDEN PARTIES

In days gone by, a gentleman named George Brown led a life of pleasure in Quebec. (I suppose that, being a purebred Englishman and a London Cockney, he must have been called George.) One drank more champagne at one of his dinners—and I can vouch for it— than in a month at the Château Saint-Louis. This gentleman, being assured of support by those whom he'd entertained, took it into his head to ask the voters of this fair city to elect him as their representative to our provincial parliament. On the day of battle none of his friends failed to show up, despite taunts of "Champagne! Champagne!" from the populace at each vote registered in favor of the *bon vivant* candidate. After all, in view of the man's generosity, his friends were merely showing their gratitude.

I'm not quite sure where this fine preamble to Governor Craig's garden parties is leading me, except to say, in all sincerity, that if I speak well of him and have expressed an opinion counter to that of my French-Canadian friends, it is *not* because of the memory of the happy hours of my youth spent at the charming garden parties at Powell Place (now Spencer Wood),[1] Sir James's summer residence on the road to Cap-Rouge.

At half past eight on the morning of a fine summer's day in July, the cream of Quebec society set out from the city in response to the governor's invitation. I say a fine day, because for three years in a row the sun shone brilliantly on these delightful parties.

James Pattison Cockburn (1779-1847) caught the sylvan tranquillity of "Spencer Wood" in this 1830 sepia wash. Here, at Governor Craig's garden parties, de Gaspé danced and wandered beneath the trees with his bride-to-be. Musée du Séminaire de Québec, photo: Pierre Soulard, Pf 986.53

On reaching Powell Place, the guests got down from their carriages on the main highway and plunged into the forest, following a path that, after many twists and turns, led to a pretty country house with a prospect of the magnificent Saint Lawrence. The river seemed to spring into view between the bordering shrubs. Tables for four, six, or eight were arranged in front of the house on an immense platform of polished timber, later to be used as an open-air ballroom. As the guests arrived, they gathered in clusters to partake of an informal breakfast. Apart from the servants and an aide-de-camp who greeted the principal guests, the small groups of close friends were left undisturbed to consume this first meal of cold meats, butter, radishes, tea, and coffee. Those who had finished left to make room for others and rambled through the gardens and surrounding shrubbery. At ten, all the tables were removed and the guests waited expectantly for the next act. Indeed, the house, like the château in *Zémire et Azor*, seemed only to await a fairy wand to bring it to life. A few minutes passed, and then the main door opened to make way for "little king

"Most beautiful among the beautiful," writes de Gaspé of his wife, Suzanne Allison, who bore him thirteen children. Early photography captured this rare likeness of Mme. de Gaspé, who died Aug. 3, 1847, at the age of 53. Archives nationales du Québec (Initial collection) 0 3Q P 600 6

Craig," followed by his staff-officers in their colourful uniforms. At this moment an invisible orchestra, perched high in some poplars, played "God Save the King." Heads were bared, and every one stood silently listening to the national anthem of Great Britain.

The most distinguished guests hurried to pay their respects to the governor. Those who, for various reasons, were unable to dance sat on the verandah where the governor held state. An aide-de-camp cried, "Gentlemen, take your partners!" and the ball began.

Sixty years have passed since that day when I, a tireless dancer, went whirling down the set of thirty couples. My feet, today so heavy and dragging, hardly seemed to touch the ground then. All the young people who enlivened that distant feast now sleep in the silence of the tomb—even she, that most beautiful among the beautiful, who shared my joys and sorrows. It was on that same day, as she was led to the dance, that she first took the hand that was to lead her to Hymen's altar—she who has long since been swept away by the inexorable torrent of death that carries all before it.[6]

Such memories bring to mind the fine passage from Ossian:

> But why art thou sad, son of Fingal? why grows the cloud of thy soul? the sons of future years shall pass away: another race shall arise. The people are like the waves of the ocean; like the leaves of woody morven: they pass away in the rustling blast, and other leaves lift their green heads on high.[J]

Why do these dark clouds sadden my soul? The children of the next generation will pass away quickly enough, and another will spring up in its place. Men are like the waves of the ocean, like the numberless leaves in the thickets of my seigneurie. The raging autumn winds strip my woodlands, but other leaves as green will crown their heights. Why then be sad? Eighty-six children, grandchildren, and great-grandchildren will mourn the old oak laid low by the breath of God. And, should I find grace before the seat of my sovereign judge, should it be granted me to rejoin the angel of virtue who added beauty to the few happy days passed in this vale of so many sorrows, we will pray together for the many descendants we have left on earth.

My reader awaits me at the garden party, however, to which I now return. At half past two we were in the middle of one of the gayest quadrilles, perhaps "speed the plow," when the orchestra suddenly stopped playing. The dancers were immobilized, some with their arms akimbo, others with one foot in the air, trying to fathom the reason for this contretemps. The arrival of Monseigneur Plessis and Lord Bishop Mountain gave us the key to the enigma. An aide-de-camp had signaled the orchestra to be silent on seeing these two dignitaries of their respective churches approach. Dancing was over for the nonce, and would only resume with the departure of the two bishops. Sir James had established this etiquette out of respect for their holy office.

At three o'clock the sound of a cornet was heard from afar, and everyone followed the governor along a path cut through the virgin forest of Powell Place. Some indeed there were who, given the length of the promenade, began to think that Sir James intended to sharpen the appetites of those who hadn't been dancing. A turning in the path suddenly revealed an immense table beneath a leafy canopy, like an oasis conjured up by some beneficent hand. Monsieur Petit, the governor's chef, had surpassed himself for the occasion. Like Vatel,^K he would have stabbed himself through the heart had he not received measureless praise on the catering of this feast, for which his generous patron had made him responsible.

Nothing could have been finer or more splendid than the arrangements for this repast, not only in the eyes of native Canadians unaccustomed to such luxury, but to Europeans as well. As guests, we nevertheless laboured under a slight inconvenience, for we were unable to recognize a single dish, so distinguished was Monsieur Petit in the art of French cuisine.

The bishops departed about half an hour after dinner, and the dancing began again. It continued with ever increasing enthusiasm until the cruel mamas called their nymphs to order, having become anxious about certain sentimental promenades undertaken by their daughters between dances, after Phoebus had disappeared from the sky. Not for them the threats or brandished spears of the goddess Calypso; instead, the mamas called irascibly to their charges, or so it seemed to the youthful cavaliers. By nine o'clock everyone was again within the city walls of Quebec.

A word about Monsieur Petit, one of the most jovial and likable Frenchmen I've ever known. Before leaving for Europe, his benevolent patron gave him the funds needed to set up a well-appointed hotel. Monsieur Petit met with the fate common to all those who tried similar ventures at that time, and he was obliged to seek his fortune in Upper

Canada after two or three years. Not many travelers visited Quebec then, even during the summer. Unless some unavoidable business demanded it, few cared to cover the hundreds of miles in ill-made calèches at a speed that could not exceed two leagues per hour, in accordance with the regulations laid down by law for the benefit of post-horse keepers. These privileged functionaries kept only the number of horses absolutely necessary for farming their land.

A traveler would arrive at a postmaster's house and ask for means of transportation.

"You'll have it in a minute," says the mistress of the house. "My husband's plowing with the horses just a step away. My little boy will run and fetch one. Won't you kindly sit down, Monsieur, and smoke a bit while waiting?"

To smoke was a synomym for having a rest or lingering awhile. The traveler waits half an hour, looks ever and anon out of the window, and finally waxes impatient.

"Is your little boy going to bring that horse, or has he gone to the back of beyond to look for it?"

"Oh, no, my fine sir!" exclaims Josephte.[7] "It's not at all far, only a short half league to the end of our land."

Sometimes the horses aren't plowing, but are out to pasture instead, or off in the woods somewhere. Not having much faith in the polite treatment that awaits them once the bit is in their mouths, they surrender only after the fiercest of battles that sometimes lasts for hours on end. The traveler hopes the driver will make up for lost time, but in vain. He tries everything; cajoling and criticism are equally useless. Jean-Baptiste remains unmoved, and never varies his response.

"Ah, Monsieur, my horse is a real fine animal. You've got to keep both hands on the reins to hold her in. She's the best trotter in the parish, but when she's pulling travelers she never goes faster than the legal rate."[1]

The reader can readily appreciate that nobody traveled for pleasure sixty years ago. In those days, people took their time about everything. No one was in a hurry, not even the courier responsible for the government mailbags, as the following demonstrates.

About four in the afternoon of December 31, I encountered one Séguin in the Rue de la Fabrique, ready to leave for Montreal with letters and dispatches. On coming out of high mass at the cathedral

274

the following day, January 1, I came face to face with the same individual. I gave a start, thinking it must be his ghost. I was soon reassured, however.

"A happy New Year to you," said Monsieur Séguin. "May you have as many as there are lady-apples in Normandy."

"The same to you," said I, "and may you have prosperity in this world and paradise in the next.

"And now, Monsieur Séguin," I continued, "how is it that I saw you on your way to Montreal with the mail last night, and find you here this morning?"

"It's very simple," he replied. "The weather got so bad by the time I'd reached Ancienne Lorette that I said to myself, it's crazy to travel in such weather; the news in my mailbag won't get mouldy by waiting a day or two! I came back here to bed, so that I could wish my friends a happy New Year this morning. Well, a happy New Year to you again."

Since Monsieur Séguin, a worthy man if ever there was one, kept his job almost until the day he died, I must conclude that his superiors didn't find fault with him—or perhaps no one even noticed the mail was a day or two late. People simply took their time about everything, and American "go ahead" was a dead letter with us.

At that time there was no post office between Quebec and Trois-Rivières. Here is how we managed in the country.

"Don't forget to make supper for Séguin," my Uncle de Lanaudière used to say to a servant in the evening. He was seigneur of Sainte-Anne de la Pérade.

Séguin would arrive after dark at the manor house, where the doors stayed open all night. He would eat supper at his ease, then take from his pouch any letters addressed to the family, and the occasional newspaper. After placing them on a table, he would continue on his way.

But I digress, as is my wont. Let us return to the subject of the scarcity of travelers at this period. "Didn't you at least have boats for summer traveling?" you ask. Yes indeed, and if the headwind weren't too strong, they could even go from Montreal to Quebec in three or four days. However, the great difficulty was to go upriver, not down. A schooner in a headwind took a fortnight on the average, and very often a month or more.

275

This reminds me of my first trip from Quebec to Montreal in a steamboat. At eleven o'clock at night in October of the year 1818, the *Caledonia*, on which I had taken passage, cleared the Quai de la Reine. About seven or eight o'clock the following morning, my traveling companion, the late Robert Christie, opened the window of his cabin and called to me, "We are going famously." We were in fact opposite Pointe-aux-Trembles, pushed by a howling tailwind, and had covered seven leagues in nine hours. We arrived at the foot of the current^M in Montreal at the end of the third day, congratulating ourselves on the speed of steam travel. Our satisfaction was in no way diminished by the fact that the ship had to use power equivalent to forty-two oxen to overcome this current, in the absence of the favourable wind that had lasted only twenty-four hours. The *Caledonia* was something of a tub, I must admit, as were most steamboats built in those days. She was a first-rate tub, nevertheless, and we said goodbye to her with regret, having had a wonderful time.

Since I have got onto the subject of boats, I will tell of my excursion on Lake Champlain, if only to give some idea of American manners of the day. We left Montreal at nine in the morning and were fortunate enough to sleep at Saint-Jean the same evening. I forget at what hour next morning we went aboard the *Phoenix*, a steamboat commanded by Captain Sherman whose courteous attention we greatly appreciated. There were several Americans on board who seemed to us as well bred as any gentleman of the best Canadian society. The servants placed a few card tables in the saloon after tea in the evening. Two American gentlemen, coming up to my traveling companion and myself, asked very politely whether we would join one of the whist tables. My friend Christie excused himself, saying he never played cards. I told them that I only liked playing whist for the enjoyment of it, but if they were used to playing for high stakes, I feared I would cramp their style.

"You can name the stake yourself, and we will abide by it," they replied.

"But gentlemen, I usually play for no more than one York shilling (fifteen sols) a point," said I.

We passed a pleasant evening with our new friends. One young man who worked in some office—I forget which—knowing that we were going to New York, said he would be glad to be of use if we had a mind to visit City Hall. The morning after our arrival in the

Empire City he gave us the full tour, not only showing us this handsome building, but introducing us to the governor of New York State. Nothing could have been more simply done than this introduction, which we had never for a moment expected when visiting City Hall. Three men stood talking, with their backs to a lighted grate, in a modestly furnished room. Our cicerone said to one of them, "Governor Clinton, allow me to introduce two gentlemen from Canada." This senior public servant came forward with the utmost graciousness, offered us his hand, and spoke to us of Canada until we felt it was appropriate to retire. I admired the tact of the young American, who did us the honours of his city in an easy, unassuming way, without otherwise imposing on us.

The governor's unaffected and cordial welcome struck us quite forcibly compared to that accorded an American gentleman by Sir James Craig in Quebec some years before.

Jonathan[8] was presented to the governor, and seeing that no move was made to shake hands, as was customary in Washington, made the initial advance and offered his own. Sir James crossed both hands over his large stomach. The American reached out to grasp a hand from the viceregal abdomen, at which Sir James dropped his arms on either side of his aristocratic breeches. Jonathan made a renewed attempt, but the governor folded his hands behind the tails of his braided coat. Since Uncle Sam[9] didn't dare rout them out from this impregnable entrenchment, I suppose he resigned himself to the thought that the British governor wasn't called "little king Craig" for nothing.

But to come back to my tale. We were told that we needed written permission to visit the navy arsenal and the warships in New York, and we therefore asked a young lieutenant called Taylor, whom we had met at the table d'hôte of a hotel in that city, how we should go about satisfying our curiosity. He replied that he would take us himself the next day. Contrary to our previous information, the formula for gaining admission appeared to be quite simple, for he contented himself with whispering in our ears, as we set foot on the first frigate, "Recollect that we are all Yankees here."

On Lake Champlain we saw the American flag flying proudly above that of England atop the masts of our fleet, captured during the War of 1812—a humiliating sight for British subjects. To forestall any untoward comments, my friend Christie thought it best to bring up the matter of our defeat first. To our great surprise, our Yankee frien‹ merely remarked, "The fortunes of war!" and changed the subject.

And now, having journeyed far afield, let me return to Monsieu Petit and his enterprise, which failed despite his emininent qualitie‹ as a culinary artist, all because of the lack of visitors to keep his hotel busy. Some young men arrived at this hotel during a July heatwave at the hour when the theatre ended, and asked for supper.

"Impossible, Messieurs," replied Monsieur Petit. "There isn't a single boarder or visitor from out of town in the house, and not a bit of fresh meat. I'm desperately sorry."

"But we're dying of hunger, Monsieur Petit. Such a distinguished artist as you can never be at a loss!"

"Very well! I will try a ratatouille," said Monsieur Petit.

He served up a stew that would have satisfied the most demanding gastronome. Perhaps he used one of his wife's old boots instead of meat. Madame Petit—now there was an English beauty! A former housekeeper in Sir James Craig's establishment, and a bit too ingratiating, perhaps—but in this case the sauce was tastier than the fish!

Silver medals and armbands were part of the formal dress of the Hurons of Jeune Lorette, described in detail by de Gaspé. Self portrait by Huron artist Zachary Vincent. Musée du Château Ramezay, Montreal. CR 3239

278

CHAPTER TWELVE

This rock, which perhaps ought to be called Seal Island,[A] lies some forty-five miles downstream from the city of Quebec. It is almost in the centre of the Saint Lawrence River, twenty-one miles wide at this point. Low tide uncovers nearly a league of the type of beach that hunters love, but when the spring tide is running only two places of safety are left to those who frequent it. Chatigny's Knoll to the northwest is covered with fir, spruce, a few cherry trees, and an apple tree planted by hunters of an earlier day. To the south lies a sandspit about one arpent long, which I will call "Sportsmen's Refuge."[1] It is here that, since time immemorial, they have built cabins on a dune at the eastern end of this sandspit. During the August spring tides I have often seen the spit submerged except for three dunes and Chatigny's Knoll. Tradition has it that unusually high water invaded even these last refuges and flooded the cabins, forcing some hunters to pass part of the night in a canoe as the only means of saving their lives.

The cabins stand on a sandy beach separated from Chatigny's Knoll by a channel running northeast and southwest for the entire length of the reef. It is only passable at low tide. Large game is hunted north of the channel, as well as on a muddy stretch called "the hunting knoll."

As I said, Chatigny's Knoll is partly covered by fir, spruce, and a few apple and cherry trees planted by hunters of other times. A family of crows has returned each year to raise a new brood for longer

279

than anyone can remember. The few trees form an evergreen cluster that ought to cheer visitors. Instead—I cannot say why—they present a melancholy sight, bringing no comfort to the soul saddened by the muddy shoals north of the channel and the arid sands to the south.

Can Chatigny's Knoll with its crown of trees be a place accursed? Why have hunters never built a cabin there, where they would be protected from the hot summer sun or the storms of spring and fall? This islet seems preferable to the bare shore where they usually camp, and the ever timid wild game would never scent the presence of hunters in the foliage covering the crest. Perhaps the voices of those birds of ill omen that cross the river each year to nest here might dampen the high spirits of hunters returning to the cabin.

In the nearly fifteen years that I visited this rock, I often asked my hunting companions this question. Equally often, I asked them why it was called Chatigny's Knoll, but the answers were always evasive. They would only tell me it was named for a certain Chatigny who used to like to hunt there, and then they would change the subject abruptly.

Toward evening in October of the year 1837, Messrs. Louis Fournier, Pierre Fournier, François Leclerc, and myself had spread out over the hunting knoll. One of them shouted to me that it was time to clear out, otherwise we would soon be cut off by the rising tide. I said I would follow shortly, but in fact ignored the warning. The wind was rising, and I hoped that some wildfowl would try to find shelter for the night in the channel. I waited there, my only companions being my dog and a crow perched on the highest branch of a fir tree atop Chatigny's Knoll. I don't know if he was displeased at having me for a neighbour, but from time to time he let out a "Caw! Caw!" as he swung back and forth with the stiffening breeze. I began to feel somewhat hungry, having been out since five o'clock. Unlike the fox in good La Fontaine's fables, however, it didn't occur to me to compliment him on his melodious voice, as he had nothing in his beak to drop—not even a piece of cheese.

I waited without success for a long time, and finally decided to go back to the cabin. However, I had to give up this plan unless prepared to swim. As I was already numb with cold, the icy October waters held no attraction whatsoever. I took refuge in the little clump of trees, and there, at the foot of a spruce, gave myself up to the sad reflections to which I was often prey, while my dog ran back and forth sniffing every corner of the wood. At that time in my life I frequently used to oscillate from frantic gaiety in the company of my friends to the bitterest moods of introspection when alone with my memories.

Very soon a storm broke in all its fury, to the accompaniment of lugubrious moans such as I had never before heard, even in the most violent hurricanes. Suddenly my sad mood gave way to a nervous exaltation in which I seemed to hear the wail of the newborn child, the cries of the invalid on his bed of pain, the lamentations of the widow at the sight of the bloody corpse of a cherished husband, the piercing shrieks of the tortured criminal, and the groans of the captive as his chains are riveted. Even as I listened with deep emotion to these mournful cries, more powerful voices—the voices of ferocious beasts—drowned out the human sounds, and now it was the roar of lions and tigers, the bellowing of the enraged bull, and the sinister howls of wolves. My dog, having sought shelter between my legs, lifted his head from time to time to yelp plaintively. The nervous system of my faithful companion was more sensitive than mine, it seemed, and this infernal din had thoroughly unsettled him.

As for me, in my gloomy state I fell to comparing the tempests of the human heart with those of the elements raging in their greatest fury.

Let the powerful hand of some genie carry this islet far, far away, over an uncharted sea! I cried inwardly. Let him surround it with storms and shoals to make it inaccessible to all oppressors of suffering humanity! Let this compassionate genie offer it as a haven for all hearts crushed by tribulation! If this asylum were capable of expanding as its population swells, it would quickly assume the proportions of an immense continent!

At this point in my philanthropic reverie, a shot fired nearby startled me out of my retreat.

"Have you decided to sleep with the crows?" shouted François Leclerc from the other side of the channel. "It's ten o'clock now, and you can get across without getting too soaked."

"Have you ever been present at a witches' sabbath?" I asked my companions when we reached the cabin. "Well! If you want a foretaste, spend three hours atop the Chatigny Knoll this evening, and you'll be able to speak with authority on the subject. Never in my life have

I heard such an uproar. I believe all the devils in hell must have agreed to meet tonight! There were the cries of children, the. . . ."

"Nonsense!" said Monsieur Louis Fournier. "If you'd hunted seals for forty years as I have, you'd know that the cries of the pups, when separated from their mothers, sound exactly like a child."

"Well, perhaps you're right insofar as your young amphibians are concerned," said I, "but were those old seals weeping and wailing, lamenting like souls in torment? Were those old seals that roared and howled like vicious beasts?"

"You heard lamentations?" asked Monsieur Louis Fournier looking disturbed.

"Indeed I did! Enough to make a Christian's hair stand on end. I could hear everything from where I was, sheltered beneath a huge, century-old spruce."

"You were sittng under the Chatigny spruce tree!" exclaimed Monsieur Louis Fournier, giving a start. "Tell me, what side were you on?"

"The southwest side, to be sure! I would't be mad enough to take refuge on the side from which that dreadful storm was raging."

"You sat at the foot of the Chatigny spruce, and what's more, on the southwest side!" declared Monsieur Pierre Fournier.

The two brothers looked at each other in consternation.

"You've said too much, Messieurs, to hide the rest now," I protested. "You're the oldest hunters on this rock, where you've been coming for sixty years, and although I've often asked about this Chatigny, you've always evaded my questions. There's some mystery that I don't understand, but I see by your looks that you judge me to be a man threatened by terrible misfortune, perhaps by sudden death. You owe it to me as friends, as Christians, in fact, to tell me what you know of Chatigny's history, so that I may be ready for whatever comes. It can't be denied that certain places have a sort of fatality attached to them. Don't be afraid of frightening me. If it's some terrible misfortune, I await it; if it's death, then I must prepare myself for it."

The two worthy old men spoke between themselves in low voices for quite some time. Then that veteran of South Shore hunters, Monsieur Louis Fournier, who at the age of eighty used to go off unaccompanied into the depths of our Canadian forests for months at a time, gave me the following account.

"You have remarked on the fact that we avoid talking about Chatigny and his regrettable history, for man is by nature superstitious and childhood impressions do not fade easily. This knoll was always considered a place of ill omen by the hunters of old, who told us its history while making us promise to give it as wide a berth as possible. As you know, I spend two months hunting seal here alone before the small game season opens in mid August. In the silence of calm nights, and during storms as well, I've often heard the lamentations you spoke of without being in the least afraid. I would pray for a soul in purgatory who lamented his fate atop this knoll for nine days, then go peacefully to my rest.

"The tragedy I'm going to recount must have happened a long time ago, for it was told me in my youth by an old man who also heard it when young—and as you see, I myself am over eighty.

"Two young men who had been friends from childhood lived in the same parish, practically next door to one another. It's hard to imagine why two men of such different character should be friends. One of them, Pierre Jean, was a bestial type, as repulsive physically as he was morally. He was a large, ungainly man, as dark as the savage from which he was descended on his mother's side, and had prodigious strength that he constantly paraded. His way of talking makes me think he must have been Acadian.[3] As for moral qualities it is useless to speak of them, for he had none.

"Chatigny, by contrast, was a handsome young man of fair colouring and somewhat taller than the average, with an expression that reflected his sweet nature. He was always polite and obliging, and to know him was to like him. Everyone found Pierre Jean detestable—with reason, as what follows will prove, for his soul must have been black indeed for him to switch suddenly and without provocation from friendship to implacable hatred of Chatigny.

"I have already said that Pierre Jean was very proud of his strength. One Sunday after vespers, when he was showing off, he lifted an enormous stone above his head and shouted laughingly to Chatigny in his Acadian patois.

"'If you're man enough, Chatigny, send back this stone that I'm going to throw at you!'

"Chatigny stepped back about fifteen feet and answered, 'Throw it; I'm ready.'

"The stone fell about twelve inches from Chatigny, who calmly picked up the massive weight and said, 'Your turn now, Pierre Jean!' And with this he threw the stone with such force that it fell virtually at Pierre Jean's feet.

"Shouts of approval from the spectators greeted this unexpected prowess. No one had suspected he was so strong. Pierre Jean was cut to the quick, but with the dissimulation of those who have Indian blood in their veins, he pretended to be pleased at his friend's success, and complimented him like the others. All the same, people thought he seemed more sullen and evasive afterward, but no one bothered much about it.

"To all appearances, the two continued to be as good friends as ever after this scene, and one day they set off for Seal Rock. Pierre Jean came back alone, however. I don't know what tale he told to account for Chatigny's absence, but people accepted it until their suspicions were awakened nine days later by a comment he let fall.

"'If Chatigny had this stew he'd wolf it down tonight!' he said at supper one evening.

"These words, spoken in a half sullen, half joking vein, together with Chatigny's long absence, began to make his family uneasy, and two of them left next day for the rock, where a sad sight awaited them. They found the unfortunate man lying beneath a spruce tree, barely alive. Nevertheless, after they had got him to swallow a little brandy, he spoke these words: 'If Pierre Jean had heard my cries he would never have had the heart to let his childhood friend die of hunger. Oh my God! Imagine my despair when I came back from hunting to find that he had singlehandedly launched a chaloupe which the two of us had barely been able to beach, and that he'd gone off. Then I guessed his cruel plan. But tell him I forgive him.'

"With this he expired, and that is why the knoll is called Chatigny, and why we avoid this ill fated spot."

"Now, Monsieur Fournier," said I, "there are a few things I don't understand about this sad story. How could Chatigny die of hunger when he had a gun, on this rock where game is so plentiful; and why didn't he send the distress signals known to all Canadians?"

"I've often thought the same thing," replied Monsieur Fournier, "but all I can tell you is what the old men told me. I think they must have made an excursion to this rock at a time when there wasn't a beak[4] about, let's say from the end of the spring hunting season until the next season opens in the middle of August. But if Chatigny hadn't any food, then couldn't he find some means of making the distress signals you spoke of at night? I can only suppose that the poor fellow had exhausted his powder, and that if he'd already killed some game Pierre Jean took it with him. What about tinder and a flint lighter?[B] Well, it sometimes happens that, of two hunters, only one comes provided, or perhaps Chatigny didn't smoke and wasn't in the habit of using one."

THE CHATIGNY LEGEND

"After telling you the story of an adventure that I think is absolutely true," continued Monsieur Fournier, "Here is one in which I haven't quite the same faith, for my authority wasn't the most truthful man in the world. He was a joker who used to spin a fair yarn.

"You probably knew Carrier," added the narrator, "the one nick-named 'woodsman,' although he might just as well have been called 'shoreman.' Like me, he used to spend most of his time hunting. You surely must have known him in your childhood, for he used to supply your family in the autumn with hare and partridge."

"The only Carrier I remember was Beaverfoot Carrier," said I.

Instead of a left hand, this Carrier, by a bizarre trick of nature, had a veritable beaver's paw at the end of a stump of arm some six to eight inches long. He managed to do all the farm chores, except for winnowing, using his right arm and a cord tied to the paw. I think I should add, as proof of the happy consequences of work, perseverance, and energy, that he went from being the poor man who felled the first tree on a concession of land in my grandfather's seigneurie, to dying a rich man, having comfortably established his large family.

"Yes," I went on. "I remember this Carrier well, for as a child I was always entranced by the sight of him digging into his tobacco pouch with this inert little paw, set in motion by the stump of an arm, as he mixed the tobacco before filling his pipe. Do you know why he was crippled like this? I've heard several versions."

"His mother always maintained that she was frightened by an Indian who threw a live beaver at her when she was pregnant," said Monsieur Fournier. "But to get back to the other Carrier, the brother of Beaverfoot: it was he who brought me to this rock when I was about eleven or twelve, and here is what he told me.

285

"'Toward nine in the evening I was alone in my cabin when I heard a wailing voice cry three times, 'Carrier! Carrier! Carrier!' I rushed down to the shore, for the tide was out and I thought a boat must have foundered on some large rocks and that someone was calling for help. Although the moon was not yet up, I could distinguish objects at a fair distance, but nothing was visible. I was going back along the path to the cabin when the same voice that I'd heard to the south called from the southwest. 'Help me! Help me! Carrier!' I ran along the dune toward it, but when I reached the place where the voice had come from I could hear nothing. I was about to retrace my steps when the voice called out from a point farther on in the same direction. I felt a sudden terror, but as the tide was rising, I thought some poor wretch, hanging onto a capsized canoe, was being carried by the current toward the channel that separates this bit of land from the Chatigny Knoll. Again I started running, and now I heard the same voice from the other side of the trees. I crossed the channel and cut through the woods to save time. There at the foot of the tallest spruce I saw the shadow of a man. I circled round the tree, but saw no one. Then my hair stood on end, for from the very trunk of the tree came a mournful cry: "Help me! I'm hungry! I'm dying of hunger!" I tried to get away but kept walking in circles and hearing cries. It was only with first light that I could leave this sinister spot. I needn't add that an hour later I was crossing to the south in my birchbark canoe.'

"I can't guarantee the truth of this story," said Monsieur Fournier. "All I can tell you is that it made a deep impression on me, young as I was, and I have looked on the Chatigny Knoll with misgiving ever since."

Let me list the merry hunters who gathered on Seal Rock around the fifteenth of August in the year 1833. The two Messrs. Fournier, already old men at the time, have long since gone to the rest reserved for the virtuous, as is the law of nature. Messrs. Charron and Félix Têtu, the same age as I and both in fine physical condition, were taken from their families in the prime of life, although with their constitutions they might have expected to live to a ripe old age. There was Monsieur Alexandre Fraser, then barely twenty, the only son and hope of his father, Simon Fraser, esquire, notary of Saint-Jean Port-Joli.[5] [C] The young Fraser, who was his father's business associate, was taken from his loving parents three of four years later. I am the only one whom death has spared.

In the evening we all gathered in the cabin. While waiting for supper we had engaged in trials of strength. Everyone except the two Fourniers had taken part, and we were boasting of our prowess. Even Monsieur Fraser had come out of it honourably, giving us proof of strength far beyond his years. When we finished supper, Monsieur Louis Fournier began to speak.

"You're boasting about your manly strength, Messieurs. I believe it, for I have the proof. But you know there are men with such prodigious strength that one can hardly credit it. I was on this rock forty years ago with my brother Pierre, whom you see here, my late brother Michel, and José Jean now dead, when we saw a canoe coming toward us from the north. It was one of our friends from Isle-aux-Coudres coming to visit us—or so we thought. The sun had just set, and a wind was rising in the south. The campfire burning at the cabin entrance was becoming a nuisance, with the sparks getting in our eyes. Someone suggested we go a little way along the beach and fetch a wild cherry tree to smother the fire. We were men in our prime, remember, and our grip had lost none of its force. My dead brother Michel, in particular, was as strong as an ox. After much effort we had to give up in disgust, for apart from being very heavy, the branches were deeply buried in the sand, and our work went for nothing.

"Night had fallen, and it was very dark by the time the man we were expecting arrived. He was a small, puny-looking old fellow, and didn't appear good for much. We didn't know who he was, but gave the best welcome we could and asked him to share our supper.

"'I won't say no, but I'll do as the Indians do, and leave you as soon as I've eaten. I don't want to lose the rising tide to get to Isle-au-Grue,' he said, adding, 'Haven't you got something to damp down that fire? The sparks are blinding you.'

"'There's a tree along this sandbank that would do, but it's so heavy that we've given up trying to pull it over here,' I told him.

"The old man sat and smoked for a few minutes as he chatted with us, and then got up. We quickly lost sight of him in the darkness. What was our surprise, our horror, when a few minutes later we saw him coming back with the tree over his shoulder!

"'There you are,' he said, throwing the tree down. 'That will damp the fire, and we'll eat supper comfortably.' The tree was so heavy

287

that we bounced a foot high in the air as it hit the ground. We firmly believed that the devil himself was paying us a visit and watched him depart after his supper with profound relief. It was only next day that we learned from Dufour of Isle-aux-Coudres that it was Goodman Grenon, not the devil, who'd supped with us. We had often heard North Shore people tell of his superhuman strength, but didn't really believe it. Now we were convinced. Since then I've been to visit old Grenon, as worthy a fellow as could be, and he was tickled to find he'd given us such a scare.

"The whole Grenon family is endowed with remarkable energy," continued Monsieur Pierre Fournier. "But only one of his daughters has inherited her father's prodigious strength. One of Grenon's sons, after a three or four years' stint with the North West Company, returned to his family laden with trophies in the form of feathers won in fights with the likes of voyageurs such as Moferant, Monargue, Dumouchel, and other redoubtable bullies from the backwoods. Someone told his father, who happened to be passing by, that his son had just gone into an inn. Old Grenon hurried to join him. When he saw that his son's back was to the door, he signaled the people of the house to say nothing. Walking quietly up behind his son, Grenon grabbed his head between his hands. The son tried to free himself but couldn't and shouted, 'It's my father. There's no other man in Canada capable of holding me so tightly!'"

Although some of the feats attributed to old Grenon must belong to the realm of legend, here is one that I believe to be true, as it has been vouched for by several eyewitnesses. In the woods one Sunday Grenon met a young bear the size of an adult. It tried to flee when it saw the man, but our Hercules thought it would be a good catch and joined battle. He got the bear down, seized it by the scruff of the neck, and arrived before mass with his prisoner at the church door of Baie Saint-Paul, where numerous spectators witnessed this rather novel scene. It would seem that the king of Canadian forests didn't relish this manner of travel, for Grenon said on arrival, "The wretch doesn't much care for the company of honest men: he clawed at all the trees and roots within reach."

The curious were soon convinced of the truth of these last words on inspecting the trail, where stripplings and roots lay strewn along the path.

Recently, I was discussing the prowess of old Grenon with a habitant called Joseph Charretier, my neighbour in the country. I mentioned that I had been assured even the daughters of this Hercules had sinews of steel.

"I never knew old man Grenon or his sons," said Charretier, "but as for one of his daughters, I know all about it. I was twenty-five years old when I first set foot on the North Shore. I was striding toward the bottom of the awesome bluffs around Baie Saint-Paul, which I would have to climb, when a young girl carrying a package under one arm passed close by me at a trot. I was at an age when one knows what to say to a girl. I took off my cap and bowed right to the ground saying, "Mademoiselle, I've two favours to ask. First, will you give me the pleasure of your company while we share the same path? And secondly, please allow me to relieve you of that package you're carrying.' You can see, Monsieur," added Charretier, "that I knew how to speak politely, like a man of the world."

"I can see you certainly know how to butter up the ladies, Father Charretier," said I. "She must have been very appreciative."

"Well, I couldn't complain to begin with," replied the old fellow. "She made me a pretty curtsey and said, 'You do me too much honour in offering me your agreeable company, and I accept with pleasure, but as for the light package I'm carrying, it's not worth your while.'

"'I wasn't brought up among the savages,' I retorted. 'We South Shore men know the respect due to the womenfolk.'

"'In that case, since you South Shore gentlemen are so gallant, here's the package,' said she.

"Thinking that this package, neatly wrapped in a white cloth, contained wool or clothing at the most, I accepted it without a second thought. To my shame, it slipped out of my hands and fell to the ground.

"'I beg your pardon!' said she. 'It was very careless of me to let the package drop.'

"I blushed furiously. Bending down quickly, I succeeded with much effort in putting her light burden on my shoulders."

"But what was in it?" I asked old Charretier.

"Nothing worth speaking of," he answered. "Merely a *minot* of salt.ᴰ

"Things went fairly well while we walked on the level, but as we climbed the slopes I began to sweat profusely. My companion chattered like a magpie, hopping from one foot to the other and making giggling excuses for the trouble I was taking on her behalf, adding that South Shore gentlemen were much more polite than those of the North. As we climbed those hellish slopes I stopped to rest on the pretext of getting her to admire various fine views.

"'We mountain people are so used to the view that we don't think much about it,' she said. "But I'm in a bit of a hurry, Monsieur. My mother's waiting for me, so please give me my package and I'll go on while you enjoy the beauties of nature.'

"I felt like sinking through the ground. My shame gave me strength, however, and I replied that I didn't wish to leave such a pleasant companion. Once more I hoisted my miserable burden, puffing like a whipped sled-dog. I was pretty well exhausted when, by a stroke of luck, we came to a crossroad. I then asked which way she was going, determined to go to the northeast if she went to the southwest. We separated, and she curtseyed prettily again and said she would never forget the gallantry of South Shore gentlemen.

"Privately, I consigned her to the devil, and at the first dwelling I stopped to ask for a beaker of milk to refresh my parched tongue. I asked the mistress of the house whether this was the land of the Amazons, and told her of my adventure.

"She burst out laughing. 'That's Marie Grenon. If need be she could have carried you as well as the minot of salt, and still gone up the hill without flinching.'"

I was reading this account of the Grenons to my son Alfred, assistant inspector in the Quebec post office, all the while regretting the lack of further information about this family.

"I think I can get you something quite quickly through Augustin Tremblay, one of our mailmen in the parish of Baie Saint-Paul," he said.

And so it was that, a few days after this conversation, the man told him the following story.

"My father, still hale and hearty although nearly ninety, knew old Grenon and his family well. One of his sons had remarkable strength, although not anywhere near that of his father, but a daughter seemed to have inherited it. The other Grenons are sturdy enough, but nothing special. As for old Grenon, everyone believed the devil helped him, as he rarely liked to show his strength in public. For that matter, he was a fine man, quiet, peaceable, and able to take a joke—although if he said, 'Enough!' the jokers changed the subject without another word, no matter how many there were. Grenon was a little fellow. My father often told me how he saw him naked one day, and was horrified to see that he was as furry as a bear, with sinews that stood out like a bull's, criss-crossing his whole body.

"One day, when Grenon had been cutting rushes by the shores of Baie Saint-Paul with several habitants, his horse couldn't make it up the steep slopes because the load of green fodder was too heavy. He lit his pipe and sat down by the roadside for a quiet smoke.

"'What are you going to do?' asked one of his friends.

"'I'm going to give my animal a rest,' replied Grenon, 'and I expect she'll get her load up the hill without any trouble afterward.'

"At this, the others left, but when night had fallen one of the habitants came back and hid near a fence to see how Grenon and his horse would manage. His hair stood on end when he saw Grenon climb the terrible bluffs of Baie Saint-Paul at a normal walk, pulling the vehicle himself while his horse followed behind, nibbling contentedly at a few mouthfuls of hay snatched from the cart. The Peeping Tom wanted to flee, believing he was looking at the devil in person, but Grenon recognized him and cried, 'I'll get you if you speak of this!' The whole parish always believed that only Satan could possess such strength."

I felt that I ought not to finish my account of the Grenons without visiting this day—February 28, 1864—my old friend, the Honourable Paschal de Sales Laterrière,[E] a member of the legislative council, in the hope of getting a few facts about the Hercules of the North. I thought he might have something to add, because he had lived for forty-five years in the seigneurie of Les Eboulements next to Baie Saint-Paul. Furthermore, he himself had possessed uncommon muscular strength in his youth, and would have been sure to ask about the feats attributed to old Grenon. My expectations were justified. He told me the following anecdote, which he had from the old men of Baie Saint-Paul.

"You must have seen some of those old fireplaces that used to be built in days gone by?" said my friend.

"Yes," I replied. "There was one in my grandfather's kitchen at the manor-house in Saint-Jean Port-Joli. You could easily burn a whole tree in it."

"Well, one of these was being built for the presbytery in Baie Saint-Paul. Eight or nine strong men had given up trying to put the mantelpiece in place—an enormous stone, six feet long, eighteen inches high, and eight inches thick. The real difficulty was not in getting it off the ground, but in setting it on the two jambs that rose four or five feet above the hearth. The workman had abandoned this Herculean labour when one of them saw Grenon pass by.

"'Hey!' shouted the workman. 'You're as strong as an ox. Come and help us put up the mantelpiece.'

"'It's my lunchtime, and yours too,' retorted Grenon. 'I'll give you a hand when we've finished our meal.'

They went their several ways, but Grenon retraced his steps once the workmen were out of the way, and laid the stone by himself.

"You know," said Monsieur Laterrière quizzically, "the devil has always counted for something in the construction of certain wonderful buildings, such as Cologne Cathedral in Europe and several churches in Canada. When the masons came back, they naturally attributed this feat to His Satanic Majesty, despite claims by the women in a neighbouring house that they saw Grenon go in and come out alone from the presbytery after the workers had gone, and that the devil wasn't with him."

I had already heard about this particular feat, but didn't know the dimensions of the stone. I see it is still remembered by the Laurentian habitants.

I have said that Grenon's muscular exploits had passed into legend. Here is one told by a wag from Isle-aux-Coudres.

Grenon was working with one of his friends in the forest near an Indian camp. When he came back to eat, the friend, who was doing the cooking, told him that a huge Indian had paid him a visit. The redskin had lifted the cover of their soup pot and insulted the brew simmering therein. Although no trace was visible, the soup had been offered a cruel and unforgivable affront. Grenon shrugged and dined in a bad mood. But when this same savage repeated the offense two days in a row, Grenon decided to do something about it and said to his companion, "I'll stay in the cabin tomorrow."

At the accustomed hour the Indian arrived and paid the same scornful tribute to the unfortunate soup as on the preceding days. Our angry Hercules grabbed the savage by the legs above the ankles and swung him around like a club, striking a tree violently several times. The Indian's head, arms, and trunk were demolished, and only the legs remained in Grenon's hands. As a child I believed the story of this exploit implicitly, and loved to hear it told. The tale is so well known in the Laurentians that one may reasonably suppose it contains a grain of truth, and that the Indian paid dearly for his bad manners.

I now return to my friend, Monsieur Paschal Laterrière. Those who see him today would find it hard to credit the anecdote I am about to relate. If this amiable and witty companion of my youth has lost none of his mental faculties, he has nevertheless undergone the physical ravages of time, as have we all. Looking at this little old man, who would believe that he once had formidably strong arms?

I think it must have been about the year 1813 that Dr. Laterrière, on leaving a ship where he was visiting professionally one morning, met a seaman who asked him what he was doing on the wharf where they were standing. The young doctor, realizing the man had been drinking, asked him politely to move aside. The sailor paid no heed, and continued to block the way, taking it upon himself to strike the doctor. Pushed too far, the doctor punched him so hard that he broke the man's jawbone in three places.

The young Aesculapius made what amends he could and had the sailor taken to a hospital that he had established for seamen in the Lower Town. Here he set the bones in the place assigned them by nature. So skilful was the operation that after six or eight weeks the patient left the hospital with his chin supported by a handkerchief knotted around his head as a precaution.

But O! the ingratitude of the human heart! The first use the sailor made of his recovery was to lay a complaint against his benefactor, and the young physician, having supplied the usual bail, appeared at the quarterly assizes to answer a charge of grievous assault and battery. I was in charge of his defense and confident of an acquittal, given the circumstances in his favour. In this, however, I had reckoned without Fletcher, the presiding judge.

The plaintiff, who was the only witness, took the customary oath and then, as initial proof of the crime, untied the handkerchief that supported his chin, at the risk of sabotaging the healing of his lower jaw.

Good God! What a chin! I can only give some idea of it by offering a comparison. Suppose that the witness's entire head resembled the shape of the globe; look at his mouth, and there you have the line of the equator.

I have read somewhere that a very eccentric English knight amused himself by gathering at his table a number of gentlemen all afflicted with the same deformity. It might be twelve London magistrates with overly large noses—noses nourished on turtle soup, roast beef, plum pudding,^F brown beer, and port wine. This kindly knight would almost split his sides laughing when, as he announced a toast, all the guests' formidable noses pointed his way.

Sometimes it was gentlemen who all had a cast in the left eye or the right. At dessert he would produce some rare object for the occasion, crying, "Look at this, gentlemen!" As the squints converged upon him, he would collapse into delightful fits of laughter.

Another time, he gathered about his hospitable board the most powerful chins of England, not excepting Scotland. The worthy knight experienced an incomparable joy when all the guests' chins advanced simultaneously, as in battle arrayed, to perform a small ablution in the little bowls provided for this purpose before dessert.

It is said, unless I'm imagining it, that at the end of the meal he always gave a small gift to the man who was most distinguished in his special line. How lucky would my sailor have been, had he been judged worthy to sit at the good knight's table! He would most certainly have acquired a life annuity, on condition that he attend forevermore the feasts for large chins.

I must come back to my unfortunate client, however, as he is patiently awaiting the jury's verdict. I have to admit that the sight of the plaintiff undermined my confidence as to the excellence of my client's case, a confidence with which I had inspired him as well.

"My dear Paschal, how did you manage to mutilate that poor devil so cruelly?"

"That pampered animal is just play-acting to get what he's after," retorted my client. "He's making the most of his chin in order to impress the court. It was big enough before the accident. Confidentially, I probably wouldn't have hit him, in spite of the provocation, if he hadn't tempted me by thrusting out his stupid great chin. A chin so out of proportion gets on my nerves. And anyway, it's impossible to set the bones in their normal position without getting some slight deformity."

"Do you call that a slight deformity? A jaw so ridiculous that the owner wouldn't be admitted to the priesthood, for fear of causing a scandal among the faithful when he officiated?"

"Stick to your own profession," said Laterrière. "I see you know nothing about anatomy and surgery."

My Aesculapius was quite right, and I remained silent.

Although large chins generally denote an egocentric nature, the sturdy sailor gave a frank and honest testimony. He admitted the threats and provocation, but added that he had not intended to hit the accused.

I saw that the sympathy of judges, jurymen, and spectators was veering toward the plaintiff's chin, and concluded that—as Hamlet said—*that* was the question. I began my interrogation with this in view.

"Witness, do you maintain, under the oath you have just taken, that it was in fact the blow which made your chin as long as it is now?"

"Certainly," said the witness.

"Did you not have a very pronounced chin before the accident?"

"I always had a long chin, but not as long as it is now."

"Have you looked in a mirror?"

"Yes. And I'm so disfigured that I'm afraid my wife will refuse to recognize me when I get back to Liverpool."

"Who cared for you, after performing the necessary operation on your jaw? Was it not the accused, and did he not give you the best possible attention? You know that it's impossible to reset broken bones without leaving some visible trace?"

"Yes, yes, I agree with all that," answered the plaintiff, "but I can't help feeling that if he'd been content with just my own bones, my chin wouldn't be as long as it is now. I think he added a handful of bones from the skeleton he has locked up in his laboratory."

Jury and spectators broke into laughter at this outburst. I was taking it as a good omen when Fletcher, the sworn enemy of French Canadians, asked the witness if he was very sure that the accused had not hit him with a stone, which he felt must certainly have been the case.

Honest Jack replied that he had seen no stone in the doctor's hand, and that Laterrière hadn't picked up one in Jack's presence.

I then made a speech on my client's behalf that seemed to me full of pathos. I said that the accused had been provoked into a fight that no young man with real blood in his veins could refuse without showing himself a coward; further, that both sides had agreed to fight of their own accord; that the accused had no way of knowing that the plaintiff's chin would be as fragile as glass; and that, if it was indeed assault, the jurors should consider it justifiable under the circumstances. A contrary verdict, said I, would have the most pernicious effects. If a surgeon who had been goaded into a fight should happen to break the bones of his antagonist, he would take care not to make any needless expenditure, as had my client, for fear that his only reward would be a lawsuit that would increase the costs considerably. I expounded on the ingratitude of men in general and of the plaintiff in particular—a man who, after receiving the most sedulous, able, and immediate attention from my client, had a soul black enough to drag him before a police court.

I was feeling rather smug about my pleading, and looking forward to the most satisfactory results for my client. Then Fletcher, the stipendiary judge who was presiding, insensible to any eloquence but his own, attacked the unfortunate physician in an exhaustive charge to the jury, declaring that it was his decided opinion that no French-Canadian arm, unless aided by a stone or some equally hard object, could have smashed a British seaman's jaw that had braved so many tempests. The jurors gave their verdict accordingly, and Fletcher had the pleasure of condemning the accused to pay ten louis to the crown, which was hardly much comfort to the plaintiff.

I have since greatly regretted that I didn't support my case by displaying the doctor's naked arm in court, side by side with the plaintiff's chin. I'm convinced that once the jurymen had seen his muscular limb, they would have rejected Mr. Fletcher's gratuitous version.

I cannot take leave of my old friend, the Honorable Marc Paschal de Sales Laterrière, without wishing him a better advocate if he is ever again overtaken by certain youthful impulses. Nor can I say farewell without mentioning the distinguished services rendered his riding in getting a road built, so that the Laurentian habitants could escape the isolation imposed by the terrain, whatever the season. In winter, the only way of getting out was by the capes (the habitants called them *câpes*), which one had to go round on foot, often clinging three or four hundred feet above the Saint Lawrence, which rumbled at the base.

The traveler, armed with a small axe, would hack steps in these Canadian glaciers, enabling him to scale the most dangerous passes by leaping like a chamois.

Monsieur Laterrière was sensitive to the great disadvantage to this part of the District of Quebec, isolated six months a year from the rest of the world. He obtained a government grant that put an end to this enforced seclusion. Hardy pioneer that he was, he headed a group of nearly a hundred men into the forest to open the fine highroad that now enables the Laurentian habitants to communicate all year long with their brothers in the various other parts of Canada.

The people of the Laurentians have always shown their gratitude for this great work, as well as for the outstanding services rendered by Monsieur Laterrière as an able and charitable doctor throughout his forty-five years' residence in his seigneurie of Les Eboulements. They have also been grateful for his constant efforts to attract settlers by opening up lumbering camps and bringing prosperity to the region. As proof of their gratitude, they returned him as their member for the provincial parliament for forty consecutive years, and finally as a member of the legislative council.

Monsieur Laterrière has reached the age when he can appreciate men for their true worth. Although recent events may appear to indicate a forgetfulness of so many good deeds, this ought to be attributed simply to the infirmities of human nature. Let him be proud to have received such an enduring proof of gratitude in the past.

CHAPTER THIRTEEN

LAC TROIS-SAUMONS IN WINTER

I suppose you'll be joining us," said my friend Monsieur Charron, merchant of the parish of Saint-Jean Port-Joli, as we emerged from high mass in December of the year 1825. "I'm going to Lac Trois-Saumons tomorrow with my friend, Monsieur Pierre Verrault, and we're counting on you."

"I've never visited our fine lake in winter," I said. "It can't be much fun to freeze in your tracks while waiting until the trout are good and ready to swallow the bait offered them in a hole dug through two or three feet of ice."

"But we'll kill hare and partridge,"ᴬ said Monsieur Charron. "We'll set traps and have better hunting at night than we would by day."

"It's very tempting," I replied, "but what will we do, cooped up in a cabin seven feet square from four-thirty in the afternoon until eight in the morning?"

"Tell stories," said my friend. "We'll recount our hunting feats and try to outdo each other with tall tales. It'll be great fun!"

"Well, in that case, I'll come—but on one condition: that we pick up old Romain Chouinard on the way. He's an inexhaustible storyteller."

"You haven't reckoned with his wife, Monsieur," said my friend. "If she takes it into her head not to let her husband leave the house, the devil himself couldn't change her mind."

"Leave it to me. I've never met a shrew that couldn't be softened by ten minutes' conversation with me."

298

"Until tomorrow, then," said Monsieur Charron with a sardonic expression. "I wish you well."

I was very fond of old Romain's company, and he usually acted as my guide when I visited the lake. He was an excellent old fellow, obliging and attentive. I had taken a special fancy to him ever since he reported having seen his brother Julien mowing his field at two o'clock in the afternoon.

"What's so extraordinary about that?" I said. "Your brother used to be my neighbour, and I've seen him mowing over a hundred times at all hours of the day."

"You may be right, Monsieur," replied old Romain, "but this is very different, for at the time I'm speaking of, he'd been dead for three days, and I'd seen him buried the day before!"

"Good God! That *does* make a difference—quite another kettle of fish, I'd say. But are you sure you recognized him?"

"As if I couldn't recognize my own brother!" snorted old Romain. "He had the hood of his homespun coat turned back on his forehead, and was wearing enormous Indian boots[1] that came up to his hips."[B]

"He must have been pretty hot," I replied. "Mowing in the heat of summer is a tough chore. The men usually wear nothing but trousers and shirt."

"The dead are always cold," said old Romain, making a long face.

Finding it impossible to refute such a confidently asserted premise, I contented myself with nodding my head, as if convinced. The reader can see that I had good reason for wanting old Romain to join our party.

When we arrived at old Chouinard's house the next day, about one in the afternoon, we found him out front splitting wood for the stove. After the usual exchange of compliments, Monsieur Charron hurried into the house with me.

"Good day, Mother. Are you as crotchety as usual?" he said.

The tendons of the old woman's neck tightened like guitar strings. White with anger, she replied, "I am when I have to be, Master Shopkeeper with your rotten wares!"

I felt extremely put out, and with reason. The old woman was just about insufferable on days when she was in a good mood, and now my friend had got the better of me by turning her into a raging she-wolf. I put a brave face on it, however, for I had boasted of being able to soften the greatest termagant, and my honour was in question.

"Pay no attention to Monsieur Charron, good Mother," said I in my most honeyed tones. "You know, he's a bit thick between the ears and doesn't know how to behave with the fair sex."

"No more do you!" snapped the old woman, whose neck tendons were beginning to quiver violently. "No more do you, great big seigneur that you think you are."

This jibe was double-edged, for I was then very corpulent, although a seigneur of scant means.

"You misunderstand me," said I, taking her hand, which was trembling with fury, in mine. "I said that he had no respect for the fair sex, that is, women, but you know that I myself am always polite to the ladies."

The old woman was somewhat mollified by this explanation, save for a few angry flashes from her eyes, as black as those of Aeolus after the storm. It seemed that calm was restored, but Monsieur Charron, seeing her soften a little, said, "We've come to take your husband to the lake."

"He shan't go," said she. "That's only for ne'er-do-wells who have nothing to do but run around the woods."

I was losing ground but didn't want to admit defeat.

"Mother Romain is right. She loves her husband and is fretful when he's away. Don't think about it any more, Mother; let's talk of something else. How is it that such a handsome creature as you were in your youth—and you're still an attractive woman, by no means on the shelf—how is it that you, who had the pick of all the young bucks in the parish—for I've heard it said that every Sunday, after vespers, your late father's house was packed with suitors asking you out for a drive. . . ."

The old woman's features began to relax.

"How is it that so beautiful a creature as yourself could prefer Romain Chouinard for a husband? You must admit he isn't a handsome man. He's as black as a savage, and you're as white as a basin."

The old woman bared her two lone eye teeth and said, "I must have been bewitched."

Old Romain turned away to laugh, and Monsieur Charron muttered, "He's going to get his way."

"But what surprises me most," I continued, "is that you could be so happily married to such an old curmudgeon."

The old woman sniggered with satisfaction. "It isn't hard when you have everthing on one side and nothing on the other."

"It's Father Romain, then, who has a world of patience," interposed Monsieur Charron.

"You old rag-seller!" rasped Mother Chouinard. "You would do better to shut up and let sensible people speak." The old woman's eyes turned as black as Erebus.

"Shame on you, Monsieur Charron," said I, "tormenting such a good woman! Can't you see she doesn't feel well and has a headache?"

As the nearest doctor lived eighteen miles away, I was often called on to administer julep, salt, and rhubarb. I felt the old woman's pulse and put on my best medical expression.

"Why didn't you send someone up to my house? I would have given you a purgative to make you feel better."

"Ah, Monsieur Philippe, you're too kind!" she exclaimed. "These remedies cost you money. . . ."

"If they cost even more than they do, can you think me hard-hearted enough to see you suffer when I could comfort you—you, my best friend? But we can still do something about it. Of course I would have liked to take your husband to the lake, but it would be cruel to deprive you of his care. Let him go to my wife, and she'll send you some good medicine."

"Go and get ready, Romain," said she, "since Monsieur Philippe[2] does you the honour of taking you with him. I'll send my little boy, who's got more sense, to get the purgative that he's kind enough to give me."

I led old Chouinard off in triumph, and two hours later we were on the shores of the lake. Despite the rigours of the season, it still wore a picturesque aspect. As far as the eye could see its surface was covered with shimmering ice, as transparent as the finest mirror. There was nothing melancholy in the ring of cedar, fir, and spruce that circled this beautiful lake and ornamented the small islands. The tufted branches of the snow-laden old trees reminded me of our old gentilhommes,[c] who always powdered their hair copiously to hide the ravages of time. The young trees, their branches trimmed with hoarfrost, reminded me, too, of my entry into society twenty years earlier, when etiquette demanded that we dress our hair as did the old men. Suddenly a puff of wind arose. All the heads quivered, and in my sometimes poetic imagination I thought for an instant that the trees, animated by the sound of this Aeolian orchestra, were about to welcome us with a woodland ball.

I was drawn from my reverie by Monsieur Charron. "Your Honour is naturally rather lazy," said he. "You have the tender hands of a young girl, so go along to the cabin with old Romain, where you'll find plenty to do. My friend Monsieur Verrault and I will do the really hard work here. Digging a trench in the ice is a pretty tiring business, what with the ice often being three or four feet thick. You have to begin with an axe and finish it off with iron chisels."

We crossed the lake to reach the cabin on the Toussaint cove, where my companion lit a fire in the stove, using the night's provision of wood. This was left by the last occupant, as was the custom. Meanwhile, I cut branches to refurbish the bed of fir that woodsmen love, after which we set snares for hare and partridge. The method is not complicated: one makes a hedge about a foot high with fir boughs stuck in the snow. The hedge runs at right angles to the hare's trail. This animal is timid by nature and only comes out of his burrow to feed at night. His instinct prompts him to run the length of the improvised hedge, rather than jump over it, until he finds an opening big enough to get through. Unfortunately for him, this opening is the trap where death awaits him—the death of great criminals, a shameful death for an animal that has led so pure and innocent a life, harming no fellow creature.

The snare to which he falls prey is as simple as can be. The hunter plants a forked branch in the snow. A long, flexible sapling is secured in the fork, about a foot from the ground. Attached to the end of the sapling is a fine brass wire forming a running noose as large as the opening in the hedge. The poor, unsuspecting hare sticks his head and shoulders through the noose. His struggles to get free make the end of the sapling spring loose from the forked branch, and the hare finds himself hanging three or four feet above the ground.[D]

You may readily imagine that two men can set several snares in a relatively short time. When our companions rejoined us in the cabin at nightfall with their catch of fish, we could look forward to an ample supply of small game the next morning.

The partridge spends the night in a hole that she makes in the snow. In searching for a suitable place to do this, she probably runs along the hedge, like the hare, rather than jumping over it. Not being strong enough to spring the trap by tugging at the noose around her

302

neck, she is usually to be found lying dead on the snow, sometimes half eaten by martens or other small carnivores, whereas the hares are out of reach.

After a supper eaten with appetites sharpened by exercise, we lit our pipes, filled our glasses with a punch liberally laced with excellent Jamaica rum, and thus fortified we settled down to an enjoyable evening. I was the one who got things going.

"You, Romain Chouinard, who journeyed such a lot in the old days, you must have seen the *chasse-galérie?*"[E]

"Only once," said old Romain, pulling a long face to show the truth of his statement.

"That's not often for a man your age," remarked Pierre Verrault.

"Not often at all," echoed Charron and de Gaspé in unison.

"One shouldn't lie," said old Romain. "True, it's only a venial sin, and you'd need as many of them to make a mortal sin as shovelfuls of snow to heat a stove, but even so it's always a bad thing."

Old Chouinard had a horror of lying.

"Well then, so as not to lie, I'll tell you that I really have heard noises in the night, in the air above my head, two or three times, but I can't swear that it was the chasse-galérie. It certainly seemed like it—but one mustn't lie. It's wicked."

We were all loud in our praises of the old fellow's scrupulous conscience, and asked him to tell us what he had really seen and heard.

"You must understand that this happened far, far away from here," said old Romain. "I was working for the agents of the Hudson's Bay Company, and was returning to a trading post after a long hunting trip. I was in a great hurry to get there, but I was so loaded down that I could hardly move."

Old Chouinard was certainly right about that, for after hearing him enumerate what he carried on his back, apart from axe, gun, and kettle, my friends estimated that his load amounted to some four hundred pounds.

"The snow was deep and still falling," continued the narrator. "My snowshoes sank at least eight inches with each step. Suddenly I heard a noise above my head. At first I thought it was an owl, but it was panting like an exhausted little animal. That's funny, I said to myself; these north-country birds pant just like four-footed creatures. I soon realized what it was, though, when I heard the sound of chains clanking, the rabid barking of dogs, and then a man's voice shouting, 'Get him! Get him! Hiyah! Hiyah!' It all happened in the sky, like a vision. My hair stood on end, and my tuque fell off into my hood before I could catch it. I tell you, it's the absolute truth."

"I believe you, Father Romain," I cried, "for I now realize that I, too, have heard the chasse-galérie. One evening, as a child, I was going out the door and heard the clanking of chains. I was terrified and went back into the house to say I'd just heard the chasse-galérie. My father told me I was silly and that it was the sound of the iron hobbles that your brother Julien was putting on one of the horses."

"Ah! *Dam*! What you say about the late Monsieur doesn't suprise me. One day I told him I'd met a werewolf with a tail at least three-quarters of a league long. He laughed in my face and said, 'You're an imbecile, my poor Romain.'"

"My father might have shown more respect for a tail that long. But for goodness' sake, tell us about your encounter with this werewolf sporting an appendage of such formidable dimensions."

"Listen, Monsieur Philippe, and you'll see that if I'm lying about the length of the tail, it's the fault of the miller you used to have at Trois-Saumons—and yet, you know, he was a very particular man in whatever he said and did.

"I was coming out of our curé's house—Monsieur Faucher's now dead, but if he were alive he'd tell you himself. I'd been to see about the funeral service and burial of my neighbour, Pierriche Moreau, who had just died. It was about eight o'clock, and although the moon wasn't up there was quite a lot of light. I had barely left the churchyard when a man went striding past me. Well, this is a bit of luck, I said to myself. When you've been seeing to the burying of a dead man, you always feel a bit shivery alone at night, and a companion on the road is most welcome. I had about two leagues to walk before reaching home, and I was on foot, my horse being lame and my mule half-broken with work.

"'Good evening, friend!' I called. 'You've come at just the right time.'

"Well, he didn't say a word. I thought he must be deaf and ran after him, but he was walking as though the devil were at his heels. I've run down moose, you know, but they're nothing compared to the man dressed in grey.

"A short time later, I felt something brush against my legs. I bent down and saw that it was the tail of an animal, unrolling itself like wool off a winder.[F] It kept going by me, but there was always more. It's a werewolf! I said to myself, and it's my Christian duty to deliver him by drawing blood. I screwed up my courage, pulled out my knife, and tried to stab the disgusting thing, but it wriggled like an eel and I missed every time. *Ma foi*, when I saw that, I gave up and hurried on.

"As I had to stop at the Trois-Saumons mill to see whether my grain was ready, it being a busy time, I asked the miller if he'd noticed a man dressed in grey go by.

"'Yes I did,' said he. 'I was helping Quénon (Etienne) Francoeur put his sacks on his sledge when he passed by. It was quarter past eight. Quénon had just asked me the time.'

"So there, Monsieur Philippe!" asserted old Romain. "Was I a liar when I told your late father about the werewolf's tail? I had hardly reached Baptiste Godrault's house when the man arrived at Trois-Saumons, and it's over three-quarters of a league from Baptiste's to your mill."

I agreed that my father had maligned him, and begged his pardon.

Although I was quite ready to keep old Romain talking, Charron said, "If you keep encouraging him to lie like this, by tomorrow morning he won't have a sound tooth left in his head to eat breakfast with."[G]

We spent all the next day fishing, hunting, and setting snares. That evening we did justice to an excellent stew of hare, bacon, and partridge, cooked by old Romain for our supper—a dish I specially recommend to hunters after much exercise. We then made ourselves comfortable, as on the previous night, determined again to pass the time agreeably. An owl perched in a neighbouring tree, the patriarch of nocturnal fowl to judge by his lugubrious voice, uttered his "Hou! Hou!" at intervals. Our gregarious habits seemed little to the taste of the venerable hermit of our forests.

"When those birds make so much noise it's not a good sign," said old Romain. "The proof is that, the night my late father died, one of those sorcerers hooted three times as it passed over our house, and ten minutes later eight orphans wept beside the corpse of the best of fathers."

The mournful cries of this solitary forest dweller and the touching words of the old man threw a melancholy shade over my soul that I sought only to deepen, for there is a certain charm in sorrowful reverie. I asked old Chouinard to tell us a good ghost story.

"Well I won't say no," he answered. But as he was about to begin, the owl hooted mournfully twice, "Hou! Hou!" The old man looked behind him anxiously and said to me, "I'm rather tired. I usually take a little nap after supper. You'll have to excuse me this evening. I'm going to bed. Good night."

I felt put out at this, then suddenly I had a bright idea.

"Wait a minute, Father," said I. "I know an excellent cure for your fatigue."

I prepared a mug of steaming punch with a double shot of rum, sugar and nutmeg—a brew capable of skinning the tongue and palate off the most ironclad jaws. But old Chouinard had a mouth as tough as a shark. He knocked back two mouthfuls of the infernal concoction without blinking, and smacked his lips, stating roundly that were was no one like Monsieur Philippe for preparing a *sangris*,[11] and that by way of thanks he would tell me a good ghost story.

OLD ROMAIN CHOUINARD'S STORY

"Give me back my biretta."

"As ye make your bed, so shall ye lie," said old Chouinard sententiously. "If Josephine Lalande had been more strictly brought up, and if her parents had taught her not to be so flighty when she was little, she wouldn't have caused them and herself so much heartache.

La Fine, as she was called by everyone, was an only daughter. Her parents, having no other child, were infatuated with her, and as a result she grew up always having her own way. If the father scolded a little, the mother took her daughter's side, and if the mother got cross the father would say, 'Why are you making the child suffer?' This didn't stop Josephine from being the prettiest girl in the parish of Sainte-Anne by the time she was sixteen, and so charming and kind to everyone, particularly the boys, that the good folk's house was never empty. Suitors vied for the love of this rich and beautiful heiress, but although La Fine played and romped with them all, or passed the time pleasantly with each in turn, it was for the fun of monopolizing the swains of the parish, hearing herself praised, and

306

infuriating the rest of the girls. You see, she'd already fallen in love with a young neighbour with whom she'd practically grown up.

"If Josephine was the prettiest creature in Sainte-Anne, Hippolite Lamonde, then twenty-eight years old, was the handsomest, as good-natured and patient as he was brave and strong. He and the young girl had become secretly engaged long before, but it hurt Lamonde, all the same, to see her flirting with every boy who spoke to her. However, he took it all without saying a word and was too proud to complain.

"Hippolite would have asked for Josephine's hand formally long before this, but his self-respect prevented him. One day he had heard the girl's father say that his daughter's hand would only be given to a young man in easy circumstances, and that he had no intention of letting her marry a beggar.

"This stung Lamonde to the quick, for although not a beggar, he had almost no prospects. His father wasn't rich and had a large family, while he himself was only beginning to live on what he earned by his trade. He was as nimble as a monkey, a good builder, and a clever carpenter.

"In the meantime, he received a letter from an uncle who lived in Upper Canada, inviting him to go there. The letter reported that there was plenty of work and few workmen in that part of the country. The uncle offered to make him a partner in a building business he'd set up for the government, and Lamonde would make a great deal of money within three years.

"He told the good news to his fiancée. She was in tears at first, but he argued so reasonably that she agreed to let him go and promised to remain faithful.

"La Fine was very sad for a few days after he left, but women are fickle, as you know, and in no time at all she was up to her old tricks.

"Coming back from a midnight party with a group of young people, she was as usual jumping and dancing about hilariously, pushing one and giving another a smart tap, and making more noise than all the others put together.

"As they came up to the church, they saw a man dressed in a surplice and a biretta standing on the steps in front of the main door. He had his head bent and his arms outstretched toward them. Everyone felt a sudden terror, but Josephine quickly recovered.

"'It's Ambroise, the verger's son,' she said. 'He's got himself up like that to scare us. I'm going to catch him and snatch off the biretta, and he'll have to come and get it before mass.'

"No sooner said than done: she ran up the church steps, grabbed the biretta, and began dancing giddily among the others and generally carrying on.

"The old folk were asleep when she got home. She tiptoed in and put the biretta in a half-empty chest in her bedroom, locking it carefully and putting the key in her pocket. When Ambroise comes in the morning, she said to herself, I'll have lots of fun telling him I lost it in the great Sainte-Anne bay and that he'd better go and find it.

"She was just about asleep when she heard a noise at the north window of her room. Opening her eyes, she saw the same figure as on the church steps, still bending forward, and pressing his lips against one of the windowpanes. She distinctly heard these words: 'Give me back my biretta!' At the same time there came a sound from the chest that sent a shiver down her spine. The moon was up by this time, and she saw, not Ambroise, but a tall young man as pale as a corpse, who kept crying, 'Give me back my biretta!' At each word, she heard a knocking from inside the chest, as if some small, trapped animal wanted to get out. Now she was really terrified and threw the blankets over her head so as to see and hear nothing. She passed a bad night, dozing off and then waking with a start. When she came to get up the next morning, she heard a noise in the chest again. Without waiting a moment longer, she grabbed her clothes and went to dress in the next room.

"When her parents saw the change in her—for she already had a burning fever—they scolded her for staying out so late the night before. The tears welled up at this, so they gave her a hug and said not to worry, that they were sorry to have upset her.

"Josephine passed the day as best she could, shivering at the slightest noise and keeping close to her mother and aunt the whole time. Toward evening, she told them she was afraid to sleep alone and asked to have a bed made up beside her aunt in the attic. This they did.

"No sooner was Josephine in bed that evening, than the aunt dropped off. But the poor girl couldn't sleep, and almost immediately noticed a shadow at the window that made her look up. It was the phantom of the night before, hanging in midair in the same way and crying, 'Give me back my biretta!' She let out a wail and fainted."

At this point in old Chouinard's story, the *nycticorax* left his solitary dwelling. We heard the sound of his wings over the cabin, where sparks were flying out of the stove pipe. The owl hooted ominously three times. Old Romain gave such a start that the pipe fell out of his mouth, although the stem had been firmly gripped between the two lone teeth in his lower jaw.

"You damned stupid animal, you almost made me jump out of my skin!" he shouted. "But you don't scare me; I've seen the likes of you in northern trading posts."

The old fellow's bravado sufficed for the occasion, thanks to the pint of triple-strength punch he'd just swallowed, and he continued his tale.

"The whole family was soon up, and after much difficulty the girl was revived. She stayed awake the rest of the night, her head on her mother's breast and her hands tightly gripping those of her father and aunt. As she was somewhat calmer by morning, her family wanted to send for the best doctor in the parish, but she insisted on having the curé.

"When the priest came, she told him the whole story in strict confidence. He comforted her as much as he could with wise counsel, saying that all he could do for the moment was send her holy relics, but that he hoped next day to deliver her from the apparition that was making her suffer.

"The good folk made a bed for Josephine in their own room, closing the shutters as she asked, and again spent the night with her. As a result she slept fairly well and was feeling better next morning when the curé came to call as promised.

"You know, Messieurs," interposed old Chouinard, "that all curés have the *Petit Albert* at hand for summoning the devil if need be."

We bowed our heads in assent to this incontestable pronouncement.[1]

"At nightfall the curé got out the *Petit Albert*, which he kept under lock and key for safety's sake, and read the proper chapter. A great noise was heard in the upper air, like a violent gust of wind, and the evil one appeared. The curé didn't much like the look of him—this being the first time he'd ever seen the devil—and he crossed his stole over his stomach to ward off harm.

"The devil had gone to a fair bit of trouble for the occasion, mind you. Not a thing was missing: black velvet coat, waistcoats, and breeches, a plumed general's hat, boots of fine leather, and silk gloves. He was pretty swarthy and his hands and feet were rather long, but you'd never pick him out of a crowd. The curé reproached him severely for what had happened to the poor young girl and accused him of having appeared in order to bring about her death.

"'My dear curé,' said the devil, 'with all due respect to your tonsure, I should think myself pretty naïve using such tactics, when I was sure to get my prey by encouraging her vanity and coquetry. Sooner or later I should have had her soul in my clutches; instead, here she is, cured of her folly for the rest of her days and about to throw herself into a life of devotion. Come now: I should have thought a smart priest like you would know more about the human heart.'

"You see, Messieurs," added old Romain, "the devil spoke politely and his reasoning was sound. Ah! *Dam!* I wouldn't have advised him to tangle with a priest, for fear he'd get a dressing-down that'd make him howl like a wild dog. However, it seemed the curé accepted his argument, for he traced the sign of the cross in the air. The earth shook and the evil one disappeared.

"When the curé saw that the devil wasn't the culprit, he took down the biggest Latin tome he could find on his bookshelf and began to read. He read for so long that he fell asleep with his head on the book, and in his sleep he had a dream. What it was I can't say, but apparently it gave him the answer. He said a mass for Josephine, and then went to her house where he found her a little better.

"'My dear girl,' said the good curé, 'you have committed a grave error, but you sinned through ignorance and I don't reproach you for it. The phantom you saw is a poor soul from purgatory who was working off a heavy penance. You interrupted it and now he can't finish it without his biretta. You must make up your mind to put it back on his head tonight.'

"'I'll never have the courage,' sobbed the unhappy girl. 'I'd fall dead at his feet.'

"'Nevertheless you must,' said the priest, 'otherwise you'll never rest, either in this world or the next. The spectre will dog your every step. There's nothing to fear, in any case. You'll be in a state of grace, and I'll be there with your mother and father. We'll tell them the whole story, so that they can comfort and protect you if need be.'

"Poor Josephine agreed after much resistance. Great was the good folk's[3] sorrow when they learned the truth, although they did their best to console their unhappy child. They spent the entire evening in the presbytery, praying fervently, and on the stroke of midnight betook themselves to the church door, where they found the spectre standing on the steps in the same position as before. La Fine was shaking like a leaf in spite of the curé's exhortations and the stole that he'd placed around her neck. Nevertheless, she went up the stairs, driven by despair, but as she was about to put the cap on the phantom's head he made as if to embrace her, and she fell fainting into her father's arms. The priest lost no time in trying to get the biretta and restore it to its rightful owner, but the girl had such a tight grip on it that he would have had to cut off her fingers.

"La Fine was soon reduced to a pitiable state. Often she thought she heard the spectre's voice. She trembled at the slightest sound, and couldn't be left alone an instant. So miserable was her existence that the pretty cheeks, once as red as Calville apples, resembled a withered white rose. The blond and naturally curly hair that was her pride hung like damp tow down her cheeks and over her shoulders. Her lovely blue eyes took on a pale, glassy look, and her whole body became so thin that one wept to see her. All the signs of death were visible in her face. The best doctors pronounced her consumptive, but said she might linger a long time.

"Where was Hippolite Lamonde all this time? It was three years since he'd left, and not a word had been heard of him. He came back, however, happy at heart and successful in business. Now he could go to Josephine's father confidently, without being afraid of a rebuff. It was nighttime when he arrived, but as soon as he had thrown his arms around his parents in greeting, he asked about La Fine. Her misfortunes were then recounted. Hippolite tore his hair in despair.

"'What!' he cried. 'Out of all those grinning idiots who made such a show of being in love with her, not one was brave enough to come to her aid! Cowards! The whole bunch!'

"He spent a sleepless night pacing the floor, talking to himself like a madman. At seven o'clock next morning he was with his fiancée. The girl sat propped up on cushions in an armchair, her feet on a little bench covered in bearskin, and her body wrapped in a thick woolen coverlet. Even so, her teeth chattered. At the sight of Hippolite she seemed to revive and reached out to him.

"'Dearest Polithe,' she said in a weak, trembling voice, 'we mustn't think about the friendships of this world any more, for when one is dying one must think only of heaven. It's a great consolation to me to see you before I die. You will mourn over my coffin with my good parents and later do your best to console them. Will you give your promise to one whom you've loved for so long? I've only one regret in dying, and that is to have behaved so badly toward you, and not to be able to make amends by giving you happiness.'

"Blinded by his tears, poor Lamonde said to her, 'My darling Fifine, chase these evil thoughts away. Hippolite is with you, and you're going to live.'

"'How can I hope to live,' she replied, 'always afraid like this, starting at the slightest noise, and as scared of the daylight as the dark? Every moment I hear the breathing of a soul in torment, reproaching me for my cruelty! I daren't ask for death to end my suffering, for the spectre is always saying, "You'll have no rest in this world or the next." Oh! It's pitiful! Pitiful!' And the unhappy girl wrung her hands in despair.

"'Josephine! Dear Fifine! Take courage for love of your parents. Take courage for love of me, too! I'll return the stolen cap to the ghost myself tonight, and you'll be free.'

"'You shan't go!' cried poor Josephine. 'Let me be the only one to die. I'm miserable enough without having your death on my conscience!'

"'I've nothing to fear,' answered Lamonde. 'I've never wronged anyone, dead or alive, so why should this phantom want to harm me? If you fell over a cliff, do you think I'd hesitate a moment to rush to your rescue, although I knew it was certain death? Fifine, I'd have myself hacked to pieces to spare you a scratch. What I have to do is child's play, and I'll be as calm as I am now.'

"Josephine pleaded with him not to risk danger for her sake; she wasn't worthy of such friendship. Hippolite wouldn't hear a word of it, and was all the more determined to carry out his resolve.

"At eleven in the evening, he asked for the key of the chest with the biretta. The cap fell into his hand almost as soon as he opened the chest.

"The night was pitch dark as he came up to the church. Only the feeble ray of the sanctuary lamp could be seen. Back and forth he paced, praying, until the spectre made its appearance. As midnight struck, he found the phantom standing before him. With firm tread he mounted the church steps to where the spectre stood in its usual position, and with steady hand he replaced the cap on its head.

"The phantom signaled him to follow, and Lamonde obeyed. The graveyard gate opened of its own accord and closed after them once they had entered. The phantom sat down on a grassy mound, motioning to Hippolite to sit down beside him. Then it spoke for the first time.

"'I'm sorry I can't offer you a more comfortable seat, my good young man. We live rather simply in a place where all are equal. Seigneur, notary, doctor—they all get the same welcome.'

"You can see that the phantom had both manners and common sense," interposed old Romain.

"Well, it surprises me to hear it, Father Romain, considering the unholy row he kicked up for his miserable biretta," I replied.

"When a man's doing heavy penance, he tends to be moody, but once it's over he recovers his good humour," asserted old Chouinard.

I couldn't gainsay so sensible a comment, and old Romain continued his story.

"'Young fellow,' said the ghost, 'for thirty years I have resided four feet under the earth where we're now sitting. I dare say you think it a sad dwelling, but I always left it at night with a sigh, when my soul came to find my poor body to make it do penance—a penance well deserved.

"'In my youth I was high-spirited and only interested in having fun. I was the parish clown, invited to every wedding, feast, and dance. If I were spending the evening anywhere, all the neighbours would come over to hear my jokes.

"'Passing by our church one day, I saw the children gathered for catechism and the curé just leaving to tend a sick person. I told them to go in, saying that the curé had told me to give the lesson until he came back. I donned a surplice, put on a biretta, and climbed into the pulpit, where I carried on so comically that the children laughed uproariously. In a word, I played the fool and profaned the sanctuary itself.

"'A week later, while I was out on the river alone in my chaloupe in calm weather, a squall hit my sails so suddenly that it tore them to shreds and my boat capsized. I succeeded in climbing onto the keel, where I had plenty of time to reflect and to commend myself

313

to God's mercy. My strength finally gave way, and a wave washed my dead body ashore.

"'I was condemned to thirty years' purgatory in the place I'd profaned. At the stroke of midnight, my soul would reenter my body and drag it to the church steps.'

"Lamonde shrank back to the end of the mound. He had thought he was dealing with a soul, but for good measure found himself in the presence of a body. He now noticed that the phantom had decidedly foul breath. The ghost paid no attention. 'You'll never understand, young man, the hardship and misery that we have to bear when we leave our resting place. The blackest nights seem as bright to us as if the moon were in the sky. As we can't hear anything four feet under, the least noise makes us shudder. It hurts our eyes and makes them smart to see the lights burning late in people's houses. The noise of passing vehicles and the shouts of travelers' laughter sound like thunder.

"'But this was the least of my miseries. What I had to endure in autumn, in the pelting rains of spring, and in the icy blasts of winter would make a stony-hearted man's hair stand on end. You see, I was a vagrant or *volontaire*,[4] and had been buried with little ceremony and less clothing. Some charitable soul had donated a sheet for a shroud, and this was all I had on when they nailed down my coffin. You will scarcely believe it, but my poor bones often used to splinter like glass in the January cold snaps.

"'I was therefore filled with joy as the last night of my penance neared its end, when a mad young girl. . . .'

"'At the risk of butting in, Mister Skeleton, I'll thank you to watch your tongue,' said Lamonde. 'I followed you without argument into this graveyard—a pretty uninviting place during the day and even more so at night. I'll admit I was somewhat intrigued: I was curious to see whether dead men are as big liars as the living, and I also wanted to find out something very important. You've been very polite up to now, and I've no regrets. So far so good. But I've no intention of letting anyone malign Fifine. You're naturally a happy ghost, having done your penance. I wish I could say the same, for I'm just beginning mine. I'm eating my heart out. So if you've nothing better to tell me, let's have done and say goodnight while we're still on good terms.'

"'Young man,' said the ghost, "I owe you too much to cause you pain, so I'll just say that Mademoiselle Lalonde interrupted me when

314

I was completing my last night of penance. It's over now, thanks to your courage, and I'm grateful to you. I'd like to prove my gratitude with something more than thanks, if it were possible. If only I knew of some treasure—but I don't.'

"'I've no need of your treasure,' said Lamonde. 'There's only one treasure I want, and that's my fiancée. If you owe me anything, restore her to life.'

"'My good young man, God alone is master of life and death.'

"'One doesn't have to come back from the other world to know that,' retorted Hippolite. 'But at least tell me if poor Josephine is really dying of consumption, and if the doctors are right in saying there's no hope of recovery.'

"'If Josephine regained her health, young man, would you still be ready to make her your wife? You deserve better than to marry a girl who might make you unhappy for the rest of your days.'

"'To each his own, Master Phantom,' returned Lamonde. 'I'd rather be unhappy with her than happy with another. You know, I don't much like having people stick their nose into my affairs. If you've no other consolation to offer, then good night.'

"He got up to leave, but the spectre motioned to him to sit down, and he obeyed.

"After a short pause, the phantom spoke again. 'The doctors have said that Josephine is consumptive, and they are right. They have pronounced it fatal, but there they are wrong. There is a remedy, although they've never discovered it, despite their much-vaunted science. Death often serves life. Take with you a handful of that herb under your feet, so that you can recognize it tomorrow. Get her to drink a tisane made of it, and in a month she'll be convalescent. Farewell; it's nearly daybreak, and I've only time to tell you that your fiancée is at peace now. I whispered in her ear that you had delivered me.'

"With that the phantom disappeared. Filled with joy, Lamonde put a handful of the herb in his pocket, leapt over the graveyard wall, and fifteen minutes later entered La Fine's house. She held out her arms as soon as she saw him, and they wept for a long time, unable to say a word.

"Those from the other world are usually never wrong," remarked old Romain, "and all came to pass just as the ghost predicted. Three

315

months later, Lamonde led the most beautiful woman in the parish to the altar."

"That's all very fine," said I, "but did they get along afterward?"

Old Chouinard said nothing for some time. "Well, he kept her in line," he said finally. "Women are great flirts, you know, and at first La Fine tried to return to her old ways. Although she adored her husband, her days as a coquette weren't entirely forgotten, despite her misfortunes. Lamonde soon saw to that, however. One day after church he declared that he was no jealous husband. He didn't mind seeing his wife surrounded by young bucks, but he'd beat the tar out of the first whippersnapper who said a word against her. What was more, he'd taken the precaution of cutting a stout maple stick, so as to be ready for the event. As he was as strong as an English bull, they all took him at his word, mindful of their backsides.

"My advice to those with fickle wives is to use the same remedy. I'm not speaking of my own, thank God. Some rascal tried to poke fun at her one day, and she let him have the Ten Commandments on his forehead with her nails, ripping the skin right down to his jaw— and she's a good woman, as you know.

"Well, when La Fine saw that no one bothered about her, she made the best of it and set about bringing up her children. After that, she only made eyes at her husband."

The next day we returned home, amply laden with trout, hare, and partridge.

Old Romain Chouinard gave me so many pleasant moments that I feel I must devote the following chapter to him.

316

CHAPTER FOURTEEN

The lake is the solitary man's confidant,
The motionless symbol of meditation.
Méry[A]

OLD ROMAIN CHOUINARD

Those who knew old Romain Chouinard, a humble and peace-loving farmer, faring along the road of life without leaving a trace of his steps, will be surprised at my taking an interest in so apparently insignificant a personage. But why should I not pay homage to virtue, though I find it beneath this rustic exterior? I knew him from earliest childhood. He, his brother our neighbour, and one Castonguay from Côte Deschênes were the best mowers in the parish of Saint-Jean Port-Joli, and my father used to retain their services for the haying season a year in advance. They were all equally good at their job and, as the habitants put it in their simple fashion, the fellow on the left didn't let the other two reap under his nose.

Like all children, I loved legends and tales, particularly the most terrifying ghost stories, although at the price of going to sleep with my head under the covers. Romain Chouinard would tell me a few whenever I could get hold of him in the evening.

"When you're grown up, Monsieur Philippe," he invariably said at the end, "I'll take you to the lake, and there in the cabin of an evening I'll tell you the best stories."

Old Chouinard kept his word during the fifteen years of my youth that I frequented Lac Trois-Saumons. But it was when I retired to the country at the age of thirty-seven that he became a valued companion on my hunting and fishing excursions to this lovely lake. Old Romain was not cheerful by nature. He was usually silent except when I engaged him in conversaton. I appreciated these qualities, for at that time I was often absorbed in melancholy reverie, and didn't like to be distracted until the cloud had passed.

Although the old fellow generally left me to my sad reflections, he sometimes made an effort to bring me out of them, but in a way that never wounded my feelings. This uncultivated soul possessed an innate sense of tact and delicacy, such as I would wish for many men who pride themselves on their savoir-vivre and good breeding.

I was sitting up quite late one night by a little fire at the door of our forest cabin, thinking of death which puts an end to all human suffering. Believing my companion asleep, I began to recite aloud bits of Hamlet's touching soliloquy, "To be or not to be."

> Whether 'tis nobler in the mind to suffer
> The slings and arrows of outrageous fortune,
> Or to take arms against a sea of troubles
> And by opposing end them. To die, to sleep—
> No more, and by a sleep to say we end
> The heartache and the thousand natural shocks
> That flesh is heir to. [B]

I was repeating these moving words for the second or third time. There must have been something peculiarly affecting in the sound of my voice, for old Romain, without understanding a word of English, was immediately by my side.

"Monsieur Philippe, what do you say we take a turn around the lake. The water looks inviting."

I was moved to tears, for I perceived Chouinard's intention, and knew he was as little disposed for a nocturnal jaunt as I am to drowning myself today.

We each took a paddle, and once on the lake a calm invaded my soul.

"Ah yes!" I reflected as I looked at the majesty of the forest and lifted my eyes to heaven, "He who created all these works of grandeur for the happiness of man will also soothe the troubled spirit."

I then began to question my companion to find out whether this man of rough education was impressed by the beauties of nature.

"Tell me, Father Romain," said I, "what do you think of, when you look at all that surrounds us tonight?"

"I think that God was very good to have dug this lake in the mountains and to have filled it with fish to feed the poor world."

"It must have been hard work to cut through this rock," I said.

"A flick of the wrist," retorted old Chouinard, tracing a furrow in the water with the tip of his paddle.

"What do you think of this fine moon that lights our way?"

"It's the lamp made by the good Lord to give light on long evenings for poor folk who haven't the means to buy oil or candles," was the old fellow's response.

We were moving along the shoreline. I said, "Do you see how the trees are reflected in the water?"

"It's the mirror given by the good Lord to those without vanity. The devil made the others that women use so often, to the perdition of their souls."

A group of picturesque islets seemed to float above the water, the effect of a mirage.

"Wouldn't you say those are floating islands, coming to meet us?" I remarked to my companion.

"Fear not," replied old Romain. "That which the good Lord has anchored so firmly won't come adrift until Judgment Day."

Knowing that he had sailed the Saint Lawrence in his youth, I remarked that he must have found the night watches long.

"Pretty long on dark nights," said my companion. "But when the moon was up and the sky clear, I always found my watch too short."

"Why?" I asked.

"Because I could see a good distance, and there was always something new."

I understood then that the old man had poetry in his soul without being able to express it in the language of Chateaubriand or Lamartine.

Often I sought the forest calm during my fourteen years in the country. There I met only friends; their church-like silence quieted my thoughts, and the roar of the storm added nothing to my agony.

I witnessed one sublime sight in all its frightening grandeur—the only time I really took pleasure in the unleashed fury of the elements. A dreadful hurricane burst upon us suddenly during the night. The trees groaned and bowed, and their debris was strewn far and wide over the virgin forest floor. The waters of the lake, hitherto as unruffled as the surface of a mirror, were convulsed to their very depths. Claps of thunder shook the base of the mountains, only to be repeated sevenfold, with the infernal noise of an immense artillery barrage, by the seven echoes of the hills to the south, their crests ceaselessly illuminated by the electrical fluid. Then, after a moment's profound silence, these terrible detonations would suddenly begin again through some trick of acoustics. It seemed as though an earthquake were rising from the depths of the lake to shake the encircling mountains.

I invoked the spirit of the storms.

Why trouble this solitude? Why topple these gigantic trees that live in peace, exempt from the passions of men, offering each other mutual support and shade? There are other exploits more worthy of your force and might! Roam the universe where numberless victims await you! See in that carefully furnished drawing room the husband and wife discussing the future of their only daughter, and talking of the joy she has brought them since infancy! How happy they are! Grief has never troubled their union!

Fly from the drawing room to the upper floor. Look at this lovely young girl just blessed by her parents, the same who, death in her heart, smilingly received her friends this very morning. Now she paces her solitary chamber with quick steps, clutching the long, disordered tresses, and throws herself on the bed, tossing and weeping!

Do you hear the sobs, capable of wringing the heart of a tiger? Have pity on her! She implores death with loud cries. Nothing can resist your power, O spirit of tempests! Carry her off in a whirlwind, far, far, from her tender parents! For tomorrow is the fatal day when she must confess to them that a miserable seducer has abandoned her to lifelong dishonour. Spend your rage on them all, and they will thank you in heaven!

See that old man in this cellar lit by a feeble glow; see with what pleasure he feels the gold pouring through his withered hands. It is a miserly moneylender. One cannot mistake him—even his skin has taken on the colour of the metal he worships. Let us leave him to his pleasure, and enter this grim house. Those two men seated at a hall table where they pass the time drinking are two bailiff's men, guarding seized effects that will be sold on the morrow. Leave them to their dissipation and let us see what is happening in that room

320

where all is in disorder. What is this man, fast failing, whose heart is breaking? A merchant, who once enjoyed great credit. Events beyond his control caused him to lose great sums, and the sharp tooth of the usurer completed his ruin. See how his kneeling wife throws her arms about him, beseeching him for the love of his children to take courage. Vain prayers! Tomorrow the noble heart of her husband will have burst his breast; she and her children will kneel beside a corpse in their dark hovel, while the strident voice of a bailiff conducts the auction of their household goods. You are all-powerful, O spirit of destruction! Blow down this house to its very foundations, and fill the usurer's vault, where he counts his riches, with the debris. Then will you have accomplished a worthwhile mission of vengeance!

What is that woman doing in this squalid dwelling on the fifth floor of a broken-down tenement? Listen, O spirit, and prepare your thunderbolts.

"Mama! Mama! Bread!" cry seven poor, half-naked children, thrusting their heads out of the straw in which they lie hidden.

"Be patient, my poor little ones; your father will be back soon, and you'll have something for supper."

A heavy step is heard on the staircase; the doorway is scarcely large enough to admit a drunken man. The children come tottering out of their wretched bed, begging loudly, "Bread! Bread! Dear Father!"

A tearing sob escapes the breast of the unhappy mother; a cudgel-blow knocks her unconscious upon the floor, and the children hide in the foetid straw.

Strike, O spirit of destruction! Put an end to their horrid torment! But strike also the rich, who let the poor die of hunger. You will have no lack of victims if you fly over that celebrated isle, so laden with riches that it could purchase the universe![1]

A light hand on my shoulder put an end to my exaltation.

"Do you think, Monsieur Philippe, that a little prayer would do you any harm?"

"You're right," said I. "We've had a narrow escape. How lucky that you took the precaution of building your cabin in this little grove of young firs. That old spruce uprooted by the wind would have crushed us beneath its debris, for its broken top fell not ten feet from where we are."

"I thought of that when I built my cabin," answered old Chouinard, "for one mustn't tempt the good Lord. But don't you think that if he wanted us to die, he would have commanded the wind to blow harder?"

In the presence of this man who referred everything to God, I, the "philosopher," felt humbled.

"Let's go in, Father Chouinard, and pray together; you're the elder: it's up to you to say the prayer."

"No, Monsieur Philippe; you've studied for the priesthood,[C] and if you didn't take orders, it's because you had no mind to. But still, you should know some fine prayers."

O vanity of man of little faith! I thought to impress him by the melancholy recital of these words:

"Man that is born of woman is of few days, and full of trouble. He cometh forth like a flower, and is cut down: he fleeth also as a shadow, and continueth not."[D]

My companion kept silent. I continued my lamentatons:

"Let the day perish wherein I was born, and the night in which it was said, There is a man child conceived. Why died I not from the womb? Why did I not give up the ghost when I came out of the belly? Why did the knees prevent me? Or why the breasts that I should suck? For now should I have lain still and been quiet, I should have slept: then had I been at rest."[E]

I expected compliments: I received a gentle reprimand.

"It's not good to lament in that way, Monsieur Philippe. It's as if you were reproaching the good Lord for the crosses he sends us. God knows better than man what's good for us, and if He punishes us it's because we deserve it. In the meantime, here's my prayer. It will be very short, for it seems you weren't in the habit of saying long ones. But as I've already said mine, and my rosary as well, we can both be content with it." And old Chouinard recited the Lord's Prayer, not in Latin, but in French. Very humbly, he then said, "I think, Monsieur Philippe, that this prayer is just as good as yours; and if you feel the same way, let's go to bed in peace."

Five minutes later, the old man had fallen into a deep sleep. As for me, I went to sleep meditating upon each phrase of that excellent prayer which contains the most moving words a man can address to his Creator.

I was very fond of this good old man, who saw God's hand in the most commonplace incidents of our hunter's life. Romain reckoned

on three *piôles* a day when we were at the lake, that is, three times
of day when the fish were rising: in the morning at sunrise, at midday,
and at sunset. One day I was at the lake with some young Quebec
friends of my own age. At the midday rise, one of them came out of
the cabin singing a snatch of song not very edifying to chaste ears.
Old Romain immediately took his line out of the water and rolled it
around his rod.

"Aren't you fishing any more?" I asked.

"No," said he, "and believe me, neither should you. The midday
rise will bring nothing after the song Monsieur has just sung."

This assertion was greeted with hoots of laughter.

"Laugh all you like," snapped Chouinard, who was then in the
full vigour of middle age, "but the good Lord is not amused."

I said to him one day, "You're very old, Father Romain; how is
it that you've lost none of the strength and vigour of youth? I suppose
you had neither great sorrow nor severe misfortune?"

"I've had my sorrows like the rest," retorted old Chouinard. "You
know, I mourned greatly when I lost my father and mother. But it
was the good Lord's will, and everyone has to face it sooner or later.
As for the rest, I've always gone my way and minded my own business.
While neither too rich nor too poor, I always had bread in my cupboard
and bacon in my salt-box, and could always do a friend a favour."

"Have you never gone to court, Father Romain?"

"I was only in court once in my life, and even that was in obedience
to the king, who summoned me as a witness. I had a bad time of it,
I can tell you. Would you believe that a dispute arose between
Toussaint and Gagnon? Toussaint was apt to fly off the handle at the
slightest provocation, while Gagnon was mild and long-suffering. I
don't know what got into Gagnon that day—life has its bad moments—
but suddenly he began calling Toussaint names, then landed him a
punch in the stomach. There they were, hard at it, and poor Gagnon
got a terrible beating. He wasn't very proud of the dressing-down
he'd received, and took Toussaint to court.

"The court was in session, and Romain Chouinard was called. I
bowed politely and presented my summons to show that I was only
there by order of the king. The clerk rudely thrust the paper back at
me and made me swear on *le book anglais*[2F] to tell the truth. Ma foi,
I said what I'd seen, without taking much notice of a great lanky

lawyer-fellow who kept shouting, 'Remember you're under oath! What? You dare say that! You dare say that before the court?'

"I was sweating like a pig, and still I could only say what I'd seen. But here was a pretty kettle of fish: three other witnesses, stout and true men of the parish, came forward to swear that it was Toussaint who began abusing Gagnon and struck the first blow.

"I couldn't believe my ears. I'd heard and seen it all as plainly as I see you now, for I was right beside them. I thought the evil one must have clouded my vision, and I was looking around in a daze when the judge said to me, 'I don't know what keeps me from sending you to jail for perjury.'

"I was shaking like a leaf, but fortunately the deceased Monsieur (Monsieur de Gaspé, *père*) spoke quietly to the judge, who changed his tune. He looked at me hard, then at the three other witnesses, and said to me, 'Get out.' I didn't have to be told twice, as you can imagine."

"My father told me all about it," I remarked. "He informed his friend, Judge DeBonne, that you were one of the most honest men he knew, and that he was sure you had told the truth. What's more, he told me that if the three witnesses whose testimony ran counter to yours had received as much hospitality from Toussaint, who is poor, as from the rich Gagnon, who kept open house and where they had lunched, perhaps they would have seen things differently."

"As for Gagnon," said old Chouinard, "he was a man with all sorts of good qualities. You couldn't criticize him. He'd put down a cask of Jamaica rum in the cellar each spring and, rich or poor, you got to taste it. But don't think, just because a man has been hospitable, you're going to lie to the court and wrong his neighbour. No indeed! You may be sure there was something pretty fishy going on that day. Of course, little white lies harm nobody—they're gone with the wind. Don't the parish jokers say that old Romain Chouinard lies like a tooth-puller?"

"Could you tell me, Father Romain, where we get that expression about lying like a tooth-puller?"

"I guess I can," said old Romain. "Unluckily I've got teeth like a shark. The roots are as tough as old oak and have made all the licensed surgeons swear mightily. One day, when I was suffering the tortures of the damned, my wife said to me, 'Go and find little Bram (Abraham); he knows more about it than all those fine gentlemen.'

"You know little Bram. He's short, as his name implies, but, Holy Mother of God! he has shoulders and wrists twice the size of yours.

"'Hello there,' said he, coming out of his shop. 'You're making faces like a witch.'

"'And with good reason,' said I. 'My tooth is so sore that I feel like bashing my head on the rocks.'

"Bram went off to look for his pincers, saying, 'Sit down on the floor. I'll fix you up with a flick of the wrist.'

"'Will it hurt very much?' I said.

"'Like a pin-prick,' he replied.

"If he'd used one of those toy instruments employed by qualified surgeons," continued old Chouinard, "I'd have been pretty leery of him. But Monsieur Philippe, just think: he was holding a pair of pincers a foot and a half long, just like a blacksmith's tongs. One twist, and presto! it'll all be over, I thought. In went the pincers— quite a mouthful—but the tooth wouldn't budge, and he began shaking me up and down like a dishmop. I shrieked blue murder and bellowed like a bull. Twice I went around the room with the pincers gripping my jaw. Then he shouted to his neighbour, who had come running to see the fun, 'Here, Coulombe, help me; climb on his back.' Coulombe had lots of practice at this sort of thing. He leapt astride my shoulders, grasped me by the forehead, and began to shout and laugh at the same time, 'Go to it, little Bram!' 'Don't worry!' cried little Bram, 'No tooth is going to make a fool of me.'

"Well, Monsieur Philippe, little Bram lifted us both off the ground three times, with such force that when I landed on the floor my backside and everything attached to it—begging your pardon—crunched like sheet-ice. At the fourth try, out came the tooth with a tearing wrench. I though my skull would burst. Little Bram was delighted and held the pincers high above his head, shouting, 'There it is! There it is! I knew that tooth wouldn't get the better of me!'

"It seems to me, Father Romain," said I, "that a man of your size and strength could easily have avoided the torture inflicted on you by little Bram."

"You think you're quite a man, but I'd like to see you with a fistful of iron in your mouth," retorted old Chouinard. "I wonder how you'd have handled it."

I've been told the same story by nearly a dozen people who encountered little Bram's tongs at serious risk to their jaws.

325

Abraham C—— earned a good living from his carpenter's trade. He only exercised his dental art to ease human suffering, and never asked for payment. As a result he was never short of patients and was proud of his skill, boasting that no tooth had ever resisted the strength of his wrist or the sturdiness of his tongs.

One day I was visiting a young doctor-friend when I heard the most awful bellows coming from the lower floor of the house.

"What is it?" I said. "Is someone being murdered downstairs without your ministrations? That's an infringement on your medical privilege."

"It's a habitant having his tooth pulled at a reduced rate," he explained. "I myself charge one écu, but as they always find this too expensive I say to them, 'Here's my apprentice who does it for thirty sols,' and I let him keep the profit.

"I can assure you he's far more popular than I am, although he's so clumsy that he's no better at it today than when he started eighteen months ago. With a little practice he'll end up doing very well."

But let us return to my old friend.

"Father Chouinard, you've just told me that you go your own way and mind your own business. Haven't you ever quarreled with the parish priest?"

"Never," said old Romain, "although the one we have now is certainly asking for it. You know, Monsieur Philippe, that I have a good wife, as mild as a lamb. Well! Each time the curé meets her, he greets her with, 'As grumpy as ever, Mother Chouinard?' That really gets her goat, and she lets him have it. Sometimes I itch to lose my temper, but the curé always laughs as if to split a gut, and I'm too taken aback to do anything."

"You do well to let Mother Romain look after herself," I remarked. "Didn't she say she can lose her temper when need be?"

"There are a lot of gossips who claim she's got more than her share of temper, but I've never seen anything of it."

This was true. He got on very well with his wife. Each time we left for a hunting expedition, he kissed her affectionately and she would reveal two eyeteeth—this being her most expressive mode of showing him that she appreciated the caress.

The first and constant victim of a shrew is generally her husband. He is usually the preferred target of her malice, although I've known several cases of the opposite. I will limit myself to one, however.

A father possessed an only daughter, as beautiful as she was sharp-tongued, who was driving him mad. His worst enemy fell passionately in love with this amiable offspring, and ventured fearfully to ask for the girl's hand. To the suitor's amazement, as to everyone else's, he received a favourable answer. The marriage took place, and the father remarked to his friends after the mass, with a nod toward his son-in-law, "I never could abide that animal. I've been trying to get my own back for ages, without success. My daughter is a malicious she-devil who has plagued me from the day she was born. I hope she never gives him a moment's peace."

O best-laid plans of men, how often they play us false! This kind-hearted father-in-law had the pain of witnessing his most hated enemy's happiness throughout the twenty years or more that he survived the wedding. When people in Quebec spoke of a happy union, a loving wife, or a good mother, they cited this worthy couple. But woe betide the outsider who fell foul of this excellent woman.

"There are those," said old Chouinard, "cleverer than I am, too, who say we should pay no attention to the parish priest when he talks of things outside his ministry. They assure us that the priests are in cahoots with the rich in order to ruin the habitant. This seems strange to me, all the same. Surely, if the habitant is rich, the curé benefits too. The tithe^G is more readily paid, more high masses are sung, and there are fewer poor folk for the curé to look after, because they find more work when the habitant is prosperous.

"You know that rain often makes wheat sprout when it is spread to dry in the field. Just last year there was a lot of damage. This summer the curé spoke about it from the pulpit, and said that if the habitants would bind their wheat in sheaves when mowing, it would be as safe from the rain as in the barn, and of much better quality. Do you know what some habitants said on coming out of church?"

"Yes, Father Chouinard. When church was over I heard some of them say, 'Monsieur le curé would do better to mind his own business. Obviously he's afraid of eating sprouted wheat.'"

"I found this so silly," said Old Romain, "that I couldn't help telling them, 'The curé won't be the one to be pitied most. He'll only eat one minot for every twenty-six harvested by the habitant. In fact, he probably won't eat any sprouted wheat. All the wheat in one parish can't be affected in the same autumn. He'll put aside the good wheat for future use, sell the damaged stuff, and let us eat our sprouted

wheat ourselves, since we seem so fond ot it.' They retorted that I
didn't know anything about business matters, and that all this talk
was just to butter up the curé."

"Now," said I, "let's talk about elections."

"I voted for the deceased Monsieur the two times he ran, and if
he didn't win it wasn't the fault of our parish, which voted for him
en masse; but as there were five parishes in the riding, we were
wiped out."

"It seems to me, Father Romain, that a good number of his censitaires
voted against him."

"A mere handful, Monsieur Philippe, not more than fifteen or so—
men without any common sense. D—— came to me and said, 'If we
vote for the seigneur we'll all be ruined.' 'Why?' said I. 'Because
the seigneurs are only interested in swallowing up the habitant.'

"You know," added old Chouinard, "I'm a peace-loving man, but
my anger got the better of me. I was in a fair way to get myself sued
when my wife came to the rescue and let him have it.

"'Animal! It's certainly not you that the seigneur is trying to ruin,'
she told him. 'Twelve years since you bought your land, and you've
not paid your *rentes* or *lods et ventes*. Your wife, who's just as mealy-
mouthed as you, tells some cock-and-bull story to the seigneur, and
he says, "That's all right, my poor woman, next year will do." And
to think, for all your stinginess in paying others, you bought your
horse a silver-studded harness that cost you at least thirty piastres
cash!'

"As the fellow saw my wife eyeing the broomstick, he slid out the
door like an otter."

I am at a loss to account for the habitants' mistrust of their seigneurs
and curés, who must surely be their most sincere well-wishers, if
only in self-interest. Is the proportion of men with plain common
sense even less that I imagine? The evidence seems to point that
way.

Of all the totally uneducated farmers who have been members of
our provincial assembly over the last sixty years, only two had enough
sense to retire as soon as possible.

"What news from the assembly?" my father asked one of them
who was on his way home.

"The news is that I must have had a screw loose when I was fool
enough to stick my nose where it wasn't wanted. There are endless

speeches by bigwigs using highfalutin language that I can't make head nor tail of. I have to pledge my conscience every two minutes by voting on questions I don't understand. The devil will be pretty smart if he can catch me again once my time is up."

The other was an emaciated giant of about six foot four, French measure,[H] who used to amuse us no end when he visited one of his relations during recreation time at the Quebec Seminary. He was a clown with a fair dose of mother wit. After holding forth in much the same terms as the member just quoted, he would add, "I die of shame when I'm in the assembly. I do my best to keep out of sight so that the spectators can't see me. I try to make myself small, but my blasted head always sticks out."

This worthy legislator was telling the truth. It was one of our games, when visiting the legislative assembly on Thursdays, to watch his efforts to avoid our teasing stares. How cruel children are!

But I must return to old Romain Chouinard, to whom I now bid adieu.

Rest in peace, good old man! Rest in peace! Not among the great and powerful of this world, but beneath the humble grass that covers the grave of the virtuous! If the dead within this lugubrious enclave could rise up some stormy night to resume life's battles, if they conjured you to take up again, like them, a life which they had left with such bitter regret, you would refuse to leave a dwelling where the silence resembles the quiet and tranquil existence you led on earth.

Sleep in peace, humble and sincere Christian! If the tempest has laid low the modest cross planted on your grave, if the passage of time has destroyed it, yet go before your supreme judge with confidence! Did you not carry that cross in your heart and on your brow your whole life long?

Romain Chouinard's character was typical of many of the peaceable habitants whom I have known in the course of my long pilgrimage in this world, where so many are the architects of their own unhappiness.

CHAPTER FIFTEEN

Force à superbe! Mercy à foible!

THE HONOURABLE LOUIS-IGNACE D'IRUMBERRY DE SALABERRY

The traveler who, at eventide, after a long and arduous journey, happens on an oasis where he finds a stream of pure and limpid waters to quench a burning thirst, does not feel as keen a satisfaction as I, in offering my countrymen a few sketches from the life of this Canadian gentilhomme—a life that flowed as unsullied as our clearest forest brook. Is not the remembrance of a citizen who was ever virtuous throughout a long life more gratifying to the chronicler, so near the grave himself, than the refreshing cup drunk by pilgrims in the desert's oases? Indeed, the chronicler has reached an age when long experience of men has taught him to appreciate them for their true worth.

No ordinary man could have inspired the homage of people from all walks of life. To watch Monsieur de Salaberry[A] pass through the streets of Quebec was a moving sight. Faces would light up as he came into view, each man doffing his hat respectfully as he went by. Monsieur Vocelle, an old and respected citizen of this city, said to me recently, "Our parents taught us from childhood to bow to Monsieur de Salaberry. He never neglected to return the compliment, be it to the smallest urchin in town."

Ignace-Michel-Louis-Antoine d'Irumberry de Salaberry (1752-1828) and his wife, Françoise-Catherine Hertel de Pierreville (d. 1824). Silhouettes by Eliab Metcalfe (1809), McCord Museum of Canadian History, McGill University, Montreal, M 972.81.21.1 and M 972.81.21.2.

Was it riches that attracted such universal deference? No indeed! Monsieur de Salaberry was then comparatively poor. Was it the high rank he held in the colony? Certainly not, for he was a mere justice of the peace at the time. The general admiration was inspired by something far more impressive: the feeling that this estimable person had ever in mind the motto engraved on the family crest: *Force à superbe! Mercy à foible!*[B]

The origin of this motto is too glorious, too remarkable, to be passed over in silence. The de Salaberry family settled in this colony over a hundred years ago, and their exceptional muscular strength is so well known to all Canadians that one must suppose this attribute was transmitted by their ancestors from time immemorial, as the following extract from the memoirs of this illustrious family would seem to prove.

"There is an ancient tradition in the family that the motto *Force à superbe! Mercy à foible!* comes from the battle of Coutras in 1587, where one of our ancestors killed a man-at-arms of notable height and strength, and wounded another. The latter asked that his life be

331

spared as he lay on the field of battle, a request that was granted. Upon the scene at this moment came the intrepid King of Navarre, always in the thick of battle. This magnanimous hero, justly appreciating these two noble exploits, cried with the gaiety habitual to him in combat: 'Force à superbe! Mercy à foible! Let it be your motto.' The king of Navarre was the great Henri IV, later king of France."

Let us pause for an instant before the illustrious figure of Henri IV, a redoubtable warrior whose sword hit hard and often. The extract I have just quoted aptly illustrates the character of this excellent prince, mourned throughout France with tears of blood. According to the historian Pierre Mathieu, "Everywhere rivers of tears sprang forth; everywhere could be heard the cries and groans of the common people. It seemed, indeed, that the blow had struck them physically, so lost and dazed did the violence of their grief render them. If one looks for the cause of this poignant sorrow, the answer is immediately clear: love. . . . These torrents of tears swept the whole country-side. . . . It is said that several died of sorrow, their names being cited."

The de Salaberry motto *Force à superbe! Mercy à foible!* well demonstrates the noble character of the prince who, in the heat of a bloody battle, beseeched one of his men-at-arms to show mercy toward his enemies. After victory, Henri IV looked upon his erstwhile foes as friends.

Among the magistrates of the city of Quebec, Captain Thomas Allison[1] was noted for his unbending attitude toward the accused, whereas Monsieur de Salaberry was remarked upon for his indulgence toward the guilty. Fault could be found with both attitudes: one judged with military inflexibility, the other, too often, with his heart. When Monsieur de Salaberry was a major in the Royal Canadians commanded by Colonel de Longueil,[2][c] the soldiers looked to him as a kind father who tempered their colonel's severity.

Of all human qualities, a kind heart is that most esteemed by the common people; hence this affection for Monsieur de Salaberry, to whom the unfortunate came in their trouble, sure of finding sympathy and compassion, even if he were unable to help them more materially. "Go to Monsieur de Salaberry," such persons were told, "and he will do all in this power to aid you."

My pleasure in paying tribute to this excellent gentleman is all the greater in that I have no fear of being contradicted, either by those

of my countrymen who knew him, or the children of those now dead—
for I am certain that the memory of his virtues has been handed down
to them by their parents.

The purpose of this chronicle being to give the reader a glimpse
of the intimate rather than public side of our Canadian men of note,
I will provide only a short sketch of his career at the end of this
chapter, so that I may deal almost exclusively with his private life.

Monsieur de Salaberry, who received an extensive education in
France, took a lively interest in the progress of his young Canadian
compatriots, not only during their school years, but afterwards as
well. Although not rich, he was a generous host, and his house was
always open to those who wished to spend a pleasant evening around
the tea table with his amiable family. Consequently the young people,
whom he liked and who found him very entertaining, made a point
of joining the frequent gatherings at his home.

When he spoke to us of his travels, recounting numerous interesting
anecdotes, we felt up to sharing in the talk, but when he led the
conversation around to Latin authors, things took a very different
turn. We made a fairly decent showing as long as he confined himself
to speaking to us in French; great was our dismay, however, when
he addressed us in the language of Cicero. We were not strong in a
language that we hadn't been accustomed to speaking in the seminary.
If our friend Vallière[3] happened to be present, we were in luck—
honour to whom honour is due. First, we would let the two adepts
begin conversing, then, one by one, we would steal away to join less
serious conclaves.

When Monsieur de Salaberry came back from France several years
before the Revolution, he was invited to watch a play, *Le Barbier de
Séville*, performed by a group of young Canadian amateurs.[D]

"Why should I go to your theatre to witness the massacre of a play
that I saw performed in Paris by the finest actors?" said he, but
allowed himself to be persuaded, nonetheless, and attended this
charming comedy more to be affable than amused. Traditionally,
many of our young Canadians have shown a remarkable aptitude for
the theatre. I can say unreservedly in their praise that, with few
exceptions, they succeeded far better than the British amateurs, as
even the English agreed.

During the first scene between Count Almaviva and the Barber,
Monsieur de Salaberry was carried away by enthusiasm for the talents

333

of his young compatriot, Monsieur Menard. He rose from his seat and cried in his fine, ringing voice, "Courage, Figaro! It's as good as Paris!"

The audience, electrified by these words, stood up spontaneously, shouting, "Courage, Figaro! It's as good as Paris!" followed by a deluge of hurrahs for de Salaberry.

O happy time, when we all knew one another in our good city of Quebec! Happy time when one was among friends, even at the theatre! When a universally-liked man could interrupt a play without impropriety and be cheered by the public!

More than thirty years after this, the Duke of Richmond,[E] who had recently arrived in Canada as governor, gave an evening party in order that the ladies might be presented. Monsieur de Salaberry, then very old, no doubt felt that he could do no less for a prince than appear at the Château Saint-Louis in the attire of the court of Louis XVI. I had just arrived with my wife when our friend, Monsieur Juchereau Duchesnay,[F] said to us in the antechamber, "There's a funny sight upstairs. My father-in-law has taken it into his head to wear the clothes in which he was presented at the court of France. Since the duke, whom few know by sight, hasn't yet made his entrance, almost all who pass by my father-in-law salute him, deceived by the richness of his dress. The gentlemen bow low, the ladies curtsey deeply, and Monsieur de Salaberry returns the honour with the dignity of a prince."

Monsieur de Salaberry was very short-sighted, and being so generally liked and respected quite naturally noticed nothing unusual. I must confess that if my friend hadn't given me prior warning, I should have bowed to Monsieur de Salaberry myself, thinking to render homage to the new governor.

The bearing of this Canadian of gentle birth was as noble and imposing as that of the Duke of Richmond, but any physical resemblance stopped there. The duke was taller, big-boned, and muscular, with a cold, severe, and morose expression that, when he entered the drawing room, brought to mind Voltaire's line: "Le Richemond qui porte un cœur de fer."[G] Those who have read his life know whether or not he was truly a man of iron heart.

Another thought immediately occurred to me: that never, in the days of chivalry, did gallant knight carry his armour so lightly or strike his enemies more cruelly than the Duke of Richmond.

334

Monsieur de Salaberry made quite a different impression. The breadth of his shoulders, which would have been the envy of a Milo of Croton, served to diminish his height. A bludgeon seemed the appropriate weapon for his herculean arm.

The characteristics of their respective forebears were admirably preserved in these two men. Toward the end of the evening they conversed at length. We formed a circle at a respectful distance, and I heard the duke repeat two or three times, "That scoundrel Buonaparte"—an Englishman always added an insulting epithet when pronouncing the name of the giant chained to the rock of Saint Helena—"that scoundrel Buonaparte stole my orange trees." He was, I suppose, alluding to the orange trees in his duchy of Aubigny. They talked in French, a language that the duke spoke as purely as his interlocutor. One would have taken them for two Parisians conversing.

I was touched, when dining for the first time at the Château Saint-Louis, by the affectionate manner in which the duke's sons treated the domestics. The young Lord Frederick Lennox, aide-de-camp to his father, motioned to one of the servants during dinner, and passing his arm amicably around his neck, spoke a few words in his ear. This was indeed the act of a true nobleman in whose veins ran royal blood. He had no fear of losing caste by treating a servant with special kindness.

His older brother, Lord William Lennox, also one of the duke's aides-de-camp, joined our Jockey Club almost as soon as he arrived in Quebec. The members had met shortly after, and he had attended the meeting. I was not introduced to him on this occasion, however. Great was my surprise, therefore, when, as we approached each other in the street next day, he crossed over and conversed with me as though we were old acquaintances.

Accustomed to the stiff and haughty bearing of English ladies, it was with considerable trepidation that we paid an initial call on Lady Mary Lennox, the Duke of Richmond's daughter. The Canadian ladies in particular felt she would crush them with her grandeur—but not at all: we saw a young noblewoman of unassuming, even affectionate manner, who only sought to put us at our ease.

This calls to mind an incident involving my cousin, Eliza-Anne Baby, widow of the late Honourable Charles E. Casgrain. Her father, the Honourable Jacques Dupéron Baby,[H] then a member of the legislative and executive council of Upper Canada over which he presided for many years, was on intimate terms with the governors of that province. One day Lady Maitland,[1] wife of the lieutenant-governor of the same name and a descendant of one of England's first families, asked to meet his daughter, then quite young. Mademoiselle Baby was somewhat fearful upon first entering this great lady's drawing room, where she expected to encounter the full British stiffness, but she was agreeably surprised by the affable and well-disposed welcome that awaited her.

Simply dressed and unpretentious in her speech, the lady soon put my cousin perfectly at ease by the grace and liveliness of her conversation.

Mademoiselle Baby was not only charmed by Lady Maitland's graciousness, but also indelibly impressed by the air of dignity and nobility that her whole person breathed. One recognized on sight, even in the simplest garb, an aristocratic descendant of the high and powerful lords of Albion.

I cite these examples in support of a long-held theory of mine, proven by lengthy experience: that those who find themselves at the summit of the social scale by birth, not promotion, are less proud in their dealings with inferiors than are those recently risen to wealth and position.

A propos the Jockey Club just mentionned, which is still functioning, it was founded about the year 1815 by the late Monsieur Narcisse Duchesnay,[J] the late Doctor Pierre de Sales Laterrière, and myself, among others, in the following circumstances.[K]

Duchesnay had a horse of whose speed he boasted much, while I owned one of mixed antecedents named Dragoon, because I had purchased it at an auction of cavalry horses in Quebec. This Dragoon ran like a deer. Laterrière convinced me that my horse, although not a thoroughbred, could hold his own over a mile-long stretch against Duchesnay's steed. A bet was made, and I was victorious. My Dragoon had won his last race, however, and the following year left me somewhat embarrassed when I made him run three miles instead of one. Rarely have I seen a horse run faster over a short distance.

The race between Duchesnay's horse and mine soon aroused the interest of three or four others, and the following year we formed a club to establish annual races, which I believe, have continued without interruption until the present day.

To return to Monsieur de Salaberry: tall of stature, as I have noted, and built like Hercules, his bearing was so imposing, his air so dignified that, without actually having fine features, he passed for a handsome man. One felt an involuntary start of admiration each time he entered a drawing room with his wife upon his arm, she being as gracious as she was beautiful, followed by his children, four boys and three girls, all unusually good-looking.

Let us consider an even more imposing sight. Monsieur de Salaberry was a fervent Catholic—despite his erudition, a philosopher might say, although a Christian might feel it was because of his profound learning—and he brought up his children in a truly Christian manner. As the church bell sounded the last stroke of the *Agnus Dei*, the mother and father would rise, and their seven children would follow them to share the Easter communion. Several people who have witnessed the whole de Salaberry family perform this religious act told me that it made an evident impresson on the congregation.

I must yield to a desire which takes me back to the wonderful days of my youth, and that is, to give the names of this family, so noteworthy and beloved of all their fellow citizens, of whatever class or origin.

Adelaide, the oldest of these demoiselles, and Amélie, the youngest who died four years ago, never married. Hermine, the second daughter, married her second cousin, Adjutant-General Juchereau Duchesnay, and left many descendants. Her daughters, Mesdames de Saint-Ours, Campbell, and Ermatinger, and her sons, the Honourable Antoine Juchereau Duchesnay and Lieutenant-Colonel Philippe Duchesnay, honorary provincial aide-de-camp, the only ones now living, are too well known to need further explanation.

The de Salaberry ladies were endowed with intellect and wit, and I cannot give a better idea of their beauty than by adding that during her youth the youngest of the three—the least handsome—was invariably called "sweet angel" by the English. Those who knew her in the last years of her life will think I exaggerate, as I do myself when people speak of many old women whose youthful beauty was much vaunted. But those who were familiar with Mademoiselle Amélie's fine spirit will think, on the contrary, that I have been sparing in my praise.

At the end of this chapter I propose to give a short biography of the oldest child, Colonel Charles-Michel de Salaberry, whom I will call Chateauguay de Salaberry in these memoirs—a title that my countrymen will perhaps give me the pleasure of adopting, should this work find acceptance in their eyes. This being the case, I will say no more for the moment on the subject of this gentilhomme whose glorious memory will live forever in the patriotic heart of true Canadians.

The careers of his three younger brothers, Maurice, Louis, and Edouard (godson of the Duke of Kent, father of our gracious sovereign, Queen Victoria) were short but glorious. Edouard was killed in 1811 at the siege of Badajoz during the Spanish Peninsular War. By a quite extraordinary coincidence, Badajoz was defended by a Canadian, Lieutenant-General Vicomte de Léry, commander-in-chief of the engineers and one of the most famous generals of Napoleon I, who held him in high esteem.

The two other brothers, Maurice and Louis, perished in the East Indies, where a monument still bears witness to the admiration of their brothers-at-arms.

Everyone knew of the senior Monsieur de Salaberry's physical strength, but it was not generally known that his sons had inherited it. About 1809 young Lieutenant Maurice de Salaberry, adjutant of the Canadian militia, was putting a company of Canadian volunteers through their drill in a shed at the foot of the Côte de la Canoterie. The shed housed a cannon, of what calibre I know not, but so heavy that after a great many attempts to lift one end off the ground the militiamen, who used to amuse themselves with trials of strength, gave up.

"If your father were here," said one of them to their young adjutant, indicating the artillery piece, "he'd soon overturn that pair of bellows!"

The common people, particularly the habitants, often referred to cannon as bellows.

"Are your bellows so heavy," said the young officer, "that men like you, Joseph Vézina, Pierre Boyer, Poussart, Guilbaut, and Thom Dorion, can't lift it? Don't worry: for the honour of Canadians I'll try."

A wag remarked in low but audible tones, "Fine feats our adjutant's going to perform, with his long, thin fingers and ladylike white hands!"

The words were hardly out of his mouth before the two aristocratic hands had lifted the enormous weight to the young officer's waist.

But to return to the principal subject of this chapter: albeit moral strength is a more precious gift than physical force, men are nonetheless prone to admire the latter greatly, especially when united to the former in the same person. I think my readers will therefore be pleased to hear about some of the muscular feats of the head of the de Salaberry family.

Fort Saint-Jean was under seige by the Americans in 1775 when a bomb exploded on top of a hut sheltering Monsieur de Salaberry and some officers. All the others had time to get out before the old building collapsed. The officers rushed to the rescue of their comrade-in-arms, under the painful expectation of dragging a lifeless body from the ruins. To their amazement, they found a new Samson, more fortunate than the first, down on hands and knees, his powerful shoulders supporting a section of the building. This is no myth, for the incident occurred in front of a hundred witnesses, three of whom recounted it to me in my youth. A few mouthfuls of blood brought some relief, but he felt the effects of this accident for many a long day, so he used to tell us.

Once I asked him if this had been the greatest test of his muscular power.

"I don't think so," he replied. "Another time, also in a life-and-death situation, I had to use even more strength. At the time of my adventure at Fort Saint-Jean, I was in a position to support an enormous weight, and nothing interfered with the use of my muscles. But under the exceptional conditions that I'm about to describe, it needed a superhuman effort to save my life, as you may judge for yourself.

"It was wintertime, a little before sundown. I had been hunting all day in the Beauport hills and was going home. As I descended a bluff on snowshoes, an avalanche from the summit buried me. The snow was above my head, but luckily it didn't knock me down. It pressed in around me, however, and I immediately found myself confined on all sides, as though in a vice, although I soon recovered the use of my arms by thrusting outwards with my elbows and pushing away the suffocating snow. In spite of this partial freedom my position was appalling, for my feet were firmly strapped, by moose-hide thongs wound twice above my heels, to large snowshoes that were covered with six feet of packed snow.

"When the full horror of my situation came home to me, I felt utterly lost and without hope. I recommended my soul to God, for there was no possibility of help from men in that lonely place, and knowing what strength was needed to free myself, I felt it was a task beyond human resources. The only way I could save myself was to snap the thongs by resting on one foot while pulling up the other with

339

all my might. As you may imagine, the more I pulled, the more the thongs tightened about the heel to be freed, causing me terrible pain. Despair doubled my strength, however, but those who can appreciate the position I was in will realize that the muscles had very little room for the movement required to break such bonds with only one leg. My confinement notwithstanding, at the end of two or three hours of persevering and superhuman exertion, I snapped the thongs—but at the cost of my two Achilles' tendons, which were stripped so raw that I nearly developed lockjaw.

"Yes, my dear de Gaspé, I may say that this was the only time I thanked God fervently for giving my physical strength, for at Fort Saint-Jean I could use my muscles properly, but my second ordeal left me nothing but the power of despair with which to break my fearful bonds, and even this was drastically reduced by my constricted position."

The following brief account may give a comparative idea of Monsieur de Salaberry's powers. He and my uncle, Gaspard de Lanaudière, also a man of remarkable strength, were at the presbytery of Cap-Santé one Sunday before mass. A group of the parish habitants were gathered around a bell whose weight I now forget. The bell was destined for the church tower, which had been destroyed by lightning. The strongest men were trying in vain to lift its heavy bulk off the ground when my uncle joined them. Not only did he lift the bell: he made it clang several times, to the astonishment of the spectators, whom he had previously showered with derision at their feeble attempts to display manly strength. Back at the presbytery, he laughingly told the curé that he had just rung the bell for mass.

"Well done, Gaspard!" said Monsieur de Salaberry. "You take after your father, the strongest man I ever knew."

They dined at the presbytery, after which the curé, consulting his watch, pronounced it time for vespers. Monsieur de Salaberry slipped out without saying a word, and a moment later the bell was heard to peal furiously. Back came Hercules, laughing.

"Well, my dear Lanaudière, you rang the bell for mass; I rang it for vespers."

My father used to describe the following scene, which he witnessed with his own eyes when serving in the British army under General Burgoyne in 1777. They were camped near the Hudson River.

"We were seated in a lean-to one evening," went his account, "when an enormous rattlesnake, attracted perhaps by the fire around which we were gathered, suddenly sprang up in our midst. We were all paralyzed with terror, but Monsieur de Salaberry, keeping a cool head, grabbed the dreadful reptile, strangled it in his powerful grasp, and tossed it into the lighted brazier of our bivouac."

Notable among the ruffians—Canadians for the most part—who disturbed the peaceful folk of the good city of Quebec and its suburbs in olden times, was a member of the Huron tribe. This fellow had frequently been thrown out of his village[L] because of his escapades, but invariably managed to return by promising to lead a more exemplary life. The Indian, Picard by name, was tall, his wide shoulders thrown back, his bearing proud and statuesque. He behaved as if he were in conquered territory when he entered a house containing only women, or men too feeble to resist. He would make them do his bidding and give him everything he asked for, especially rum, for which he had a decided preference.

But where were the police, thinks my reader? The only policemen during my childhood were the soldiers on duty who happened to be within call. The troublemakers had usually made off by the time they arrived.

Monsieur de Salaberry was coming home one day when he heard the terrified screams of the women of the family coming from his house[4] at the corner of Stadacona and Desjardins, almost opposite the Ursuline church. This house had a long verandah six or seven feet above the ground, as was then the custom. Monsieur de Salaberry went up the stairs to the dining room four steps at a time. Here he found Master Picard, who had taken possession of a wine carafe and now wanted the women to hand over the keys to the cupboards. Justice was short and swift. In his initial rage at the sight of his family in distress, the magistrate seized the Huron by the flanks and sent him sailing through the window, over the balcony, and across the Rue Desjardins.

Reason quickly succeeded this terrific burst of anger, and he rushed to the aid of the savage whom he fortunately found still alive after his aerial journey, although considerably the worse for wear. Picard hobbled away muttering, "He's bad *Charivary!*"[M]

"You've forgotten the most amusing detail of all," remarked my old friend, Monsieur Barthélemy Faribault,[5][N] to whom I recently read this account. "When Monsieur de Salaberry helped Picard up, he said, 'Have I hurt you, dear child?'"

This perfectly illustrates the character of that excellent man.

Monsieur de Salaberry always carried a huge cudgel, a sort of herculean bludgeon.

"It's a good thing, Colonel, that you're so very strong," I one day teased him. "Anyone else would be dead tired after a day of carrying around such a weight."

"It isn't for my good deeds that I always carry this ridiculous club," said he. "It's my guide and mentor, for I have a quick temper. This cudgel is forever crying, 'Don't do anything rash, de Salaberry!' and I come to my senses. An ordinary cane wouldn't have the same effect. I can put up with personal insults, but to see the strong oppress the weak makes me furious."

One day, when he was living at Beauport, news was brought to him that a backwoods bully who had been terrorizing the parish for some time was at that moment in the presbytery, kicking up an infernal row. Arriving on the spot, the magistrate easily distinguished oppressed from oppressor, for the curé, Monsieur Van Felson,° was dabbing the blood on his chin with a handkerchief, while the tough swore mightily that "may S[atan's devil]s twist my soul on the end of a poker"[6] if he didn't exterminate all priests and bishops who dared say a word about his goings on.

It seemed the curé had advised his parishioners to shun this man, who was creating havoc in the parish and never opened his mouth but to swear and blaspheme. Hence the vengeance that he had just wreaked on the pastor.

"Wretch!" cried Monsieur de Salaberry. "How dare you strike the anointed of God!"

"I'll do the same for you," retorted the bully, advancing toward the magistrate with raised fist.

Hardly had he pronounced these words than a powerful arm launched him like a cannonball over table and chairs, to be picked up in a state of collapse.

Thereafter everything was settled amicably. The curé agreed not to take the man to court if his assailant would agree to leave the parish of Beauport within twenty-four hours—a condition which the bully was only too glad to fulfil after his rough lesson.

In earlier times it was not unusual in the District of Quebec to encounter bullies employed by the North West Company, who came down from Sorel, L'Assomption, and other District of Montreal parishes for the sole purpose of provoking brawls with worthy opponents, regarding themselves as wolves among the sheep of the Lower Saint Lawrence. If they went home with black eyes, they would console themselves with their eternal boast: "No ladies' man gave me a shiner like this!"

One last detail about Monsieur de Salaberry's strength, and I shall close the subject for fear of boring readers who don't care for this sort of prowess. He put four fingers into the barrels of four grenadier's rifles and held them horizontally, his arm straight, for several seconds.

The service record of this brave gentilhomme shows that he amply repaid the debt every citizen owes his country: first to the land of his ancestors by serving as a cadet in the French army at the age of fourteen, and subsequently, in fighting as a volunteer under the banner of Great Britain, to be wounded three times during the rebellion of the American colonies.

In 1796 he was named major of the first batallion of the Royal Volunteer regiment commanded by Colonel de Longueil,[7] which was re-formed in 1802. Here, too, he tempered the rigid discipline of his colonel. In 1812, during the last American war, he commanded the first regiment of select embodied militia raised at that time.[P] He was twice elected to our provincial parliament, and subsequently named by his sovereign to the legislative council. But let him speak for himself in the autograph note that I have before me:

> No Canadian subject has made such painful sacrifices for his king. Of four sons, I have lost three in the army—surely a most cruel proportion, and the cause of ineradicable sorrow! The only son left to me has served the army with the 60th in various parts of the world, continually and with honour, since the age of fourteen. Among other actions was the glorious affair at Chateauguay, for which he received from His Majesty several marks of distinction and a seat on the legislative council, in defiance of the established rule of never having a father and son sit at the same time. I trust that we both will be the government's staunchest supporters, be it in council or with sword in hand, despite my advanced age.

I cannot end this profile better than by publishing one of the many autograph letters of the Duke of Kent, father of our gracious sovereign,

Queen Victoria, written to Monsieur de Salaberry. The letters addressed to the father are all written in French and signed "Edouard," whereas those to the son are written in English and signed "Edward." The de Salaberry family archives also contain several letters in Latin from His Royal Highness to Monsieur de Salaberry senior, which to my great regret I have been unable to procure. One of these epistles would be sure to intrigue men of letters of our own day, as it offers a curious picture of the kind of classical education then given the princes of England's royal family. If wielding the rod constituted a sure method of teaching them Latin, the Duke of Kent must have been an excellent Latinist, for he said one day to a colonel in the engineers at Quebec. "Do you remember, B——, the thorough canings administered by your respectable father, our private tutor, when he taught us Latin?"

One must conclude from this that it was not the custom in German courts to beat a common child in the presence of young princes as an encouragement to study, but rather that the latter were submitted to the same form of correction as other pupils. But to return to the letter which terminates this biographical sketch:[Q]

Kensington Palace,
March 15, 1814.

My dear de Salaberry,

On December 31 I received your interesting letter of November 10, acquainting me with the dispatches reporting the advance of the Canadian army, October 27, and the brilliant affair of the previous day, in which your son was victorious.[R] At the same time, I received letters from him supplying the details, and do not hesitate to state that, not only are you justfied in being proud of the victory gained by my protégé against forces so superior in number to those under his command, but that in his preparations, and during the battle, he displayed a judgment and talent rarely found, even among veterans.

I was sorry to see that the adjutant-general's report did not do him sufficient justice, as it did not show that the success of the operation was exclusively due to the preparations carried out by your son. But you may take comfort in the thought that everyone here accords him all the honour of it, and that he is regarded as the hero who saved the province of Lower Canada by his decisive measures, and by the steadfastness with which he opposed his small corps of select militia to enemy troops of such superior numbers. I have even discussed it with the Duke of York, who seemed perfectly convinced that all the credit is due to your son. I have no doubt that, given the opportunity, the Duke will try to reward him in a manner that accords with his desires and merits. You will realize that he would not feel this way, were it not for the reports of English officers who were present and who witnessed the affair. . . .

With the same friendship as always, my dear de Salaberry,

Your most affectionate,

EDOUARD, DUKE OF KENT

Monsieur le colonel De Salaberry,
    senior, Beauport,
      Quebec.

As we live in an era when happily one may speak the truth without fear of passing for a disloyal subject, I will add that the English, in spite of themselves, were bound to do Colonel de Salaberry justice in giving him full credit for the victory at Chateauguay, but with this small modification: that he owed the victory to the light-infantry corps composed almost entirely of Englishmen.[5] It must have required unabashed arrogance to foist such a lie on an entire province! Some six months after this celebrated battle, I was visiting an English family. The lady of the house said to me, in all seriousness, that it wasn't at all surprising that Colonel de Salaberry had achieved such a brilliant success, considering the light-infantry corps was three quarters English.

"Madame is surely joking?" said I.

"Oh, no," said she, looking askance. "Just ask my husband."

"Nonsense!" exclaimed the husband, turning red and changing the subject.

I subsequently had reason to believe that at least two thirds of the English population believed this fable, or pretended to, at any rate.

All the world knows that during the war of 1812 the British element in Lower Canada was scarcely sufficient to fill the required complement of officers in English militia battalions, and that it is only since the Irish exodus that it has increased in such notable proportions. Let us be just above any other consideration, and accord their share of

345

glory to the small number of English militiamen who fought shoulder to shoulder with their French-Canadian brothers. Let us grant to Upper Canadians the glory acquired during this war in their own province, but let us leave to French Canadians the honour of having saved Lower Canada.

CHATEAUGUAY DE SALABERRY

Canadians in my youth spoke only with pride of their young compatriot, Charles-Michel de Salaberry,[T] son of Monsieur de Salaberry, when he was but a lieutenant in the British 60th regiment. They knew that the honour of their race was in good hands and that he would not allow it to be insulted with impunity. Of this he gave a shining example at the very beginning of his military career.

The officers' corps of the 60th was made up of men from various nations: English, Prussian, Swiss, Hanoverian, and two French Canadians—Lieutenants de Salaberry and DesRivières.[U] That any degree of harmony should exist among such disparate elements is difficult to imagine; the Germans, in particular, were a quarrelsome, hot-tempered lot, much given to dueling.

Lieutenant de Salaberry was breakfasting with some brothers-at-arms when a German officer came into the room, looked at the young Canadian with an insolent expression, and said, "I have just dispatched a French Canadian to the other world!"

He was alluding to Lieutenant DesRivières, whom he had just killed in a duel.

De Salaberry rose up like a tiger, but checking himself quickly, said calmly, "Very well, Monsieur. We will breakfast and then you shall have the pleasure of dispatching another French Canadian."

The combat was long and relentless. Lieutenant de Salaberry was very young, whereas his antagonist, the German captain, was older and an accomplished swordsman. The young Canadian received a sabre cut on his forehead, the scar of which he bore ever after. His friends wanted to put an end to the duel, but the wounded man persistently refused. He bandaged his head with his handkerchief and the fight resumed with increased ferocity. I can truthfully say that the German captain has never since slain a French Canadian, or anyone else for that matter.

At the time of the last American war, the British governor felt the need of conciliating the French Canadians, roused to indignation by

LT-COL. CHARLES DE SALABERRY.

Lt.-Col. Charles-Michel d'Irumberry de Salaberry, the hero of Chateauguay, masterminded one of the crucial battles of the War of 1812, routing the invading Americans with the Voltigeurs Canadiens militia. Engr. The Burland Desbarats Co. of Montreal, in L.-O. David, *Biographies et portraits* (1876) the persecution of their most eminent compatriots under the recent Craig administration. The task was not difficult: it sufficed to give public recognition to the courage of brave Jean-Baptiste to make him forget all. How, in effect, could one continue to resent a government that, when the militia was raised, put French Canadians almost exclusively in command—those very men whom it had previously hounded as traitors to the crown of England?

I think I should add that one of the measures that touched the pride of French Canadians most was to see Captain de Salaberry of the 60th given the responsibility, at first with the rank of major, of raising a select corps from among his compatriots, to be called the Voltigeurs Canadiens. The quota for this regiment was soon filled, each man wishing to serve under a gentilhomme of whom they were proud. The real difficulty, however, lay in disciplining a corps of men, made up in large part of young fellows who had once been the rowdies of their respective towns, suburbs, and villages—places that had become positively somnolent after their departure.

A little sketch will give an idea of the spirit of independence and insubordination possessed by the new recruits from the city of Quebec, before the iron hand of their commandant had bent them to military discipline. One day he entered a shed used for drilling, to witness a strange spectacle for a man accustomed to the severe discipline of the English army. God himself could not have been heard above the uproar, despite the efforts of officers and subalterns to establish order.

A man called Rouleau, one of the most formidable bullies of the Saint-Roch suburb, stood naked to the waist, his face contorted with fury, challenging everyone present.

In my mind's eye I can still see this Rouleau who, because of his continual brawls, was a regular occupant of the dock when the court of quarter sessions was sitting. He was tall, thin, and toothless, a thing of sinew and bone, with a meagre layer of skin to cover the skeletal frame—in a word, a walking spectre of ferocious mien. Rouleau used to boast that the loss of his teeth owed nothing to sweetmeats, adding that "it wasn't nightingales" that had thus cleared his gums of their stumps.

"Get dressed, Rouleau!" thundered the major.

"That'll be the day when a shrimp of an officer like you can make Rouleau obey!" vociferated the unruly recruit, foaming at the mouth with rage.

These ill-considered words were hardly out of his mouth before an iron hand, bearing down heavily on his shoulder, crushed him to the floor like a mere child. No one was in the least prepared for this muscular feat, Major de Salaberry being a man of middle height. The bully's anger dropped away as though he had been hit on the head. He rose limply to his feet.

"All right, all right, Major! I'll get dressed. Where's my shirt?"

This scene was recounted to me by a soldier in the Voltigeurs— Côté was his name, I believe.

"We thought Rouleau had gone through the floorboards," he said. "The major squashed him like a bedbug. He consoled himself quickly enough, however, by announcing that it wasn't any nightingale that had mashed him, and, what was more, 'If you don't believe me, try it for yourselves.'"

There is no doubt that it took a commanding officer of uncommon military ability and great energy to turn a group of raw recruits into a regiment as distinguished as the Voltigeurs Canadiens. In no time at all they equaled the best troops of the regular army in discipline and combat performance. Our Canadian hero was a born soldier, and seemed to have drawn in a whiff of gunpowder with his first breath. I have often heard it said that his company, and that commanded by Captain Chandler,[8] [V] also Canadian, but of British origin, were the best disciplined in the 60th regiment.

The Voltigeurs were scared to death of their commanding officer, as is shown by the following song about him, quite droll and typically Canadian in its straightforward simplicity:

> It's our major,
> Full of the devil,
> Who'll be the death of us.
> There's no tiger or wolf
> Under heaven's wide roof—
> There's no one quite like him,
> So rustic[9] and grim.

Although the Voltigeurs feared their commandant, they nonetheless regarded him with pride and affection. Those whom I knew after the War of 1812 were all agreed.

"It's very true that Colonel de Salaberry kept a whip hand over us, but he was a fair man: everyone got the same treatment and there was no favouritism for either officers or enlisted men. Our grievances were always heard. If the officer was in the wrong, he was severely reprimanded. No preference was shown his relatives, although there were several among the officers."

I regret being unable to quote in its entirety the song composed by our light-hearted Voltigeurs, in which several of the officers and subalterns were treated to either praise or derision. I knew only the first and last verses. Here is the latter:

> By the time our song is ended
> Three jolly fellows
> Are clapped into jail;
> Nor meat nor bread have they,
> Nor anything they want—
> Haven't even got a cent
> To buy a b[lood]y drink. W

Although the colonel evidently made insubordinates toe the line with the utmost severity, their high spirits were undiminished and their poetic verve increased in consequence.

As with the father, I shall end this biographical sketch of the son with an autograph letter in English written by His Royal Highness, the Duke of Kent, after the brilliant victory at Chateauguay.

This letter is too important for me to give it in translation only. The reader will be surprised to learn on reading it that two French Canadians of the highest merit received little credit for the signal services rendered their sovereign, in spite of the protection of a royal prince of England. It is true, of course, that the Duke of Kent was not on the best possible terms with his brother, the Duke of York, commander-in-chief of the British army, and that the latter perhaps allowed himself to be influenced by those wishing to forward the interests of friends in the British army stationed in Canada during the last American war, to the detriment of the French Canadians.

Such memories are painful, but why should they be passed over in silence if they belong to the immutable pages of this colony's history? The impartial writer must speak of them, if only as an object lesson for his compatriots. Colonel de Salaberry saved Lower Canada from a formidable invasion by fighting with his brave Canadians against forces ten times the strength. He received, in the touching words of his father that I have already recorded, "several marks of distinction from his sovereign"—not very telling marks, no doubt, what what does it matter? If the weight of centuries has not prevented the name of Leonidas from being joined with Thermopolae, then the name of de Salaberry and his courageous Canadians will alike be joined to Chateauguay by our great-nephews, unless future geographers, jealous of the Canadians' glory, should efface Chateauguay from the map of Canada.

Herewith the Duke of Kent's remarkable letter:[x]

Kensington Palace,
25th March, 1814.

My dear de Salaberry,

It was on the 22nd of December that I received your letter of the 28th October; and a few days afterwards the details of your brilliant repulse of the enemy, through your worthy father, and your brother in law Duchesnay.

As in the enclosed letter for your father, which I send under flying seal, in order to unable [sic] you to withdraw the postscript, or not, as you may see fit, you will see my sentiments upon that business; it will be needless for me to say more in this, than that I appreciate as highly your distinguished conduct on the memorable occasion in question, as if it had been noticed by those, whose duty it was to notice it in a manner commensurate to your merits. It is easy to form an opinion why more ample justice was not done you; but upon this head, it may perhaps be more prudent to be silent; more especially as you may take my word for it, that here there is but one opinion as to the credit you have done yourself, and the remuneration you are entitled to.

It is a great satisfaction to me to find that the Canadian Militia, both embodied and sedentary, have behaved so well; and when it is considered how insufficient the Militia Laws are to the proper government of the men, upon military principles, I think your merit in having brought your Voltigeurs[10] to the state of perfection, which I understand they have attained, is beyond all praise.

With respect to yourself, I will tell your [sic] candidly my wish is, when a proper opportunity offers, to get you promoted to the rank of Colonel, by being nominated an honorary aide-de-camp to the Prince Regent; and then some day, or other, appointed *colonel-propriétaire* [*sic*] of the Canadian Regiment, which will then trive [*sic*] under you, and enable you to remain in your own country, with benefit to that, and honour to yourself. So, do not think of quitting the army upon any consideration, which [*sic*] there is not a chance of your being removed from the defense of your Dieux Pénates. As to your worthy father, the granting him his full pay for life upon retirement, was but an act of justice; and the withdrawing that grant afterwards, most injustifiable [*sic*]; and I do not wonder it should have hurt you. But times may alter, . . .

Repeating, as I conclude, the sentiments of friendship and esteem, with which I ever am, my dear de Salaberry,

Yours faithfully,

(Signed) Edward.

Men of the stamp of the de Salaberry father and son would have felt an injustice to the depths of their fine souls, yet the father nevertheless ended the autograph note quoted earlier with this remarkable sentence: "I trust that we both will be the government's staunchest supporters, be it in council or with sword in hand, despite my advanced age."

CHAPTER SIXTEEN

We are in the month of December, 1865. I open one of memory's pigeonholes to discover what the good citizens of Quebec were thinking about during the same month in the year 1806, only to find, to my surprise and chagrin, that after a lapse of fifty-nine years, the mind of the masses hasn't changed a wit. Blind, lame, sick, and disabled French Canadians used to sit day and night outside the door of a great faith healer who had appeared from nowhere, and who cured people miraculously by the laying on of hands.[1A] In vain did the clergy thunder against the imposter: the marvelous cures continued unabated, in spite of the many practical jokes inflicted on the miracle-worker by young fellows suddenly become blind, deaf, and lame, afflicted by all the ills ever to escape Pandora's box. The authorities put a timely end to these farcical cures by indicating to the imposter that, unless he decamped forthwith, his next miracle would be performed within the four walls of a cell. The improvised saint took them at their word, hired a sturdy carriage, and disappeared into the night, laden with spoils garnered from the sheep of Quebec. I could tell numerous anecdotes that would scarcely be appreciated by the descendants of this imposter's victims. My French-Canadian compatriots will perhaps grumble that I have been unsparing in my treatment of their ancestor's frailties in this regard, but as I hardly spare myself when occasion demands, I expect total amnesty from them.

Nevertheless, just in case my fellow citizens of the other origin feel they have just cause to complain that I have neglected them in favour of my countrymen, I will discuss *their* principal preoccupation of the period. The subject is certainly worthy of study, for it concerns nothing less than the coming of the Antichrist, the beast of the Apocalypse in the person of Napoleon I. The prophecy had at long last been fulfilled.

Before enlarging on this subject, however, let us cast an eye on present-day happenings in our good city of Quebec.

My compatriots are not now besieging the door of some faith healer in search of a cure for their physical ailments, for the very simple reason that such a benevolent personage is currently unavailable. Nonetheless, let it be said in passing, they are the dupes of all the political charlatans who exploit the populace for their own ends.

And what are my fellow citizens of the other origin doing? They don't believe in miracles—not they!—and would no more seek health from a faith healer nowadays than they did in the past. They will, however, go to hear a lecturer prove, as two and two make four, that Napoleon III is the Antichrist, the beast of the Apocalypse. One must admit that the Bonapartes are a greedy lot: two Antichrists in the same family within the space of half a century are a bit much! Evidently, although my English friends don't believe in miracles, they do swallow some extraordinarily tall tales now and then.

Let us come back to the first Antichrist in the family, whom I have mentioned as being an object of interest fifty-seven years ago. Here is the actual text of the Apolcalypse, thirteenth chapter:

"And . . . I saw a beast rise up out of the sea, having seven heads and ten horns, and upon his horns ten crowns, and upon his heads the name of blasphemy."[B]

Certainly Napoleon, being born in Corsica, came out of the sea and did in fact wear as many crowns. Those who doubt it need only consult a history book to be convinced. Indeed, they will find that there was perhaps a surfeit of crowns.

As for blasphemy, the man who—according to the English papers, and even certain French-language newspapers and pamphlets published outside France—occupied his leisure moments in hitting, pinching, or scratching everyone who so much as mentioned it, as for blasphemy, say I, he must have been used to it. But let us continue:

"And the beast which I saw was like unto a leopard . . . and the dragon gave him his power . . . and great authority."[C]

Again the description fits. Does not Napoleon mean lion of the desert in Italian? As to the power and great authority, one can't deny him these two attributes.

"And it was given unto him to make war with the saints, and to overcome them: and power was given him over all kindreds, and tongues, and nations."[D]

Napoleon had made war on His Holiness Pope Pius VII, and was master of Europe in his day.

"And I beheld another beast coming up out of the earth; and he had two horns like a lamb, and he spake as a dragon.

"And he exerciseth all the power of the first beast before him, and causeth the earth and them which dwell therein to worship the first beast."[E]

The mitre worn by Talleyrand as Bishop of Autun before becoming prime minister to the Emperor Napoleon marks him out most aptly as the beast with two horns, emblems of the lamb he supposedly resembled in gentleness, while speaking like the dragon. The English papers immediately seized the allusion.

"And that no man might buy or sell, save he that had the mark, or the name of the beast, or the number of his name."[F]

The continental blockade was then in operation. No mistake was possible: the wretch was indeed the Antichrist. The Holy Scripture ends thus:

"Here is wisdom. Let him that hath understanding count the number of the beast: for it is the number of a man; and his number is Six hundred threescore and six.[G]

Those possessed of wisdom and intelligence were convinced that, according to some Hebrew, Chaldean, Syriac, or I know not what calculation, the number of the beast formed the actual letters of Napoleon Buonaparte. Observing most shrewdly that Napoleon had dropped the "u" in order to Frenchify his original name, or perhaps to give the lie to Holy Writ (for the impious scoundrel was quite capable of it!) they maintained that the said Napoleon was the beast of the Apocalypse. Nothing could be clearer, and to them redounded the credit for this ingenious discovery. There were indeed a few incredulous dunces here and there who didn't find this argument conclusive, but the majority, which as you know is always right, silenced them. As for me, an enthusiastic young man with a passion for the supernatural, only laziness prevented me from studying Chaldean, Hebrew, and Syriac so as to count the number of the beast.

So now, my worthy lecturer of November 1863, burn your thesis: your Antichrist is an apocryphal being. It was the first who was genuine!

Let us go back two years more in that earlier time. It was then that I left the Quebec Seminary and went to live as a boarder with the Reverend John Jackson,[H] a Church of England minister who used to run an excellent school. I didn't know a word of English at the time, and my father felt that, while taking my philosophy course at the seminary for two years, I would learn the language more easily in a house where only English was spoken.

I was the only French Canadian among either the boarders or day scholars, but this made no difference, and I warmed to them immediately. At seventeen I was pretty much the same light-hearted scapegrace as at twelve, and this quickly earned me numerous friends.

The mores of my new schoolfellows were, I found, somewhat different from those of the young men among whom I'd lived at the Quebec Seminary. They had a natural inclination for boxing, and at the slightest quarrel would be off to settle their differences on the ramparts near the Palace Gate. The schoolmaster closed his eyes to these peccadilloes, whereas we had been severely punished at the seminary when we took it into our heads to blacken each others' eyes, as we did from time to time. I remained outside these battles, however, although often asked to sit in judgment on their quarrels. A philosopher must preserve some dignity, and I was no longer the little street urchin who used to come home with the occasional shiner.

The first thing that surprised me was to find a high Anglican minister calling his dog Toby. It seemed exceedingly profane when applied to a four-legged creature, but one of my friends having informed me that the story of Tobias was apocryphal, I was convinced that the reverend gentleman had acted in good faith.[1]

The second thing that struck me was the way the pupils, at the beginning of Holy Week, eagerly awaited the arrival of Good Friday. I already knew enough English to understand that "good" meant *bon*, and "Friday" meant *vendredi*. And as there was only one *vendredi* in the current week, I concluded with great sagacity that "Good Friday" meant *le vendredi saint*. Having sorted out this difficulty, I asked them why they should look forward to Good Friday more than any other day of the week.

"Because," they told me, "we have hot cross buns for breakfast on Good Friday, and it's the only day of the year that we get such a treat."

We were more ascetic at the seminary: even those who were not obliged to fast would voluntarily undertake a small penance on that day. As I, however, had already adopted the principle of never interfering with other men's consciences, I found this liking for Good Friday cakes perfectly natural.

I spent two happy years in this boarding school. Those who have read *The Vicar of Wakefield* will have some idea of the excellent Mr. Jackson and his wife. Their manners were as unaffected as those of the Primroses in Goldsmith's small masterpiece.

These worthy people always showed me the utmost consideration. Never did the slightest allusion to my religion wound my Catholic susceptibility. I would have been more than sensitive to the least joke about Catholicism, for even in my years of lukewarm adherence— dare I say of unbelieving?—I would never have borne any insult to the religion of my forefathers in which I had been raised. I have always respected the religious beliefs of others and have insisted on the same respect for mine. But during the happy days of my youth, fanaticism was a monster almost unknown in Quebec. My Protestant friends were numerous, and if I passed near my church during the hours of worship, their only remark was, "Go into your church, bad Catholic!" I would say the same to them when we went by a Protestant place of worship.

One cannot think without trembling of the ills brought about by religious intolerance! Of the rivers of blood shed by fanaticism! Or that might one day be shed in this fortunate colony! Certain races[1] have remained as fanatic as their forebears of a hundred years ago, but I here proudly proclaim that this sentiment is a stranger to the hearts of my French-Canadian countrymen.

A little scene that my friend, the late Robert Christie, witnessed when a member of the provincial parliament, and that he used to recount with his accustomed verve, fits in naturally here.

Two men, old friends who typified Canada, the Honourable Denis-Benjamin Viger and the Honourable John Neilson, were strolling in a corridor one evening while waiting for the house to sit. Monsieur

An anonymous watercolour, circa 1818, shows the Esplanade, an area just inside the Saint-Louis Gate that was a popular place for taking the air. National Gallery of Canada, photo: Hans Blohm. 16627

Viger was a Catholic, Mr. Neilson a Protestant, and the following dialogue took place between them.

Mr. Neilson: Catholics are better Christians than we are.

Monsieur Viger: What do you mean by that?

N: Don't Catholics believe that all Protestants are damned as heretics?

V: Easy! Easy! if you please. My friend, the. . . .

N: Well, well! Have you forgotten the precepts of your religion: No salvation outside the church?

V: You mustn't take. . . .

N: I repeat, you believe that as heretics, Protestants will roast in hell for all eternity.

V: Do you take us for Iroquois?

N: Boil, if you prefer, in Satan's big cauldron. Yet this doesn't prevent you from liking us, or from praying for us unceasingly, particularly during your Sunday mass. The Protestants, on the other hand, believe that Catholics will grill in hell as idolaters, and far from pitying you, their hatred is such that they rejoice in it.

At that Mr. Neilson gave vent to his habitual sardonic laugh, echoed by Monsieur Viger.

The memory of the parliamentary battles fought by these two great men under the same banner, in defense of our most sacred rights, is graven on the heart of every sincere friend of Canada.

I applied myself to the study of the English language with all the energy of which I was capable, and Mr. Jackson seconded me with every power at his command. He was versed enough in French to realize my faults of translation, but when it came to style, the budding philosopher took charge. The first translations he set me were the two touching episodes from Sterne: "The Story of Le Fever" and of "Poor Maria."[K] I was enchanted with the simple, conversational style of the author of A Sentimental Journey, a style since made fashionable by Walter Scott and imitated by novelists of other nations. After six months' study I could read Pope fairly easily. But from Pope to Shakespeare there was a mountain to be climbed, and I must admit that it took me ten years to be able to appreciate the beauties of this prince of poets.

I have a naturally poor ear, even for the harmonies of fine French poetry. Great and profound thoughts are what I care for, whereas I find rhyme wearisome. Pity me, my dear countrymen! Pity me, charming Canadian poets! How I would drink in your vivid imagery, your ingenious and touching thoughts that so often move me, if only you could drop the monotonous rhyme that drives me to distraction! 'Tis an infirmity with me: pity then my misery! In return, I advise you to read Shakespeare—the English text, not the translations. If, young poets, you have not already mastered the language of this sublime author, get to work at once. The task will be hard, but what a reward awaits you! At each moment you will be astonished at the depth of this prodigious man's genius.

The French poets who have translated Shakespeare have not done him justice, in my opinion. To really appreciate him, one must read the actual text or else a prose translation, as close, word for word, as possible.

While my tutor gave me English lessons, I, on my side, initiated him further into the French language, lending him our classics and coming to his aid when necessary.

The method of English tutors at that time consisted of beating children over the head in order to instil Greek and Latin authors more deeply. But to my knowledge, the worthy Mr. Jackson rarely inflicted such punishment, and then only to one pupil who made a habit of bedeviling him.

Only death severed the ties that bound me to Mr. and Mrs. Jackson. What pleasure it gave me several years later, when I had my own home, to show them that their kindness hadn't been wasted on an ungrateful object. This respectable couple had only one child, a lovable little boy whom all the scholars delighted in. His premature death at about the age of twenty embittered the last years of these good parents, so kind, understanding, and affectionate.

The reader may find an old man's memories of little interest. The old man, by contrast, enjoys bringing to life on these pages those whose virtues have won his heart or who have treated him with consideration and tenderness.

My entry into the adult world could be dated from this same period, for it was then that I began to mingle with the best society, although it wasn't until I did my law training that I was really initiated into it.

The scene I am about to describe took place some years before I had stopped boarding at the Quebec Seminary.

English society, not very numerous at the time, valued that of the French Canadians, which was infinitely more lively than their own. In fact, Canadians had as yet lost none of the unaffected and somewhat turbulent gaiety of their ancestors. One of my maternal aunts, Marguerite de Lanaudière,[L] then about twenty years old, as lovely as she was light-hearted and vivacious, was exceedingly popular, particularly among the English. I don't know how it was possible with such beautiful and regular features, but she managed to assume an expression of age, idiocy, or any other that she wished to personify, and to make her naturally soft voice unrecognizable. It was during her frequent visits to the country that she usually enacted these little comedies. Needless to say, in disguising herself she only sought to mystify those who knew her well.

A few friends would arrive at my father's house and ask after Mademoiselle Marguerite, only to be told that she was absent. A quarter of an hour later she would make her entry into the drawing room dressed as a habitant's wife come to consult the seigneur about a legal action she wished to take, or with which she was threatened, or about the quarrels with her husband, or with her landlord about the payment in kind that she was obliged to make him annually. Never was a real Josephte[2] better portrayed.

Sometimes it would be a halfwit whose family had dumped her on her relations. She excelled in this role. Her face was the picture of utter and pitiful idiocy, and her audience was treated to the most ridiculous remarks and nonsensical questions.

But I return to the promised scene.

Her Quebec friends had often heard of these practical jokes, and had long defied her to trick them, whatever the disguise. Her sister-in-law, Madame Charles de Lanaudière, proposed an opportunity for putting them to the test. The occasion was to be a dinner at her house, and those who had thrown down the gauntlet were to be invited.

Invitations were accordingly sent, my Uncle de Lanaudière making a point of personally delivering one to Mr. Sewell, the attorney general.[M] He said as he left that he was most anxious for Mr. Sewell to be there. An old seigneuresse, his friend Madame K——, had arrived the evening before to consult a lawyer on a suit that could compromise her children's fortune, and he had advised her to see Mr. Sewell, the most eminent lawyer in Quebec. The old dame[N] had thanked him, and he had suggested making the introduction under his own roof. They could then arrange a day for showing Mr. Sewell the many title deeds and papers, and acquainting him with the facts of this important case.

"As I am only too happy to show her this consideration," added Monsieur de Lanaudière, "I killed two birds with one stone and invited some of our friends as well. The old lady is very rich, and will pay you generously."

"It will be a real pleasure to oblige a friend as well as rendering a service to this old seigneuresse," said Mr. Sewell. "You may count on me. As to fees, you know how disinterested I am and that I don't act for love of profit." And—rare exception—this was true!

I should observe here that Mrs. Sewell[O] had been the most outspoken challenger of her childhood friend, Marguerite de Lanaudière.

At six o'clock in the evening all the guests were assembled. Mesdames

361

Smith, Sewell, Fynlay,[P] Fargues,[Q] Mountain, Taylor,[R] de Salaberry, Duchesnay,[S] Dupré, and so on, were at their posts.

"Where is Marguerite?" asked several ladies at once.

"Would you believe," said the mistress of the house, "that she has taken it into her head to have a horrid migraine this evening, and has written me a note to say she can't go out?"

The more indulgent sympathized with the sufferings of their friend, whereas others emitted a torrent of abuse against the churlish Marguerite and her wretched migraine, which she could quite well have put off until the morrow.

At this point Monsieur de Lanaudière said to a servant, in a voice loud enough to be heard by all the company, "Tell me directly the Seigneuresse K—— arrives, so that I can greet her as soon as she steps down from her carriage."

After a pause of several minutes, he reentered the drawing room with his sister on his arm. This was no longer the young and lovely girl who was the admiration of all Quebec, but an old lady, walking hunched over, her face unrecognizable, her fine, ebony eyebrows so disproportionately elongated that they met in the middle. Her face was heavily rouged in the fashion of the time of Louis XV and dotted with black taffeta beauty patches, while most of her nose had disappeared beneath a plaster made of these same black patches, once so much in vogue. Her costume was that of the court of Louis XV, with such an accoutrement of gems, rings, bracelets, diamonds, and earrings hanging down to her shoulders, that the old lady blazed like the sun. Every jewel case in the family had been turned upside down. After the customary introductions, to which she replied with sweeping curtseys, she spoke:

"I will soon reach an age when all desire to please must cease, but this doesn't prevent me from feeling considerable embarrassment at having to present myself in the pitiful condition that you see—the result of a most aggravating mishap, which I must blame on the rigours of the season. My poor nose covered with patches will explain my sad misadventure. Monsieur de Lanaudière can testify that this same nose, which is so shamefully disguised this evening, has turned the head of many a gallant beau in other times, and—were it not for fear of making our hostess jealous—I would add that the seigneur of La Pérade[3] himself did not escape without severe wounds, for at that

362

time, my dear de Lanaudière, you used to break hearts right and left."

The old lady sighed two or three times and batted her eyelashes tenderly in the direction of her old friend. Then she drew from her pocket an immense and magnificent gold box, from which her great-great-grandfather must frequently have snuffed Spanish tobacco. Rising majestically, she made a tour of the room, stopping with a deep curtsey before each person present. "D'ye take snuff?" The curtsey was punctiliously acknowledged by everyone, loth to be found wanting in politeness toward the venerable dowager. Every ten minutes she went through the same thankless task, snuff box in one hand and a handkerchief in the other, saying "D'ye take snuff?" to the accompaniment of many curtseys, which were returned with equal graciousness. The guests were all in torment, being obliged to smother their bursts of laughter, whereas my Uncle de Lanaudière allowed his mirth full vent in an adjoining room, where he was followed by several friends, indignant at his discourteous behaviour.

"We're surprised, de Lanaudière, that a gentleman of your breeding could, under your own roof, be so lacking in the consideration due to age and to a lady of such respectability!" said Messrs. Sewell, de Salaberry, and Major Doyle.[4]

"What do you expect?" said my uncle. "My dear friends, I can't help it. The good woman is so ridiculous that it's impossible not to laugh."

Very soon a highly animated conversation was in progress between the young ladies and the dowager. Each complimented her on her toilet with the most serious air in the world, and the old lady enumerated all the conquests that her crimson velvet gown had made in days of yore. Mrs. Smith, widow of the chief justice of that name as well as being Mrs. Sewell's mother, and herself an elderly woman, expressed unfeigned admiration for raiment similar, she said, to that which she had seen her grandmother wear. She very much regretted being unable to speak French so as to converse with the worthy seigneuresse.

It was only after much conversation, and forcing those around her to endure politely her various absurd or eccentric antics, that the seigneuresse said:

"You've been kind enough to take me back to the wonderful days of my youth, alas! so fleeting, and it is with much regret that I find myself obliged to give a few minutes to a serious matter concerning

363

my family's future. The attorney-general has been good enough to take an interest in the fate of a poor old woman threatened by a ruinous suit that could send her to the grave. With your permission, I shall profit from his kindness to give him a little glimpse of this deplorable business that has aged me fifty years in the space of a month. Yes, ladies, little more than a *fortnight* ago, the roses of youth were upon this withered face. I could even have passed for the younger sister of this lovely lady,[5] wife of the celebrated attorney-general who is ever ready to come to the aid of the unfortunate."

Mr. Sewell lent himself good-naturedly to the wishes of the dowager, who treated him for at least twenty minutes to a loud and voluble account of the finest case of chicanery every invented by equivocating, cross-grained Norman. Racine's Comtesse de Pimbesche in *Les Plaideurs*[T] was but a simpleton compared with my dear aunt. She was never at a loss: the names of the notaries who drew up the deeds, the exact dates, passages quoted from the said deeds—all flowed forth with an abundance that astonished the learned lawyer who listened to her.

Supper was announced. It was then, and even twenty years later, the fashion to sing at dessert,[6] the gentlemen alternating with the ladies. Madame de Lanaudière asked the old seigneuresse if she would be so kind as to favour them with a song.

"Not three days ago, my voice was as sweet as it was at twenty," said the dowager, "but this horrid cold weather that froze my poor nose has, alas! affected my lungs. However, I will do the impossible to add to the pleasantness of this charming party." And forthwith she intoned, in the deep but rough and broken voice of an old man, the following drinking song, with a heavy accent on the first word:

> Ba-a-a-chu-u-us (Bacchus) sitting on a cask,
> Bade me drink no water."

There followed a general explosion among those members of the company who, until now, had with difficulty preserved their gravity, while the more sober stuffed their handkerchiefs in their mouths to keep from bursting out laughing.

"Ring down the curtain and go wash your face, Marguerite," cried my uncle. "The game is up."

Thereupon the young ladies all began to cry out at once, "Oh, Marguerite, you she-devil! How you made us suffer!"

Then, arming themselves with handkerchiefs, fans, and whatnot, they pursued the fugitive from room to room—for she had fled from the table once unmasked—and dragged her back to her place amid an uproar over which even God couldn't have made Himself heard.

"Mademoiselle Marguerite," stated Mr. Sewell, once calm had been more or less restored, "it is you, not I, that our sovereign should have appointed attorney-general, for never have I heard a more ingenious or entangled case of chicanery expounded with such lucidity, even by our oldest attorneys in the city of London."

"You forget, Mr. Attorney-General, that my ancestors were Norman, and that a little of it must have rubbed off on me," she replied.

I was not present on this occasion, being too young at the time. It was so often described to me by my family, however, that I thoroughly grasped the salient details. Chief Justice Sewell himself told me, laughing at the joke twenty years later, that my aunt would have driven judges wild had she been born a man and followed a career at the bar.

My aunt, Charles Marguerite de Lanaudière, born in 1775, died at Quebec at the age of eighty-two after breaking a leg. She was the youngest of nine children of my grandfather, the Chevalier Charles de Lanaudière, and survived her brothers and sisters. Although her qualities of mind didn't equal those of her two older sisters, Madame Baby and my mother, she nonetheless possessed a spirited wit with a particular talent for satire. Such was the opinion with regard to the three sisters expressed by the distinguished prelate, Monsiegneur Plessis, an intimate friend of my family. Yet if she had not the superior intellect of the oldest sister, or the quick mind and measured judgment of my mother, she possessed all the former's strength of character, and the will to overcome all obstacles. In the ten or fifteen years preceding her death she lived in retirement, but governors and prominent persons traveling in Canada still came to visit this ancient and final relict of a generation whose light is now extinguished. Was it the curiosity of conversing with a representative of the old *noblesse*[7] [U] that motivated the visitors?

My old aunt took these visits seriously, and always looked forward to them. Lord Elgin (who did not use the term *noblesse* with scorn) also paid her a visit.

"And how is milady?" inquired Mademoiselle de Lanaudière.

"Why, very well," was the answer.

"I'm delighted to hear it, milord. When I was younger, I never omitted to pay a courtesy visit to the representatives of my sovereign, but since old age has prevented me doing so, all the governors and their wives have condescended to visit the granddaughter of the second Baron de Longueil, governor of Montreal before the Conquest."

Lady Elgin[V] called on the old demoiselle a few days later.

Some Canadians still recall today a regiment stationed in Quebec more than sixty years ago, so many were the unfortunate memories it left behind. The major commanding this corps of rowdy officers was a young man of twenty-two, of the same stamp as his men. The civil governor of the period was totally unable to restrain them. In all fairness it must be said that, to my knowledge, all the officers of other regiments that I knew treated ladies with the utmost respect, with the occasional and rare exception of a particular individual overheated by wine. The man who behaved otherwise would have been sent to Coventry. But the conduct of the regiment in question was very different, and several ladies were known to have been insulted by certain of its officers.

It was a spring day on which services were being held in the cathedral. The streets, then unpaved, were in a terrible state, and a group of officers was monopolizing the crown of the road in the Rue de la Fabrique, obliging passers-by to trample through the mud and water. The women were making what progress they could, stepping gingerly down the middle of the street, their dresses hitched up to mid calf, all the while assailed by the jeers of these gallant gentlemen. Mademoiselle de Lanaudière, then very young, came up to the group with three or four of her friends who, at the sight of the hostile phalanx closing ranks as at Fontenoy, desired to go back the way they had come. Not a wit disconcerted, she went on alone. With the superb bearing of an empress, she said, "If there is a single gentleman among you, let him make way for the ladies." This stinging reproach had the desired effect, and the way was immediately cleared.

Like the Irish brigade that so effectively helped break through the English column at Fontenoy, the young Canadian girl had broken the British ranks. I cannot help quoting a passage from the very detailed and authoritative memoirs of the Marquis d'Argenson on the subject of this battle, if only to show the high esteem in which the French held the ebullient courage of green Erin's sons:

Lord Elgin made a point of calling on de Gaspé's aged aunt, Marguerite de Lanaudière, when he arrived in Canada—a custom observed by previous governors. James Bruce, Earl of Elgin & Kincardine, circa 1850. Musée du Château Ramezay, Montreal. CRX 978.26.1

Winter costume: A portrait of Catherine Chaussegros de Léry (1771-1847) shows winter dress of 1798-99. Catherine became the mother of George-René Saveuse de Beaujeu, who married de Gaspé's daughter Adélaïde. Wilhelm Von Moll Berczy. Musée du Château Ramezay, Montreal. CR3282.5

The king called for the reserves and the brave Lordendall, but there was no need of them. Another reserve charged. It was the same cavalry which had charged in the beginning uselessly—the king's household troops, the carbineers, those of the French guards who had remained stationary, and the Irish, *excellent above all when they march against the English and Hanoverians.* It was Monsieur de Richelieu who gave the advice, and executed it, of advancing on the enemy like hunters, or like foragers, pell-mell, hands low, arms shortened; masters, valets, officers, cavalry, infantry, all together . . . it was an affair of ten minutes to win the battle with this unexpected offensive. ^W

To return to the little scene of which my aunt was the heroine, I myself belong to the old school, and always make a point of allowing ladies to pass on the higher portion of the street, even though it often means stepping in the mud. In days gone by, anyone who showed such consideraton, even a young man, was thanked with a slight nod of the head. In our progressive century, however, I get small return for my outlay in politeness at the age of seventy-nine, and my friends chide me for excessive courtesy toward the fair ones. My answer to that is, "When one has been properly brought up it's difficult to become inconsiderate in old age." This brings to mind the retort of a reprobate Canadian friend of mine to a young Englishman who expressed surprise at seeing him say his evening prayers: "I cannot, my dear friend, break myself out of it [sic]."

When the French frigate *La Capricieuse*^X touched on Canada's shores nine years ago, Captain de Belvèze did not omit to call on Mademoiselle de Lanaudière. The conversation turned mainly on France, a highly interesting subject for the old Canadian lady, but she finally said to him, "Our hearts belong to France, but our arms to England." There, *Messieurs les anglais*, you see an example of that old French nobility who respected the oath of loyalty to the sovereigns of Great Britain taken by her father and brothers.

An officer called Gaulthier, belonging to this same frigate, somehow knew that before the Conquest one of our aunts had married a royal physician of that name.^Y I saw somewhere that the latter was the discoverer of the Canadian tea to which he gave the name Gaultharia— the same tea, I suppose, that is being experimented with nowadays. The said officer therefore claimed kinship with the old lady, who good-naturedly lent herself to the idea. He laughingly called her "my

aunt," and she jokingly referred to him as her nephew. But my dear
aunt was in the habit of dressing down her nephews severely, as the
author of these memoirs can testify, having at the age of sixty still
been afraid of her. To return to my cousin of *La Capricieuse*, as I
suppose I must call him: thinking no doubt to flatter the old aunt,
he made some remarks hostile to England in her presence.

"My nephew, you are not being a good and faithful subject of your
emperor—of whom I'm not very fond, incidentally—since you exhibit
hostile intentions toward his allies, especially at a time when they
are receiving you so cordially."

In spite of her despotic nature, my dear aunt had a kind heart,
and I cannot remember that she ever broke with a single one of her
friends—quite the contrary. I knew well two Englishwomen of gentle
birth, childhood companions of hers who fell on hard times after their
father's death, going from opulence to a condition bordering on poverty.
Thereupon they were abandoned by almost all their acquaintance,
but nonetheless remained the close friends of my aunt, who often
took them with her to spend part of the summer with my mother in
the country. When, later, she kept house with her brothers in Quebec,
the first invitations were always to these poor ladies. I can confidently
add that my whole family felt the same way.

A propos my aunts, one of them, Agathe, who died unmarried like
her sister Marguerite, was called Charlotte Corday by the family after
her heroine, because she often said that she would have liked to be
born a man in order to assassinate some of the scoundrels who shed
so much innocent blood during the Revolution of '93. My dear Aunt
Agathe deserves a place here, by reason of her fearlessness. Thirty
years ago, a well-organized band of thieves spread terror throughout
the countryside among the rich or reputedly so. People must surely
remember the daring burglaries committed by these brigands: how
during the night persons living alone, or whole families, would be
tied up and horrible deeds perpetrated. My Aunt Agathe de Lanaudière,
co-seigneuresse of Saint-Valier,[82] and generally thought to be wealthy,
lived alone with her servants in a bay of the parish, isolated from all
neighbours. A pretty but thickly-wooded grove extended for some ten
arpents along the shore, giving these communist brethren every facility
for hiding themselves as well as their chaloupe during the day, should
they have wanted to take advantage of the tide and land during a
moonless night not a hundred feet from my dear aunt's dwelling.

As was natural enough for a person in her position, during this reign of terror she felt she might be attacked from one night to the next. She had even been warned that a chaloupe containing evil-faced men had been seen in the vicinity for some time. She had mounted her defenses accordingly, and was continually on the lookout, prepared for anything. She slept alone in the northeast wing of the house, separated by a protruding shed from her farmer, who occupied the other end of the building. Her two servants lodged with the farmer and his family, the kitchen being in this section also.

At dusk one evening, she came into the kitchen after her usual stroll in the environs, to find a man standing alone with his back to the fireplace, in which a few embers burned. She asked what she could do for him. Jean-Baptiste, being a great practical joker, by way of answer began poking around the room, giving vent to some rough remarks that were ill-received by our heroine, who thought she saw in him an emissary of the fearsome band trying to reconnoitre the house.

"I had no weapon at hand," she used to say, "and was afraid to bend down for the poker lest he hit me on the head. But fortunately I had my hob-nailed clogs with me,[9] and I hit him so hard in the stomach that he tumbled into the embers, to the great detriment of his breeches. I was about to give him more of the same when he yelled, while brushing off the hot sparks, 'It's me, Mademoiselle Agathe! It's me, Peltier, your farmer's friend come to ask for lodging.'"

My aunt was quite overcome and apologized profusely for having jumped to conclusions, but she also scolded the poor wretch roundly, for in view of the number of robbers skulking about the countryside, he'd asked for it. She made what amends she could (for she was as good-hearted as she was quick to act), by ordering the farmer's wife to prepare a good supper for their guest at the expense of the seigneuresse. I believe the *foncière*, as she was called, even extended her generosity to the point of having the luckless breeches replaced, as they were full of holes.

A few evenings later, toward the end of October, I arrived at the home of my bellicose aunt. As we were having a quiet chat after supper, her maid and manservant came into the drawing room carrying a bundle of cords. These were attached to each of the shutters, already closed, and, having traversed all the rooms, were finally brought together in the bedroom of Mademoiselle Agathe de Lanaudière.

Curious to see what it was all about, I followed her into this room, where she immediately started tying the cords to four little bells, which she hung on the four posters of her bed. She then opened a cupboard, took out four pistols, placed two on a small table, and presented me with the others.

"I loaded these weapons myself, so they won't backfire if we're attacked by rascals tonight," she said.

"My dear aunt, Vauban himself never fortified a citadel as well as you!"

"You see, my boy," she replied, "I've never feared a man when I was on my guard, but those cowards might come upon me in my sleep, although I defy them to do so now. In spite of being well armed, I couldn't get any sleep until I had the happy idea of protecting myself from a surprise attack."

"Well, dear aunt, you're certainly a niece worthy of our two Verchères great-aunts[AA] who led the other women in successfully defending a fort from Indian attack in 1690 and 1692."

"Ah, my boy!" she sighed. "If only heaven had seen fit to have me born a man!"

I couldn't help admiring so much courage in such a small, frail body.

When in the country, the two sisters indulged in activities that, to my way of thinking, are the exclusive preserve of the male sex. I greatly admire the sight of a man of virile physique adroitly handling a pair of mettlesome horses, but I feel conversely ill at ease seeing the women of our day engaging in such an exercise. The inherent weakness of their sex deprives them of all charm when holding reins in delicate hands more suited to tracing graceful flowers on canvas or running lightly over the piano keyboard, than to reining in a horse likely to bolt at the slightest untoward noise or at the sight of some frightening object. Riding I will accept; some ladies certainly do acquit themselves with grace. As for my two dear aunts, breaking in horses was one of their favourite rural pastimes.

CHAPTER SEVENTEEN

Odds and ends.

THE RECLUSE

Great reverses of fortune do not affect all men equally. Some, as though struck by lightning, succumb within minutes to misfortune. "He died heart-broken," say the English, or "of a broken heart." Indeed, this malady is reported to be more common among them than other nations, perhaps because, engaging particularly in trade as they do, they are more prone to financial disaster.

There are those who survive their misfortunes for many years, dragging out a miserable existence, their hearts steeped in blood, until death ends their suffering. Others, steel-hearted, harden themselves to misfortune and resume the battle with renewed vigour, often triumphing at last.

"Be so good as to take the sum of money contained in these three packets to Mr. Roxburg,"[A] said my employer, Monsieur Olivier Perrault, in whose office I was finishing my law training about the year 1809. My first employer, Attorney-General Sewell, had been named chief justice.

"In that case, I'll hand the money over to his nephew," I replied, "for you know that Mr. Roxburg is a hermit who never admits strangers, a recluse who hasn't seen the sun for twenty years, except through his dormer windows."

L'HONORABLE JUGE JEAN-BAPTISTE-OLIVIER PERRAULT

Judge Jean-Baptiste-Olivier Perreault, in whose law office de Gaspé articled. From P.-G. Roy, *Les Juges de la Province de Québec* (1933)

"It's absolutely imperative that you see him yourself," explained Monsieur Perrault. "Your interview must be private." And he told me what I must communicate.

"What if he refuses to see me?"

"You're on your mettle as a future lawyer to succeed," answered my employer with a laugh.

Mr. Ritchie at first thought it was a young man's idea of a joke when I asked to see his uncle. But after much insistence, and the assurance that I was entrusted with an important message for his relative, he finally said he would do his best to overcome his uncle's unwillingness and persuade him to see me.

The conference between uncle and nephew seemed very long. I could hear loud remonstrations, and it wasn't until a good half hour had passed that I was shown into his reputedly inviolable sanctuary.

The venerable air of the recluse impressed me profoundly. There really was something quite imposing in that pale, suffering visage etched with wrinkles, no doubt premature, as well as in that high, wide brow, seat of a strong intellect, and that long, snow-white hair falling smoothly to his shoulders. Mr. Roxburg must have been very tall, although it was difficult for me to judge, as he was seated almost immobile in his armchair throughout our interview. In spite of the severe look that he consciously assumed on seeing me, I felt that his expression must usually be one of great gentleness. I was expecting to see an unkempt bear, but found myself in the presence of a perfect gentleman, who for twenty years had been consumed by affliction without ending his moral suffering, which only death could terminate.

"Young man, there must indeed by very cogent reasons (he used the word "cogent") to induce you to disturb my solitude," he said.

I felt ill at ease, but more distressed than intimidated, and my voice shook with emotion as I replied that I was following the orders of my employer, the lawyer, Monsieur Perrault.

He sighed as he motioned me to a seat near a book-laden table by which he sat. Amid these books a large family Bible drew my gaze, for it was open at the Book of Job. A new expression of suffering appeared on his wan face, and it was with a reserve tinged with impatience that he said, "Speak, sir."

"These three sealed packets," said I, putting them on the table, "contain sums of money that I have been directed to give you, while at the same time asking your indulgence in pardoning the one or ones who stole them from you."

"What can anyone steal from me?" he exclaimed bitterly, looking about the room. "The very bed on which I seek repose does not belong to me."

"This theft was carried out by one or several persons in your employ while you were the associate of Mr.———. That is what I have been instructed to tell you."

I had struck a highly sensitive chord. The old man clasped his hands, lifted them for an instant to the level of his brow, and then pressing the left side of his breast cried, "Ah, yes! That is what broke my heart!"

Despite efforts to hide my emotion, my eyes filled with tears. The old man, prey to dark and sorrowful memories, kept silent for a long while. No doubt he was thinking of the happy days of his youth and his dashed hopes, of his first successes in business and his vain struggles to stave off inevitable failure. Dreadful indeed must have been the travail of this great soul during the thirty years and more that he cowered in a lonely garret, an old man hidden from the stares of his fellows, whom he now found an odious sight. Without that excessive sensitivity that made him fear a reproach in each glance of his fellow man, Mr. Roxburg could have repaired his fortunes, freed himself from former debts, and begun life anew, for—as I learned after this interview—he was a man of superior talent, and the generosity of his English countrymen, always ready to help one another, would certainly not have failed him.

At that point I knew nothing of Mr. Roxburg's previous history, but the heart-rending exclamation that escaped him revealed the venerable old man's long agony. "Ah, yes! That is what broke my heart!" I was waiting in respectful silence for him to say something else, when he said to me. Sir, I do not know whence came this money and cannot honourably accept it. The one or ones who stole it would never be so imprudent as to give it to your employer!"

"Catholic priests oblige their penitents to make restitution," I replied. "The latter put the money in the hands of their priests under the seal of the confessional, and a third of it, to avoid suspicion, is usually returned to the rightful owner. Monsieur Perrault, like myself, has no idea who is behind this restitution."

"Do you not think it would be dishonest of me, even in these circumstances, to accept such a sum?" said he.

This unwillingness of a poor man to take such money revealed to me all the sensitivity of his noble soul. Mr. Roxburg, the victim of insufficient vigilance on his part, doubtless feared that someone was offering him charity.

"Consult your heart, sir," said I, "rather than take the advice of a young man like myself. It will tell you how cruel it would be to refuse to accept restitution, when it would relieve repentant sinners of an enormous burden on their conscience—repentant sinners who have erred in their youth and who ask your pardon."

"Your heart," he repeated bitterly, pressing his hand to the organ that he believed had withered long ago. Then he added, with a painful effort, "Leave the money and see that they are told that I forgive them for this theft."

I then produced a waiver drawn up by my employer, which I requested him to sign, adding that as Monsieur Perrault and myself were but proxies, this document would be proof of restitution having been made, as well as of the generous pardon that he granted the guilty parties.

He glanced quickly at the paper. "You belong to the de Lanaudières on your mother's side. I knew the family well, and you have their sensitivity. Do not think, young sir, that I compliment or congratulate you on having a kind heart. On the contrary, happy is he—a thousand times happy!—who possesses a heart of brass, since he is constrained to live among men. Farewell," he added, disdainfully throwing down the pen with which he had signed the waiver.

"You are not angry with me, Monsieur?"

"I bear no man ill will," he stated, "and especially not you, who have acquitted yourself with delicacy of a disagreeable errand."

"Goodbye, my father," said I, tears in my voice.

He stared at me with such astonishment at first, that I thought I must have wounded him, but he said in a gentle, melancholy tone, "God bless you, my son!"

I believe I am the only stranger who ever gained access to this recluse whose seclusion lasted over thirty years. When I told my friends of how I had not only seen Mr. Roxburg, but had even held a lengthy conversation with him, they could scarcely credit so unlikely a circumstance.

It took many years to end the torment of this fine spirit, broken by misfortune. Old Time was hard put to snatch the last breath, stop the last beat of a crushed heart that had survived for a third of a century before death could release it from its tortures.

SEIGNEURS AND CENSITAIRES

> I am sinking in every respect, although I
> am still alert enough to realize the fact
> without being at all sorry. I'm quite
> content to be senile.
> Madame de Staal[B]

Several great and no doubt sincere patriots made virulent speeches against seigneurs at the time seigneurial tenure was abolished. Despite or indeed because of this, I feel it incumbent upon me to give a brief sketch of the relations between seigneurs and censitaires of other times in the old District of Quebec. At that period there was a genuine sense of fraternity among them, and if it has weakened year by year over the last half century, who is to blame if not the censitaires themselves? People motivated by envy have sown dissension in order to break the bonds of affection, most often founded in gratitude, which linked the censitaires to their seigneurs. Human nature and the low rate of *cens et rentes* combined to help achieve this work of ill will.

The censitaire of the District of Quebec is the most independent man in the world. The richest in terms of land needed only pay a dozen shillings annually to his seigneur, and he might scoff at him with impunity. Why should we show consideration and respect, they naturally must have thought, for a man who has no power over us? It's very true that this seigneur and his fathers before him have always been ready to do things for us and help us when we needed it. They've never come down hard on us for their *cens et rentes* and *lods et ventes*. But what of it? Hasn't the son of Quénon Bellegueule[C]—his father made him study hard and he can read big books as easy as falling off a log—hasn't he told us for sure that the seigneurs do all this just to get on our good side and make men raise their hats when the seigneur goes by?

That old apple-polisher Leclerc replies that *he* certainly wouldn't be the one to wear his hat out by doffing it—that he's acquired so much self-respect since he began wearing thin-soled shoes and a suit with pockets that he doesn't even return the greeting of a habitant who takes off his hat to him; upon which young Bellegueule drives it home that polite manners are a foolishness invented by the seigneurs to gain the flattering homage of the habitants. And what's more, one Sunday after vespers didn't that eminent legal light, Pousse-chicane[D] preach that all men are equal and that it was debasing to salute a seigneur? After all, he's only got two eyes in his head and isn't any different from a habitant!

In this manner they have succeeded in severing the bonds of good will, charity, and disinterested affection that existed on one side, and the ties of gratitude felt on the other.

In my youth I knew all the seigneurs of the District of Quebec, as well as a great many of those in the other districts that then formed the province of Lower Canada. I can state with confidence that they were almost all similarly considerate of their censitaires. Take as a case at random the seigneurs of Kamouraska. I can't remember a time when I did not know Monsieur and Madame Taché.[E] Their son Paschal, of the same name as his father, and the late Dr. Couillard of Saint-Thomas, were my two oldest friends. Death alone severed an unclouded friendship formed at the most tender age.

I paid frequent and lengthy visits to my friends in Kamouraska, and witnessed the consideration, respect, and love with which they were regarded by their censitaires. My young friend Paschal, as lovable as he was gentle, was on terms of familiarity with the habitants such as might have exposed him, one felt, to occasional unpleasantness, especially on the part of the young people. But not at all: they were never lacking in the respect that they considered due their young seigneur, child though he was.

Often I have accompanied Madame Taché and her son on her frequent visits to the poor and sick of her seigneurie. She was welcomed as a benevolent divinity in their homes. Apart from the abundant alms that she distributed to poor families, she took wines, cordials, and biscuits, which they could not otherwise have procured, to speed the convalescence of censitaires who had fallen ill, and provided all the little comforts that her ingenious generosity could devise. Thus, through ties held dear of love and gratitude, she reigned supreme in her seigneurie.

When church was over and Madame Taché emerged, the habitants who were ready to leave suddenly reined in their horses, and, taking their pace from hers, followed in a long line of vehicles until she turned into the avenue leading to the seigneurial manor. Even though her back was to them, those who continued on their way still took off their hats as they passed by the avenue, as though she could see this courteous act. One day, nevertheless, I witnessed a violation of this universal deference.

It was the Kamouraska parish feast day of Saint-Louis. As usual after mass, Madame Taché was leading a long escort of her censitaires, when a young fellow, heated by the frequent libations that some were in the habit of imbibing during country parish feast days, left the cortège and overtook the seigneuresse's carriage as fast as his horse could carry him.

Madame Taché ordered her carriage stopped, and turning toward those who accompanied her, cried out in a loud voice, "Who is the insolent person who drove by me?"

"It is my son, Madame," said an old man tearfully, stepping forward, hat in hand. "Unfortunately, he's had too much to drink, but you may be sure that I'll bring him to ask your pardon, and in the meantime, I beg you to accept my apologies for his rude behaviour."

I should add that the whole parish subsequently expressed indignaton at this young man's conduct. The delinquent had, in fact, offended doubly: first in showing a lack of respect for their benefactress, and secondly, in flouting a deep-rooted local custom by overtaking a vehicle without requesting permission. [1]

This reminds me of a little adventure that I will now relate. I was returning from the Kamouraska circuit court in the year 1812, accompanied by my lawyer friend, Monsieur Plamondon, to whom I had offered a seat in my cabriolet. Harnessed to the aforementioned cabriolet was a high-spirited and particularly fast horse given me by my father-in-law, Captain Allison. I knew the country customs too well not to request permission to pass from the habitants going in my direction, despite urgings to the contrary by my mischievous and lively friend. He knew that nothing could shock a habitant more than to overtake his vehicle without first asking leave to do so, and that, after such an insult, a race would ensue to my advantage, during which my companion would hurl at the vanquished driver a few of the jibes that the victor was wont to employ in such circumstances. These rarely failed to arouse the ire of the rustics—touchy fellows on the subject of their horses—and put them in a fury.

"Hey there, friend! Is the axle of your cabriolet broken? Are you busy making another, that you don't move forward?"

Or perhaps: "If your whip is worn out, why don't you beat your old screw with the handle?"

Again, it might be: "Don't hurry, friend! There's plenty of time to get home before nightfall."

Nevertheless, although we were as frisky as puppies in those days, I was too well known along the South Shore to risk giving my friend this pleasure. However, when we reached the bay at Berthier and came in sight of a habitant driving his horse at a walk, I felt I could pass by without asking permission. His cart was laden with five sacks of flour, and in such circumstances one usually didn't bother with the formalities. Jean-Baptiste was too proud of his magnificent chestnut to submit to such an affront, however, and shot forward with all possible speed to dispute the way. The resulting jolt caused a peg holding a plank at the back of the little cart to break, and the plank fell to the ground followed by one of the sacks of flour that it supported. The sack split from end to end, spilling its contents.

"Hey there, friend!" shouted Plamondon. "Are you unloading your cart to make it easier for your nag? Wise man—you're afraid your rotten old screw will work up a lather!"

"Go to the devil, you d----d jumped-up puppy!"[2] vociferated the habitant, whipping his horse for all he was worth. At this unexpected punishment the horse first reared and then took off at a gallop with all the force of its supple hocks. This second jolt brought down another sack, which suffered the same fate as its predecessor.

"Hey, friend!" called Plamondon. "If you lose all your flour, the wife won't be able to make any pancakes to console you for the insult to your jackass."

Throughout this interchange we were hurtling along with Jean-Baptiste in hot pursuit, fuming with rage as he tried to hang on to a third sack. This followed its brethren, however, and he then decided to give up a contest that brought him more loss than profit. I doubt if there were a better trotter on the whole South Shore than my antagonist's horse, but he had no chance against mine, which the carters used to call "Captain Allison's devil."

I have strayed from my subject, however, lured by youthful memories so pleasant to an old man. The founders of the two branches of the Taché family whom I knew as a child were Monsieur Charles Taché, father of Sir Etienne Taché, our present prime minister, and Monsieur Paschal Taché, seigneur of Kamouraska[F] and great-grandfather of Monsieur Ivanhoë Taché. The latter is the present owner of this seigneurie and the husband of my granddaughter, Theresa Power. Her father was the late Honourable William Power, judge of the superior court, of whom the memory will ever remain fresh in the parishes of the District of Quebec where he dispensed justice to the general satisfaction of the inhabitants. I have no fear of being accused of partiality in this little paean of praise, as I know how highly esteemed by all who knew him was this worthy and virtuous man.[G]

Sir Etienne Taché is too well known for my humble voice to add to the great respect in which he is held by his fellow citizens. Is he not part of this colony's history, one of its most ardent defenders during the War of 1812, as well as in subsequent parliamentary battles where he championed the most cherished rights of his countrymen?

Sir Etienne Taché[3] was what the English call "a self-made man." The founders of the two family branches that I mentioned were not equally favoured as to fortune. The seigneur of Kamouraska was rich and had only one child, whereas his relatively poor brother was burdened with a large family and consequently unable to provide them with as liberal an education as he wished. Sir Etienne, however, carried all before his iron will and overcame every obstacle. He became an able physician through perseverance and energy. More than this, he disciplined his own nature. His friends, knowing the inherent violence of his character, feared he might become embroiled in parliamentary battles, but with unbending will he succeeded in mastering his temper, as combustible as saltpeter, and showed himself to be consistently calm, cool, and deferential in his political dealings with fellow citizens and in parliamentary debate. To conquer one's own nature seems to me the greatest, noblest, and most difficult of triumphs.

The Taché family has ever been endowed with great powers of intellect, but one had to know the two founders well in order to do them justice, for Messrs. Charles and Paschal Taché were certainly the most absent-minded men I have ever met. A discussion would be under way and one of them would at first take a lively part in it, only to fall suddenly silent. The debate would pursue its way for a while, then the subject would change, and the rain and fine weather be canvassed. Perhaps twenty minutes later Monsieur Taché, not having heard a thing, would resume the discussion at the point he'd left it, to the immense surprise as well as the amusement of his friends. The stories of the two brothers' wool-gathering were legion.

A propos absent-mindedness, our forefathers were much diverted by this characteristic as exhibited by a one-time citizen of Quebec. Monsieur A was already in his declining years. As soon as he had dressed in the morning, and while waiting for his breakfast, he was in the habit of visiting his old friend and neighbour, Monsieur B, whose house was just across the street. One fine morning—I suppose it must have been summer—he got up, put on his shoes, stockings, and possibly his dressing gown. As for his breeches, however, he calmly tucked them under his arm, crossed the street, which was most likely deserted, and installed himself without ceremony in his neighbour's parlor. There, seated in a comfortable armchair, he was beginning to put on his breeches, when Madame B entered the room unexpectedly. "Goodness me, neighbour!" she cried, bursting out laughing, "Another time, would you mind finishing the most indispensable part of your toilet at home, for decency's sake!"

Monsieur A had only half finished his task, but he hurried back across the street holding up his "indispensables," as the English prudishly refer to them.[H] One presumes he had finished his toilet by the time he breakfasted in the bosom of his family.

The remarkable thing is that absent-minded people are generally highly intelligent, as was Monsieur A.

THE *LAUZON*

I walked along the ramparts today and was reminded of the *Lauzon*.[1] This was the first steam ferry to ply between Quebec and Pointe-Lévis. In those days the steamboat captain used to call out the orders, and it was only later that a bell was installed to signal the engineer.

The first captain of the *Lauzon* was an excellent ferryman from Pointe-Lévis: Michel Lecourt *dit* Barras. Considerable practice was needed to understand the thrust of steam power and to calculate the speed, so as to prevent the vessel from smashing against the wharves on either side of the Saint Lawrence. It frequently happened that the unfortunate steamboat would bound forward like a ram when the captain had failed to shout soon enough to the engineer, whose name was Joseph, "Stop her, Joe!" In vain did he then cry "Reverse her, Joe!"[4] to cushion the shock; it was too late, and the wretched boat,

The old boatmen mistrusted "those dogs of English inventions," but nevertheless steam gradually superseded sail and paddle on the Saint Lawrence. Anonymous watercolour of Quebec taken from the Lévis shore about 1846. Public Archives Canada. C-41657

like a billy-goat with its head lowered, bounced against the obstacle before it and came away with its sides badly bruised.

Another time the captain would shout "Stop her, Joe!" when the boat was too far from shore. The engineer would stop the engine and the steamboat would be carried far from port by the current. The captain would then have to shout "Start her, Joe! Another stroke, Joe!" until eventually, after a series of little jerks, we would approach the wharf with the passengers firmly clutching the rail for fear of being launched into space. One always did get there in the end, it must be admitted. I knew the Barras family well, as they had been ferrymen from father to son for my family for a hundred years, and I often took the captain of the *Lauzon* to task for the awful jolts he gave us.

"What can you expect, Monsieur," Barras would say. "One needs such a lot of practice to understand the temperament of these dogs of English inventions that have killed off our canoes, and are as capricious as those who invented them with the help of the devil."[J]

384

The advent of the *Lauzon* completely changed the habits of the citizens of the good city of Quebec, of which more than three-quarters had never set foot on the southern shore of the Saint Lawrence. Everyone wanted to visit this unknown strand on which only two houses, still standing today, were visible: the house belonging to the Bégin family at the foot of the hill, to the northeast, and that of the Labadie family looking across to the old Lower Town market in Quebec. The poorest people would save their money to procure the pleasure of a Sunday walk on the other side of the river, and on returning in the evening our worthy citizens, each another Christopher Columbus, would hold forth on the wonders of this new continent.

One anomaly that I am at a loss to explain is the striking contrast, observable in my youth, between the male population of the parish of Pointe-Lévis, and that of the opposite sex. Few localities produced such good-looking men, whereas the women—I fear I may be un-gallant—were decidedly less favoured by nature as to their charms, although they have since compensated for this lack. They were pious women, however, and many of them used to frequent our markets wearing solid silver crosses, six inches long and a third of an inch thick, hung about their necks, this being the one luxury they allowed themselves.

But to return to the *Lauzon*: if men welcomed it with open arms, there was a breed of animal that must have rejoiced even more. A herd of beef cattle would often have to travel twenty to thirty leagues on the hoof in the middle of sweltering heat to get their throats cut in Quebec. This seemed an already hard enough task for so cruel a fate, but it was merely the beginning of their trials. To add to their misery, they were obliged to swim the Saint Lawrence. Yes! A fine river a quarter of a league wide! A magnificent river, no doubt, but one with a fast current that offered formidable resistance when the tide was ebbing. Impediments notwithstanding, the townsfolk of Quebec liked their meat fresh: the English for their roast beef, and the Canadians for their soup and *boeuf-à-la-mode*. The impatient butchers awaited their victims on the ramparts, sharpening their long knives the while.

The bellowing herd is on the strand at Pointe-Lévis, innocent then of wharves. As carefree as the Pope's lamb that licks the hand about to slaughter it, the cattle philosophically contemplate that agglomeration of houses called a town on the north side of the river. What goes on in the brain of an ox? I don't know. Perhaps the wisest among them think that men must indeed be mad to bury themselves alive in a heap of stone and mortar, when the green fields and forest offer so many attractions.

"All aboard! All aboard!" cries the ferryman, paddle in hand. Each man whom he is to take across arms himself with a long pole, a switch, or a cudgel in the form of an oar or paddle, to help yoke the cattle to the canoe according to their age and apparent strength, tying them by the horns to the cross-benches of the canoe as it lies pulled up on the shore. It is rough work, but once completed the remaining burden falls on the quadrupeds. First, however, they must be persuaded to pull the canoe to the water's edge, aided by a liberal application of blows and resounding oaths. But the most difficult thing is to get them to leave terra firma and submit to the mercies of another element. They put up a stubborn fight, but once in the water the poor animals become resigned to their fate and swim vigorously, as much out of an instinct for self-preservation as to avoid blows from the long poles whose powers of persuasion they have already sampled.

A stranger seeing a canoe crossing the river at great speed, without sail, oars, or paddles, would call on all the saints to explain the phenomenon—until he spied a dozen head of cattle rising out of the water like tritons. He would never have suspected their presence around the sides of the canoe from a distance. The poor beasts were generally so exhausted by the time they drew near the beaches of the Lower Town that only their muzzles could be seen above the water.

I have never heard of any accidents happening to those who crossed the river in this primitive and ingenious manner. If an animal at the end of his strength became unmanageable or was struggling against death—although according to the canoemen this rarely happened— the rope tying it to the canoe was cut, and if the beast's owner wanted the hide, let him look for it at Ile d'Orléans, Cap Rouge, or elsewhere.

I am, therefore, correct in saying that the bovine breed had as much cause for rejoicing as humankind at the sight of the *Lauzon*, for the cattle could henceforth cross the Saint Lawrence easily, en-countering nothing more unpleasant than a few blows of the long pole now and then to prod the lazy in boarding and disembarking from the steamboat.

Often, when walking down the Rue des Glacis in the Saint-Jean ward, I find myself glancing at the first few houses in the Rue d'Aiguillon, but I look in vain for the one that gave me such a thrill as a child. In other days, a life-sized grenadier painted in dazzling colours on the front door drew the attention of the passer-by, and it was almost impossible not to stop a moment if the door of the enclosed porch chanced to be open.

This masterpiece came from the brush of old Marseille, founder of the marionette theatre in Canada's capital, who died in his nineties some sixty-seven years ago.[K] Dead indeed, alas! as are all the young schoolfriends that, like myself, gazed down on the stern visage of this old man who, for fifty years, had made so many spectators roar with laughter as they listened eagerly for the witty dialogue spoken through his dolls.

Here is how he came to be honoured with a visit that would no doubt have flattered him some ten years earlier, but to which he was now insensible.

It was a Thursday in the height of summer, and all the seminary boarders were joyously on their way to La Canardière[5] for the day. On turning into the poplar-lined road leading to the old Dorchester Bridge, we saw a group of women in front of a shabby house on the east side of the king's highway. One of them, the wife of a local hotelkeeper called Frederick, told us that old Marseille, the former puppeteer, had departed this life.

Old Marseille was hardly more than a legend to me. I had, of course, heard my parents speak of the delight that he and his wife had given them in their own childhood, often praising these two renowned performers highly when comparing their theatre to that of their successor, Barbeau. I felt a sudden desire to see the remains of this man about whom I knew, but had thought long dead.

Although I was the most boisterous child in the seminary, or perhaps because of this invaluable asset, Monsieur Bedard had a great weakness for me, and I used to take frequent advantage of it by soliciting favours for which the others wouldn't have dared ask.

"I've never seen anyone dead," I said. "Please, won't you let me look at old Marseille?"

"If I thought such a sight would have a salutary effect, I'd gladly let you see him," retorted Monsieur Bedard.

La Maison Jacquet, 1851. De Gaspé lived in this house on the corner of the Rue Saint-Louis and Rue des Jardins during his early married life. Watercolour by Edwin Whitefield. Musée du Québec, photo Patrick Altman. G5390D

The atmosphere of old Quebec is admirably caught in this oil by William Sewell, son of Chief Justice Jonathan Sewell. "View of the Rue Sainte-Ursule," 1842. Musée du Québec. photo: Patrick Altman. 83.53

"You may be sure that it will," I answered, winking at my comrades. "That's all I need to make me behave like an angel."

The schoolmaster pursed his lips and said, "Those who wish to enter this house may follow me."

Only a dozen of the youngest scholars entered that funereal hovel. Monsieur Bedard uncovered the face of the dead man.

"Look upon death," he said, "and reflect seriously, for one day, perhaps not far distant, the same fate awaits you."

It is difficult to remember now what I felt when I first saw death. Twenty years later, I, like Hamlet in a cemetery as he handled Yorick's skull, might have tried to discern in that ashen visage, in that large, aquiline nose, and in that long chin, bound with a band of white linen to hold shut the immense mouth of the corpse—I might have tried, I say, to discern a single trait in the old puppeteer's rigid countenance that would give some clue to his former calling. Had the mouth not been pressed shut, I might have cried, like the young Danish prince, "For half a century you made others laugh: now mock your own grinning!"[L]

"Well, Gaspé," said the master, "are you thinking that tomorrow perhaps you, boisterous as you are, will be as lifeless as this old fellow?"

"I won't be so ugly, anyway," I said by way of consolation.

"Get on with you, madcap!" exclaimed Monsieur Bedard.

The master said tomorrow, and here we are, almost seventy years since this scene took place. And yet this is indeed tomorrow: the worthy man was not mistaken! If I am given the chance to count the last minutes as life slips into death, I will no doubt remember my former schoolmaster's prediction, and I shall say, "He was right about tomorrow!" The vigour, the rising sap of youth, the singing in my blood all spoke to me of long life then, and yet my tomorrow is already here, for it seems to me that I have lived but a day. After all, what is seventy years in the infinite stretch of eternity?

But I come back to that house, that grenadier, which I seek in vain today. The marionette theatre, source of so much merriment for the children, opened regularly at six in the evening on the second feast of Christmas (there were then three feasts of Christmas), only closing on Ash Wednesday. The price of admission was not much: for the sum of six sols a child could drink in the delights offered. The theatre, not being as capacious as Covent Garden[M] in London or the Odéon in Paris, closed its doors as soon as all the seats were filled, and those who arrived later or who hadn't already gained admittance waited patiently in the snow for two hours. The second show followed the first without intermission, and occasionally there were three shows in one evening.

There is no need to add that, from the time Master Marseille and his wife introduced marionettes to this city until the closing of this brilliant theatre twenty-five years ago, these dancing and talking dolls were relished by several generations of children for more than a century. For the sum of eight piastres, Marseille and his wife, while their health permitted, would carry their theatrical company to the homes of the leading families in Canadian society when the paterfamilias wished to entertain his children and their friends. The other parents were invited to these parties, which invariably ended with a supper, and often with both a supper and a ball.

Like all famous actors, the Marseilles had their night of great triumph, to be remembered all their lives. His Royal Highness the Duke of Kent, father of our gracious sovereign, was kind enough to honour their theatre one evening with his presence. Something new had to be thought of for so great a personage, and the Marseille genius was not found wanting on this solemn occasion. As the prince had rénted the theatre for himself and his guests several days in advance, the players had time to prepare everything for the surprise that they had in store.

The curtain falls. The puppeteers have already succeeded in making the prince laugh, but are determined to melt his heart as well, and must needs follow comedy with moving drama. Madame Marseille is seated at the foot of the stage as partner to her worthy husband, as is usual during the performance. Near her is the orchestra, which has been enlarged for the occasion by the addition of a fife to the customary lone violin and drum. Madame Marseille rises, curtseys deeply to the Duke of Kent, and says:

"My Prince, there are no more marionettes: the devil has carried them all off." Effectively, His Satanic Majesty, in the guise of a prairie chicken,[N] has just swept the stage clear of Punchinello and his company in the midst of a whirling dance, and Mother Marseille has drawn the curtain.

"However," she adds, "to make up to Your Principality for so great a loss, we shall present for your entertainment the siege of Quebec by the Americans in 1775, and show you the proper beating that the English and Canadians gave them so they'd learn to treat their neighbours with respect." Having delivered herself of this bellicose speech, Mother Marseille probably amuses the prince by singing "Malbrouk s'en va-t-en guerre, mirliton, mirlitaine,"⁰ from the first verse to the last.

The curtain rises and the spectators view with astonishment the city of Quebec. True, the miniature town is made of cardboard, but there is no mistaking it. Atop the high citadel floats the British flag. Soldiers and citizens line the ramparts, and cannoneers are at their posts, wick alight. The American battalions begin the assault, the cannon roars, the sound of rapid firing is heard, the besiegers take flight, and the city is saved.

The orchestra plays "God Save the King," at which the entire English royal family parades on stage: King George III leads the way, mounted on a thoroughbred with Queen Charlotte riding pillion on its wide rump. The two sovereigns, wearing crowns, are followed by their large family of princes and princesses seated on high-stepping steeds. But let Mother Marseille, be it only to console her shade, describe this scene so gratifying to her self-esteem.

"When the prince recognized his dear father and mother whom he hadn't seen for so long, he could barely control his feelings, but when he saw his little brother, Rodolph, he broke down completely and hid his face in his handkerchief." Mother Marseille's eyes become misty at the recollection of all this, and she takes a strong sniff of tobacco to clear her vision.

As Master Barbeau, the Marseilles' son-in-law and successor, refused to take his marionettes to people's homes, one of us (I was paterfamilias by this time) used to rent the theatre. For the sum of four piastres he would give a special performance at five in the evening, to which only ourselves and our guests were admitted. It was understood that after the show we would spend the evening at the home of the person who had hired the theatre. Laughter is contagious, as everyone knows, but I have rarely seen all the company laugh as heartily as at a particular one of Barbeau's marionette performances. I was the one to rent the theatre that year, and among the guests I included Madame Pierre de Sales Laterrière, *née* Bulmer. As the young Englishwoman had recently arrived in Canada, she had no idea of what she was about to see. Noticing that we were at first fairly indifferent to the antics of Master Punchinello and his consorts, which we'd seen a hundred times, she made a superhuman effort—and even pinched herself—to keep a straight face. At last there was no help for it: she burst into gales of laughter, rocking in her seat and crying, "It is *so* ridiculous!" Laughter being contagious—as I have observed—the success of Barbeau's performance has never since been equalled. As for our young Englishwoman, she spent the evening at my home with my other friends, and each time she thought of Master Barbeau's theatre she burst out laughing. When we asked her the cause of this hilarity, she replied, "It's so ridiculous!" and was again convulsed.

Some anecdotes are so trivial that they ought to be quickly forgotten, yet here is one dating from at least sixty years ago, about which people are still talking. During the Continental War, the guard was so strictly maintained that one would have thought the French were encamped on the Plains of Abraham. As of nine o'clock at night, one had to answer the challenge of the sentries posted on every street corner in Quebec. Lamentable tales were even told of sentries firing on people who didn't know any English and had failed to reply "Friend!"

Three young Canadian sisters between the ages of twelve and fourteen were coming gaily home from Master Barbeau's theatre about nine o'clock one evening, when the sentry posted at the Saint-Jean Gate cried in stentorian tones, "Who comes there?" [*sic*] Whether through terror or their ignorance of the required response, the young girls continued to advance. Upon a second challenge in a voice even more thunderous than before, the oldest of the three replied tremulously, "Trois petites Dorionne come from de Marionettes!" Seeing the three girls, the sentry laughed and said, "Pass, trois petites Dorionne come from de Marionettes!"

The marionettes, like all the things that made up the joys of my childhood, exist only in memory now, for the hand of a despot raided the theatre during the troubles of 1837 and 1838. It was feared, I suppose, that Punchinello would swell the rebel batallions with his troupe. There were indeed some redoubtable warriors among these dolls. "Bring on the Germans!" would cry Barbeau, master of ceremonies, and immediately out would come a dozen Teutons, male and female. After dancing about brandishing bared sabres, the men would end by battling among themselves, to the great distress of the German ladies, until two or three of the combattants lay upon the ground.

392

The police, once they had demolished and pillaged the theatre of Sasseville, Barbeau's successor, marched about the streets for some time, bearing their spoils on their shoulders and yelling, "Here is rebel A!" or "rebel B!" or "rebel C!" naming the leaders of the alleged rebellion. Revolt was certainly non-existent in the District of Quebec, much to the regret of the French Canadians' enemies, who were trying to goad them into an uprising by all manner of vexation. The reign of terror is over, fortunately, but the English seem to have forgotten that even in the District of Montreal only a very small number of French Canadians took part in the 1837 Rebellion, whereas in Upper Canada, populated by Anglo-Saxons, the extent of the rebellion was far greater. Let us, however, quickly draw a veil over this disastrous time. The French Canadian of noble and generous heart may feel insults deeply, but he is equally ready to forget when his enemy tenders the olive branch.

Although generally easy-going, I was never inclined, even in my youth, to swallow a number of myths that most men digest with the credulity of ostriches. I have never believed in the fine freedom on which the English pride themselves.

"But," my friends used to say, "what about habeas corpus, that great bulwark of English liberties?"

A fine privilege indeed, if it weren't suspended at the drop of a hat to butcher hundreds of wretched Irishmen who only claim the liberty that their British fellow subjects enjoy. Have I not seen, even here, some of our great patriots unjustly imprisoned and clamoring for the privilege of a judicial inquiry without success? And did not the government, for the sake of peace and quiet, finally have them expelled from prison by the turnkey, since it had no grounds on which to charge them?

"As proof of the liberty that all British subjects enjoy," my friends would add, "you may often see a gentleman, even a lord, take off his jacket in the streets of London and have a knock-down fight with some barefoot rascal or surly lout whom he has insulted, or who has insulted him. What do you say to that?"

"In the first place, I say that I'd prefer the protection of a policeman for the insulted party, as is done on the Continent. Furthermore, I'm utterly convinced from my own experience that a gentleman or a lord wouldn't be mad enough to take on a barefoot rascal or surly lout unless he were sure of being a better boxer—a talent acquired at the cost of a guinea a lesson. It's only for the glory of applause from the unsuspecting populace (who don't see that they're being mocked even while being knocked on the head), as well as the congratulations of his friends at the club that evening, that the said lord, most haughty and arrogant of aristocrats, consents to make a spectacle of himself. Were he not certain of victory over his ragged antagonist, he wouldn't hesitate to call on the police for protection."

"It's impossible to make you forego your French prejudices," my friends would say.

"Taken all round, my dear fellows, I prefer my prejudices to yours."

A few scenes witnessed by me have afforded an opportunity of appreciating the real worth of the fine theories regarding British liberties, of which my English friends were so proud. Two men were slugging it out in the Quebec Lower Town. The strongest, a sort of Goliath, was soundly belabouring his adversary, despite the latter's pleas for quarter, when along came a young Englishman. He was pale, weak-looking, and delicately built, and his clothes were the last word in London foppery. At the sight of this brutal treatment he told the giant not to hit a defenseless man.

"And who'll stop me?" demanded the assailant.

"I will," said the young man.

"You'd do better to climb back onto your nurse's lap. You're not weaned yet!" roared the other, glaring angrily at him.

"I'd really love to teach this oaf a lesson," mused the Cockney, as though to himself. And so saying, he removed his white kid gloves with the utmost coolness, folded them carefully, put them in the pocket of his coat, the sleeves of which he turned back, gave his hat to one of the spectators, and said, "Come and wean me now."

The battle was short-lived. Two punches applied with lightning speed blinded the latterday Cyclops, who then struck out at random and was quickly reduced to asking for mercy. He retired with his face as crumpled as a baked apple. Although I was young, even then I reflected that the fop would never have been fool enough to stand up to a man four times his strength, had he not counted on the advantage that his knowledge of the art gave him over his adversary.

Some years after this a young Anglo-Canadian, very small and slight of build, returned to Quebec after studying in England, and commenced his sojourn by knocking down one Paul Clifford, the most formidable bully in the city and its suburbs. Everyone was astonished

"Bonsoir la compagnie." Philippe-Joseph Aubert de Gaspé near the end of his life. Archives nationales du Québec (Montreal) 06M. P54/19/315°

that the young aristocrat had beaten Clifford who, although not the same man whom Captain Marryatt[P] made the hero of one of his charming novels, was nonetheless considered to be the strongest man in Quebec.

It must have been in the year 1808 that I was leaving a dinner party with three of my young friends, Lieutenants Butler and Loring of the 49th, and young Mr. Burke,[6] nicknamed "Château Burke" because he was staying with Governor Craig. We were walking alongside the wall of the barracks opposite the houses of the Rue de la Fabrique, a short distance from the guard-house. I gave my arm to Burke, and the two officers were following, when we encountered five or six apprentice shoemakers.

"You shoved me," said my companion to one of them.

"*You* did," was the reply.

Burke, like every English gentleman, prided himself on being an excellent boxer. In vain did I represent to him the impropriety of fighting in the streets of a small city like Quebec, where we were known to everyone. He put up his fists and the battle commenced. However, as it was exceedingly dark, our friend lost much of the advantage his art would otherwise have given him. Crispin, the apprentice, dealt him such a cuff on the nose that Burke was immediately covered in blood. Those who have been graced with a "bloody-nose," as is the English expression, know how the loss of blood can sap one's strength and courage. Consequently, our friend proposed to his adversary that they should put off the contest to the morrow, to be held in a less public place of his choosing. But the young apprentice, deaf to all reason, retorted that he couldn't choose a more convenient spot to administer two black eyes, or a better time to do it than right now. With this, he began to hit afresh, whereupon our friends and Burke himself threatened to call the watch. This threat effectively intimidated young Crispin, who went off, protesting nevertheless that the watch had no authority over him, and that we'd do better to call a justice of the peace.

The losers turned in at the officers' mess of the 49th, only a few steps from the scene of the brawl. The messman hurried off to get a basin of water to bathe our friend's nose, while a servant ran to the Château Saint-Louis to fetch a shirt, waistcoat, breeches, and a coat to replace the bloodied raiment of our athlete. After endless ablutions, Burke, despite a nose that had suffered somewhat in combat and that he occasionally felt to see whether it was still swelling to formidable proportions—Burke, I say, having sworn vengeance sooner or later upon the rascal who had insulted him, was, notwithstanding, one of the liveliest and most amiable of the companions who supped with us.

This last scene dispelled any doubts I may have had. I was convinced that an English gentleman, like any other, would ask for police protection when he was the weaker, and that your man of the people is an ass to believe that such gentlemen knock him down out of a feeling of exalted patriotism, in order to instil in him a high opinion of the liberty he will enjoy under British government.

For myself, I have little enthusiasm for a species of liberty that can only profit vagabonds. My sympathies are all on the side of respectable men. Perhaps, in this independent age, it is an error in judgment on my part, but it is not given to everyone to feel the republican spirit that dominates our continent.

If my countrymen wish to retain the estimable reputation of *peuple gentilhomme* that they still possess, I strongly advise them above all not to hanker after that degree of liberty which our neighbours now enjoy.

I here terminate these memoirs, written at the request of my friends, which can have no merit except as a complement to the notes to my first work, *Les Anciens Canadiens*. If they interest my compatriots in this respect, I will be amply repaid for the labour that I have been tempted to interrupt a hundred times, when discouragement loomed. Although prey to such disheartenment, I was nevertheless upheld by the patriotic desire to transmit to a new generation the anecdotes, activities, and scenes that my seventy-nine years have vouchsafed me. This being said, I now break a quill too heavy for my enfeebled hand, and end with this refrain from an old song: "Bonsoir la compagnie."[Q]

THE END

NOTES

ABBREVIATIONS

ATM   Pierre-Georges Roy, *A travers les* Mémoires *de Philippe Aubert de Gaspé* (Montreal: G. Ducharme, 1943)

BRH   Bulletin de recherches historiques, ed. Pierre-Georges Roy (Lévis: 1895——)

DCB   *Dictionary of Canadian Biography*, eds. George W. Brown et al., (Toronto: University of Toronto Press, 1966——)

DNB   *Dictionary of National Biography*, eds. Leslie Stephen and Sidney Lee, in 21 vols. with supplement (1885-1890; reprint London: Oxford University Press, 1921-1922)

Enc. Brit.   *The Encyclopaedia Britannica*, 11th ed. (London and New York, 1910-1911)

Enc. Can.   *Encyclopedia Canadiana* (Toronto: Grolier of Canada Ltd., 1970)

GLE   *Grand Larousse encyclopédique*, ed. Claude Dubois (Paris: Librairie Larousse, 1960)

Littré   Emile Littré, *Dictionnaire de la langue française* (Paris: Editions Jean-Jacques Pauvert, 1956-1958)

LJ   Louis-Marie Le Jeune, *Dictionnaire générale du Canada* (Ottawa: University of Ottawa, 1931)

MDCB   *Macmillan Dictionary of Canadian Biography*, 4th ed., W. Stewart Wallace, ed., revised, updated and enlarged

	by W. A. McKay (Toronto: The Macmillan Company of Canada Limited, 1978)
Mémoires	Philippe-Joseph Aubert de Gaspé, *Mémoires*, 1st ed., (Ottawa: G. E. Desbarats, 1866; facsimile edition, New York: Johnson Reprint Corporation, 1966)
Morgan	Henry J. Morgan, *Sketches of Celebrated Canadians, and Persons Connected with Canada, from the Earliest Period in the History of the Province Down to the Present Time* (Quebec: Hunter, Rose & Co., 1862)
OED	*Oxford English Dictionary*, Sir James A. H. Murray et al., eds., corrected re-issue of *A New English Dictionary*, 1888-1928 (Oxford: Clarendon Press, 1933)
Shorter OED	*The Shorter Oxford English Dictionary on Historical Principles*, rev. 3rd ed., William Little et al., eds. (1933; rpt. Oxford: Clarendon Press, 1964)
Story	Norah Story, *The Oxford Companion to Canadian History and Literature* (Toronto: Oxford University Press, 1967)

NOTES TO TRANSLATOR'S INTRODUCTION

1. Jacques Castonguay, *La Seigneurie de Philippe Aubert de Gaspé* (Montreal: Fides, 1977, 11, 61).

2. Philippe-Joseph Aubert de Gaspé, *Les Anciens Canadiens* (Quebec: Desbarats et Derbishire, 1863). The work has been published in English under several titles, based on two English versions originally entitled *The Canadians of Old*, translated by Georgiana M. Pennée (Quebec: G. and G. E. Desbarats, 1864), and G. D. Roberts (New York: D. Appleton and Company, 1890), the latter currently available in Stewart McClelland's New Canadian Library series. See David Hayne, "Bibliographie critique des *Anciens Canadiens* (1863) de Philippe-Joseph Aubert de Gaspé" *Papers of the Bibliographical Society of Canada*, 3 (1964), 38-60. Id., *Mémoires* (Ottawa: G. E. Desbarats, 1866) and a second edition prepared by the author's son, Alfred (Quebec: N. S. Hardy, 1885). Pocket "integral" French editions of these two works have been published by Fides in recent years. All page references to the French *Mémoires* are to the facsimile of the first edition, on which the present translation is based.

3. Raymonde Gauthier, *Les Manoirs du Québec* (Quebec: Fides, 1976), cover and 165. Castonguay, *La Seigneurie . . . de Gaspé*, 57, 155.

4. Castonguay, 141.

5. Ibid., 141-142.

6. Henri-Raymond Casgrain, *De Gaspé et Garneau* (Montreal: Librairie Beauchemin Limitée, 1912), 45-46. Casgrain's account of his role in promoting the initial publication of de Gaspé's work should be viewed with considerable reservations, as Luc Lacourcière has demonstrated in detail. However, Casgrain is one of the very few published sources that enable us to see de Gaspé in the flesh, so to speak, which is why his description of several scenes from the author's life have been included in this introduction. Luc Lacourcière, "L'Enjeu des 'Anciens Canadiens,'" *Cahiers des Dix*, 32 (1967): 223-254.

7. Casgrain, *De Gaspé et Garneau*, 17.

8. Ibid., 34.

9. Ibid., 33.

10. Léon Tolstoï, *Enfance, adolescence, jeunesse*, trans. M. J. W. Bienstock and P. Birukov (Lausanne: La Guilde du Livre, 1937), 42, 43, 60, 61.

11. J. Ross Robertson, ed., *The Diary of Mrs. John Graves Simcoe* (1911; facsimile edition, Toronto: Coles Publishing Company, 1973), 262, n.

12. Ibid., 66, 69, 73, 76, and 78, to cite a few examples.

13. Castonguay, *La Seigneurie . . . de Gaspé*, 135-136. He is described as the "son of Sieur Aubert . . . intendant of fortifications of the city of Amiens."

14. Ibid., 26.

15. Ibid., 38.

16. For a comprehensive view of this much-debated incident, see Marcel Trudel, "L'Affaire Jumonville," *Revue d'histoire de l'Amérique française*, 6 (1952-1953): 331-373; also Robert C. Alberts, *The Most Extraordinary Adventures of Major Robert Stobo* (Boston: Houghton Mifflin, 1965), 48 n.

17. Castonguay, 53.

18. Ibid., 61.

19. Philippe-Joseph Aubert de Gaspé, *Les Anciens Canadiens* (1863; Montreal: Librairie Beauchemin Limitée, 1913), 340.

20. Laurence Sterne, *The Life and Opinions of Tristram Shandy, Gentleman*, eds. Melvyn New and Joan New (1762; Florida: The University Presses of Florida, 1978), 5 and 8.

21. True autobiographers are prone to note the unpredictable play of memory (which is complex and disordered instead of structured or linear) while often making excuses for not adopting a chronological narrative. Philippe Lejeune, *L'Autobiographie en France* (Paris: Librairie Armand Colin, 1971), 77.

22. Casgrain, *De Gaspé et Garneau*, 28, citing *Les Anciens Canadiens*.

23. Castonguay, *La Seigneurie . . . de Gaspé*, 66.

24. P. G. Roy, *La Famille Aubert de Gaspé* (Lévis: J. E. Mercier, 1907), 115 n. 1.

25. Castonguay notes that de Gaspé's mother lived at 20 Rue Sainte-Anne, within sight of the Quebec prison, on the basis of a death announcement in the possession of Professor Luc Lacourcière. P.-G. Roy earlier believed that the de Gaspés lived on the Rue des Ramparts, as was later the case. Castonguay, *La Seigneurie . . . de Gaspé*, 67 n. 11.

26. *DCB*, 10:19.

27. Luc Lacourcière, "Aubert de Gaspé, fils (1814-1841)," *Cahiers des Dix*, 40 (1976), 280.

28. Roy, *La Famille Aubert de Gaspé*, 115 n. 1.

29. De Gaspé, *Les Anciens Canadiens*, 153-154.

30. *DCB*, 10:21.

31. Casgrain, *De Gaspé et Garneau*, 16-17.

32. Castonguay, quoting a published interview with his grandmother, Mme. A.-D. Castonguay. *La Seigneurie . . . de Gaspé*, 63.

33. Casgrain, *De Gaspé et Garneau*, 51.

34. W. J. Anderson, "On Canadian History and Biography, and passages in the lives of a British Prince and a Canadian Seigneur," *Index of the Lectures, Papers and Historical Documents published by the Literary and Historical Society of Quebec* (Quebec: L'Evénement, 1927), 30.

35. William Notman, *Portraits of British Americans, with Biographical Sketches by Fennings Taylor* (Montreal: William Notman, 1866-1868), 3:247.

36. Recent literary criticism has explored the distinction between memoirs and "true" autobiography, which is seen as a development of Western European literature coinciding with the emergence of the concept of the individual as unique. See Northrop Frye, *Anatomy of Criticism* (Princeton: Princeton University Press, 1957), 307; Lejeune, *L'Autobiographie en France*, 13, 65; and Roy Pascal, *Design and Truth in Autobiography*

(London: Routledge and Kegan Paul, 1960), 21. Significant earmarks include a sincere attempt to represent a true picture of the author's personality, implicitly if not explicitly (Pascal, 189-195); the relatively large amount of space given the account of childhood (Lejeune, 19); the selective shaping of the narrative to include people, events, and anecdotes that in some way exemplify the author's personality (Lejeune 72); the "grave idealizing of heroism and purity" (Frye, 306); and the presence of an "autobiographical pact," wherein the author states early in the narrative his intention of writing his personal story, while often putting forward acceptable reasons for doing so, such as being representative of a class or generation (Lejeune, 81).

37. Pascal, *Design and Truth in Autobiography*, 55.

38. Frye, *Anatomy of Criticism*, 264.

39. Jean-Jacques Rousseau, *The Confessions* (1781), trans. J. M. Cohen (1973; reprinted Harmondsworth: Penguin Books, 1979), 119.

40. Jean-Jacques Rousseau, *Les Rêveries du promeneur solitaire* (1782), ed. Henri Roddier (Paris: Editions Garnier Frères, 1960), 99, 65, 62.

41. Frye, *Anatomy of Criticism*, 263.

42. Jacques Castonguay, *Au Temps de Philippe Aubert de Gaspé: Lady Stuart* (Ottawa: Les Editions du Méridien, 1986).

43. Casgrain, *De Gaspé et Garneau*, 64-66. Casgrain noted that at his death the author had 115 children and grandchildren (p. 62 n. 1).

44. James Reaney, "Tales of the Great River: Aubert de Gaspé and John Richardson," *Proceedings and Transactions of the Royal Society of Canada*, 4th series (Ottawa: Royal Society of Canada, 1980), 17 (1979): 170.

CHAPTER 1

Author's Footnotes to 1866 Edition

1. I was aged two years and five months when my paternal grandmother, Marie Anne Coulon de Villiers, passed away.

2. Philippe Villiers de L'Isle-Adam, died 1534, Grand Master of the Order of Saint John of Jerusalem, defended Rhodes for five months from attack by 200,000 Turks with 400 war machines under the command of Suleiman. In 1530, after eight years' wandering, the vanquished hero obtained from Charles V the complete sovereignty of the islands of Malta and Gozzo for his order.

3. It would be unfair to class Lady Simcoe, wife of the general who was governor of Upper Canada, as a bluestocking. On the contrary, her literary tastes were most discriminating. One evening my Aunt Baby had no other book to lend her but the Lenten sermons of Massillon. Lady Simcoe, in spite of being a Protestant, was so taken with this masterpiece that she expressed a desire to read all the sermons of our famous preachers, and subsequently took great delight in Bossuet, Bourdaloue, etc.

4. *Frater*, adopted from the Latin, and formerly used to designate a surgeon's assistant. It was also used to describe an inept surgeon, either in fun or sarcastically: "He's just a *frater*. He's a bungling *frater*." *Dictionnaire de l'Académie.*

5. Our habitants, remembering their origins, consider everything French superior to anything provided by other nations. This belief is sometimes manifested in a curious fashion. My friend, the late Dr. Couillard, once wanted to vaccinate the child of a prosperous farmer. "No, no, *Monsieur le docteur*," said Jean-Baptiste, "none of those English inventions; give him some of our good French pox."

6. The author is possibly alluding here to Madame Perrault de Linière. *Editor's note.* [This is a reference to the daugher of Madame de Montenach, Wilhelmine Dudding de Montenach (1817-1901), wife of Olivier-Joseph-Elzéar Perreault de Linière (d. 1870), and subsequently of the Honourable Thomas Ryan, a Canadian senator. *ATM*, 24.]

CHAPTER 1

Translator's Annotations

A. Jean de Joinville, "Histoire de Saint Louis," in *Historiens et Chroniqueurs du Moyen Age*, ed. Albert Pauchilet, vol. 48 of Bibliothèque de la Pléiade (Paris: Gallimard, 1952), 372. The Sire de Joinville (1224-1317) accompanied Saint Louis, king of France, on a crusade in 1284. His memoirs (1305-1309) are an early and noted example of autobiographical writing. *GLE*, 6:372.

B. Nicholas Boileau-Despréaux, "Satire III" (1665), in *Oeuvres complètes de Boileau Despréaux* (Paris: Lefevre, 1835), 191.

C. Philippe-Joseph Aubert de Gaspé, *Les Anciens Canadiens* (Quebec: Desbarats et Derbishire, 1863).

D. During most of the period described in the *Memoirs* "Canadians" meant French Canadians. It was not until the mid-nineteenth century that the English in Canada referred to themselves as Canadians, thereby making it necessary to distinguish "French" Canadians. Serge Gendron, *Quebec and Its Historians, 1840-1920*, trans. Yves Brunelle (Montreal: Harvest House, 1982), 102, citing Benjamin Sulte, *Histoire des Canadiens français, 1608-1880* (Montreal: Wilson, 1882), 8:149.

E.   Charles-François-Xavier Tarieu de Lanaudière, or de la Naudière (1710-1776), seigneur of La Pérade, son of Marie-Madeleine Jarret de Verchères, the Madeleine de Verchères of popular legend. He married twice: Louise-Geneviève Deschamps de Boishébert in 1743; and Marie-Catherine Le Moyne de Longueuil, daughter of the second Baron de Longueuil, in 1764. His widow died in 1788. *DCB*, 4:728-729; *LJ*, 2:58.

F.   Mrs. (not "Lady") Simcoe, born Elizabeth Posthuma Gwillim (1766-1850). She became "the esteemed and talented wife" of John Graves Simcoe, appointed first lieutenant governor of Upper Canada in 1791. The Simcoes were in Quebec from November 1791 to June 1792. The threat of war with the United States brought her again to Quebec between September 1794 and March 1795. A propos de Gaspé's note (chap. 1 n. 3), Mrs. Simcoe's *Diary* mentions dining with Madame Baby a number of times during these two periods, and describes her as "one of the most agreeable people in Quebec." Madame Baby (née Marie-Anne Tarieu de Lanaudière) was de Gaspé's aunt and the wife of the Honourable François Baby, a member of the legislative and executive councils of Lower Canada). Robertson, *Diary of Mrs. Simcoe*, xi, 7, 262; LJ, 1:110.

G.   Giovanni Pico Della Mirandola (1463-1494), Italian philosopher known for his vast erudition, legendary powers of memory, and precocious talent. *GLE*, 8:463.

H.   Joseph Painchaud (1787-1871) was a "popular practitioner with the people of Quebec, and from morning to night was to be seen travelling the streets of the city." He helped establish the Quebec Medical Society (1826) and the Quebec Medical School, where he taught obstetrics and the treatment of women's and children's diseases. *DCB*, 10:563.

I.   La Canardière (a *canardière* is a duck blind) was the name of a beach on the far side of the Saint Charles River, which runs into the Saint Lawrence immediately east of Quebec. Sir James Le Moine has left us a description of the site that sets the scene for this and a later anecdote. "One of the most conspicuous landmarks . . . at La Canardière . . . is Maizerets; a long two story [*sic*] farm house, belonging to the Quebec Seminary, where their blue-coated boys, each Thursday, spend their weekly holiday, since time immemorial, walking back to the city with the descending shades of evening and awakening the echoes of the Beauport shore with their jolly old French songs." The house was burned by the Americans in 1775 but rebuilt in 1778. The name "Maizerets" was only given it in 1850. James MacPherson Le Moine, *The Explorations of Jonathan Oldbuck, F.G.S.Q., in Eastern Latitudes* (Quebec: L. J. Demers et Frère, 1889), 7-8.

J.   This refers to the expanse of land between the ruins of the intendant's palace and the high water mark of the Saint Charles River. See Joseph Bouchette, "surveyor-general of the Province," *Topographical Map of the Province of Lower Canada* (London: W. Faden, 1815), map of the City of Quebec, n. pag.

K.   De Gaspé gives a number of anecdotes involving a variety of river craft. Modern readers may be surprised at a canoe being used as a dinghy. He uses the word *canot* (a term more recently applied to a wooden riverboat) both here and in a description of early ferries in chap. 17. J. M. Le Moine, writing in English, confirms the use of canoes in the latter instance: "For the enlightenment of future generations, let us note here . . . the old style of ferrying passengers. . . . In summer, birch bark canoes were used; in winter, wooden boats, scooped out from the trunk of large pines, all in one piece. . . . In 1843, the 'dug-outs' met with rivals. Messrs. Julien & Gabriel Chabot of Levi used the first 'built' canoes, made something like a long and strong whale boat." Le Moine, *The Chronicles of the St. Lawrence* (Montreal: Dawson Bros., 1880), 344-345.

L.   De Gaspé was proud of his parents' intimacy with the Dorchesters, who appear in several anecdotes of the *Memoirs*. Lady Dorchester had been educated in France (see introduction, n. 11). Lord Dorchester (the former Guy Carleton) had a long association with North America, having taken part in the siege of Louisburg (1758), been wounded at the Plains of Abraham (1759), and held office as lieutenant-governor (1766) and governor (1768-1778) of the Province of Quebec. He had been knighted following the defense of Quebec against invading Americans during the Revolutionary War. He received the later title of baron at the time of his appointment simultaneously as governor-in-chief of British North America (1786-1798) and governor of the then Province of Quebec, subsequently Lower Canada. *DNB*, 3:1003.

M.   *Soupirant* (literally "one who sighs for"), although a surname, often had a slightly ridiculous connotation in eighteenth-century comic writing, echoed in this Molièresque anecdote. *Littré*, 7:356.

N.   Fréderic-Guillaume Oliva (*c.* 1749-1796) came to North America as surgeon major with one of the German regiments assisting the British in the American revolutionary war. He was considered particularly knowledgeable in the field of contagious diseases. *DCB*, 4:589.

O.   A *censitaire* had permanent possession of his land, the title of which he held from the seigneur, to whom he owed certain duties and the annual payment of the *cens et rentes*, usually in kind. Payment took place on a specified day, usually Michaelmas (Nov. 11), and was the occasion for an important social gathering. The seigneur had responsibilities toward his censitaires, such as building a flour mill. If the centisaire sold his right in the land, he paid a mutation fine called *lods et ventes*. Seigneurial tenure was abolished in Quebec in 1854. W. B. Munro, *The Seigniorial System in Canada* (New York: Longmans, Green and Co., 1907), 95.

P.   Joseph Morrin (1792-1861), born in Scotland, came to Canada as a child. A respected Quebec physician and citizen, he helped found Morrin College for Protestant working-men in 1862. *DCB*, 9:572.

CHAPTER 2

Author's Footnotes to 1866 Edition

1.   Prince William Henry landed at Quebec on August 14, 1787. His official capacity was that of a frigate captain, but he was received with all the honours attached to the title of prince. At noon, all militia troops were drawn up, the cannon on the ramparts sounded an eighty-four gun salute in four volleys, and in the evening the whole town was illuminated.

2.   It was the English who introduced the thick woollen sock worn over the shoe during winter, as well as the "spencer," a waistcoat worn over a tail coat.

3.   She was the daughter of the Chevalier de Saint-Luc.

4.   Monsieur Jean-Baptiste Couillard de Lépinay, seigneur of Saint-Thomas on the Rivière du Sud, and a keen gardener.

5.   It is regrettable that the Canadians have not kept the fine name Côte de Léry, now changed to Hope Hill. On this same hill there still stands the oldest house in Quebec, built by the de Léry family.

6.   My father was alluding to the time a detachment of Wolfe's army, in which Colonel Fraser served as a lieutenant in the 78th Fraser's Highlanders, burned all the dwellings on the South Shore from Rivière-Ouelle to Saint-Jean Port-Joli, including my grandfather's manor and mill.

7.   Niger was a magnificent sheep dog given my father by Lord Dorchester before leaving Canada. He and his wife left little mementos with their friends in Canada, and I still have a small mahogany table that Lady Dorchester gave my mother. Although they were not wealthy, this noble couple was nonetheless generous.

CHAPTER 2

Translator's Annotations

A. The Prince of Wales, later Edward VII (1841-1910), visited Canada from July to September 1860 as the representative of Queen Victoria. *DNB*, 2d suppl., 1:554-555.

B. Probably the Pointe-aux-Trembles (now Neuville) on the North Shore of the Saint Lawrence, some 25 kilometres upriver from Quebec, not the Pointe-aux-Trembles just east of Montreal.

C. At the time of his visit to Quebec (1787) he was not yet Duke of Clarence, this title being conferred on May 20, 1789. William IV (1765-1837) served in the navy as a young man, and was appointed captain of the frigate *Pegasus* in April, 1786. He had served in the West Indies under Nelson, who wrote admiring reports. The prince's subordinate officers did not share this admiration, and "made what interest they could to get out of the ship." He is described as a "self-willed and opinionated young captain." *DNB*, 21:325-327.

D. De Gaspé refers to the *chronique d'Halifax*. See "Quebec, August 16," *The Nova Scotia Gazette and the Weekly Chronicle* 4 Sept. 1787.

E. Charles-Louis Tarieu de Lanaudière (1743-1811), son of the de Lanaudière mentioned in chap. 1 (n. E) by his first wife, and therefore de Gaspé's half-uncle. He was known as "the celebrated Chevalier de Lanaudière," and is a recurring figure in the *Memoirs*. At sixteen he fought on the Plains of Abraham and at Sainte-Foy, spending some months in the care of the nuns of the Hôpital-Général as a result. He returned to France with his regiment after 1760, and in 1767 went to London with the French ambassador. From there he returned to Canada, married Elisabeth de Lacorne (1769), and became aide-de-camp to Guy Carleton, later Lord Dorchester. He was with Carleton when the latter fled Montreal (1775) at the approach of the American revolutionary forces under General Montgomery. After a further period in England, he returned to Quebec with Lord Dorchester in 1786, and in 1791 became a member of the newly created legislative council. LJ, 2:58; *DCB*, 5:791.

F. "Sans Bruit" is mentioned by Mrs. Simcoe as being on the Sainte-Foy road, about two miles from Quebec (*Diary*, 58). Richard Murray was the nephew of General James Murray, successively military and civil governor of Quebec after the Conquest. He managed his uncle's Canadian property during the latter's absence from Canada after 1766, and occupied "Sans Bruit" between 1766 and 1774. *BRH*, 27 (1921): 171.

G. Madeleine Coulon de Villiers (1734-1799), daughter of Nicolas-Antoine Coulon de Villiers, was married three times, lastly to Joseph D'Amours (or Damours) de Plaine. LJ, 1:466; *ATM*, 34.

H. Richard Montgomery (1736-1775), Irish-born, served in the British army under Wolfe, and was present at the capture of Louisburg and the capitulation of Montreal in 1760. He subsequently emigrated to New York, and took the revolutionary side in the War of Independence. He commanded the expeditionary force that captured Montreal in November 1775, and in December met with Benedict Arnold's forces before Quebec. He was killed in an attack on New Year's Eve, 1775. De Gaspé appears to confuse him with his older brother, Alexander, the Captain Montgomery who supervised the burning of French homesteads along the Saint Lawrence in 1759 under Wolfe's orders. A. Doughty, *The Siege of Quebec and the Battle of the Plains of Abraham* (Quebec: Dussault and Proulx, 1901), 2:224 n. 1; LJ, 2:298; *MDCB*, 522.

I. Montgomery was found, his body almost covered with snow, the morning after the battle, and his sword was picked up by Sergeant James Thompson, a veteran of the Conquest. At the latter's death in 1830, at the reputed age of ninety-eight, the sword passed to his son, Assistant Commissary-General James Thompson (d. 1869). The sword then passed to a nephew, was displayed in the museum of the Quebec Literary and Historical Society, and in 1878 was purchased by the Marquess of Lorne, who presented it to Montgomery's wife's family in New York. *BRH*, 20 (1914): 162.

J. General Wolfe is said to have intended "to burn all the country from Kamouraska to Pointe-Lévi," and on August 23, 1759, "the destruction of property threatened by the British was now put into terrible effect." Doughty, *The Siege of Quebec*, 2:222, 223. Colonel Malcolm Fraser, in a rare journal of the siege, describes how "the barbarous Captain Montgomery, who commands us, ordered to be butchered in a most inhuman and cruel manner" the few prisoners taken, after which "we set about burning the houses with great success." Colonel Malcolm Fraser, "Extract from a Manuscript Journal Relating to the Siege of Quebec in 1759," in *MSS Relating to the Early History of Canada, recently published under the Auspices of the Literary and Historical Society of Quebec* (1868; reprinted Quebec: T. J. Moore and Company Ltd., 1927), 13.

K. *Piastre* is a French-Canadian colloquial word for dollar, originally from the Italian, and applied to the Spanish *peso dura* or piece of eight that circulated in the Americas. *OED*, 8:815

L. "Un grand homme sec, là, qui me sert de témoin,/ Et qui jure pour moi lorsque j'en ai besoin." Jean Racine, *Les Plaideurs* (1668), 1.6.10-11.

M.   Presumably de Gaspé meant 25° below freezing, as the Réaumur thermometor is based on 0° as the freezing point.

N.   The "sheriff in question" was de Gaspé, who received his commission as sheriff of Quebec May 9, 1816. *DCB*, 10:19.

O.   Sir Isaac Brock (1769-1812), the hero of Queenston Heights, came to Canada with his regiment in 1802, and in 1806 assumed temporary command of troops in Canada, with headquarters at Quebec. *DCB*, 5:111.

P.   The De Meuron was a Swiss mercenary regiment that entered British service in 1796, and was sent to Quebec in 1813 during the War of 1812. Story, 207.

Q.   Malcolm Fraser (1733-1815), author of the journal mentioned in note J, came to Canada in 1757 with the 78th Foot, and settled on the Lower Saint Lawrence after the Conquest. The character of Archibald Cameron of Locheill in *Les Anciens Canadiens* bears some resemblance to Fraser. *DCB*, 5:330; LJ, 1:658,659.

CHAPTER 3

Translator's Annotations

A.   The Canadian Recollets (or Recollects) were members of a reformed branch of the Franciscan order. At the instigation of Samuel de Champlain, priests and lay brothers began arriving in New France in 1615. They traveled with the explorers and eventually established centres at Quebec, Trois-Rivières, and Montreal, as well as visiting country parishes and military garrisons on a regular basis. The last Canadian *commissaire* was Father Félix de Bérey Des Essarts (see note F), and the last priest was Father Louis Demers, who died in Montreal in 1813. The last Canadian Recollet, Brother Marc Comptant, is reported to have died at Saint-Thomas de Montmagny in 1849 (Story, 700), not far from de Gaspé's parish of Saint-Jean Port-Joli (cf., anecdote at the end of this chapter). LJ, 2:512-515.

B.   Sir James Monk (1745-1826), born in Boston, was named attorney-general of Quebec (1776), attorney-general of Lower Canada (1792), chief justice of the Court of King's Bench in Montreal (1794), and subsequently became a member of the legislative and executive councils. He was a friend of Jonathan Sewell, in whose office de Gaspé first articled as a law student. P.-G. Roy, *Les Juges de la Province de Québec* (Quebec: Rédempti Paradis, 1933), 383; Story, 532.

C.   The Ursulines, an order of teaching nuns, was established in Quebec in 1693. Their church and convent reflected the prestige achieved by the order. Daughters of the colony's elite were educated in this institution, and in 1786 Lord Dorchester sent his daughter there for lessons in French and embroidery. The nuns record that "lady Carleton" asked if she might accompany her daughter. Catherine Burke and Adèle Cimon, *Les Ursulines de Québec depuis leur établissement jusqu'à nos jours* (Quebec: Presses de C. Darveau, 1863-1866), 1:17, 19.

D. See the watercolour, "View of the Ruins of the Monastery of the Recollects taken from the Garden, 1799," in Gerald Finley's *George Heriot: Painter of the Canadas* (Kingston: Agnes Etherington Art Centre, 1978), 42.

E. Luke 12:19, 20.

F. Father Félix Berey Des Essarts (*DCB*, 4:231) or "Father P. Félix de Bérey" (*Diary of Mrs. Simcoe*, 78), (1720-1800), was born in Montreal, the son of a military officer. Mrs. Simcoe writes, "The heads of the French clergy dined with Coll. Simcoe—the Bishop, Monsr. Gravé the Vicar-General, Père Barré, etc. Père Barré quite an Irishman and too jocose for his station."

G. "Your adversary the devil, as a roaring lion, walketh about, seeking whom he may devour." 1 Pet. 5:8.

H. *Oeufs à la tripe*, a dish consisting of chopped hard-boiled eggs with onions.

I. De Gaspé describes "la gazette de Nelson" (*Mémoires*, 67) as the sole newspaper in the District of Quebec. It most probably refers to John Neilson's *Quebec Gazette*, "the earliest Quebec newspaper," founded in 1764. At the time of the anecdote it was a bilingual weekly containing local news and advertisements. John R. Bone, et al., *A History of Canadian Journalism* (Toronto: The Canadian Press Association, 1980), 148.

J. Georges Louis Leclerc, Comte de Buffon (1707-1788), a proponent of the scientific approach to nature study based on observation and classification. He wrote and edited a voluminous *Histoire naturelle* (1749-1788). *GLE*, 2:431.

K. *Deux quarts* (*Mémoires*, 77). A *quart* was a small barrel commonly used for transporting and storing a wide variety of goods. Nicole Genêt, Louise Décarie-Audet, and Luce Vermet, *Les Objets familiers de nos ancêtres* (Montreal: Les Editions de l'Homme, 1974) 40-41, 215.

L. A *demiard* was a standard measuring cup that equaled a half pint, usually a pewter or tinware vessel. Genêt et al., *Les Objets familiers*, 107.

M. The point was that, apart from julep as a sweetener, each of the ingredients in the royal purgative was a powerful cathartic. *OED*, 4:206, 6:128, 8:633, 9:455.

N.   A drawing and description of a dog-powered spit is given in Genêt et al.,
     Les Objets familiers, 251.

CHAPTER 4

Author's Footnotes to 1866 Edition

1.   The worthy Monsieur Louis has died since I wrote this passage.

2.   As everyone knows, Henri IV was a native of Béarn, the domain of the
     house of Albret. It was united with France by Louis XII.

3.   My Uncle de Lanaudière nevertheless continued to receive emoluments
     of 500 pounds as *maître des eaux et des forêts* until his death.

4.   This was the Anglican bishop, Jacob Mountain, father of the second bishop
     of that name who died recently, mourned by all classes of society for his
     goodness and charity to the poor. [Jacob Mountain (1749-1825) was
     appointed first Anglican bishop of Quebec in 1793, a post he held for
     over thirty years. *MDCB*, 534. His son, George Jehoshaphat Mountain
     (1789-1863), was third Anglican bishop of Quebec (1837-1863), first
     principal of McGill College (1824-1835), and founder of Bishop's University,
     Lennoxville, Quebec (1843). *DCB*, 9:581.]

CHAPTER 4

Translator's Annotations

A.   Quoted from the shipwreck scene, Henri Bernardin de Saint-Pierre, *Paul
     et Virginie* (1788; Paris: Editions Bordas, 1970), 117.

B.   Jacques Panet (1754-1834), is described as curé of "Lislet et de Saint
     Jean," for a brief sojourn (1780-1781), and of L'Islet until 1829. Jean-
     Baptiste Perras was curé of Saint-Jean Port-Joli, 1793-1799. Angéline
     Saint-Pierre, *L'Eglise de Saint-Jean Port-Joli* (Quebec: Editions Garneau,
     1977), 201. The other members of the Panet family mentioned are Louis
     Panet (1794-1884), who became a legislative councillor in 1852, and his
     father, Jean-Antoine Panet (1751-1815), who was elected to the first
     legislative assembly in 1792, was its first speaker, and held both these
     elected positions until his death. LJ, 2:400.

C.   These two uncles were half-brothers. The elder was Charles-Louis Tarieu
     de Lanaudière (see chap. 2, note E), son of Charles-François Tarieu de
     Lanaudière and Louise-Geneviève des Champs de Boishébert. The younger
     was Charles-Gaspard Tarieu de Lanaudière (1769-1812), son of Charles-

François and his second wife, Marie-Catherine, daughter of the Baron de Longueuil. Other children of this second marriage included de Gaspé's mother, Marie-Catherine (1767-1842), and his aunt, Marie-Anne (1765-1844), wife of the legislative councillor, François Baby. LJ, 2:58.

D. Ignace-Michel-Louis-Antoine d'Irumberry de Salaberry (1752-1828) visited Paris in 1785. An influential cousin enabled him to attend the launching of a Montgolfier balloon, and presented him at court, where he kissed the hand of the dauphin, son of Louis XVI. LJ, 2:609.

E. Louis-René Chaussegros de Léry (1762-1832) born in Paris and educated at the Little Seminary in Quebec, was a cavalry captain in Louis XVI's bodyguard from 1784 to 1789. He then served with emigré forces in Germany, later moving to Brussels, and then England, from where he returned to Canada in 1794. Here he served in various military and civil posts, becoming a legislative councillor in 1818. LJ, 1:379.

F. Sir Robert Shore Milnes (1746-1836) was appointed lieutenant-governor of Lower Canada in 1797, although he did not arrive in the colony until June 1799. LJ, 2:277.

G. Abbé Jean-Baptiste-Antoine Ferland (1805-1865), historian and archivist, was professor of Canadian history at Laval University (1855), dean of the faculty of arts (1864), and the author of Cours d'histoire du Canada (Quebec, 1861-1865), lectures on the French régime. He was a contributor to Le Foyer canadien and Les Soirées canadiennes, both of which he helped found (Story, 252). These popular journals were a stimulus to de Gaspé's writing.

H. François Dupéron (or Duperron) Baby (or Bàby) (1733-1820) was the son of Montreal fur trader Raymond Baby and Thérèse Lecompte-Dupré. He married de Gaspé's aunt (see note C) and settled in the city of Quebec. De Gaspé's wife, Suzanne Allison, was also connected to the Baby family, being the granddaughter of Francois's brother, Jacques Dupéron Baby (1731-1789), a loyalist who moved from Detroit after the American War of Independence and who founded the Upper Canadian branch of the family.

I. The old French law had complex and specific rules governing inheritance. Simply put, half a man's estate automatically went to his legitimate heirs. A child's legitimate portion (his or her légitime) was the equal share of this half. Henry des Rivières Beaubien, Traité sur les lois civiles du Bas-Canada (Montreal: Ludger Duvernay, 1832), 2:25, 105. Although freedom of willing was introduced by the Quebec Act (1774), the old rules pertained where no will existed.

J. Charles-Gaspard Tarieu de Lanaudière (see note C) was sent to London in 1776 at the age of seven. His ailing father died in the same year, and

413

his half-brother, the elder by twenty-six years, appears to have assumed responsibility for him. LJ, 2:58.

K.   This appears as "Convent Garden" in the 1866 edition (*Mémoires*, 101).

L.   De Gaspé mentions only four in all: Louis-René (note E); Charles-Etienne (1774-1842), a member of the executive council (1826-1837) and of the special council (1838-1841); François-Joseph (1754-1828), a military engineer who was made a baron under Napoleon and a vicomte under the Restoration; and Gaspard-Roch-George (1771-1831). Note the English "George," presumably for the British monarch. Cf., Brian Young, *George-Etienne Cartier: Montreal Bourgeois* (Kingston: McGill-Queen's University Press, 1981), 6. This brother studied military engineering in France. In 1799 he formally renounced his place in the family succession. He became a tutor for a noble family and later for the children of the Russian emperor. A fifth brother, Alexandre-André-Victor (1778-1818), was admitted to the Quebec legal profession in 1808, at about the same time as de Gaspé. He then took up a military career in France, and died in Guadeloupe. LJ, 1:376-380.

M.   Not only the vicomte's great-grandfather, but his grandfather and father were military engineers. The grandfather, Joseph-Gaspard (1682-1756), a pupil of the famous French military engineer Vauban, came to Canada in 1716, where he participated in the fortification of Quebec and Montreal. The father, also Joseph-Gaspard (1721-1797), built Fort Beauséjour in Acadia, still visible today near Sackville, N.B. LJ, 1:379.

CHAPTER 5

Author's Footnotes to the 1866 Edition

1.   In the past, French Canadians were exposed to all manner of insults, and were unable to clear themselves because of the lack of French-language newspapers in which to respond.

2.   These three Canadian officers were the uncles of the author's wife.

3.   The author's grandfather.

4.   This Mr. Mabane, who was made a judge, was an Edinburgh surgeon, whereas there were then in Quebec eminent legal men of Canadian origin. [Adam Mabane (1734-1792).]

5.   This [*greton*] is a piece of pork fat, which Canadians consider a delicacy, particularly when frozen.

CHAPTER 5

Translator's Annotations

A. These century-old memoirs were first published around the time de Gaspé's books appeared. There were two versions: *Mémoires et journal inédit du Marquis d'Argenson, ministre des Affaires étrangères sous Louis XV, publiés et annotés par M. le marquis d'Argenson* (1857-1858), and *Journal et mémoires du marquis d'Argenson, publiés pour la première fois d'après les manuscrits autographes par E.-J.-B. Rathéry* (1859-1867). Alexandre Cioranescu, *Bibliographie de la littérature française du dix-huitième siècle* (Paris: Editions du Centre nationale de la recherche scientifique, 1969), 1:247. René Louis de Voyer, Marquis d'Argenson (1694-1757), was minister of foreign affairs under Louis XV. His great-uncle, Pierre de Voyer, Vicomte d'Argenson, had been a governor of New France (1657-1661).

B. This English rendering is from William Kirby's novel, *The Golden Dog* (first authorized edition 1896; Toronto: McClelland and Stewart, 1969), 67.

C. Nicolas Jaquin, *dit* Philibert, a Quebec merchant, was killed in January 1748 by Pierre-Jean-Baptiste-François-Xavier Legardeur de Repentigny (1719-1776), an officer in the French colonial regular army before the Conquest. They had reportedly been quarreling over a billeting order. *DCB* 4:448. Repentigny was condemned *in absentia* by a Quebec court in 1748, "in view of his quality of gentleman, to have his head cut off." This judgment was reversed a year later by the king, "restoring . . . his good name and fame, imposing silence upon all officials, and cancelling all judgments and fines except those of civil origin." A. G. Doughty, *Quebec of Yesteryear* (Toronto: Thomas Nelson and Sons, 1932), 151-153.

D. Anon., *Reminiscences of Quebec derived from reliable sources; for The use of Travellers by an old inhabitant* (Quebec: Printed at the Mercury Office, 1858). This version does not name de Repentigny. It alleges that the inscription on the Golden Dog was directed at Indendant Bigot, "and Mr. Phillibert [*sic*] received, as the reward of his verse, the sword of an officer of the garrison through his back, when descending the Lower Town hill. The murderer was permitted to leave the colony unmolested," and was later killed in a duel in Pondicherry by the victim's brother (pp. 4-5). De Gaspé attributes the authorship of this pamphlet to Alfred Hawkins (1802?-1855), who published "several works of real historical value" (*MDCB*, 343). One of these contains an account of the Philibert killing very similar in wording and substance to the anonymous *Reminiscences*, and names "M. de R——, a French Officer of the garrison." Alfred

Hawkins, *Hawkins's Picture of Quebec with historical recollections* (Quebec: Printed for the proprietor by Neilson & Cowan, 1834), 259-260.

E. Probably "Caroline, Légende canadienne," by Amédée Papineau (1819-1903), son of Louis-Joseph Papineau, "which appeared in July 1837 in the short-lived *Le Glaneur* of St. Charles. James Huston included the story in the first volume of *Le Repertoire national* (1848)." Yves Brunelle, ed. and trans., *French Canadian Prose Masters: The Nineteenth Century* (Montreal: Harvest Houst Ltd., 1978), 18.

F. Madame Bailly de Messein died at Saint-Thomas de Montmagny in 1834, at the age of eight-five. She was Geneviève, the wife of Michel Bailly de Messein (m. 1772), and the daughter of Ignace Aubert de Gaspé (the author's grandfather) and Marie-Anne Coulon de Villiers. *BRH*, 23 (1917): 195.

G. Three watercolors of this scene are in the possession of the Royal Ontario Museum. Finley, *George Heriot, Painter of the Canadas*, 40, 42.

H. These three were the sons of Jacques-Dupéron (or Duperron) Baby (chap. 4, note H), fur trader, friend of Pontiac, and superintendant of Indians, who settled in Detroit after the Seven Years' War, but moved to Sandwich, Ontario, as a loyalist after the American Revolution. His daughter, Thérèse (d. 1839), married Captain Thomas Allison, and was the mother of de Gaspé's wife, Suzanne. The first brother mentioned, Daniel Baby (Detroit 1778-London 1858), rose to be a general in the British army. His natural son, Daniel-Antoine Baby (b. England, 1826), also had a military career. The second, Louis (Detroit 1782-Ile Bourbon 1812), served in the East Indies with the British army, and became a captain in the "Bourbon Corps" before being killed in a duel. The third, Antoine-Dupéron Baby (Detroit 1779-Tours 1863), served with the British army in India, Mauritius, and the Ile Bourbon (now Réunion Island) in campaigns against the French, becoming a half-pay officer in 1816. *BRH*, 7 (1901): 313, and 29 (1923): 63.

I. Francis Maseres, *Occasional Essays on various subjects, chiefly political and historical; extracted partly from the publick newspapers, during the present reign, and partly from tracts published in the reigns of Queen Elizabeth, King Charles I., King Charles II., and from Bishop Burnet's history of his own times* (London: printed by Robert Wilks; sold by John White, 1809), 407-411. Francis Maseres (1731-1824) was attorney-general of Quebec, 1766-1769, but otherwise spent most of his life in England. He was of Huguenot origin (*MDCB*, 563). De Gaspé's translation is occasionally free, and the order of the introductory sentences slightly rearranged (cf., *Mémoires*, 121); the extract as given here reproduces the Maseres text with its awkward style and spelling.

416

J. Of the type of incident described in this anecdote, Hugh Gray wrote, "It is certainly enough to startle a stranger, to see a person . . . come running up, with a handful of snow, calling out, '*Your nose, Sir,—your nose,—* you are frost bitten;' and, without further ceremony, either themselves rubbing it without mercy, or making you do so." Hugh Gray, *Letters from Canada written During a Residence There in the Years 1806, 1807, and 1808* (London: Longman, Hurst, Rees, and Orme, 1809), 293.

K. Lady Anne Howard, elder sister of Lady Dorchester, was the first wife of Lord Dorchester's younger brother, General Thomas Carleton (1735-1817), governor of New Brunswick. LJ, 1:310. Lady Anne was reportedly proposed to by Lord Dorchester when he was Sir Guy Carleton, but she refused him. He later proposed to Lady Maria (Lady Dorchester), who had been heard to say, "I only wish he had given me the chance." Robertson, *Diary of Mrs. Simcoe*, 261. Lady Anne is recorded as having spent a year in retreat in the Ursuline convent in Quebec (1787-1788), where the nuns were impressed by her equable and affectionate nature. At the request of her family, she returned to London in July 1788. Burke and Cimon, *Les Ursulines de Québec*, 3:184.

L. Robert Prescott (1725-1816), came to Lower Canada in 1796 as lieutenant-governor. He succeeded Lord Dorchester as governor-in-chief of Canada in 1797, and was promoted to full general in 1798. He returned to England in 1799, although he retained his appointment until 1807. *MDCB*, 677.

M. The "ordre royal et militaire de Saint-Louis" was created by Louis XIV as a reward for virtue, merit, and services rendered. It was significant as being the first such award accessible to the bourgeoisie, that is, officers who had come up through the ranks. *GLE*, 9:523.

N. Louis Coulon de Villiers (1710-1757) was the officer to whom George Washington capitulated at Fort Necessity, July 3, 1754. This capitulation avenged the death of Louis' brother, Villiers de Jumonville, reputedly killed on Washington's order while under a flag of truce (see introduction, n. 16). De Gaspé gives the details in his "notes et éclaircissements" to chap. 14 of *Les Anciens Canadiens*. *DCB*, 3:148.

O. Louis de Bonne de Missègle (c. 1717-1760) was wounded on April 28, 1760, in the Battle of Saint-Foy, and died the following day. His son, Pierre-Amable de Bonne (1758-1816), was a prominent member of the Canadian party in the legislative assembly. *DCB*, 3:69, 70, 736, and Morgan, 163.

P. Lieutenant-Colonel François Vassal de Monviel (1759-1843). *DCB*, 5:45, 1041. The "late adjutant-general of the militia of Lower Canada, was one of the few remaining individuals who figured in the most stirring and memorable scenes of the history of this province. . . . His father, captain in the Royal Roussillon, was descended from one of the old noble families of France, and fell whilst fighting at the side of Montcalm on Abraham's Plains." Morgan, 92.

CHAPTER 6

Author's Footnotes to the 1866 Edition

1. The common people referred to the agents of the North West and Hudson's Bay companies as "bourgeois," and this term is used even today to denote those who employ the working class. They still say, "I'm working for a *bon bourgeois.*"

2. When I was a child, the present Côte de la Prison was called the Côte à Moreau.

3. Mr. Tanswell, having studied at I know not what Jesuit college in Europe, was believed by the English to have belonged to this eminent order. He was twice married in Quebec in a Catholic church. ["Although he may have studied at a Jesuit college in Europe, James Tanswell himself records only that he spent 'the Twenty first Years' of his life 'in acquiring a universal Education.'" *DCB*, 5:789.]

4. There being no police force at this time, the garrison was called upon to maintain order.

5. Around the year 1797, a troupe from Ricket's Circus of London spent part of the summer in Quebec. It was the first circus to come to Canada.
   When I was a child the venerable and much-mourned Father Demers, a priest attached to the Quebec Seminary, asked me one day where I had been. "I've been doing *acrobatatic* tricks [*tours de soupletesse*]," I replied. "Oh, the wretch!" cried Father Demers, laughing until the tears came. "He's been doing acrobatatics!" He never forgot this muddled expression. If, in the philosophy class that he taught us twelve years later, anyone used mangled French, he would call out, still laughing at the memory, "That's not nearly as good as de Gaspé's acrobatatics!"

CHAPTER 6

Translator's Annotations

A. This passage occurs in the opening lines of *Oina-Morul*, a poem of "Ossian" supposedly translated by Scottish writer James Macpherson. These widely popular poems, "a central influence in the early Romantic movement," purported to be a collection of verse by Oisin, the ancient Irish warrior poet, translated by Macpherson from third-century texts. Although subsequently shown to be the poems of Macpherson himself, these works (*Fingal* in 1762 and *Temora* in 1763) enjoyed an enthusiastic reception. *New Enc. Brit.: Micro*, 7:611. See "Oina-Morul: a poem," in *The Poems of Ossian: translated by James Macpherson, with notes* (Edinburgh: Centenary Edition, 1896), 187.

B. Assistant Commissary-General James Thompson was the son of that James Thompson (chap. 2, annotation I) who picked up Montgomery's sword. He was a fellow member of the Club des Anciens (*DCB*, 10:21), and the brother of Judge John Gawler Thompson (1787-1868). According to P.-G. Roy, the brothers were twins, James dying less than a year after John. He should not be confused with another brother, W.A. Thompson (1786-1838), also an assistant commissary-general. Morgan, 168; Roy. *Les Juges de la province de Québec*, 547.

C. The costume of the Little Seminary students "was composed of a blue cloth tunic [i.e., a fitted coat] with a white piping on the seams. The braided sash of the early days was later replaced by the green sash still in use." Adam Shortt and Arthur G. Doughty, eds., *Canada and its Provinces* (Toronto: Glasgow, Brook and Company, 1914), 16:390.

D. Justin McCarthy (1786-1832), "lawyer and author, was born at Montmagny, Quebec . . . and was admitted to the bar of Lower Canada in 1812. While still a law student, he published a *Dictionnaire de l'ancien droit du Canada* (Quebec, 1809)." As the *Memoirs* show, McCarthy became an alcoholic and a vagrant. In 1820, he announced the forthcoming publication of a *Dictionnaire des lois du Canada*. It never appeared, and he died at Quebec in June 1832. *MDCB*, 485.

E. "The bat in the fable" of La Fontaine (bk. 2, fable 5) posed alternately as a bird and a mouse to escape predators. Jean de La Fontaine, *Fables*, eds. Edmond Pilon and Fernand Dauphin (Paris: Librairie Garnier Frères, n.d.), 52.

F. This is not the coniferous hemlock tree, but *conium maculatum*, a poisonous weed. After flowering, "the poisonous substance appears to concentrate in the ripening fruits," which is perhaps why the author and his companions suffered no ill-effects from the fifes and flutes made of the dried stalks. The plant has a carrot-like root, and *carrotte à moreau* is given as its common name by the Montreal Botanical Gardens. *Enc. Can.*, 8, 125. Lauren Brown, *Weeds in Winter* (New York: W. W. Norton and Co. Inc., 1976), 118.

G. The Cul-de-Sac was a small inlet between wharves on the Lower Town waterfront. Bouchette, "City of Quebec," *Topographical Map of the Province of Quebec*, n. pag.

H. Through the generosity of its founder, Bishop Laval, the Quebec Seminary possessed, among its extensive North Shore properties, "two considerable farms" at Saint-Joachim, at the foot of Cap Tourmente: "the upper farm, called today the large farm, and the lower or small farm. . . . The pupils ordinarily took . . . their vacations at Saint-Joachim, the students in theology and philosophy going to the large farm, and the rest of the pupils to the small one."

These holidays usually lasted from August 15 to October 1. Although religious observances and farm work occupied part of the time, amusements included excursions up Cap Tourmente, sailing, fishing, and hunting the wildfowl that descended in their "thousands upon the reefs" in September. This custom was interrupted by the hostilities preceding the Conquest, but was resumed "in 1779, with the inauguration of the Château Bellevue at Petit-Cap" in Saint-Joachim. Shortt and Doughty, *Canada and its Provinces*, 16:332, 378, 391. Noël Baillargeon, *Le Séminaire de Québec sous l'épiscopat the Mgr de Laval* (Quebec: Presses de l'université de Laval, 1972), 119.

CHAPTER 7

Author's Footnotes to the 1866 Edition

1. It is actually "carpenter" in the song, but we thought "shoemaker" more amusing.

2. For some reason that I cannot explain, in France a girl of noble family who married a commoner was called *demoiselle*, and could not use the title *dame*.

3. Joseph Toussaint drowned in this cove nearly a hundred years ago. He was alone with his eleven-year-old son, Charles, when the ice gave way beneath his feet. With the aid of pieces of wood thrown by his son, he kept afloat almost a quarter of an hour, but in the end disappeared. The child traversed the forest by himself to reach the first dwellings, a fair distance from the lake, and give the alarm. Toussaint's body was taken from the water, which was fairly shallow at this point, with a cod hook.

    Charles Toussaint himself often told me the sad story of his father's death.

4. Biscuit was made of wheat flour mixed with milk, or if none were available, with water. In the forest, where no spoons were to be had, it was usually eaten with wooden pallets, oriental fashion.

5. My old friend, Doctor Painchaud, can testify to the wonderful echoes of Lac Trois-Saumons, although those who visit this fine lake nowadays

speak of them without enthusiasm. This is perhaps because their favourite fishing spot is in the Toussaint Cove on the south side, whereas we used to camp on the north.

6. Canadian hunters often make a small notch on the bark of trees to guide them through our immense forests, particularly if they intend to return by the same path.

7. Manitou: the malevolent spirit of Indian lore.

CHAPTER 7

Translator's Annotations

A. Jacques Montanier, *dit* Delille (1738-1813), was a prolific poet and translator of poems on the subject of nature and man, including works by Virgil, Pope, Milton, and Shakespeare. These lines, which set the tone for this chapter, are from his original poem, "L'Homme des champs" (song 2, lines 17-18), which are in turn a reference to his translation of lines in Virgil's *Georgics*, bk. 2. Virgil is speaking of his family estate, taken away by Augustus, but subsequently restored. The context echoes circumstances in de Gaspé's own life—his loss of freedom, his subsequent reinstatement in society after years of prison, the simple pleasures of youth and life in the seigneurie. *Oeuvres de J. Delille*, "nouvelle édition" (Paris: L. G. Michaud, 1824), 2:93, 138; 7:253, 283.

B. *Omelette à la bajoue* (*Mémoires*, 178). Smoked pig's cheek or pork jowl (*bajoue de porc fumée*), also known colloquially as *la gourgane* is mentioned in the *Glossaire du parler français au Canada* (Quebec: L'Action Social Limitée, 1930), 374.

C. Arpent refers to a French linear measure, the equivalent of about 190 English feet (as against the French foot), used in areas mainly settled by French Canadians. Although it also refers to a square measure of about one acre, its linear use was fairly common in the early nineteenth century. Walter S. Avis, et al., eds., *A Dictionary of Canadianisms on Historical Principles* (Toronto: W. J. Gage Ltd., 1967), 16.

D. De Gaspé's word *huard*, a variant of *huart*, as well as the behaviour and cries of these birds, make it clear that he is speaking of the common loon (*Gavia immer* or *huart à collier*). These birds have a swan-like outline (cf., the quotation at the beginning of the chapter), although it is perhaps an exaggeration to call them "our superb Canadian swans." J. M. Le Moine stated that European authors had given this flattering name to the Canada Goose, and noted the presence of this waterfowl in the area of Saint-Jean Port-Joli. David Rogers, *Dictionnaire de la langue québecoise rurale* (Montreal: VLB Editeur Inc., 1977), 146. W. Earl Godfrey, *The Birds of Canada* (Ottawa: Printing and Publishing Supply and Services Canada, 1966), 9. J. M. Le Moine, *Ornithologie du Canada*, 2d ed. (Quebec: n.p., 1861), 1:78, 79.

E. This is possibly a variant of *patliache*, meaning "patriarch" in French-Canadian popular speech. N.-E. Dionne, *Le Parler populaire des canadiens français* (Quebec: Laflamme et Proulx, 1909), 488.

CHAPTER 8
Author's Footnotes to the 1866 Edition

1. This was written before the death of Mr. Hamond Gowan, taken from his many friends a couple of years ago. [Possibly Hammond Gowen, *DCB*, 8:353.]

2. Mr. William Philips, carried off so suddenly from his excellent family and a wide circle of friends by a cruel death.

3. This game is of Breton origin, however, and is still called *criquet* in Britanny.

4. A Canadian calèche has only two wheels.

5. The O'Hara Hotel, replaced by government offices, at the corner of the Rue du Fort and the Rue Sainte-Anne. The present gallery did not then exit.

6. Mr. John Ross, prothonotary of the court of king's bench, was as goodnatured and amiable as he was sincere in friendship. He died young and universally regretted.

7. Madame Laterrière was still alive when I wrote this chapter last winter. She had read my book, *Les Anciens Canadiens*, with great pleasure, and I was planning to send her this chronicle when I learned of her death from her brother-in-law, the Honourable Paschal de Sales Laterrière.

8. Dr. Pierre de Sales Laterrière published a pamphlet written in English, entitled *A Political and Historical Account of Lower Canada* in London in 1830.
   This patriotic pamphlet caused a sensation among his Canadian compatriots.

CHAPTER 8

Translator's Annotations

A. Henri Benjamin Constant de Rebecque (1767-1830), Swiss-born French writer and liberal politician under the Restoration, is most noted for his novel *Adolphe* (1816), with its innovative exploration of human follies and failings in the youthful protagonist-narrator.

B. "Queenston-Hight" (*Mémoires*, 209).

C. De Gaspé writes "*cricket* (jeu de la crosse)" (*Mémoires*, 216), a somewhat confusing reference; lacrosse could certainly not be a game "unknown to us French Canadians," as it originated in Canada. Cricket, although a word of uncertain etymology, is considered to be the same game as the French *criquet*, and to have been popular in England since the early eighteenth century. *OED*, 2:1171,1172, 6:17.

D. Canadian calèches, essentially two-passenger, open carriages, were described by George Heriot, who was deputy postmaster-general of British North America between 1799 and 1816, as "small vehicles with two wheels, of a homely and rude construction hung upon Bands of leather, or Thongs of unmanufactured Bull Hides, by way of Springs." The wheels were very high. Finlay, *George Heriot, Painter of the Canadas*, 57, 58.

E. Pierre de Sales Laterrière (1785-1834). His Languedoc father, a successful Quebec doctor, apparently adopted the name De Salles Laterrière, and had a romantic but chequered career between arriving in Canada as a young man in 1766, and settling down in 1810 as the elderly seigneur of Les Eboulements on the North Shore of the Saint Lawrence. The younger Laterrière was educated at the Quebec Seminary and was sent to London to study medicine. There he married Mary Anne, daughter of Sir Fenwick Bulmer, in 1815. Although he returned to Canada to die of diabetes, his wife and family remained in England. Evelyn Waugh's diaries contain an intriguing mention of meeting "a Mrs Grub and Mrs de Sales de la Terrière," the owners of a decayed castle, in Ireland in 1949. *Enc. Can.*, 6:78; *DCB* 5:735-738; *The Diaries of Evelyn Waugh*, ed. Michael Davie (Boston: Little, Brown and Company, 1976), 677.

F. Jonathan Sewell (1766-1839), generally an unpopular figure with his French-Canadian contemporaries because of being associated with the repressive policies of Governor James Craig, was chief justice of Lower Canada from 1808 to 1838. He had earlier been appointed solicitor-general (1793) and attorney-general (1795), and was a member of the provincial parliament from 1796 to 1808. He came from an old New England Loyalist family that had gone back to England after the American

Revolution. Sewell, however, returned to New-Brunswick in 1785 to study law, and in 1789 moved to Quebec. He was first president of the Quebec Literary and Historical Society, founded in 1824, and a keen amateur musician. He is described as being distinguished not only for his legal ability, but "by the variety of his talents, the charm of his conversation, and the kindness of his heart." William Notman, *Portraits of British Americans*, 2:247, 250, 266. A photograph exists of the Sewell house, built in 1803 at 87 Rue Saint-Louis, where de Gaspé mentions going to parties. Sewell married Henrietta, daughter of Chief Justice William Smith, in 1796. They had twenty-two children. Fournier, *Lieux et monuments historiques de Québec et environs*, 199.

G. John Ross (1783-1826) was the son of a member of the Fraser's Highlanders who had came to Canada with Wolfe's army. He began practising law in 1803, and became prothonotary for the District of Quebec, conjointly with Joseph-François Perrault, in 1812. "Mr. Ross, brought up among the French Canadians of Quebec, spoke French like his mother tongue. Very sympathetic to our race, he had as many friends among the French Canadians as among his own compatriots." P.-G. Roy, *Fils de Québec* (Lévis: n. pub., 1933), 3:17.

H. Richard Cartwright (1759-1815), a distinguished Loyalist, legislative councillor, and successful Upper Canadian businessman, "was a kind and loving father and husband." He married Magdalen Secord, sister-in-law of Laura Ingersoll Secord, heroine of the War of 1812. "He . . . suffered a crushing blow from which he never really recovered when his two eldest sons—James and Richard—died in 1811." *DCB*, 5:168, 171.

I. De Gaspé writes "Ashley" (*Mémoires*, 234). Sir Astley Paston Cooper (1768-1841) made medical history in the days before antiseptic surgery, lecturing at St. Thomas's Hospital in London, and after 1800 became surgeon at Guy's Hospital. *Enc. Brit.* 6:444.

CHAPTER 9

Author's Footnotes to the 1866 Edition

1. In Canada we always said *couette* rather than *queue*.

2. Judges of the Court of Queen's Bench used to wear ermine robes.

3. John Ross, advocate, was prothonotary of the court of king's bench at his death.

4. The Honourable John Gawler Thompson, now a judge in the Gaspé.

CHAPTER 9

Translator's Annotations

A. The famous leader of the Patriote party, Louis-Joseph Papineau (1786-1871), whose dates coincide with de Gaspé's, was born in Montreal and attended both the Montreal and Quebec seminaries. The lives of the two men, while divergent in many ways, have some interesting parallels. See Gérard Parizeau, "Deux Seigneurs: Philippe Aubert de Gaspé et Joseph Papineau," in *Assurances*, 40, nos. 3 and 4 (1972). Fernand Ouellet has provided a penetrating article on Papineau and his background in *DCB*, 10:564-578.

B. The Petit Séminaire or Little Seminary is the background for many of the scenes of de Gaspé's youth. It was founded in 1668 by Bishop Laval to provide vocational training and secondary education for French and Indian boys, with a view to their entering the Grand Séminaire or Grand Seminary to be educated for the priesthood.

   The term "Quebec Seminary" is often used to indicate either or both of these institutions. In fact they shared many facilities, and were under the same overall administration. The seminary buildings, standing near the Upper Town market-place, housed the two branches in separate wings giving onto a common courtyard. The administration included a superior and, usually, five "directors." The boys boarded at the Little Seminary, where they received "moral and religious training," and performed various menial and administrative tasks. For academic instruction, they originally attended the Jesuit College. When this closed in 1763, the Quebec Seminary "opened its doors to all youths wishing to undertake the study of the humanities and the sciences," and has done so ever since.

   As in the Jesuit College, the secondary level covered five years or "classes," beginning at the fifth and progressing through three years of Latin grammar to humanities in "second" and rhetoric in "first"—i.e. the final year. In addition, "the syllabus included French, English . . . literature . . . physics and chemistry," as well as mathematics. Post-secondary students who did not go in for the priesthood might board out and take philosophy courses at the Grand Seminary, as did de Gaspé. Baillargeon, *Le Séminaire de Québec sous l'épiscopat de Mgr de Laval*, i, 97-99, 110, 113, 114. John Lambert, *Travels through Canada and the United States of America in the years 1806, 1807, and 1808*, 2nd. ed. (London: C. Cradock and W. Joy, 1814), 1:60. Shortt and Doughty, *Canada and its Provinces*, 16:367, 368, 387, 390.

C. Joseph Papineau (1752-1841) typified the rising professional French Canadian middle class that began to seek greater political representation at this time. Born in Montreal, he was educated at the Montreal and Quebec

425

seminaries, and was twice elected to the legislative assembly (1792-1804 and 1809-1814). He purchased the seigneurie of La Petite Nation, which he sold to his son in 1818. *MDCB*, 643; *DCB*, 10:564.

D.   Note the missing line, after "with easy art": "Melting they fall, and sink into the heart!" which the author also omitted in his translation. The transcription in the *Mémoires* contains slight differences from the original, notably "accent" instead of "accents," and "wandering" instead of "wondering," although de Gaspé has translated the original sense correctly. Cf., *The Iliad of Homer in the English Verse Translation by Alexander Pope* (New York: The Heritage Press, 1943), 55.

E.   One of Dr. Painchaud's eccentricities was that of "making his house calls on horseback and wearing long Wellington boots and silver spurs." *DCB*, 10:563.

F.   De Gaspé refers to *casque* and *chapeau* for winter and summer wear respectively (*Mémoires*, 252). There was no regulation headgear in the period he describes. Before 1726, Little Seminary pupils wore a *tapabor* (a hat, sometimes of oiled silk, with a large brim that could be turned down and tied in bad weather). After 1842, a regulation peaked cap was adopted. Between the two dates, however, "the headgear depended upon the pupil's taste."

In warmer weather, pupils might wear a soft, peaked, cap such as worn by the youths of a later generation in the painting "La Chasse aux tourtes" by Antoine Plamondon (Art Gallery of Ontario). John Lambert, in his *Travel*, depicted a seminary student of about 1806 wearing a top hat with the sides curled up. Canadian historian Benjamin Sulte thought this was probably a beaver or silk hat. In the same drawing, an adult in winter dress is wearing a high, peaked, fur cap or *casque*, somewhat military in appearance. Léonidas Bélanger, "Le Capot d'écolier," *Saguenayensia*, no. 1 (Jan.-Feb. 1973): 29-30. Lambert, *Travels . . . 1808*, 1: facing page 60.

G.   Arnaud Berquin (1747-1791), author of popular works for children such as *L'Ami des enfants* and *Lectures pour les enfants. GLE*, 2:91.

H.   Joseph-Rémi Vallières (or Vallière) de Saint-Réal (1787-1847), chief justice of Montreal when he died, was "universally respected and beloved" (Morgan, 420). As a child, he had accompanied his parents to Windham in Upper Canada. His father, a Quebec blacksmith, had been recruited to settle there with the group of French émigré colonists brought out by the Comte de Puisaye. He returned to Quebec after his father's death in 1799 to live with his maternal aunt, Charlotte Cornelier Amyot, wife of a cooper. Le Jeune 2:752; *MDCB*, 852; P.-G. Roy, *Les Avocats de la région de Québec* (Lévis: Le Quotidien Ltée., 1936) 445.

I.   Prosper Jolyot Crébillon, *dit* Sieur de Crais-Billon (1674-1762), author of blood-and-thunder plays, reportedly said, "Corneille took heaven, Racine earth, and I was left with hell." *GLE*, 3:629.

J.   The long pigtail or *couette* of the habitant was remarked upon by John Lambert and Isaac Weld in their respective *Travels*. Weld saw "a queue bound with eel skins that reached the whole way down his back." To have it cut off (*se faire couper la couette*) was a terrible insult. Gerald Craig, ed., *Early Travellers in the Canadas* (Toronto: The Macmillan Company of Canada Limited, 1955), 25, 29. Dionne, *Le Parler populaire*, 189.

K.   Louis Plamondon (1785-1828), was admitted to the bar in 1811 and appointed clerk of the registry office and of crown land for Lower Canada in 1826. An obituary notice in the *Quebec Gazette*, January 3, 1828, praised him for "the extent of his legal knowledge, the graces of his elocution and the polished amenity of his manners and his wit." Although de Gaspé describes him as the first of his seminary contemporaries to die, in fact Louis Moquin died earlier, in 1825. Roy, *Les Avocats de la région de Québec*, 354.

L.   Sébastien Roch Nicolas (*dit* "de") Chamfort (1740-1794), disillusioned revolutionary and cynic, wrote the caustic *Pensées, maximes et anecdotes* (1803). *GLE*, 2:823.

M.   Louis Moquin (1786-1825), admitted to the bar in 1813, was reportedly considered "one of the most brilliant lawyers of his time." At his funeral, Chief Justice Sewell remarked on his skill and knowledge, as well as the "severe integrity of his conduct" in his profession. The portrait mentioned by de Gaspé was probably destroyed in the Quebec courthouse fire of 1873. A likeness is reproduced in *BRH*, 3 (1897): facing page 161. Roy, *Les Avocats de la région de Québec*, 309; *BRH*, 1 (1895): 172; 2 (1896): 54-58.

N.   *Baston* is a variant of Boston. *Glossaire du parler populaire*, 101.

O.   Andrew Bulger (1789-1858) was born in Newfoundland and studied at the Little Seminary in Quebec. He joined the Newfoundland Regiment of Fencible Infantry in 1804 and received a lieutenant's commission in the Royal Newfoundland Regiment in 1806. He served heroically in the War of 1812, and became governor of Assiniboia or the Red River district in 1822. *DCB*, 8:111-113.

P.   *Le Lutrin, poème héroï-comique* (1674) by Boileau, mentions ever hungry canons in the *chant premier*, although it is their master, the fat young Bishop of Coutances, who is described in the glowing detail mentioned by de Gaspé: "Youth in its flower shines upon his visage,/His chin upon his breast descends in double stage." Boileau, *Oeuvres*, 256.

Q. John Fletcher (1787-1844), "provincial judge of the district of St. Francis, Lower Canada, one of the justices of the Court of Queen's Bench, for that district, and also of the Provincial Court of Appeals," had emigrated from London, where he had also "become distinguished as an eminent man of science" (Morgan, 231). He became a judge of the sessions court in Quebec in 1815, shortly before de Gaspé became sheriff of Quebec. An attempt in 1831 to remove him from his functions was unsuccessful, and "his faults were rather his eccentricities." Roy, *Les Juges de la province de Québec*, 209.

R. Marie de Brinon (d. 1701) was the superior of the school for young ladies at Saint-Cyr, placed there through the influence of Madame de Maintenon, the morganatic wife of Louis XIV. De Gaspé had possibly read this anecdote in the memoirs of the Marquise de Créquy, whom he cites in another context (see chap. 16, author's note 1). *GLE*, 1:377.

S. Boileau, in *Satire III* (1665), describes a dinner consisting of a succession of unpalatable dishes, elaborately presented. As in de Gaspé's anecdote, the host asks the guests what they think of the meal, praising it fulsomely himself. Boileau, *Oeuvres*, 190-193.

T. "Beneath the sheltering beech"—a facetious reference to a line in Virgil's poem about the shepherdess Amaryllis and her swain Tityrus (Eclogue 1): "Tityre, tu patulae recubans sub tegmine fagi." ("Tityrus, here you loll . . . beneath a spread of sheltering beech.") *The Eclogues of Virgil*, trans. C. Day Lewis (London: Jonathan Cape, 1963), 9.

CHAPTER 10

Author's Footnotes to the 1866 Edition

1. My respectable friend, Mr. C. T., when reading these memoirs, will recall our conversation on this subject in Rimouski. [This probably refers to Joseph-Charles Taché (1820-1894), nephew of Sir Etienne Taché. He practised medicine in Rimouski and represented the riding from 1847 to 1857. Significantly, he was also an active essayist, a founder of the *Soirées canadiennes*, in which de Gaspé's work first appeared, and possibly one of the author's earliest literary advisers. LJ, 2:686. *ATM*, 181. Lacourcière, "L'Enjeu des 'Anciens Canadiens,'" 237-238.]

2. It is known that Volney's real name was Chasseboeuf [cowherd], indicating his origins and the profession of his family.

3. Madame Baby, née Susanne De la Croix-Réaume, was a native of Detroit, where she had married the Honourable Jacques Dupéron Baby in 1760. He had served in the French army during the wars of the Conquest and,

as an officer in the Canadian militia, was present at the battles of Monongahela, Abraham, and Sainte-Foy.

He settled in Detroit after the Conquest, occupying the highly influential post of superintendant of Indians. In recognition for his services he was appointed a judge in 1788 by Lord Dorchester. He died shortly afterward, leaving a large fortune to his family.

He was the grandson of the first and only member of that family to come to Canada: *honorable homme* Jacques Baby, Seigneur de Ranville, and officer of the Carignan regiment, who arrived in the colony in 1664.

4. This was written before the Honourable Mr. Justice Charles Mondelet had presided over the session of the Quebec criminal court ending February 24, 1865. The honourable judge should certainly be proud of the high praise that appeared in all the Quebec newspapers, for it was indeed merited. With talent and admirable tact, he was able to work on the minds of the jurors so effectively that their verdicts restored a measure of security to the law-abiding citizens of this city, prey to attacks by the riff-raff that infested the outlying areas of our suburbs.

CHAPTER 10

Translator's Annotations

A. Louis de Fontanes (1757-1821). This French statesman and author embraced radical principles early in the French Revolution, but later became a leading figure in the movement to restore traditional political and religious principles, rather like the young man in the anecdote de Gaspé is about to recount. *GLE*, 5:105.

B. The *Coutume de Paris* was the primary compilation of French customary law before the Revolution. It dealt with private law (property and civil rights), and was formally introduced into New France in 1664. After a period of confusion following the Cession, the place of this body of law "in the constitution of Canada . . . was assured by the imperial legislation popularly known as the 'Quebec Act' of 1774." Civil matters in Quebec are generally governed by French legal tradition as originally embodied in the *Coutume de Paris* and the Civil or Napoleonic Code. The confusing number of authorities to which de Gaspé refers was presumably reduced with the adoption of the Quebec Civil Code in 1866, the year of the publication of the *Mémoires*. John E. C. Brierley, "Quebec's Civil Law Codification: Viewed and Reviewed," *McGill Law Journal* 14 (1968): 522.

C. Joseph Levasseur Borgia (1773-1839) was admitted to the Quebec legal profession in 1800. He took an active part in politics, and was a member of the provincial assembly from 1808 to 1820, and 1824 to 1830. Borgia, one of the founding members of *Le Canadien*, was arrested in 1810 by order of Governor Craig, "who had already stripped him of his rank in the militia in 1808." He was later reinstated. Roy, *Les Avocats de la région de Québec*, 52.

D.   At this period (around 1806), there was no bar—that is, a recognized professional corporation governing the admission of members to its ranks. After a period of articling, aspiring lawyers were sworn in before the court. It was customary, however, to refer to the legal profession as "the bar." The bar of the province of Quebec was formed in 1849, and the earliest bar in Canada was the Law Society of Upper Canada, formed in 1797.

E.   *Les Ruines ou méditations sur les révolutions des empires* (1791), by Constantin François de Chasseboeuf, Comte de Volney (1757-1820). Volney studied medicine and law, and traveled in Egypt and Syria. Although imprisoned during the Terror, he retained his liberal ideas and later flourished under Napoleon and Louis XVIII as a historian, scholar, and statesman. *GLE*, 10:887.

F.   Eliza or Elisa-Anne Baby (1803-1871) married Charles-Eusèbe Casgrain, son of the seigneur of Rivière-Ouelle, near Saint-Jean Port-Joli. She wrote a set of memoirs, chiefly a portrait of her husband and his political activities destined for her children, based in large part on correspondence. This, with an evocation of Madame Casgrain written by her son, the historian Henri-Raymond Casgrain who also acted as literary adviser to de Gaspé, was published in 1891, under the title, *Mémoires de famille: C.-E. Casgrain. DOLQ*, 1:483.

G.   This probably refers to the library housed in a room of the old bishop's palace established after the Conquest at the governor's behest, which included the works of eighteenth-century philosophers. The Roman Catholic bishop was obliged to accept this innovation, although the church in Canada did not favour liberal thought or "the spirit of Voltaire." *DOLQ*, 1:xviii.

H.   Since the Conquest criminal matters in Quebec have been governed by the British Common Law tradition. De Gaspé's use of the expression "English criminal code" is merely a general reference to the body of criminal law, not to an actual code.

I.   De Gaspé was present at the Quebec trial of a group of Irish Catholics for the murder of an Irish Protestant, Richard Corrigan. The unexpected verdict, on February 18, 1856, of "not guilty" aroused such a storm of indignation, especially in Canada-West, that a commission of inquiry was set up. De Gaspé was among those who submitted testimony to the commission, regarding a conversation that he had with a juror after the trial. Philippe Sylvain, "L'Affaire Corrigan à Saint-Sylvestre," *Les Cahiers des Dix*, 42 (1979), 133, 134, 141-143.

CHAPTER 11

Author's Footnotes to the 1866 Edition

1. *Knack.* The Academy [l'Académie française] ought to enrich the French language with this word, which is impossible to translate. The words *habilité, dextérité, talent, adresse,* etc., give a very imperfect rendering of this essentially British word.

2. I believe that French authors are beginning to enrich our language with the word *humour,* which is very difficult to render, even by circumlocution.

3. Major LaForce was subsequently promoted to the rank of lieutenant-colonel.

4. Monsieur Perrault, then a practising lawyer, was later named a judge of the court of king's bench. [Jean-Baptiste-Olivier Perrault (1773-1827) was named a judge of the court of king's bench in 1812. The incident referred to here took place in 1808. *Les Juges de la province de Québec,* 437.]

5. Colonel François Vassal de Monviel, created adjutant-general of the militia in 1812. [See chap. 5, annotation P.]

6. In 1811, the author married Susanne, daughter of Thomas Allison, a captain in the 5th British infantry regiment, and Thérèse Baby—hence a double relationship with the Baby family. In Detroit, then part of Upper Canada, three officers of the same regiment, Captains Allison, Ross Lewin, and Bellingham, since Lord Bellingham, married three sisters, the daughters of the Honourable Jacques Dupéron Baby. The latter was also the great-grandfather of my friend, the Abbé Casgrain.

7. Josephte: a nickname given to farmers' wives by city folk.

8. Nickname given to Americans from the United States.

9. Uncle Sam: another nickname given to Americans.

CHAPTER 11

Translator's Annotations

A. The notary Pierre Pépin (1776-1836), *dit* LaForce or Laforce, was arrested under the Craig administration for "treasonable practices." In 1812, he was "one of the first to go the front," and was promoted major in the active militia. He later became a lieutenant-colonel in the Quebec militia, but his penchant for joking and his caustic wit personally offended Governor Dalhousie, who had him dismissed from this post. *BRH*, 6 (1900): 58; Roy, *ATM, 196-198.*

B. The Chevalier Robert-Anne d'Estimauville de Beaumouchel (1754-1831) was born in Louisburg and served in the French army. He emigrated to Germany after the French Revolution, then to England, and later returned to Canada. During de Gaspé's period as sheriff of Quebec (1816-1822), the Chevalier d'Estimauville served as assistant chief inspector of highways and assistant surveyor-general. *BRH*, 10 (1904): 112, 114.

C. Andrew Stuart (1786-1840), a distinguished lawyer and jurist, was born in Upper Canada but practised law in Quebec. In 1810 he acted for Pierre Bédard, imprisoned by Sir James Craig in connection with *Le Canadien*. His son, Sir Andrew Stuart, chief justice of the superior court of the province of Quebec, married de Gaspé's daughter, Charlotte-Elmire, in 1842. Morgan, 510-514. G. M. Rose, ed., *Representative Canadians: A Cyclopaedia of Canadian Biography, being chiefly Men of the Time* (Toronto: Rose Publishing Company, 1866-1888), 2:641. See also portraits, Castonguay, *Lady Stuart*, 39, 64.

D   *Mitasses* (*Mémoires*, 332). These were "a kind of gaiter" worn by the Indians, and later adopted by Europeans, covering the leg between the knee and ankle. They were often decorated with ornaments. A watercolour by J. Crawford Young shows an Indian, "probably . . . of Lorette," wearing a red pair. E.-Z. Massicotte, "Le Costume civil masculin à Montréal au dix-septième siècle," *Mémoires de la Société royale du Canada*, 33 (1939), 137. J. Russell Harper, *Everyman's Canada: Paintings and Drawings from the McCord Museum of McGill University* (Ottawa: Roger Duhamel, Queen's Printer, 1962), 17.

E. Alexandre Vassilievitch Souvorov (1729-1800), (cf. Sowarow, *Mémoires*, 335), was a distinguished Russian general, veteran of the Seven Years' War in Europe and numerous other conflicts. He campaigned in Italy against French revolutionary forces until 1799. *GLE*, 11:948.

F. The principle founders of *Le Canadien* were Pierre-Stanislas Bédard (1762-1829), the speaker of the legislative assembly Jean-Antoine Panet (1751-

432

1815), Jean-Thomas Taschereau (1779-1832), Joseph Levasseur Borgia (1773-1839), François-Xavier Blanchet (1776-1830), Louis Bourdages (1764-1835), and Joseph-Bernard Planté (1768-1826), all of whom were arrested March 17, 1810. Craig had earlier (1808) shown his displeasure by dismissing these men from their posts in the militia. *BRH*, 8 (1902): 33; 10 (1904): 145. Pierre de Grandpré, ed., *Histoire de la Littérature française du Québec*, revised (Montreal: Librairie Beauchemin Limitée, 1971), 1:108. LJ, 1:189, 224, 294; 2:400, 699. Morgan, 245. *ATM*, 207.

G. Thomas Allison (1757-1822) was the eldest son of John Allison of Forcett Park, in the North Riding of Yorkshire. He entered the army, rising to the rank of captain. He sold his commission in 1798, a few years after his marriage to Thérèse Baby, daughter of Jacques Dupéron Baby of Detroit, and settled in Quebec. His daughter Susanne (see author's note 6 in this chapter) or Suzanne (Roy, *La Famille Aubert de Gaspé*, 130) married the author September 11, 1811.

On March 17, 1810, Captain Allison, on the orders of Governor Craig and in the capacity of justice of the peace and magistrate, commanded the picket that seized the printing press of *Le Canadien*, and arrested Bédard, Blanchet, and Taschereau, as well as the printer, on a charge of treason. *BRH*, 7 (1901), 313.

H. The full text of this speech appears in the work by de Gaspé's friend, Robert Christie, *A History of the Late Province of Lower Canada* (Montreal: Richard Worthington, 1866), 1:317 n. The work first came out between 1848-1855.

I. "Powell Place was owned by Sir Henry Watson Powell, who resided there from 1780-95. It was renamed Spencer Wood by the Honorable Michael Henry Percival," who died in 1812. "The situation was most picturesque, about two miles from the city walls, on the south side of the St. Louis Road. It is now the residence of the Lieutenant-Governor of Quebec." Robertson, *Diary of Mrs. Simcoe*, 85 n. This residence, later called Bois-de-Coulonge, was destroyed by fire some years ago.

J. This quotation, with some very minor differences, is from "Berrathon," one of the alleged poems of Ossian (cf., chap. 6, annotation A).

K. François Vatel, major-domo to the powerful seventeenth-century prince known as *le Grand Condé*, killed himself in despair when the fresh fish failed to arrive for a dinner given for Louis XIV at Chantilly.

L. "But in Canada the average pace is only five miles an hour. In Ireland it is seven, and the time is acccurately kept, which does not seem to be the case in Canada." Anthony Trollope, *North America* (New York: Harper and Bros., 1862), 53. Trollope, a senior official of the British post office and a former rural post office inspector, was well qualified to judge.

M.   The powerful St. Mary's Current was a major navigational hazard along the main shore of the Island of Montreal.

CHAPTER 12

Author's Footnotes to the 1866 Edition

1.   The author dares to hope that the hunters of Saint-Jean Port-Joli and L'Islet will adopt this name, in memory of the sole survivor among those who used to hunt on that portion of Seal Island fifty years ago—unless, of course, they prefer to call it "Gaspé's Rest."

2.   I have said history rather than legend, as I believe it to be true in every detail.

3.   The old Acadians, who sought refuge in Canada and whom I knew during my childhood, retained their patois until they died, whereas their children gradually lost it through contact with the purer language of the Canadian habitants. Even so, scarcely twenty years ago I knew two old men born in Canada, but of Acadian stock, who when excited would let fly a few words in the patois learned from their fathers. For example, "Pourquoi m'insultions?" One of them said one day to his son, who had sold me a valise, "Pourquoi vendions sans ma permission? Etions de valeur de donner son butin pour rien." An Acadian of old, instead of saying to a woman, "Vous êtes belle," would say "Etions belle." ["Canada" in this context refers essentially to what is now Quebec and Ontario, in contrast to the separate areas of Prince Edward Island, New Brunswick, and Nova Scotia, where the Acadians originally settled. As no number for this note appears on p. 375 of the 1866 or 1885 editions of the *Mémoires*, the translator has inserted it at an appropriate place.]

4.   *Pas un bec*: an expression current among hunters, signifying absence of game.

5.   Monsieur Simon Fraser is too well known in the District of Quebec for it to be necessary to add my word of praise, but I must in all gratitude mention that he managed the seigneuries of my family for over forty years with the utmost probity and good sense.

CHAPTER 12

Translator's Annotations

A.   "From time immemorial, it has been known to the English as Seal Rocks or Seal Islands; to the French, as *Battures-aux-Loups-Marins*," says J.

M. Le Moine. Note that De Gaspé uses island in the singular. "At low tide, five miles long, by one mile broad," it is reduced by the high August tides to "about one mile in length and seven acres [arpents] in width. At the north-west point there exists a . . . knoll" known as "Chatigny's Knoll." In addition, "the other portion of Seal Rocks, bare at high water . . . is very properly styled the *Sportsmen's Refuge*." Le Moine, *The Explorations of Jonathan Oldbuck*, 221.

It may help the reader of this chapter to know that the Saint Lawrence River flows northeast here, and that Isle-aux-Coudres and Isle-au-Grue (de Gaspé's spelling varies) lie about fifteen kilometers to the north and southwest respectively of Seal Islands. See *Canada Ordinance Map "Baie-St-Paul, Quebec*," Edition 1, comp. 1959 (Ottawa: Department of Mines and Surveys, 1962).

B.   *Tondre et batte-feu* (*Mémoires*, 378). *Tondre* is the Norman word for tinder, of Scandinavian origin. *Batte-feu* was a lighter consisting of an iron ring used to strike sparks from a stone. Genêt, et al, *Les Objets familiers de nos anêtres*, 44. Albert Dauzat, et al, *Nouveau Dictionnaire étymologique et historique*, 3d ed., revised and corrected (Paris: Librairies Larousse, 1971), 751, hereinafter cited as *Larousse étymologique*.

C.   The notary Simon Fraser (d. 1855) was born at Beaumont on the Lower Saint Lawrence, the son of Augustin Fraser and Marie-Françoise Adam. He established himself as a notary at Saint-Jean Port-Joli and lived there until his death. This Simon Fraser was possibly a grandson of Malcolm Fraser (chap. 2, annotation Q) and Marie Allaire, of Beaumont. Castonguay, *La Seigneurie . . . Gaspé* 72. LJ, 1:659.

D.   A *minot* was a unit of capacity for dry measure, equal to about four bushels of salt or three bushels of grain. Genêt, et al, *Les Objets familiers de nos anêtres*, 164.

E.   Marc Pascal (var. Paschal) de Sales Laterrière (1792-1872) was a doctor, like his father and brother Pierre (chap. 8, annotation E), seigneur of Les Eboulements, and a politician. After a long political life he was defeated at the polls (a circumstance de Gaspé refers to obliquely toward the end of the chapter) on the issue of Confederation, which he opposed. *DCB*, 10:431.

F.   "Plumb-pudding" (*Mémoires*, 394).

CHAPTER 13

Author's Footnotes to the 1866 Edition

1.   The Canadians call footwear without soles, like moccasins, "Indian" boots

or shoes, to distinguish them from the "French" shoes that they buy in shops.

2. The habitants of Saint-Jean Port-Joli always said simply "Monsieur" or "Madame" when speaking of the seigneur or seigneuresse, but I was "Monsieur Philippe," and the old folk still refer to me in this way.

3. Good folk [*bonnes gens*, *Mémoires*, 423] means father and mother in the homely language of the habitants.

4. In the country, *volontaire* was the name for those with neither hearth nor home.

CHAPTER 13

Translator's Annotations

A. Partridge or *perdrix* (*Mémoires*, 401) does not refer to the European or gray partridge, although this has been introduced to Canada. It is a popular term for varieties of native grouse, particularly the ruffed grouse (*gélinotte huppée*), a year-round resident of wooded areas in southern Quebec. Its rapid takeoff makes it difficult to hunt with firearms, but it is valued for its flavour. Dionne, *Le Parler populaire des canadiens français*, 494. W. Earl Godfrey, *Les Oiseaux de Québec* (Montreal: Editions de L'Homme, 1972), 194-196.

B. A *capot* (*Mémoires*, 403) was a hooded, knee-length coat, tied at the waist (Massicotte, "Le Costume civil masculin," 133). Says Lambert, "The dress of the Habitant is simple and homely; it consists of a long-skirted cloth coat or frock, of a dark grey colour, with a hood attached to it, which in winter time or wet weather he puts over his head. His coat is tied round the waist by a worsted sash of various colours ornamented with beads. His waistcoat and trowsers are of the same cloth. A pair of moccasins, or swamp-boots, complete the lower part of his dress." Although a lighter summer outfit was sometimes worn, "it oftener happens that the dress which I have described is worn the whole year round." John Lambert, "French Canadian Character and Customs (1806-08)," *Early Travellers in the Canadas*, 28-29.

C. Although *gentilhomme* can usually be understood as "gentleman," in the restricted sense of a man who is well bred or of gentle birth, in this instance the author may be referring to a rank of minor, untitled nobility. This rank was awarded for military and civil services in New France, and passed to all the children of the recipient. In Canada, a gentilhomme was not exempt from ordinary taxes, as he was in France. On the other hand, the Canadian gentilhomme was "free to engage openly in any branch of industry or trade," which was not permitted in France. Shortt and Doughty, *Canada and its Provinces*, 2:570.

D.   See the drawings of this type of snare (*collet*) in Louis-Alexandre Bélisle, *Dictionnaire nord-américain de la langue française au Canada*, 2d ed., (Quebec: Bélisle, Editeur Inc., 1979), 181.

E.   *Chasse-galérie* generally refers to a canoe flying by the devil's power, and figures frequently in Canadian legends. It is also defined as a "noise heard in the air towards midnight; sometimes the galloping of horses, the barking of dogs, the sound of trumpets or the cries of hunters; sometimes a sound of confusion and disorder, which must be the witches' Sabbath." Edward C. Woodley, "La Chasse-galérie," *Legends of French Canada* (Toronto: Thomas Nelson and Sons Ltd., 1931), 10. *Glossaire du parler français au Canada*, 192.

F.   A *dévidoir* (*Mémoires*, 413) or winder, standing beside the spinning-wheel, was a common sight in a habitant household. Used for winding wool into skeins, it was made of wood and resembled a paddle-wheel of four blades with a handle for turning, supported on a small stand. Genêt et al., *Les Objets familiers de nos anêtres*, 109

G.   This is a reference to the French expression, *mentir comme un arracheur de dents* (literally, "to lie like a tooth-puller," expressed in such English idioms as "to lie like a trooper" or "to lie through one's teeth").

H.   *Sangris* (*Mémoires*, 415) or *sang-gris* generally describes a mixture of wine or brandy with sugar and hot water. Dionne, *Le Parler populaire des canadiens français*, 591.

I.   The *Petit Albert* was a popular compilation of "alchemy and magical practices" originally published in 1704 in Geneva (Story, 634). De Gaspé no doubt intended a certain irony in old Chouinard's remark, as the clergy in fact disapproved strongly of the book. In addition to being mentioned in old Chouinard's story, it plays a central role in the early French-Canadian novel, *L'Influence d'un livre* (Quebec: William Cowan et fils, 1837), by de Gaspé's eldest son, Philippe-Ignace-François Aubert de Gaspé (1814-1841). De Gaspé senior is believed to have contributed significantly to this novel, of which a much-edited version was brought out by the Abbé H.-R. Casgrain in 1864 under the title *Le Chercheur de trésors ou l'Influence d'un livre*.

CHAPTER 14

Author's Footnotes to the 1866 Edition

1. It is not my intention to reproach the English for the cries of sordid misery that escape their mighty realm, but at least they should refrain from casting stones at other nations. One of my English friends, returning from a trip to the Continent, drew for me a lamentable picture of the misery of the Italian populace, and took the opportunity of blaming it on the Pope and the King of Naples.

    "But," I demurred, "isn't the poverty of the English lower classes much worse?"

    "Are you speaking of Ireland?" he queried.

    "Not at all. I'm alluding to old England. Have you visited the cellars of Liverpool, or seen the poor of Spitfield [Spitalfields], St. Giles, and Saffran-Hill [Saffron Hill] in London?"

    "No indeed," he replied, "I've never visited the districts to which you refer."

    What a singular propensity the English have for thinking all's well at home and finding fault abroad! And yet my friend is a distinguished and highly educated man.

2. Many uneducated Canadians of old felt that an oath sworn on *le book anglais* [the St. James Version of the Holy Bible] was not binding. This misunderstanding was eliminated fifty years ago by putting a cross on the cover of the Bible. The error arose from the pronunciation of the word "book," resembling the French *bouc* [billy-goat], an animal held in derision by Canadians.

CHAPTER 14

Translator's Annotations

A. Joseph Méry (1798-1865), French liberal journalist, poet, playwright, novelist, and librettist.

B. Ham. 3.1.57-63. All Shakespeare quotations are from G. B. Harrison, ed., *Shakespeare: The Complete Works* (New York: Harcourt, Brace and Co., 1952). De Gaspé gives a French translation, probably his own (*Mémoires*, 436).

C. Apparently a reference to de Gaspé's having attended philosophy classes at the Grand Seminary.

D. Job 14:1,2.

E. Job 3:11-13.

F. Alexis de Tocqueville, author of *La Démocratie en Amérique* (1835) visited Quebec in 1831, and described such a Bible. "Witnesses were produced. Some kissed the silver Christ that covered the Bible and swore in French to tell the truth; others swore the same oath in English and, in their quality of Protestants, kissed the other side of the Bible, which was plain." Jacques Vallée, ed., *Tocqueville au Bas-Canada* (Montréal: Editions du Jour, 1973), 92.

G. The dîme or tithe, "an ancient tax for the support of the . . . parish priest or curé, . . . is still legally binding on Roman Catholics in the province of Quebec." Begun under the French régime, "the right of the curés to collect tithes . . . was recognized by the 'Quebec Act.'" Its value was established at one twenty-sixth of the grain crop (Story, 798). Unlike France, where tithes in the Old Regime were calculated and levied in the actual field, in Canada the habitant delivered his tithe (usually wheat) to the curé, and in bad times was often unable or unwilling to make full payment. Sometimes the curé would postpone payment, or in other ways alleviate the poverty that he often shared. Gagnon, *Quebec and its Historians: The Twentieth Century*, trans. Jane Brierley (Montreal: Harvest House Ltd., 1985), 157.

H. The *pied français* or French foot was an old unit of linear measure, also called *pied de roi*, divided into twelve "inches." It was slightly longer than the English foot (.3248 metres as against .3048 metres). *GLE*, 7:475.

CHAPTER 15

Author's Footnotes to the 1866 Edition

1. Captain Thomas Allison, of the 5th regiment of foot, British army, then retired, was the author's father-in-law.

2. Colonel Dominique-Emmanuel-Lemoine de Longueil, the author's great-uncle.

3. The Honourable Vallière de Saint-Réal, who has since become chief justice.

4. This house burned down two years ago, but has since been rebuilt.

5. The scholarly Canadian archeologist, whose research has contributed so greatly to our history.

6. This oath was much in vogue among those who served the North West Company.

7. My maternal great-uncle, Colonel Dominique-Emmanuel Le Moine de Longueil, had also served the French government before the conquest, in the capacity of assistant medical officer.

8. Captain Chandler died seigneur of Nicolet, after serving with honour in the British army.

9. The common people used the word "rustic" [*rustique, Mémoires,* 487] to express "crotchety, hard to live with."

10 The Duke of Kent, a great martinet as the English say, seemed surprised that one could command soldiers without submitting them to the extremely cruel discipline of the time. I imagine he must be alluding in this passage to the praise accorded the Voltigeurs Canadiens by General Prevost, during a review of 14,000 men, for their fine military discipline and conduct in action.

CHAPTER 15

Translator's Annotations

A. Ignace-Michel-Louis-Antoine d'Irumberry de Salaberry (1752-1828), officer, member of the legislative assembly, magistrate, superintendant of Indians, executive councillor, legislative councillor, inspector of forests, and colonel, studied in France and at the Quebec Seminary. He served in the war against the American revolutionaries, and was taken prisoner in 1775 at Fort Saint-Jean after being wounded.

   In 1785 he visited Paris (chap. 4, annotation D). Upon his return to Quebec, he was elected to the legislative assembly, and simultaneously appointed a justice of the peace. In 1795, he was named major in the newly recruited Royal Canadian militia regiment. In 1812, although advanced in years, he again took up arms and served as colonel in the first batallion of the select embodied militia.

   De Salaberry and the Duke of Kent became "intimate acquaintances" in 1791, when the prince arrived in Quebec as commander of the 60th regiment. They later became "fast friends and correspondents." LJ, 2:609. Fennings Taylor, "Colonel the Honorable Charles Michel D'Irumberry de Salaberry, C.B.," in *Portraits of British Americans,* 3:251.

B. "Conquer the mighty! Show mercy to the weak!"

C. Joseph-Dominique-Emmanuel Le Moyne de Longueuil (1738-1807) (note de Gaspé's variant spellings) was a career soldier under both French and British regimes. He was for some years styled Baron de Longueuil, following the death in 1755 of his third cousin, the third baron. In 1776 a Paris court conferred the title on the third baron's only surviving child, the young Marie-Charlotte-Joseph Le Moyne. He was named inspector-general of militia in 1777 and promoted colonel of the Royal Canadians in 1796. As his only son died in infancy, he left his property, including the seigneuries of Soulanges and Nouvelle-Longueuil, to his nephew, Jacques-Philippe Saveuse de Beaujeu, whose son and heir married de Gaspé's daughter, Adelaide-Suzanne-Catherine. LJ, 1:139; 2:166.

D. *Le Barbier de Séville* (1775) by Beaumarchais was staged March 2, 1791, in a makeshift theatre "on the second floor of a house on the corner of the Rues des Jardins and Saint-Anne." A group of French-Canadian amateur actors had staged a season of plays, and "was honoured that evening by the presence of General Clarke and a numerous and brilliant assembly of ladies and gentlemen, both English and Canadian," according to the *Quebec Gazette* of March 10, 1791. *ATM*, 227-228.

E. De Gaspé, who had an understandable interest in genealogy, may be forgiven for being impressed by Charles Gordon Lennox (1764-1819), "fourth Duke of Richmond, Earl of March, and Baron Sittrington in the peerage of England; Duke of Lennox, Earl of Darnley and Baron Methuen in the peerage of Scotland, and Duke d'Aubigny in France." In addition, the duke was the great-great-grandson of Charles II of England and Louise de Kerouailles, who bore the English title of Duchess of Portsmouth, and the French title, conferred by Louis XIV, of Duchesse d'Aubigny. His mother was the daughter of the fourth Marquis of Lothian. The duke was therefore of royal lineage, and connected to the highest English and Scottish nobility. He succeeded Sherbrooke as governor-in-chief of Canada in 1818, and died in Upper Canada of hydrophobia, the result of a bite by a pet fox, in August 1819.

Despite "dignified bearing and a graceful and courteous manner," the fourth Duke of Richmond, like his father before him, was extraordinarily outspoken and prone to quarrel, often with those of superior rank. He had fought duels with the Duke of York and Jonathan Swift, and during his short period as governor in Canada took it upon himself to harangue the legislative assembly in "violent language." LJ, 2:524-527. Morgan, 241-243. *DNB*, 11:923-927.

F. Michel-Louis Juchereau Duchesnay (1785-1838), the son of Antoine Juchereau Duchesnay and Catherine Lecomte-Dupré, attended the Little Seminary in Quebec and followed a military career, distinguishing himself in the battle of Chateauguay. In 1808, he married Charlotte-Hermine-Louise-Catherine, the daughter of Monsieur de Salaberry. LJ, 1:542; 2:609.

G. "Le Richemond qui porte un coeur de fer: (*Mémoires*, 464) refers to the line from Voltaire's long poem about Joan of Arc, *La Pucelle d'Orléans* (1762): "Le Richemont qui porte un coeur de fer" (chant 1.298). Arthur

III (1398-1458), Comte de Richemont and Duke of Britanny, was constable of France under Henri VII, and partly responsible for the recovery of part of Aquitaine and all of Normandy from the English. Voltaire describes him as very outspoken, regardless of rank (chant ii.342-345), a trait that the Duke of Richmond shared. Although the connection drawn by de Gaspé between Richmond and Richemont is coincidental, Voltaire's poem contains a fortuitous reference to the future Charles II and "la belle Portsmouth" (chant xiii. 398), the duke's ancestors. Theodore Besterman et al., eds., *The Complete Works of Voltaire* (Geneva: Institut et Musée Voltaire, 1970), 7:273, 291, 481. *GLE*, 1:613.

H.　The Honourable Jacques Dupéron Baby (1762-1833) or "James Baby" (Morgan, 277) was the eldest son of the loyalist Jacques Dupéron Baby of Detroit and Sandwich, Ontario. His daugher, Eliza-Anne (chap. 10, annotation F), and de Gaspé's wife were therefore first cousins. *Representative Canadians: A Cyclopaedia of Canadian Biography*, 3:230. *DOLQ*, 1:483.

I.　Lady Sarah Lennox, second daughter of the Duke of Richmond, married Sir Peregrine Maitland (1777-1854) in 1815. She was his second wife. In 1818 her husband was appointed lieutenant-governor of the province of Upper Canada. After the duke's unexpected death, Sir Peregrine "administered the government of Lower Canada until the arrival of the Earl of Dalhousie, the governor general." Morgan, 244.

J.　Antoine-Narcisse Juchereau Duchesnay (1793-1851), a veteran of the War of 1812, was the son of the seigneur of Beauport, and "a member of the gilded youth of the early years of the nineteenth century in Quebec." His father and Michel-Louis Juchereau Duchesnay (annotation E) were half-brothers. *ATM*, 232. *LJ*, 1:541-542.

K.　"Who would have thought that the Quebec Jockey Club had three French Canadians as founders?" asks archivist P.-G. Roy, pointing out that this club was once well known and composed almost exclusively of English members. *ATM*, 230.

L.　This was probably the village of Jeune Lorette, where the remnant of the Huron tribe established themselves in 1697. *LJ*, 1:782. *ATM*, 225.

M.　The charivari or "shivaree" was a feature of nineteenth century life in Canada—a form of hell-raising that has not entirely disappeared in rural Quebec areas. Originally a noisy nighttime demonstration to show disapproval of certain marriages, it came to mean a noisy disturbance in general, with a rough and occasionally violent side to it. Bélisle, *Dictionnaire générale de la langue française au Canada*, 193. *Enc. Can.*, 2:314.

N.　Georges-Barthélemi Faribault (1789-1866) played a vital part in the collecting, preserving, copying, and cataloguing of early Canadian material.

His vicissitudes as an archivist are vividly portrayed in Yvan Lamonde's article for *DCB*. A lawyer by training, he was appointed clerk of committees and parliamentary archives for the legislative assembly of Lower Canada in 1815, and occupied the senior post of assistant clerk of the assembly from 1835 to 1855. After his retirement in 1855, he continued to be active in the Quebec Literary and Historical Society and in the *Club des anciens*, of which de Gaspé was a member. *DCB*, 9:249-251; 10:21.

O. Antoine Van Felson, or Vanfelson (1776-1829) became curé of Beauport in 1808, remaining there until his death. *ATM*, 234.

P. In 1812, "the army in Canada" consisted "of British Regulars, Canadian Fencibles (Regulars) and Canadian Militia including Incorporated, Select Embodied, Embodied and Sedentary)." A. Fortescue Duguid, *History of the Canadian Grenadier Guards, 1760-1964* (Montreal: Gazette Printing Co. Ltd., 1965), 12-13.

Q. The Duke of Kent's letter was written in French. The English version given here is the translator's.

R. The battle of Chateauguay took place in the vicinity of Grant's Ford on the Chateauguay River, south of Montreal, on October 26, 1813. The invading American force, a division of 7,500 men and fourteen guns, was repulsed by a defending force of 1,100 men, including 200 Indians. "Lt.-Col. Charles Michel de Salaberry, Commanding the Voltigeurs" was appointed "to command a special composite brigade to meet the invading force." His ability to prepare the terrain, confuse the enemy, protect his men from unecessary exposure to an enemy of superior strength, and act promptly once battle was joined, completely routed the Americans, who retreated to the other side of the border. Duguid, *History of the Canadian Grenadier Guards*, 20.

S. "Like the population from which it was drawn, the Militia comprised men of both French and British origin, with the former in great majority. Attacked by a superior force, it had fought and won an outstandingly successful action, unaided by British regular troops." Duguid, *History of the Canadian Grenadier Guards*, 12-21. LJ, 1:374.

T. Charles-Michel d'Irumberry de Salaberry (1778-1829), known as "the Canadian Leonidas," lieutenant-colonel, Companion of the Order of the Bath, legislative councillor, and seigneur of Chambly and Beaulac, was born at the Beauport manor house near Quebec. He became a volunteer in the British army at fourteen, under the aegis of the Duke of Kent. Commissioned by Sir George Prevost in 1812 to raise a select corps from among his countrymen, he recruited and trained the light infantry corps named the Voltigeurs Canadiens, of which he was lieutenant-colonel and his father colonel.

A gold commemorative medal of the battle of Chateauguay was struck in his honour, and he was named Companion of the Order of the Bath as well as receiving a vote of thanks from the upper and lower houses of Lower Canada. In 1818, he was named a member of the legislative council, his father also occupying a seat. Duguid, 13-21. LJ, 2:549, 610. Morgan, 197-201. Taylor, "Colonel . . . de Salaberry," 3:247-266.

U. Possibly Hippolyte Trottier Des Rivières of Montreal, born 1769, who entered the 60th regiment in 1791, was promoted lieutenant in 1795, and captain in 1797, but whose name does not appear in the Army List after 1801. *ATM*, 236.

V. Kenelm Connor Chandler (1773-1850), born in Quebec, entered the army early and served with the 60th regiment for eighteen years. He bought the seigneurie of Nicolet in 1832. *ATM*, 238.

W. Seven verses of this song, of which de Gaspé gives the fourth and seventh, with slight variations, were repeated to E.-Z. Massicotte by the nephew of an 1812 militiaman. *BRH*, 26 (1920): 189-191.

X. De Gaspé gives the duke's letter in the original English, followed by his French translation (*Mémoires*, 491-493).

CHAPTER 16

Author's Footnotes to the 1866 Edition

1. The Marquise de Créquy reports in her *Souvenirs* that a few years before the Revolution, a charlatan had similar success with the laying on of hands, which gives us the consolation of knowing that Parisian idlers were as witless as their Canadian counterparts. In the countryside today one still finds imposters who, according to their dupes, perform marvelous cures. That's what's called *guérir du secret*. [See *The French Noblesse of the XVIII Century translated by Mrs. Colquhoun Grant from Les Souvenirs de la marquise de Créquy*, 1834 (New York: E. P. Dutton and Co., 1904), 247.]

2. Josephte, nickname given by townsfolk to country women.

3. Charles de Lanaudière, Sieur de La Pérade.

4. Major Doyle had married a Miss Smith, sister of Mrs. Sewell. He died a general in the Peninsula, I believe. [Major, later General, William Doyle, married Mary, daughter of Chief Justice William Smith, March 27, 1799. He was an officer in the 24th regiment, garrisoned in Quebec. *ATM*, 250-251.]

5. Mrs. Sewell was a woman of great beauty.

6. Even the most reserved English allowed this in their houses. On Epiphany, about the year 1812, we were gathered at the home of Lord Bishop Mountain, father of that Bishop Mountain who died recently and was so universally regretted. The evening was rather flat at first. Mrs. Mountain and her children were alone in the drawing room when we arrived, and after the usual salutations we sat down in chairs placed around the edge of the room: the gentlemen on one side, the ladies on the other. The Lord Bishop then made his entry, and after a short fifteen minutes' tour of the room, during which he had a friendly word with everyone present, he retired and was seen no more. A few ladies then went to the piano, where they played and sang until the supper hour. As at that time there were, I believe, only three pianos in the city of Quebec—in the homes of the Anglican bishop and of my two uncles de Lanaudière and Baby—the lady musicians were soon obliged to excuse themselves; and since cards were forbidden in the episcopal palace, we made conversation as best we could, without leaving our seats until the supper hour. The Twelfth-night cake was handed round in the English manner. The king and queen [of the Twelfth-night feast] raised their glasses to their lips in vain: no one cried, "The king drinks, the queen drinks," as was the custom at our Canadian gatherings. Nevertheless, a few songs were sung; but I cannot remember whether Mrs. Mountain was present at the supper in the absence of her husband.

7. Many Englishmen, in speaking of a Canadian of noble extraction, say "he is *noblesse!*" with scornful sarcasm, no doubt very witty—although when referring to one of their own countrymen of similar background, they say "a nobleman."

8. This fine property now belongs to my son-in-law, the Honourable Charles Alleyn, who bought it to keep it in the family. [De Gaspé's eighth child, Zoë (1825-188), married Charles Joseph Alleyn, lawyer and politician, who became provincial secretary in 1858 under the Cartier administration. Roy, *La Famille Aubert de Gaspé* 165. Morgan, 634.]

9. The crampons on clogs used to be an inch long in those days.

10. See Charlevoix's history of New France. [Pierre-François-Xavier de Charlevoix (1682-1761), *Histoire et description générale de la Nouvelle France, avec le Journal historique d'un voyage fait par ordre du roi dans l'Amérique septentrionale* (Paris, 1744).]

CHAPTER 16

Translator's Annotations

A. The circumstances of this anecdote are substantiated in a pastoral letter issued by Bishop Plessis, dated March 17, 1808. *ATM*, 238-240.

B. Revelation 13:1.

C. Revelation 13:2.

D. Revelation 13:7.

E. Revelation 13:11.12.

F. Revelation 13:17.

G. Revelation 13:18.

H. The schoolmaster and Anglican clergyman John Jackson (1765-1839) arrived in Quebec about 1795, and in 1799 bought a house of considerable size on the ramparts. Although an "excellent schoolmaster," his lack of business acumen resulted in debt, and 1822 he sold the house and returned to England. *ATM*, 248; *DCB*, 5:496, 1013.

I. De Gaspé possibly found the name strange for a dog because *Tobie* is the French for Tobit or Tobias (a saint of the Septuagent)—a blind Jew whose sight was restored by the angel Raphael. "Tobias and the angel" was a popular scene in church iconography. The name "Toby" is, of course, a popular English name for a dog, and calls to mind the trained dog with a frill around its neck that became a feature of the Punch and Judy puppet shows in the first half of the nineteenth century. *Enc. Brit. Micro.*, 10:18. *GLE*, 10:359-360. *OED*, 11:98.

J. A reference to the White Boys and the implacable hatred between Irish factions that a number of Irish immigrants to Canada brought with them.

K. De Gaspé writes: "l'histoire de LeFêvre et La Pauvre Marie" (*Mémoires*, 503). "The Story of Le Fever," appears in vol. 6, chaps. 6-10, of *Tristram Shandy* (see also vol. 9, where the same character is called "Le Fevre"). "Poor Maria" appears in vol. 9, chap. 24, and also in *A Sentimental Journey*. Laurence Sterne, *The Life and Opinions of Tristram Shandy, Gentleman*, eds. Melvyn New and Joan New, (1762; Florida: The University Presses of Florida, 1978), 499-513, 746, 780-784. Laurence Sterne, *A Sentimental Journey through France and Italy by Mr. Yorick*, ed. Gardner D. Stout, Jr., (1766; Berkeley: University of California Press, 1967), 268-279.

L. Charlotte-Marguerite or Charles-Marguerite (*Mémoires*, 513) Tarieu de Lanaudière (1775-1856) was the youngest daughter of Charles-François-

Xavier Tarieu de Lanaudière by his second wife, Marie-Catherine le Moyne, daughter of the second Baron de Longueuil. *DCB*, 4:728-729. *ATM*, 251.

M. *Procureur du Roi* (*Mémoires*, 506). As this party must have taken place after Sewell's marriage (September 1796), de Gaspé possibly means *procureur-général* (attorney-general), Sewell having been named to this post in 1795. Roy, *Les Juges de la province de Québec*, 499. Fennings Taylor, "The Honorable Jonathan Sewell, LL.D.," in *Portraits of British Americans*, 2:254.

N. "Dame" was the title given to the wife of a seigneur. Bélisle, *Dictionaire nord-américain de la langue française*, 238.

O. Harriet or Henrietta Smith, daughter of the Loyalist, Chief Justice William Smith, formerly of New York, married Sewell, who was then thirty, in September 1796. *DCB*, 4:716. LJ, 2:641. Story, 771.

P. This may refer to the wife of Hugh Finlay (1732-1801), executive councillor and postmaster-general for British North America (1774-1799). LJ, 1:630.

Q. P.-G. Roy expresses surprise that de Gaspé does not mention Madame Fargues at greater length, since she was a very popular member of Quebec society for many years. Born Marie-Henriette Guichaud, the daugher of a Quebec merchant, she married the "rich Huguenot merchant Pierre Fargues." Widowed early, in 1783 she married Thomas Dunn (1729-1818), a prominent Quebec fur-trader, executive and legislative councillor, and judge of the court of king's bench (1775). Mrs. Dunn died in 1839 at the age of eighty-six. LJ, 1:554. *ATM*, 248-249. Roy, *Les Juges de la province de Québec*, 195.

R. Possibly the wife of "Henry Taylor, the owner of a Quebec distillery" during the last part of the eighteenth century. *DCB*, 4:399.

S. Possibly Catherine Lecomte-Dupré, second wife of executive councillor Antoine Juchereau Duchesnay (1740-1806) (see chap. 15, annotation F). LJ, 1:541; 2:127.

T. The people of Normandy, from whom many French Canadians are descended, have a reputation for litigiousness that was given comic expression by Racine in *Les Plaideurs* (1668). The play depicts the litigious eccentricities of the Comtesse de Pimbesche, aged sixty, and Monsieur Chicaneau (a *chicaneur* is a person given to lawsuits). Like the Seigneuresse K——, the comtesse is particularly eloquent on the subject of her lawsuits. Racine, *Les Plaideurs*, 1.7.55-62.

U. "Rank in the noblesse" in New France was acquired "only through special letters patent from the crown," issued "usually as a mark of appreciation for military or civil services rendered," with the rank of *comte* and *baron*.

Many Frenchmen "were already members of the noblesse at home, and. . . . retained their rank and quality. The king, moreover, gave the rank of *gentilhomme* to many Canadian seigneurs." The title of *chevalier* could refer either to a member of a military order of merit, or to a younger son of a noble. Shortt and Doughty, *Canada and its Provinces* 2:569-570. *BRH*, 8 (1902): 36.

V. Lady Mary Louisa Lambton (1819-1898), was the second wife of James Bruce, eighth Earl of Elgin. She married him at the beginning of his term as governor-general of British North America (1846-1854). She was also the eldest daughter of the first Earl of Durham (governor-general of British North America, 1838, the author of the Durham Report, 1839). *DNB*, 7:104; 32:23-25. Patricia Godsell, ed., *Letters and Diaries of Lady Durham* (Canada: Oberon Press, 1979), 157 n. 7. Story, 236, 237, 240.

W. *Journal and Memoirs of the Marquis d'Argenson*, ed. E. J. B. Rathéry, trans. K. P. Wormely (Boston: Hardy, Pratt and Co., 1902), 1:389. The italics in this passage are de Gaspé's. The spelling "Lordendall" is presumably an error in transcription. The passage is contained in a letter of May 15, 1745 from d'Argenson to Voltaire, and reads "Löwendahl." (Ulrich Frédéric Valdemar, Comte de Löwendahl, was made a marshall of France after the battle of Fontenoy.)

X. *La Capricieuse* was "a French naval vessel . . . sent on a goodwill mission to Quebec in 1855 to mark the Anglo-French alliance that had been brought about by the Crimean War, and was the first ship since 1760 to enter Quebec harbour wearing the French flag." The emotion and enthusiasm which greeted *La Capricieuse* found expression in Octave Crémazie's poem, "Le Vieux Soldat," published during the visit, which lasted from July 13 to August 25. Story, 150. *ATM*, 255-257.

Y. Jean-François Gaulthier or Gaultier (1708-1756), a royal physician in New France, "did outstanding work in botany, natural history and entymology. The wintergreen plant *Gaultheria procumbens* was named after him." In 1752 Gaulthier became the third husband of Marguerite de Lanaudière's aunt, Madeleine-Marie-Anne (1707-1776), oldest daughter of Pierre-Thomas Tarieu de Lanaudière, *dit* "de la Pérade," and Marie-Madeleine Jarret de Verchères. When Gaulthier died, his widow sent money and her husband's medical books to his nephew, who was studying medicine in Paris. All this occurred a century before the arrival of *La Capricieuse*, and the French officer's connection, if any, must have been fairly distant. P.-G. Roy lists a Gauthier (assistant-surgeon) aboard *La Capricieuse* as well as a Gaultier (ship's officer). *DCB*, 3:676. *Enc. Can.*, 7:8. *ATM*, 258-259.

Z. The manor house of Saint-Vallier (or Saint-Valier) de Bellechasse was built by Charles-François-Xavier Tarieu de Lanaudière, de Gaspé's maternal grandfather, "around 1767," on land acquired from the nuns of the Hôpital-Général. Raymonde Gauthier, *Les Manoirs du Québec* (Québec: Fides, 1976), 178.

AA. De Gaspé must mean his great-great-grandmother and great-grandmother, Marie Jarret de Verchères and her daughter, Marie-Madeleine Jarret de Verchères (1678-1747). In 1690, Marie, then thirty-three, directed the defense of the Verchères manor against an Iroquois attack. The legendary Madeleine, at fourteen, directed a similar defense in 1692. At the time the author was writing, the story of Madeleine de Verchères was not well known, and it was only in 1901 that the incident began to receive wide publicity. Madeleine married Pierre-Thomas Tarieu de Lanaudière, Sieur de La Pérade (1677-1757), in 1706. *DCB*, 3:308-313.

CHAPTER 17

Author's Footnotes to the 1866 Edition

1. It is still the laudable custom in our rural areas never to overtake a vehicle without excusing oneself or requesting permission. May we always preserve these old and touching customs, this fine French courtesy handed down to us by our fathers, the most polite of men!

2. *Sauteur d'escalier* [*Mémoires*, 535]: pejorative name given by the habitants to city youths, who all too often insulted them in the streets of Quebec.

3. This biographical note had scarcely been written when death struck this great man, plunging all Canada into mourning.

4. *To reverse*: to make the paddle wheels rotate in the opposite direction.

5. Country house belonging to the Quebec Siminary [see chap. 1] annotation I].

6. This young gentleman was the son or nephew of the famous Edmund Burke.

CHAPTER 17

Translator's Annotations

A. Possibly "William Roxburg, of Quebec, merchant," whose death on May 28, 1818, is recorded in the act of burial (the equivalent of a death certificate in Quebec) in the registers of Saint Andrew's Church, a Presbyterian church on the Rue Sainte-Anne. *ATM*, 263.

B.	Marguerite Jeanne Cordier, Baronne de Staal de Launay (1684-1750) (not to be confused with the famous bluestocking, Madame de Staël). Madame de Staal's *Mémoires*, dating from the mid eighteenth century, are considered the forerunner of the autobiographical narrative epitomized by Rousseau.

C.	*Bellegueule*: bigmouth.

D.	*Pousse-chicane*: troublemaker.

E.	In 1785, Paschal-Jacques Taché (1757-1830) married Marie-Louise-Renée de Charnay (d. 1813), widow of Jean-Baptiste Magnan and co-seigneuresse of Kamouraska, which was thus brought into the Taché family. Their only child, Paschal (1786-1833), was the father of Louis-Paschal-Achille Taché, whose murder in 1838 by Dr. Holmes of Sorel forms the subject of Anne Hébert's novel, *Kamouraska* (1970). P.-G. Roy, *La Famille Taché* (Lévis: n. pub., 1904), 131, 135, 161.

F.	Two brothers, Paschal-Jacques (*supra*) and Charles Taché (1752-1826), inherited the seigneurie of Mingan from their father, Jean-Paschal Taché (1697-1768), but the family fortunes had been virtually ruined by the Seven Years' War. As noted, Paschal-Jacques married the comparatively wealthy seigneuresse of Kamouraska. Charles, however, settled at Saint-Thomas de Montmagny, "and raised a family of ten children," including the future Sir Etienne Taché, "on the inadequate income brought in by leasing the Chicoutimi trading post." Sir Etienne-Paschal Taché (1795-1865) became prime minister of Canada in 1755, during the period of Union. His untimely death has obscured his important role in Confederation, although the date, July 30, 1865, gives us internal evidence as to the writing of chap. 17. *DCB*, 9:774. LJ, 2:685. Roy, *La Famille Taché*, 11, 15, 21, 22, 131.

G.	On December 15, 1829, de Gaspé's oldest child, Suzanne (1812-1882), married William Power (1800-1860), a member of an Irish Catholic family that had settled in Newfoundland. Power was sent to Ireland for his schooling, and came to Lower Canada to study law. He became a member of the legislative assembly (1832-1838) and a superior court judge (1857). A daughter, Thérèse-Catherine Power (1837-1890) married J.-B.-J.-Paschal-Ivanhoë Taché (1835-1887) on November 25, 1856. (He was the oldest son of the murdered Taché (annotation E). Roy, *La Famille Aubert de Gaspé*, 131, 132. Id., *La Famille Taché*, 165. Id., *Les Juges de la Province de Québec*, 449.

H.	"Indispensables" *(Mémoires, 539)*, was a colloquial euphemism (1841) for trousers. *Shorter OED*. 992.

I.	The *Lauzon*, launched September 30, 1817, had a capacity of 310 tons, with a 28 h.p. engine. She began regular crossings in the spring of 1818.

taking between "nine or fifteen minutes. Everything depended on the wind and tide." *ATM*, 280.

J. The "dogs of English inventions" ended by killing Barras as well as the canoes. He died in 1853 when the *Sainte-Pierre*, of which he was captain, blew up, killing seven of the nine persons aboard. Ibid., 282.

K. The marionette theatre was opened by a former soldier, Jean Natte, *dit* Marseille, after his place of origin. He died at the age of sixty-nine on July 12, 1803. Ibid., 270-273.

L. "Alas, poor Yorick! . . . Where be your gibes now? . . . Your flashes of merriment that were wont to set the table on a roar? Not one now, to mock your own grinning?" Hamlet 5.1.201-211.

M. "Convent-Garden" (*Mémoires*, 547).

N. *Perdrix de savane* (*Mémoires*, 549) possibly refers to the Sharp-tailed Grouse, often called "prairie chicken" after a similar bird. The presence of this grouse in the Saguenay and Quebec City areas is mentioned in "old records." Its dramatic courtship dance involves "rapid stamping . . . ruffled plumage, and a low booming sound." Godfrey, *The Birds of Canada*, 113, 114.

O. "Malbrouk is going to war, Mirliton, mirlitaine"—an old French soldier's song. "Malbrouk" or "Malbrough" refers to John Churchill (1650-1722), first Duke of Marlborough. The translator saw an old plate displayed in the library of Blenheim Palace in 1980, bearing a verse with music, beginning: "Monsieur d'Malbrough est mort./Mironton, ton, ton, Miron-tai-ne." *Dict. usuel Quillet-Flammarion*, 858.

P. The novel *Paul Clifford* (1830) was written, not by Captain Frederick Marryat (de Gaspé writes "Marryatt," *Mémoires*, 556), but by Edward Bulwer Lytton (1803-1873). P.-G. Roy states that one Thomas Clifford was a well-known bully in Quebec, citing his act of burial in the records of Saint Paul's Anglican Church, Quebec. Clifford died October 20, 1850, "from exposure of cold want of necessaries of life and habitual drinking." Sir Paul Harvey, comp. and ed., *The Oxford Companion to English Literature*, 4th ed., rev. Dorothy Eagle (Oxford: The Clarendon Press, 1967), 499. *ATM*, 275.

Q. "Good night, fellow guests." P.-G. Roy gives the following verse (ATM, 285):

Lorsque d'ici je sortirai,
Je ne sais pas trop où j'irai;
Mais en Dieu je me fie,
Il ne peut me mener que bien.
Aussi je n'appréhende rien;
Bonsoir la compagnie.

[When from hence I do depart,
I know not whither I shall go;
But in God I put my trust,
For he can bring me nought but good.
And, therefore, I shall not fear;
Good night, fellow guests.]

INDEX

This index gives names of persons occuring in the narrative and the author's notes, with a few exceptions (e.g., names of dogs, boats, Lac Trois-Saumons) that figure significantly in the narrative. Spelling reflects the author's text, except where it is necessary to clarify entries. For the benefit of the general reader, family names with several components are listed under the one most familiar (e.g. Gaspé, Salaberry, and so on).

454

Toussaint (of Saint-Jean Port-Joli), 323-324
Toussaint, Charles, 421
Toussaint, Joseph, 160, 421
Tremblay, Augustin, 290
Trois-Saumons mill, 42, 43, 305, 318
Trois-Saumons, Lac, 80, 154, 158ff., 194, 298, 317-320, 323, 421
Turgeon, Monseigneur Flavien, 197

Ursuline convent, 70

Vallière de Saint-Réal, Joseph-Rémi, 206-212, 233, 235, 246, 247, 255, 256, 333
Van Felson, curé of Beauport, 342
Vassal de Monviel (fils), Colonel François, 129, 432
Vassal de Monviel (père), Captain, 128
Vatel, 273
Vauban, 372
Verchères ("great-aunts"), 372
Verrault, (merchant of Saint-Jean Port-Joli), 77
Verrault, Abbé, Principal of Jacques Cartier Normal School, 77

Verrault, curé of Saint-Roch, 66, 92
Verrault, François, 154
Verrault, Pierre, 298, 302, 303
Victoria, Queen, 40, 344
Viger, Denis-Benjamin, 357-359
Villiers de L'Isle-Adam, 37, 404
Villiers, Marie-Anne Coulon de. See Mme Pierre-Ignace Aubert de Gaspé
Villiers, Monsieur de Coulombier de, 128
Vincelot, Seigneur, 72
Vincent, the Indian, 178
Vocelle, 330
Volney, de, 242, 243, 244, 429
Voltaire, 242
Vézina, Joseph, 338

Wales, Prince of, 52
Walker, 192, 193
Waller, Sam, 134
Washington, George, 258
William IV, 53, 54, 408
Wolfe, General James, 59, 408

Yorick, 389
York, Duke of, 345

Zémir et Azor, 270

DOSSIER QUEBEC

Life of the Party
Gérard Fortin & Boyce Richardson

The Milton-Park Affair
Canada's Largest Citizen-Developer Confrontation
Claire Helman

A Man of Sentiment
The Memoirs of Philippe-Joseph Aubert de Gaspé
1786-1871
Translated & annotated by Jane Brierley

The Passionate Debate
Ideas of Quebec Nationalism (1920-1945)
Michael Oliver
(forthcoming Fall 1988)

Printed by the workers
of Editions Marquis, Montmagny, Qc
in 1988